Patisserie

L. J. HANNEMAN
F.Inst.B.B., F.H.C.I.M.A., F.C.F.A.(C.G.), A.M.R.S.H.

*Formerly Head of Department of
Service Industries
Lancaster and Morecambe College
of Further Education*

Patisserie

HEINEMANN : LONDON

William Heinemann Ltd
10 Upper Grosvenor Street, London W1X 9PA

LONDON MELBOURNE JOHANNESBURG AUCKLAND

First published 1971
Reprinted 1975, 1977, 1979, 1983, 1984, 1985, 1986

ISBN 0 434 90707 3

Filmset and printed by
BAS Printers Limited, Over Wallop, Hampshire

Preface

This publication is designed to be used by all interested in patisserie. Designed especially for students who will need to learn patisserie as part of courses in catering, domestic science, and confectionery, it would also prove of great value to the practising chef and patissier, as well as the ambitious housewife.

The examination requirements of the following are also covered:

Union of Lancashire and Cheshire Institutes:
  Basic Patisserie
  Advanced Patisserie
City and Guilds of London Institute (Patisserie section only)
  705 General Catering
  706/1 Basic Cookery for the Catering Industry
  706/2 Cookery for the Catering Industry
  706/5 Advanced Cookery for the Catering Industry (Pastry)

Precise instructions as to the method are given to help the student to use this book in preparation for the above examinations.

The quantities given in this book are fairly small, being mostly calculated for eight persons. However, for larger quantities it is an easy matter to divide the yield given into the required number and multiply the recipe by the factor which results.

Metric as well as Imperial units have been given throughout. For simplicity, however, ounces have been calculated as being equivalent to 30 grammes instead of their value of 28·35 grammes. Since we are dealing in ratios in a recipe, this discrepancy does not alter the recipe and is small enough not to affect the yield appreciably.

Obviously no book can cover every aspect of patisserie the world over, but a serious attempt has been made to include most of the basic and a variety of the better known specialized, advanced dishes, many of which are Continental in origin.

Illustrations have been included to show not only finished goods but also the techniques used.

This book is offered in the sincere hope that it will prove of great value to all those who enjoy good patisserie.

L. J. HANNEMAN

Lancaster

Acknowledgments

No author can produce a book of this type without the help of others. My grateful thanks are given to the following:

The Governors and Principal of the Lancaster and Morecambe College of Further Education, who allowed me the facilities of the College for the preparation of part of this book.

My staff in the Department of Food and Catering, in particular Mr. Arthur Green, F.Inst.B.B., and Mr. Bryan Popplewell, who gave me valuable advice and also helped in producing some of the examples of work shown. Also M. André Boutin for proof-reading of the French.

Mr. Edward Roberts, F.Inst.B.B., of the Liverpool College of Craft and Catering, to whom I am indebted for the assistance he gave in the chapter on sugar work and for some of the illustrations.

Mr. Taylor, Secretary *Le Salon Culinaire International de Londres* for permission to reproduce the photograph of the sugar basket of fruit shown in Figure 119.

Lastly, but by no means least, to my dear wife who acted as my secretary. Besides this important task, I wish to thank her for her valued advice and criticism.

L.J.H.

Contents

1. Patisserie Equipment, Ingredients, and Hygiene

EQUIPMENT

Obviously to get the best use of equipment, it must be kept in good repair and in a clean condition. The latter is especially important as far as food is concerned. Although this applies to the whole range of equipment used by the patissier – from an oven to a patty pan – some items merit special attention as follows.

Bain-marie

When in use, the main precaution is to see that the pan is never allowed to burn dry. When not in use, the bain-marie should be emptied, cleaned inside and out, washed in hot detergent water, then rinsed and dried.

Baking Sheets

These are made of either aluminium or steel.
Aluminium. This has the advantage of being light in weight, rustless, and able to conduct heat more quickly. Its main disadvantage is that it is a softer metal and is, therefore, not so durable. It must, therefore, be treated with care. When scraping off food soils never use a steel scraper as this will scratch the surface and may remove some of the metal. The best method of cleaning is to use water with a mild disinfectant. If a scraper has to be employed, use either a celluloid or nylon one.
Steel. Although this will stand up to more harsh treatment, its obvious disadvantage is its liability to rust. If water is used to wash the tin, always thoroughly dry, afterwards. Often the cause of rust can be traced back to buns being left on the tin to cool. When this happens, the steam trapped between the tin and the bun condenses to water and, if left, rusts away that part of the tin under the bun.

Of whatever metal the baking sheet is made, make sure that the corners are really well cleaned. It is here that the particles of food accumulate and if left will bake onto the surface of the tin to leave a soil which is difficult to remove. When cleaning baking tins, concentrate on the corners and the centre will clean itself.

Brushes

These need washing and thoroughly drying at regular intervals. If left, there is a build up of food particles adhering to the bristles which quickly reduces the efficiency of the brushes. This is particularly prevalent with board brushes used for brushing such commodities as flour which, when wet, forms a tenacious paste which dries hard on the bristle.

1

Cake Machines and Attachments

These should be regularly serviced and lubricated to ensure freedom from breakdown. One of the most annoying faults with these machines is the leakage of oil which tends to drip into the mixing. If this happens when sponges or meringues are being made, they could be completely ruined. Cleaning of machines after each use is desirable but, if moving parts like the blade of a mincer are involved, thorough drying is essential to prevent rust formation. Traces of mixings left on the handles, etc. of the machine are not only unhygienic but can contaminate other mixings. It is important that these mixers should not be overloaded. This can easily happen by allowing them to mix stiff pastes and doughs. It is better to mix these by hand if in doubt.

Bowls, whisks, beaters, etc. should always be washed in very hot water to eliminate traces of grease which can have disastrous consequences to mixes such as meringues and sponges.

Chopping Boards

These are used a great deal by the patissier and should be kept in good condition by regular washing and drying, the latter in a relatively cool place, otherwise warping could result. It is important to keep certain chopping boards for specific purposes to avoid contamination. For example, fruit and chocolate, both of which readily pick up foreign odours such as onions. It is always advisable that vegetables and onions should not be chopped on a board used for fruit.

Cloths (Muslin, Jelly Bags, and Piping Bags)

These should be regularly laundered and sterilized. Often pastry is left wrapped in a damp cloth. It should be remembered that such practice increases the risk of attack by mould and could infect the goods with this micro-organism and others.

Cutters

Pastry cutters are usually very poorly cared for. They are comparatively fragile utensils and, with misuse, quickly lose their shape. Always ensure that cutters are put away in their boxes clean and dry. If cutters are replaced in their boxes without proper cleaning, the food particles adhering can go bad without anyone noticing. When cleaning, special attention should be given to the rim where food particles can easily become lodged. If the cutters are washed, make sure that they are really well dried out before replacing in their boxes; otherwise rust will soon be apparent.

Docker

This is a wooden disc with protruding points used to make a number of small holes in pastry. When cleaning it, it is essential to remove any food soil from the points.

Dredgers

These are used for giving a light dusting of flour, icing sugar, etc. Since the same kind of dredger is used for these materials, it is important to have some means of identification; otherwise the flour could be mistaken for sugar and vice versa. Regular cleaning is again recommended with a regular change of contents.

Fryers

Many goods are deep fried by the patissier. For the best results it is essential that frying oil should be as fresh as possible and screened free of foreign matter. The oil used by the patissier should never be used by the chef because of the risk of contamination from such commodities as fish and onions. The fryer should be cleaned out and restocked with fresh oil at regular intervals.

Knives

Besides ensuring that these are kept clean and free from rust, French knives, etc. need to be kept sharp for their efficient use. To achieve an edge, a stone should be used first, after which the knife edge should be kept keen by the use of a steel.

Moulds

These should be kept in a clean condition both inside and outside, particularly if stacked. Never use a knife to scrape off adhering particles as this will damage the surface and could spoil the mould for future use – especially Easter egg moulds.

Patty Pans

The cleaning of these is often neglected. Because they are stacked it is very easy to contaminate clean tins with dirty ones. If placed on a dirty tray, dirt becomes transferred to the underside of the tin which, if stacked in an unclean condition, makes the clean patty pan into which it nests also dirty. Always place these patty pans on a clean tray and ensure they are thoroughly cleaned before stacking.

Piping Tubes

These should always be washed immediately after use. This is especially important if icing like royal icing is used, because of its rapid drying action. To remove hard sugar from piping tubes, they should be soaked in water, then either brushed out or a thin jet of water directed into the nozzles.

Provers

These are cabinets in which steam can be generated and in which trays of fermented goods are left to prove. The steam can be made either by allowing a pan of water to boil (gas or electric ring) or injecting steam from a steam boiler. With the presence of so much water, deterioration by rust is a real problem in metal provers. Wiping out and drying after each use can greatly reduce this risk.

Rolling Pins

The best rolling pins are mounted on ball bearings at the handles and rolling is accomplished by applying pressure and moving the handles away from the person. Obviously in such appliances it is important to prevent the ball race from rusting by the occasional application of lubricating oil. Most rolling pins are made of beech because of its non-splintering properties. Since all woods tend to warp if left too long in a wet condition, rolling pins should be dried as quickly as possible after washing. On no account should any pastry, etc. adhering to the surface of the rolling pin be removed with a knife or similar sharp instrument. This would damage the soft wooden surface of the pin and the impression of this damage would be left upon the paste being rolled out.

Refrigerators

The most common abuse a refrigerator gets is in allowing it to operate without regular defrosting at appropriate intervals of time. When operating, ice is built up around the evaporating coils inside the refrigerator. This reduces its efficiency and overloads the motor, risking unnecessary break-downs. A regular defrosting, at least once a week, should be programmed and the inside wiped over with a weak solution of bicarbonate of soda then dried, before putting the refrigerator back into operation.

Deep Freeze

Never overload a deep freeze especially if fresh foods are to be frozen. Here it is not only the temperature which is important but also the speed at which goods can be frozen. With baked goods like rolls and cake, staling is at its most rapid at temperatures around zero, and the aim must always be to get goods to the deep freeze temperature as rapidly as possible to prevent premature staling. It is essential that a deep freeze should not be overloaded for this reason.

Siting of refrigerators and deep freeze cabinets should receive careful consideration. They should always be sited in a relatively cool place so that the compressor and its coils can effectively be kept cool. Ideally this piece of equipment is best sited outside the patisserie room, in the open air under suitable cover to prevent ingress of rain.

Salamanders

The bars and draining trays should be regularly cleaned with hot water containing a grease solvent. After rinsing, they should be replaced and the salamander turned on for a few minutes to dry out. Prevent waste of fuel by never having the salamander alight unnecessarily.

Saucepans

The type of pan used by the patissier is usually either copper or aluminium.

Copper pans are sometimes lined with tin. For these pans it is dangerous practice to leave them empty on too hot a stove since the tinning can melt. Copper has the advantage that food cooks more quickly and burns less easily because of its good heat conduction. Tarnishing is a problem which can only be eliminated by repeated use of a cleaning paste. Copper pans should be thoroughly washed in boiling soda water, scoured with a brush, wire wool, or powder, rinsed, and then placed upside down to dry.

Aluminium is suitable for most cooking purposes but there is a risk of discoloration of some foods when prepared in aluminium pans. The use of metal spoons and whisks should be avoided, a wooden spoon always being used to prevent risk of discoloration. This type of saucepan may be cleaned in the same way as copper except that a detergent should be used instead of soda.

Savoy Bags and Tubes

These are available in either nylon, plastic, or cloth. Of these the plastic bags have a definite advantage in that they are not porous and, when used for creams, etc., no liquid can seep through. Whatever their composition savoy bags require to be sterilized before each use, especially when used for fresh cream and jelly concoctions (*see* Food Hygiene, page 9). After sterilizing in a suitable solution or by boiling, they should be thoroughly dried and stored in a very clean place. Tubes are made either of plastic or tinned metal; in the latter case rust must be guarded against.

Sieves

These may be very fine hair sieves, large meshes for sieving flour, or larger still for draining dried fruit after washing.

Sieves should be washed immediately after use. If this is not done, the food or liquid dries in the mesh, making it difficult to remove. To wash, the sieve should be placed upside down under running water, tapping vigorously with the bristles of a stiff brush. Always store sieves in a dry place to prevent risk of rusting the wire mesh.

Spatulas and Wooden Spoons

These are usually made of beech and require the same treatment as rolling pins.

Steamers

For efficient working, this piece of equipment should be checked periodically by a qualified engineer to ensure that it is working correctly.

The trays, runners, and the inside of the steamer should be washed in hot detergent water and then rinsed. When not in use the steamer door should always be left open to allow free circulation of air.

Storage Bins

These may be made of metal or plastic; the latter is not as robust as metal but has the advantage of being more easily cleaned; they are often moulded with no corners in which food particles can be trapped. There should be a regular programme of cleaning. No storage bin should be refilled until it has been thoroughly washed in hot detergent water, rinsed, and dried. Storage of such goods as onions, spices, etc. should be confined to the same bin since washing is not always effective in removing the pungent aroma of such foods and this can easily be passed on to other commodities via the bin.

Tables

The surfaces of these may be wood, melamine, stainless steel, or marble.

Wooden tables can be scrubbed with hot soda water to remove grease, rinsed, and wiped dry to prevent undue warping. They must not be scraped with a sharp scraper as lumps might be gouged out. The other surfaces should be washed in hot detergent water, rinsed, and dried.

Chopping or cutting should never be done on work surfaces; chopping boards are supplied for these purposes. Hot pans should be placed on wooden triangles and never directly on the table.

Marble tops require special care to ensure they do not crack. Heavy concussion such as hitting with a rolling pin can cause this to happen.

HYGIENE

Hygiene is playing an ever increasing part in our daily lives, especially in so far as it affects our food. The patissier must be particularly conscious of the need for hygiene because many of his preparations have to be handled and passed on to the customer without being sterilized by heat. Many of his commodities, e.g. eggs and cream, make ideal breeding grounds for food poisoning organisms and the greatest care must be taken to keep their growth to the minimum. Thus the patissier bears a heavy responsibility to see that the materials he uses are sound, that they are processed in conditions which are as clean as possible, and that they reach the customer in a fresh state.

Of course, there are now regulations on Hygiene but this is a difficult subject for which to legislate. It should become an attitude of mind or a habit to carry out the recommendations of the regulations.

Food Hygiene can be broken down into three headings: Personal; Premises and Equipment; and Handling of Food. One aspect is useless without the others. It is no use the patissier being clean if the premises in which he works and the utensils which he uses are dirty or constructed in such a way that cleaning is made difficult. And if he has no knowledge of how to handle the food in a hygienic way, the cleanliness of his person and the premises will be of no avail.

Personal Hygiene

Good personal hygiene stems from a healthy person, so that this is the first requirement. Apart from an inherited constitution there is much that can be done by an individual to promote health in his person. Good clean living habits, a good regular diet, plenty of fresh air, exercise, and sleep are all requirements which should receive the utmost consideration.

Washing. Regular washing and bathing is necessary to prevent germs from being transferred from the body to clothes and thence to food. Hands especially should be washed frequently, particularly after using the toilet and before food is handled.

Watches, rings, and jewellery should not be worn when food is being handled. Apart from the risk of their being lost in the food, particles of food could be caught underneath which would provide a breeding ground for bacteria which could be transferred to the food.

Finger nails must be kept short and clean to prevent transfer of harmful bacteria to the food.

Hair. This should be washed regularly and kept covered. It should not be combed, scratched, or touched in the kitchen as germs, loose hair, and dandruff could find their way into the food.

Mouth and Nose. These organs are the source of much harmful bacteria and should not come into contact with food or the utensils used. Tasting should be done with a separate spoon, washed well after use. Coughing or sneezing over food must be avoided. The use of a handkerchief to trap the germs is essential, paper handkerchiefs being more hygienic.

Sores and Cuts. It is very important that any opening of the skin be kept covered with a waterproof dressing. People who suffer from septic sores must not handle food.

Cosmetics. These should not be applied to dirty skin or put on in such a manner that they could find their way into food. They should never be applied in the kitchen.

Spitting. This dirty habit must never be allowed as germs can easily spread.

Smoking. Smoking must never take place where food is being prepared. Apart from the risk of ash and cigarette ends finding their way into food, germs can be transmitted if the butt is put down on working surfaces. It is now an offence against the law.

Protective Clothing

Every person handling food must wear clean protective clothing. It should be light weight, washable, strong, absorbent, and of a suitable colour. Most chefs' coats, overalls, aprons, hats, and trousers are made of white cotton because it has most of these qualities. White clothing has the advantage of showing the dirt more easily and keeping one's person cool.

Premises

The use of premises which are clean and can be kept clean is essential for the preparation of food.

Floors. These should be of some easily washed, durable, and non-permeable material. Ideally they should be tiled, but terrazzo and granolithic surfaces are almost as good. They must be kept clean with repeated washes of hot detergent water.

Walls. The same requirements as with the floor, except that they should be light in colour. Tiles, special painted, or Melamine surfaces are best because they have an impervious smooth surface which can be washed easily. Corners should be rounded or coved for ease of cleaning.

Ceilings. These should be smooth without cracks or flaking.

Ventilation. Circulation of air is important for the well-being of the staff. Stale air and fumes must be taken away by extractor fans but these are a potential source of dirt and must be kept clean.

Lighting. Good lighting is essential to avoid eye strain and to detect dirt. Natural light is best but where artificial lighting is used some thought should be given to the type employed. Generally fluorescent lighting is best but this sometimes makes food colours look peculiar. If decorative patisserie is being carried out, this factor must be considered.

Windows. These should be cleaned inside and out to admit the maximum light. If opened for ventilation purposes, they may have to be screened against entry of birds and insects.

Water and Sanitation. A plentiful supply of hot and cold water should always be available. Separate toilets for men and women must be provided away from the rooms in which food is prepared. Facilities for washing hands must be furnished, separate from food preparation sinks.

Equipment

This should be designed so that it is easily cleaned. It should be hard and smooth so that food materials cannot be absorbed, and it must be resistant to rusting and chipping. The materials of which the equipment is made must not be toxic, e.g. lead.

FOOD POISONING

Food poisoning may be defined as an illness which can cause stomach pains, acute diarrhoea, and vomiting within 1 to 36 hours after eating infected food. Such food might be infected by:

(*a*) Chemicals which may have entered the food accidentally during its processing in cooking.

(*b*) Bacteria which have contaminated food from animal, human, or other sources. Either the bacteria themselves or the toxins produced by them cause the food to be harmful.

Chemicals

Arsenic. Sometimes to be found in fruit after it is treated by special sprays during its growth.

Copper, Antimony, or Zinc. Acid foods can sometimes become contaminated if stored in poor quality enamelled galvanized containers or copper containers.

Lead. Water in contact with lead for long periods can become contaminated.
Poisonous Plants. Certain fungi, rhubarb leaves.

Bacteria

Bacteriological contamination of food is by far the most common cause
of food poisoning. Bacteria are microscopic single cell organisms which
are present practically everywhere but can only be brought into contact
with food by an outside agent, i.e. human, air movement, insects, etc.

The toxins or poisons are produced by some bacteria outside their own
bodies and thus the food itself is poisonous causing very rapid symptoms of
food poisoning. Other bacteria produce the toxins in their own bodies and
this is not released until the bacteria die. In these circumstances food
poisoning is delayed until the bacteria die in sufficient numbers.

Some of these toxins are very resistant to heat; bringing food to boiling
point may not be sufficient if the food has become heavily contaminated
with this type of toxin.

Given the right conditions, bacteria will multiply at a fantastic rate,
dividing into two every 20 minutes at room temperature so that, within 12
hours, one bacterium can multiply into several hundred million.

Some bacteria, like lactic, acetic, etc., are beneficial to humans and are
utilized in the making of cheese and vinegar.

Diseases other than food poisoning are caused by certain types of bacteria,
e.g. typhoid, paratyphoid, and dysentry. This type of bacteria does not
multiply in the food like the food poisoning bacteria, but it can be carried
by the food, thus causing the disease.

The symptoms of food poisoning are not always immediately apparent;
the time between the consumption of the contaminated food and the onset
of the illness depends upon the type of bacteria which has caused the
illness.

Conditions for the Multiplication of Bacteria

1. The right type of food
2. Suitable temperature
3. Adequate moisture
4. Sufficient time

Foods which are resistant to Food Poisoning

Sterilized foods – in tins, cans, etc.
Preserved foods – high concentration of sugar, salt, or vinegar

Foods which are Susceptible to the Growth of Bacteria

Stock, sauces, gravies, soups, jellies, custards
Meat and meat products
Egg and egg products
Milk and milk products
Coconut

All foods which are handled
Re-heated foods

Temperature

The most rapid multiplication of the bacteria occurs about body temperature, 98°F (37°C). Below and above this the rate decreases until at about 170°F (76°C) they begin to die. At cold temperatures they are not killed but lie dormant. All food should therefore be kept in a cool room or refrigerator.

Although boiling will kill the bacteria some types can produce heat resistant spores which require 4 to 5 hours boiling to eliminate them. Some of the toxins produced can only be eliminated by at least $\frac{1}{2}$ hour boiling. Thus it is necessary to boil for sufficient length of time to ensure that the food is safe from contamination. Foods which cannot be boiled require extra care.

Food which may have to be taken out of the refrigerator, and left at room temperature for some time, should not be returned to the refrigerator for further use as it may have become contaminated.

Moisture

Bacteria cannot grow on dry food but requires some moisture. Jellies, custards, creams, and sauces make ideal breeding grounds.

Time

The longer food is left in warm conditions, the more prone it is to produce food poisoning. In five hours, one cell can multiply into 16 777 216 given ideal conditions. If food has to be stored for any length of time, it should always be in a cool room or refrigerator.

TYPES OF BACTERIA WHICH CAUSE FOOD POISONING

The Salmonella Group

This group includes the bacteria which cause typhoid and paratyphoid fevers which can result in death. By far the most common types, however, require large numbers to be ingested with food and drink to cause food poisoning. The food poisoning of this group is by living bacteria which are present in the intestines and are found in excreta. Anything coming into contact, either directly or indirectly, with such excreta may become infected. For example, contaminated water supplies could spread the infection.

Salmonella infection is caused by man or animals eating food contaminated with infected excreta originating from man or animals, thus completing a cycle of infection. Such contamination may be caused by:

(*a*) Vermin: droppings, fur, hair, feet, etc.

(*b*) Insects, especially flies which land on infected excreta and carry the infection to the food itself.

(*c*) Infected food, e.g. coconut.

(*d*) Cross contamination, e.g. by using an unsterilized savoy bag which is infected from a previous mixing.

(*e*) Food can be infected either by a person who has the disease or by one who is a carrier (a person who does not suffer from the disease but who carries the bacteria and can, therefore, contaminate others with whom he comes into contact).

Staphylococci

These cause food poisoning by the toxins secreted by the bacteria. They are present in the human skin, sores, spots, and the nose and throat. Food becomes infected by too much handling by infected persons.

Meat pies, custard, etc. are the foods most frequently infected by this type of bacteria.

Clostridium Welchii

This is another bacterium also found in the intestines and excreta of humans and animals and also in the soil. Since the spores of this bacterium can survive light cooking, it is often to be found in meat products.

PREVENTION OF FOOD POISONING

The food handler must prevent the bacteria from multiplying and spreading from one place to another.

This means that the source of the bacteria is eliminated and the conditions for their development, i.e. temperature, time, and moisture, are minimized. For this to be achieved, a high standard of hygiene is essential in the person, the premises, and the way in which food is handled.

SPREAD OF INFECTION

Human

People who are feeling ill, suffering from diarrhoea, or vomiting, who have colds, sore throats, or weeping sores, or are carriers, must not handle food. If the person is aware that he is a carrier of an infection, the person responsible for the premises must be informed and he must then inform the Medical Officer of Health.

Animal

Domestic pets or vermin can bring infection into the patisserie room. By far the most dangerous are rats and mice and every effort must be made to ensure that access to food by these vermin is barred. Tell-tale signs of their presence are droppings, gnawing marks, grease marks, paw marks, and damage to stock. To prevent such infestation, stock should be moved regularly and always kept covered. The premises should be kept in good repair and in a clean condition. No scraps of food should be left lying about. The Public Health Inspector should be contacted as soon as premises become infested with rats or mice.

Insects

By far the most dangerous insect is the *house fly* which will settle on filth, contaminate its legs, wings, and body and deposit this on the food which it also contaminates with its own excreta and saliva. Since flies breed in rubbish and filth in warm moist places, rubbish bins must be kept clean and covered. Combustible rubbish should be burnt, whilst the use of a waste disposer for stale scraps of food is recommended.

Flies can be controlled by:

(*a*) Screening openings with a wire mesh.

(*b*) The use of special paints which contain insecticides.

(*c*) The use of a special electric fly exterminator, fitted over entrances.

(*d*) The use of insecticide where it cannot come into contact with food.

Other insects which can carry harmful bacteria are: cockroaches, silver fish, and beetles. All can be controlled by the use of special insecticides.

Birds

Entry of birds must be prevented, since food can be contaminated by their droppings.

Dust

Bacteria can be carried by dust so that where possible food should always be kept covered.

Inanimate Objects

Towels, dish cloths, and utensils should be regularly washed. Cloths especially need boiling between uses. The old-fashioned roller hand towel is a potential source of danger and if possible paper towels should be substituted.

FOODS WHICH REQUIRE SPECIAL CONSIDERATION

Meat and Poultry

Made up dishes such as meat pies require special care to ensure that they are properly cooked and kept in a cool place for short periods of time before use. If meat products need to be re-heated, they must be heated to over 150°F (65°C) and kept at this temperature before use.

Fish

Danger here is usually to re-heated fish dishes where the same conditions as those of re-heated meat dishes apply.

Egg

Duck eggs are more susceptible to food poisoning bacteria than hens' egg and so must be thoroughly cooked. Dried egg has been known to be contaminated and any reconstituted solution should be used immediately and not left for future use even if refrigerated.

Milk Products

Dishes in which milk is used, i.e. custards, puddings, etc., should be used straight away. If required to be left, they should be placed in a refrigerator and used soon afterwards.

Synthetic Cream

If left in a warm condition for any length of time, food poisoning bacteria could develop. It should always be kept in a refrigerator.

Coconut

This has been a source of food poisoning but today it is usually pasteurized. If in doubt as to whether this processing has been done, it is wise not to use it in decoration especially where cream is concerned.

Sauces, Jellies, Custards, etc.

These should never be left in a warm condition for any length of time since they make an ideal breeding ground for bacteria.

COMMODITIES USED IN PATISSERIE

WHEAT FLOUR AND CEREAL PRODUCTS

Wheat Flour

This may be obtained either white or brown as follows.

White Flour

This flour is milled from the white floury *endosperm* of the wheat berry, the husk or *bran* and embryo *germ* being removed. According to the blend of wheats from which it is milled, this flour may be either: weak (soft), strong (hard), or medium.

Weak Flour. Milled from predominantly English wheats, this flour is low in protein (gluten) content, i.e. 8%, and is ideally suited to rich cakes and sponges and especially short pastry. The flour may be labelled 'Biscuit', 'Cake', or merely 'English'. Some Australian flours are also soft and ideal for the making of cakes. Special Cake Flour is specially milled to a fine particle size to have great moisture absorbing properties and is used for cakes having a high liquid/flour ratio.

Strong Flour. Canadian and American wheats are usually used for the major part of the wheat blend from which this flour is milled. Their high protein (gluten) content enables a dough to be made which will hold its shape and become aerated with the gas of fermenting yeast, thus producing good bread and rolls. This flour is used for all fermented goods, and for puff pastry when a special puff pastry fat is used.

Medium Flour. Between these two extremes we have a flour milled to provide medium strength. Such a flour is suitable for goods which have to be chemically aerated, i.e. with baking powder. It is strong enough to withstand the pressures of gas which can cause aeration, yet weak enough to prevent undue toughening in the crumb of such goods.

Self-raising Flour

This is usually a medium strength flour in which has been blended a proportion of baking powder, at the rate of approximately ⅓ oz (10 grammes) to 1 lb (480 g) flour. Although this flour is handy for the novice to use to produce cakes, it is not recommended because:

(*a*) The baking powder will react with dampness so that, if such a flour has been kept for a long time, its aerating properties will be seriously affected.

(*b*) The proportion of baking powder required in mixings will vary to such an extent that this flour could not be used on its own anyway. The patissier would either have to add some plain flour or extra baking powder for certain goods.

It is best to use plain flour and baking powder. When the quantities of baking powder required are very small, a special blend may be used called Scone Flour made up as follows:

1 *lb* (480 g) *medium flour*   1 *oz* (30 g) *baking powder*
Sieve together at least 3 times.

Hand Test for Flour Strength

Weak and strong flours may be identified by squeezing some in the hand. A weak flour will cling together after the hand is opened. A strong flour will crumble to flour again as soon as the hand is opened.

If a strong flour has to be used for goods which are best made from a weak flour, some of the strong flour may be replaced with cornflour (up to 50%).

Wheatmeal

Most of the brown flours on the market are wheatmeals. That is they are made by blending a certain proportion of the brown skins of the wheat berry bran with the white flour. Such flours may be used for items like scones and rolls.

Wholemeal

A true wholemeal is made from the whole of the wheat berry and contains the embryo *germ* in addition to the bran and white endosperm. Its use in patisserie is usually confined to scones and rolls.

Malted Meal

Several proprietary brands of malted wheatmeals are on the market which may be made into fruited malt loaves and served as slices with butter.

Cornflour

This is a white powder milled from *maize* and consisting mainly of starch. It is the well-known thickening agent for all culinary purposes because in the presence of boiling water it forms a thick jelly. In patisserie it is used for thickening all types of sauces, glazes, and custards and may also be an ingredient in some special cake mixes.

Arrowroot

This is mainly pure starch and therefore has the same properties of thickening as cornflour. However, because the jelly formed by boiling it in water is not as opaque as the cornflour gel, it is widely used for making glazes.

Rice

There are several types of rice but the type used for patisserie is the short grained soft Carolina. It should be perfectly white and free from any adhering husk and specks.

Riceflour

This is finely milled rice. It has several uses:

(*a*) As an ingredient in various puddings and cakes. Its function in some cakes is to absorb moisture. In macaroons its use can reduce the cost of the mixture and at the same time help to produce a good looking macaroon biscuit with a crack on its surface.

(*b*) In baking powder it is a useful additive to absorb any dampness and so keep the powder free flowing and inactive.

Rice-cones

These are rice granules, i.e. not milled so finely as riceflour. Their use is confined to dusting purposes, e.g. marzipan and bread.

Semolina

Obtained from wheat, it is really the product from the first break mill of the flour mill and consists mainly of the starchy endosperm minus the bran and germ. Use mainly for puddings.

Tapioca

This is the hard white grains of the cassava plant. Its use is confined to puddings.

Oatmeal

This product from oats is obtained milled as coarse, medium, or fine (pinhead), and is used in goods such as parkins and scones. Rolled oats are the oats partially cooked and put through rollers and flattened. These are used for making flapjacks. Any of the varieties of oats may be made into porridge.

SUGAR

Many different types of sugar are available to the patissier as follows.

Icing Sugar

This is merely crystalline sugar crushed to a fine powder. There are usually several qualities, the best being of superfine texture and pure white in colour. Inferior brands are more gritty and grey in colour. For royal icing the superfine grade is recommended, whilst if an icing sugar is required in a cake mixing, the poorer and cheaper qualities can be used. Sometimes a small quantity of calcium chloride is added to absorb any moisture and improve its free flowing properties.

Pulverized Sugar

This is really a poor quality icing sugar having a coarse, gritty texture and grey in colour. It is useful in goods like shortpastry where it can easily dissolve in the small amount of liquid available.

Castor Sugar

Consists of small crystals of sugar evenly graded. It can be obtained either as fine, medium, or coarse grained according to the crystal size. For goods which are aerated by beating in air, e.g. sponges, the coarse (or hard) grained sugar is the best.

Granulated Sugar

Here the crystals are larger. Such sugar may be used in any goods in which there is sufficient liquor for it to be dissolved, i.e. syrups and general sweetening of sauces, etc.

Nib Sugar

This is sugar crystals in clusters to form lumps about $\frac{1}{8}$ in. (3 mm) diameter. It is used for decoration mainly in such goods as bath buns.

Cube and Preserving Sugar

For sugar boiling, it is best to use a pure sugar not contaminated with dust in order to prevent the formation of scum. These types of sugar are best used for this purpose.

Demerara Sugar

This is pale amber and really only suitable for decorative effect or for flavouring purposes. Because of its hard crystalline state it is not suitable for cake making unless it can be dissolved first.

Raw Sugar

This can be obtained in a variety of shades of brown. It is of a fine crystal size and ideal for making cakes such as Dundee, Christmas, wedding, etc. The darker the sugar the more pronounced the flavour. Because of the syrup which adheres to the sugar crystals, this type of sugar will form into a hard solid lump if left in store for too long a period.

Confectioners' Glucose

This is a thick viscous, clear, transparent syrup used by sugar confectioners in all types of boiling sugar preparations. It is a complicated mixture of various simple sugars and dextrin and must not be confused with the pure glucose available as an anhydrous powder at the chemist. There are four different types of viscous confectioners' glucose available, defined by their dextrose equivalent (D.E.) namely, D.E. 34; 42; 55; 63.

The types having the low D.E. figures have a low sugar content with a corresponding high percentage of dextrin gum and are the types which should be used in sugar boiling, since the dextrin has an inhibiting effect on the premature crystallization of sugar.

The glucoses having the high D.E. figures have a low dextrin content with a corresponding high percentage of glucose sugar; and since they are very hygroscopic they may be used to advantage in cakes to keep them moist. D.E. 63 is especially useful in this respect. Dried glucoses are now on the market and, because of their superior handling qualities, are likely to supersede the viscous syrups which have been used in the past.

Golden Syrup

This should not be kept too long in storage before it is used since crystallization can occur and the syrup may become discoloured. It should be perfectly clear and transparent and of a pale amber colour.

Fondant

Although this can be readily made by the patissier, fondant purchased from a manufacturer is usually of much superior quality. It should be pure white, plastic, and devoid of any hard crust if packed properly by the manufacturer. Fondant should be used as soon as possible and not left too long in store.

Dry Fondant

Fondant may now be purchased as a powder like icing sugar, only requiring a certain quantity of water or fruit juice to reconstitute it. The use of fruit juice makes an icing of much superior flavour.

Honey

Obtained either as a clear, golden-coloured, thin syrup or as a thick opaque crystalline mass. For most patisserie uses, the clear thin syrup is best because it will blend more readily with other ingredients. There is no difference in flavour of either type.

Storage

All sugar products are hygroscopic, i.e. they absorb moisture from the atmosphere. This is an advantage in the actual goods which contain sugar because it contributes to their keeping properties, but in storage dampness can cause considerable trouble. Dry storage is essential even if some form of heating has to be installed.

MILK AND MILK PRODUCTS

Milk

Most patissiers will use fresh milk whenever necessary, but there are other milk products on the market which may be used either when there are shortages or when special circumstances arise.

Sterilized and Ultra Heat Treated (U.H.T.) Milk

This will lack the flavour of fresh milk but has a much longer storage life and is a useful standby in case of shortages.

Milk Powders (Spray Dried and Roller Dried)

Available as full, half, or skimmed, this product is a very useful one and has a wide use in many recipes. It may be added in powder form or re-constituted as follows:
1 pint (6 decilitres) water to 2 oz (60 g) milk powder.
Whisk the milk powder into the water for a solution free from lumps.

The skimmed milk powder has the longest shelf life and its use is recommended in preference to the full and half cream variety which will soon deteriorate in storage. If skimmed milk powder is used, the patissier can easily replace the butter fat which is removed in its manufacture. The spray dried product is the best.

Evaporated Milk

For many recipes such as creams and sauces, this product gives superior results because it is concentrated and smooth. To get the same degree of concentration, milk powder would have to be used and this would give a gritty result. Storage approx. 3 days once tin is opened.

Condensed Milk

Similar to evaporated but has high concentration of sugar. If this sweetness is required, condensed milk may be used with advantage. Once the tin is opened it has a much longer storage life than evaporated milk.

Fresh Cream

This is the butter fat separated from fresh milk. There are three types depending upon the percentage of butter fat present, i.e.

Single cream   – 18% butter fat
Double cream   – 48–50% butter fat
Whipping cream – 35–40% butter fat.

All three types of creams may be whisked to thicken them but the degree of thickening will depend upon the percentage of butter fat present. Although the double cream will give the thickest and most stable cream, it will not give an economic volume and so the whipping cream is recommended.

A suitable whipping can be made by whipping together 1 part of single cream and 2 parts of double cream.

If liqueurs or fruit juices are to be added to cream for flavouring purposes, double cream should be used on its own. The amount of liqueur used should not exceed $\frac{1}{4}$ of the amount of cream.

Fresh cream should be stored at 40°F (4·5°C) and also whisked at this temperature for the best results.

Cream and milk must be handled in a hygienic way and refrigeration used to keep them cool. Given sufficient time in a warm temperature they are subjected to the action of *lactic acid bacteria* which will quickly turn them sour and unfit for use in most patisserie recipes. In extreme circumstances the milk will curdle as the protein becomes coagulated by the acid formed. Sometimes this can happen to stale milk when warmed in a pan or when it has acid added, e.g. lemon juice. It is essential to use fresh milk in all recipes in which milk needs to be heated.

Imitation Cream

There are several products on the market which may be whipped to a stable thick cream resembling fresh whipped cream in texture and looks (though lacking in flavour). These creams contain milk solids but the butter fat is replaced with a vegetable fat which is finely dispersed by a homogenizer. To all intents and purposes such creams behave like fresh cream except that they will keep much longer, up to one month in a refrigerator, and the foam is more stable. However, they are subject to attack by lactic acid and other bacteria and, therefore, the same hygienic handling precautions should be taken (*see* page 9).

EGGS AND EGG PRODUCTS

Shell Eggs

All varieties of birds' eggs may be used in cooking but the hen provides the bulk of our requirements. Fresh or pickled eggs in shell may be used but they must be sound, without any musty smell, and with a strong glutinous white. The weight of a hen's egg varies from $2\frac{3}{16}$ oz (70–75 g) to below $1\frac{1}{2}$ oz (40–45 g) according to grades from 1 to 7. Since the weight of the yolks is approximately half that of the whites, a small standard egg with a total weight of $1\frac{3}{4}$ oz (53 g) would give approx. $\frac{1}{2}$ oz (15 g) yolk and 1 oz (30 g) whites.

Both egg whites and egg yolks form a skin and dry if exposed to the air for long. They should always be covered with a damp cloth and placed in a refrigerator until required to prevent this and also for hygienic reasons.

Frozen Egg

This is marketed in tins of approx. 14 lb (3·5 kg) and must be kept frozen at a temperature of approx. -5°F (-20°C) until required. When the egg is needed it must be slowly defrosted, preferably by leaving it overnight in the kitchen. Alternatively, it may be placed in the sink and *cold* water allowed to trickle over for several hours. Once defrosted, frozen egg should be used as soon as possible. It is dangerous practice to re-freeze any surplus egg (*see* page 9).

Frozen Whites and Yolks

Both frozen whites and frozen yolks are obtainable and the same defrosting precautions apply.

Dried Egg

Dried egg is reconstituted at the rate of 1 oz (30 g) to 3 oz (90 g) water when it makes a thick liquid, having nearly the same properties as fresh egg. Such egg lacks the whipping property of fresh egg and recipes in which this is required must be supplemented with baking powder. Once reconstituted, the egg must be used immediately and not left for any length of time before use (*see* page 9). Such egg is a useful standby although it will not make such a good product as fresh egg. It also has the disadvantage of a limited shelf life.

Dried Whites or Albumen

This is obtainable in either powder or flake form, the former being preferred since it reconstitutes much more quickly. It is reconstituted at the rate of 3 oz (90 g) to 1 pint (600 g) water. The solution should stand for a few hours prior to use because it does not readily dissolve immediately.

Processed Albumen

Several products are now on the market under various proprietary trade names. Used as directed, they may be reconstituted into albumen solutions from which meringues, royal icing, and other goods in which egg whites are used may be made. However, such albumen solution lacks the stability that fresh egg whites enjoy and therefore is not recommended for such goods as bavarois, japonaise, etc.

FATS AND OILS

Butter

Used for all high class patisserie. There are two types of butter available: *Sweet Cream*. This type has the longest storage life but is not so strongly flavoured as the other type. New Zealand, Australian, and English butters are usually in this group.
Soured. This has a limited storage life but is superior in flavour since it is made from soured cream. Danish is an example of this type of butter.

Salted and Unsalted

Most butters contain some salt to enhance the flavour and also prolong their storage life. For certain goods however, e.g. buttercream, the unsalted variety must be used. This is usually available in Normandy and Dutch butters.

Margarine

In many respects in cakemaking, margarine is superior to butter in every respect except flavour. It can be specially prepared for specific purposes:

Cake margarine   – Suitable for all cakes

Pastry margarine   – Tougher than cake margarine and ideally suitable for manufacture of puff pastry

Saltless margarine   – For use in creams.

Shortening (White or Yellow)

This is ideal for most cooking purposes in which flavour is not of paramount importance. It may be used with advantage in all short pastry goods and small quantities may be incorporated with margarine or butter in cakes where it improves the shortness of the crumb.

Lard

Used for savoury pastry where the flavour is especially valued. It also imparts a shortness in pastry unequalled by other fats. It is unsuitable for use in cakes because it has poor creaming qualities.

Cooking Oils

The use of oil is mostly confined to frying purposes where it can be heated to quite high temperatures without deterioration and the absorption rate of the goods being fried is kept to the minimum. Most of these oils are manufactured specifically for this purpose from blends of various nut and vegetable oils. Some oils are sold under their own name, e.g. Arachis or ground nut, Cottonseed, Palm nut, Corn oil, etc.

Suet

Recommended for suet puddings, dumplings, Christmas puddings and mincemeat. It is now available in a shredded form which makes it easily usable.

Dripping

Savoury pastry can be made with this commodity but it will not give such good pastry as the use of lard.

DRIED FRUIT

Dried fruits not only refer to Currants, Sultanas, Raisins, and Peel, but also to Figs, Dates, Apricots, Peaches, Apples, Pears, and Prunes. Sometimes glacé cherries and other glacé fruits are included in this general term.

Currants and Sultanas

These should be of good size and colour and free from dirt, stones, and stalks. They may be obtained already washed and selected but another sorting and washing should always be given before use.

It is a good idea to wash this fruit in hot water and, if the fruit is very dry or hard, to actually soak it for 10 minutes to soften it. The fruit should then be well drained in a sieve, placed on a clean cloth, and left to dry for 12 hours or so before use. In this way a soft, juicy fruit will be obtained which will enhance the goods in which it is used.

Raisins

These are of two types, seedless and the larger ones with stones (Muscatel). For most goods, the seedless raisins are used, but in puddings the use of large stoned raisins will give a better flavour. This fruit will also benefit from the washing procedure previously described.

Dates

These are usually packed with the stones already removed and no further treatment is necessary before they are used.

Figs, Apricots, Peaches, Apples, Pears, Prunes

Before these can be used they need a preliminary washing and then at least a 12-hour soaking in water. For compote, the fruit should be cooked in the liqueur in which it has been soaking.

Candied Peel

Three types are available: Orange, Lemon, and Citron.

A mixture of all three makes an interesting blend of colour. The peel should be cut finely into small cubes approx. $\frac{1}{4}$ in. ($\frac{1}{2}$ cm) and mixed in with the other dried fruit used.

Glacé Cherries and Other Glacé Fruit

These are usually packed in thick syrup which must be washed off before their use in a mixing. The fruit may be used whole or chopped into pieces.

Ginger in Syrup

In this product, the ginger rhizome is preserved in a heavy syrup. This preserved ginger may be used cut into pieces or crushed.

NUT PRODUCTS

Almonds

There are many types of almond products available to the patissier. The types prepared for decoration are as follows:

Unblanched whole almonds	– May be roasted and salted
Split almonds	– May be roasted and salted
Strip almonds	– May be roasted

Flaked almonds   – May be roasted
Nib almonds   – May be roasted or coloured.

Ground Almonds

When the true flavour of almonds is required, the use of a proportion of ground almonds is recommended in place of some of the flour used in the recipe. Ground almonds are also the main ingredient used for macaroons and almond paste.

Other Nuts

The composition of most nuts is very similar and many products which are traditionally made with almonds can also be made with other types of nuts.

Walnuts. Available as broken or halves. May be used either as an ingredient in cakes or for decorative effect.

Brazil. Available as broken or whole.

Hazelnuts. These may be used as decoration either blanched, unblanched, or roasted. Ground hazelnuts may be used in place of almonds in macaroon goods.

Pecan. Very useful as a decorative nut. Available as halves or broken.

Coconut. This is available as: strip (thread), desiccated, or flour. It can be used in place of ground almonds in many recipes. The desiccated coconut may be roasted to make an attractive decorative medium.

Chestnuts. These must first be cooked either by roasting or boiling. They can be made into a sweetmeat by preserving in sugar – marron glacé. This may be crushed or made into a purée and used to flavour many types of sweet dishes.

Peanuts. Ground peanuts may be used as a substitute for ground almonds but are not a very satisfactory alternative.

Raw Marzipan

This product is made by mixing sugar and almonds in the proportion of $\frac{1}{3}$ sugar and $\frac{2}{3}$ almonds, cooking the mixture by steam heating, and milling it into a stiff paste, light grey in colour. It may be used for making modelling pastes and macaroons by the addition of sugar and may also be incorporated into a cake to achieve a flavour of almonds. This is a bakers' and confectioners' product and may not be readily known to many patissiers.

Praline

If croquant (nougat) is milled to a paste through granite or steel rollers, a product called praline paste is made. It can be made from any type of nut although usually almonds and hazelnuts are used. Praline is used for flavouring purposes.

Almond Paste

Although this can easily be made (*see* page 251), many patissiers may wish to purchase this commodity already manufactured. The quality of the almond paste depends upon its almond content, the best being approx. 40%. It is also available either neutral or in various colours.

Macaroon Paste

This product is made from ground almonds, sugar, and egg whites. It may be made into a macaroon mixing by the addition of water, egg whites, or egg, in accordance with the instructions supplied by the manufacturer.

Storage of Nut Products

On prolonged storage, nuts are very prone to become rancid and become ravaged by weevils and moth. They are best stored in an airtight tin or jar in a cool, dry place.

Marzipan and almond paste readily forms a skin when exposed to air. To avoid this it should be wrapped in waxed paper or a plastic bag. However, raw marzipan will rapidly go mouldy if stored too long in a plastic bag. The real solution is not to keep marzipan for any longer than necessary but obtain fresh supplies from the manufacturer as and when required.

FLAVOURING MATERIALS

Besides the obvious natural flavours the patissier imparts to his goods by the use of butter, chocolate, fruit, etc., there are many materials which may be added, either to reinforce or modify the natural flavour. These materials may be classified into Extracts, Essential Oils, and Essences.

Extracts

These are derived from the natural flavouring material. The flavour is extracted by macerating the natural source in ethyl alcohol and so such extractions contain its true bouquet. An example of such an extract is vanilla. These extracts are not only the best flavouring materials to use but, as one would expect, are also the most expensive.

Essential Oils

All fruits, nuts, and flowers yield an oil which contains the principal flavour. However, only a few materials such as spices and citrus fruits can be used to yield this oil economically. The most useful of these are lemon and orange. Since these oils will withstand high temperatures without deterioration their use is favoured in biscuits which are baked at a high temperature.

Essences

Many flavours can now be made artificially from coal tar products; although the flavour does not have the true bouquet of the natural products, used with discretion, they are useful to reinforce natural flavours and are fairly inexpensive. They will not withstand high temperatures however, so their use should be confined to flavouring cream, jellies, icings, etc.

Blended Flavours

Some of the most popular essences are compounded from both natural and artificial sources. Such essences have the true bouquet of the natural flavour, reinforced with the strength of the artificial essence.

In general the quality of essences may be indicated by the cost. The better essences will always be the most expensive.

Essences, extracts, or essential oils cannot always imitate the natural flavour on their own and may require certain additions. An example of this is in the use of lemon or similar fruit flavour which usually accompanies an acid taste. For the true flavour citric or tartaric acid should also be introduced.

Spices

These are available in three forms:
Spice oils   – The essential oil of the spice
Ground spice – Finely ground to a powder
Preserved   – Ginger.

Fruit Pastes and Concentrates

These are first class products which impart the true flavour of the fruit. As one would expect such products are expensive but their use to flavour creams, etc. cannot be excelled.

Spirits and Liqueurs

These are used in high class patisserie to impart flavour. In Britain, because of the high excise duty, these special flavours are expensive and therefore should be used with discretion. Their use should be confined to creams, icings, etc., and they should rarely be used as ingredients in goods which are to be baked, since spirits and liqueurs are volatile substances which can vaporize when heated. If a spirit like rum is required to flavour cakes such as Christmas and wedding cakes, it is best added by pouring onto the cake after it is baked.

These products should always be stored in well-stoppered bottles.

Storage

All these flavouring materials have a limited storage life and should be used as soon as possible after purchase. If left in the presence of air for a period of time, they undergo a chemical change known as oxidation and objectionable off-flavours will develop. All flavours whether in liquid or powder form should be stored in airtight containers away from strong sunlight.

Chocolate and Cocoa

Chocolate Couverture. This is available either as Milk, Plain, or Blended. Before it may be used satisfactorily, it must be tempered (*see* Chapter 18, page 244).

Block Cocoa. This is chocolate devoid of sugar. Its use is confined to the flavouring of icings which are themselves very sweet.

Cooking Chocolate. Available in either Milk or Plain, this chocolate does not need to be tempered before use but merely warmed (not above 110°F (43°C)).

White Chocolate. This is really manufactured from cocoa butter, milk powder, and sugar, but must be treated in the same way as couverture.

Cocoa. There are two types available, ordinary and superfine, the latter being superior.

Cocoa Butter. When the natural fat of chocolate is extracted the result is cocoa butter. It is used to thin couverture for use as a coating medium but can also be used to glaze marzipan fruits.

Coffee

Available as a flavouring agent in three forms:
1. Normal solution extracted from coffee beans in the normal way
2. Concentrated extract of coffee
3. Instant powdered coffee

Where flavour is required without dilution due to water only, products 2 and 3 can be used.

The product 2 may have chicory added.

BAKING POWDER

Baking powder is made as follows:

2 parts Cream of Tartar or substitute (acid)

1 part Bicarbonate of Soda (alkali).

Sieve together about 6 times to ensure uniform dispersal. Store in an airtight tin in a dry atmosphere.

Cream of Tartar Baking Powder

This type of baking powder is now practically unavailable to purchase and can only be made up by the patissier. Its great virtue is that it leaves no aftertaste in goods in which it is used and so these goods have a superior flavour. However, it reacts rather quickly once in contact with water, giving off its carbon dioxide gas. Therefore, goods containing cream of tartar baking powder need to be baked off fairly quickly.

Substitute 'Cream' Powders

Most of these are derivatives from phosphoric acid (phosphates) which, whilst harmless, imparts an aftertaste or 'bite' to goods in which this baking powder is used in large quantities, e.g. scones. Phosphates have the advantage that they do not react very quickly with water and so goods containing phosphate baking powder may be left standing prior to baking. The appearance of goods in which phosphate baking powders are used is usually superior.

Glucono Delta Lactone (G.D.L.)

Another type of acid substitute for cream of tartar is G.D.L. This is superior both from the point of view of flavour and its slowness to react in the cold. Like phosphates, goods can be left standing prior to being baked.

VOL

This is ammonium bicarbonate. When heated this chemical produces carbon dioxide gas, ammonia gas, and water. Although it appears to be an ideal aerating agent, it can only be used in biscuits which have little moisture content and are thin and baked at a high temperature. In goods like cake, it is difficult to get rid of the ammonia gas which leaves an objectionable taint in the baked goods.

JAMS AND CURDS

Although these may be made by the patissier and there is a section dealing with this on page 287, probably most patissiers will use a product made by a reputable manufacturer. The price is a guide to quality but there are now regulations governing the minimum quality of jam. The use of a good full fruit jam will always pay dividend because of its flavour.

Storage

These products should not be stored for longer than absolutely necessary. They are prone to attack by moulds and yeasts.

If the product has not been packed hot in sterile containers or has been opened, mould or yeast spores can settle on its surface and bring about its deterioration. Mould will form a coloured growth (usually green) on the surface and can be removed, leaving the product perfectly usable afterwards. Yeast, on the other hand, will ferment the product and make it completely unsuitable for further use.

JELLIES

Jellies may be divided into:

Concentrated Gelatine or Agar Jellies

Available in various flavours and colours, these are used for making jellies by the addition of a quantity of boiling water. Provided they are stored in a dry place, they should not deteriorate.

Piping Jelly

Ideal medium for decorative uses. Available in various flavours and colours.

Glazing Jelly

This is similar to piping jelly but is neutral in colour and is used as a glaze for fruit flans, etc.

Quick Set Pectin Jelly

This product is in the form of a syrup which will set to a jelly once a certain measured amount of citric acid is stirred in. It is an ideal jelly for the glazing of fruit flans.

A novel way to glaze flat areas, such as torten and gâteaux, is explained on page 118.

Jellying Agents

Gelatine. Available either as a coarse powder or in sheets. For the best results, the leaf gelatine should be used. A preliminary soaking in water is always recommended before the gelatine is used in various goods. Although heat is required to dissolve gelatine thoroughly in water it is a mistake to subject it to prolonged boiling as this will weaken it.

Agar. Available as a coarse powder or as strips. This is a difficult commodity to get into solution which can only be achieved by prolonged boiling. Its use is confined mainly to marshmallow.

Pectin. This is used to increase the setting properties of jellies and jams made from various fruits naturally deficient in pectin. Two types are available: either dry or liquid. The dry pectin powder is the most convenient to use and has the greater strength.

Gum Tragacanth. This gum is available either as flakes or as a powder. With water it forms a mucilage which is used to stiffen various mixtures such as sugar and almond paste. The powder form is recommended for use in patisserie.

Gum Arabic. This is also a gum which forms a solution only with difficulty. It is usually in powder form and has to be dissolved in hot water for use.

DECORATING MATERIALS

Sugar-preserved Fruits and Flowers (and Jellies)

Many decorating materials are fruits or flowers which are preserved in sugar or syrup. There are two groups:

Confiture Fruits. In this category are glacé cherries, angelica, pineapple and ginger. These should be kept moist in store, preferably in a heavy syrup. Before use the syrup should be washed off and the fruit dried.

Crystallized Fruits and Flowers. Rose, lilac, violet petals, and mimosa are in this category. With crystallized fruits, the preserving sugar they contain has been allowed to crystallize. Keeping such goods in perfect condition requires a dry atmosphere. Dampness in store could cause the sugar crystals to soften and eventually dissolve away.

Jellies

Many decorations are made from pectin jelly shapes usually covered with sugar crystals. The most popular of these are orange and lemon slices which are available either natural size or smaller. Pineapple slices are also imitated in jelly.

Coralettes and Vermicelli

These are very useful decorating mediums. They can be made from a variety of materials as follows:

Chocolate. Available as plain or milk.

Almonds. Nib almonds coloured in a variety of tints.

Sugar. Coloured icing dried in the form of short threads or very small grains.

Other materials which are used for decoration in a similar way to coralettes are flaked, nibbed, or strip almonds, and desiccated coconut. Both these may be roasted prior to their use.

YEAST

This is available as a grey plastic solid which can be easily broken into lumps. Its storage should not be prolonged more than absolutely necessary; it is always best used fresh. If it has to be stored, a cool moist place should be chosen, e.g. in a refrigerator at approx. 40°F (4·5°C).

BREAD

Many patisserie items contain bread and this commodity is usually purchased from the baker. It is essential that the bread chosen should have a stable and firm crumb to enable it to be cut (e.g. for charlottes). The best type to purchase is usually the sandwich loaf.

Storage

Bread is best kept stored at room temperature. As bread stales more rapidly at temperatures around the freezing point of water, it is a mistake to think that placing it in a normal refrigerator will delay its staling rate. Deep freeze, i.e. −5°F (−20°C), will keep bread indefinitely.

FRUIT

For high class patisserie, choice ripe fruit should always be used. Choosing the best fruit for the purpose required is not always an easy task, especially if it is outside the fruit's normal season.

Apples

These are of two types: dessert and cooking.

Dessert Apples. These should be sweet and juicy and of good flavour. They may be: hard – Cox's Orange Pippin, medium – Laxton's Superb, soft – James Grieve.

Cooking Apples. These are sour and more suitable for cooking purposes. The best known and most reliable is Bramley's Seedling which has a season from October to March.

The number of different varieties of apples is considerable and even a normal English catalogue would list about fifty. Many of the apples sold on the market are imported from France, Italy, South Africa, Canada, U.S.A., Australia, and New Zealand; therefore, with our own season, apples are available all the year round.

Selection and Storage. Apples easily bruise when handled roughly or knocked against something hard, and this is enough to start the deterioration of the apple to the state when it is rotten. If apples have to be stored for any length of time, they should be individually wrapped in oiled tissue so that if decomposition sets in it will be confined to that particular apple only. One rotten apple will easily cause adjacent sound apples to turn rotten also. Always store in a dry place.

Use. Once the apple has been cut open and exposed to the air, oxidation occurs which causes the surface to brown. The use of lemon juice, salt, or ascorbic acid prevents or retards this action but sliced apples should not be exposed to the atmosphere for too long a period before use.

Pears

Most of what has been written about apples can also refer to pears.

The most well known are Conference, Doyenné du Comice, and William Bon Chretien.

Selection and Storage. To be in the correct condition for eating, a ripe pear should be soft but with the flesh still firm, sweet, and juicy. Pears readily become over-ripe with a soft sleepy interior sometimes starting at the centre. For this reason, it is unwise to store pears for too long. Storage in a refrigerator slows down the ripening of pears but with some varieties, e.g. William Bon Chretien, they can become over-ripe with a sleepy interior in spite of the outside being firm.

Usually pears are purchased slightly under-ripe and allowed to ripen by the patissier. If a dessert pear yields to slight pressure at the stalk end, it is ready for eating.

Apricots, Peaches, and Nectarines

Most of these are imported, Italy being one of the main exporting countries. These fruits readily bruise and are usually carefully packed wrapped in tissue paper in moulded trays. If possible they are best purchased in this way to eliminate handling by a third person. Choice ripe fruits should be semi-firm but juicy.

Storage. In a refrigerator or cold store.

Cherries

These are mostly home-grown. There are many different varieties with colours ranging from yellow to very dark crimson, almost black. Most cherries are dessert but the one exception is Morello, which is in great demand for making jam, tart fillings, etc.

Unless preserved in some way the cherry season is a short one, the dessert varieties being available in June and July and the Morello in August and September.

Storage. In a dry cool place and remove any blemished cherries as soon as they appear.

Plums, Greengages, and Damsons

These are also mainly a home crop although a few large dessert plums are imported from abroad, mainly Italy. Like the cherries, there are many varieties of varying sizes and with colours ranging from green, yellow, blue, purple, and almost black. Most of the plums are suitable for either dessert or cooking purposes and a few, such as damsons, for cooking only.

The season for plums is fairly short, from July to September depending upon variety. When ripe, the flesh should be very juicy and fall away from the stone.

Storage. This fruit does not keep for long in store without becoming rotten. A cool, dry store is required and any plums showing signs of decay should be removed at once to prevent contamination of the rest.

Gooseberries

This is another home-grown fruit. The unripe green gooseberry is available from the end of April and is used extensively for cooking purposes. As the gooseberry ripens it also becomes sweeter and it may then be used for dessert purposes. Some varieties of ripe fruit are milky white in colour, others are yellow-green or deep red.

Storage. The unripe gooseberries will have a fairly good storage life provided they are kept dry and cool. The ripe fruit will rapidly deteriorate and should not be kept too long in store. Any blemished fruit should be removed at once as soon as it becomes apparent.

Use. Before use, gooseberries need to be washed and 'topped' and 'tailed'.

Soft Fruits (Raspberries, Loganberries, Strawberries, Blackberries, Blackcurrants, Red Currants, and White Currants)

All the above soft fruits are very perishable and great care should be exercised in their selection. Mould will rapidly manifest itself especially if picked in wet weather. When buying, examine the underneath of the container. The presence of fruit stains is a sure indication that the fruit at the base is wet or damaged.

Storage. Soft fruits should be stored in shallow trays in a cool dark place or a refrigerator. Even with every precaution, deterioration will set in within three days from the time of picking.

Selection—

Raspberries and Loganberries. When purchasing make sure the fruit looks really fresh and clean and of good colour. The fruit should be firm but juicy without blemishes.

Strawberries. The same considerations as for raspberries. If the strawberries are to be used as a dessert fruit, the calyx and leaves should still be attached.

Blackberries. This fruit is liable to go bad very quickly so if possible it should be eaten or cooked on the day of purchase.

Black Currants, Red Currants, and White Currants. When these are purchased, check that they are firm, clean, and glossy, not withered or dusty looking. Ensure that there are not very many leaves or strings without berries on them. Black currants should not be bought which have more than 15 per cent of dark berries or 5 per cent green berries turning red.

Citrus Fruits (Oranges, Lemons, Limes, and Grapefruit)

These have to be imported, the main exporting countries being Spain, South Africa, and Israel.

Oranges. These may be sweet or bitter. Among the different sweet types available are Mandarins, Tangerines, and Clementines which are small, Navels which are seedless, and the large thick skinned and very juicy Jaffas. Seville is the most widely known bitter orange which is used extensively in preserves.

Lemons. These should be full of juice with a fresh clear skin. Since the zest is often used for flavouring patisserie, this latter point is important.

Limes. These are like small green lemons widely used for flavouring purposes and for preserves.

Grapefruit. This fruit should be large and firm and full of juice. Brown marks which appear on the skin indicate that the grapefruit is perfectly ripe for eating.

Melons

There are several types, the following being the most widely known and used:

Cantaloup. These are large round melons with a rough skin mottled orange and yellow. The flesh is light orange in colour. These melons are imported mainly from France and Holland in the late summer.

Honeydew. Imported from North Africa and Spain in the late summer, autumn, and winter. These melons are oval-shaped with dark green skins. The flesh is white with a greenish tinge.

Charentais. This melon, which is imported from France in the late summer, is small and round with a mottled green and yellow skin. The flesh is orange coloured.

Water Melon. These are not often to be found in this country because they rapidly deteriorate. They are grown in the warm Mediterranean regions where there is an abundance of water. They are rather large, about the size of a football and green in colour. The flesh is very sweet, red, and juicy with a certain crispness. When chilled or refrigerated, a slice of this melon makes a very refreshing 'drink'.

Selection and Storage. Care must be exercised in buying melons. They should not be either too under- or over-ripe. The ripeness can be detected by gently pressing the top when it should be soft. If the melon is under-ripe, it should be stored until the top softens.

Quince

This is not unlike an apple in appearance. It has a golden-yellow skin and a tough yellow flesh which turns pink on cooking. Because of its high pectin and acid content, quince is used extensively in making preserves.

Prune

Prunes are dried plums and require first soaking and then cooking to make them suitable for eating. They may be obtained graded in different sizes. The large Californian prune is one of the best but also the most expensive.

Banana

Most of our bananas are imported from the Windward Islands. Here they are cut down in an unripe green condition and, with carefully controlled temperature conditions, are allowed to ripen to a golden yellow (tinged with green at the ends), before being placed in the shops for sale.
Selection. If bananas are required to be cooked, they should be as just described. For eating, however, it is best to wait until the skin has begun to show freckles of brown. This is the stage at which the banana is fully ripe and at its best.
Use. Once exposed to the air, banana slices will quickly brown and become unsightly. To prevent this they may be dipped in lemon juice or the slicing may be left to the last possible moment. Besides slicing bananas in various ways, they may also be pulped and incorporated into such dishes as ice-cream.

Grape

Although grapes may be grown in a hothouse in this country, the bulk of our requirements are imported from the Mediterranean countries, particularly North Africa. Supplies also reach us from South Africa and America. Four types are usually to be found on the market: large blue-black, large green, medium-sized red, and small sultana. The last variety is the least expensive and is ideally suitable for macédoine of fruits. The first variety above is usually the most expensive.
Selection. Make sure the grapes are sound, the bunch not containing any bruised or mouldy ones. Before use, the grapes should be washed and allowed to drain thoroughly and dry. Large grapes included in a fruit salad may have their skins and pips removed.
Storage. In a refrigerator or a cold dry store.

Rhubarb

Although not strictly a fruit, this is treated as such. Forced rhubarb is usually available in January. It has slender, light pink stems. The garden grown variety is much darker in colour and has thicker stems. After washing, the rhubarb stems should be cut into suitable sized lengths, after removing any unwanted fibre or skin. It requires a considerable amount of sweetening to overcome the acid taste and to make it palatable.

Pineapple

These have to be imported into this country. The largest and best are obtained from Hawaii but the fresh variety is very expensive.

Selection. The flesh should be of a deep yellow colour with a noticeable fragrance. When ripe the leaves or spikes at the top should loosen easily when pulled.

Except for special sweets in which the outside case of a fresh pineapple is required (e.g. Ninon), the tinned variety fulfils the needs of most patissiers. Tinned pineapple may be obtained in the following cuts: small slices or rings, large slices, cubes, titbits, and crushed. The first two types may also have a fancy cut at the edges of the ring.

Fig

Although figs are grown in this country, they seldom ripen sufficiently to become the delicious dessert fruit that they undoubtedly are. Fresh figs may be cooked in the same way as plums.

Selection. Most of the figs used by the patissier will be the dried imported variety. These should not be too dried and should be fairly clean.

Uses. Dried figs may be used in three ways:

(*a*) Soaked in water and then stewed until soft (same as for other dried fruit).

(*b*) Chopped into pieces and incorporated into puddings, etc.

(*c*) Chopped or minced and cooked with a little water to make a paste to use as a filling.

Dates

This is the fruit of a certain species of palm which grows in hot climes, i.e. North Africa, Western Asia, etc.

Fresh dates are never available in this country but the dessert dates loosely packed in small boxes, unstoned, are a very acceptable substitute.

Selection. Apart from the dessert type which are used for petits fours, etc., dates may be obtained stoned and packed in bulk in a solid pack. Once washed, they are quite acceptable for cooking purposes.

Dessert dates should be very moist and purchased in as fresh a condition as possible. If kept too long in storage these dates will dry out and lose their palatability.

Tinned Fruits	*Sizes of tins*	*Approx. net weight*
	Picnic	8 oz
	A 1	10 oz
	E 1	14 oz
	No. 1 Tall	1 lb
	1 lb Flat	1 lb
	A 2	$1\frac{1}{4}$ lb
	A $2\frac{1}{2}$	$1\frac{3}{4}$ lb
	A 10	$6\frac{3}{4}$ lb

Note. At the time this book was written, no metric sizes of tinned fruits had been decided. Indeed, the weights given here are approximate only, since the canning industry have not standardized on tins.

Selection. When selecting tins of fruit, make sure that they are not dented, punctured, or 'blown'. Rust indicates that the tin has either been in store for a long time or has been stored in a damp place; all such tins should be discarded.

Uses. Once opened, the fruit should never be left in the tin. It should be transferred to a clean basin, preferably china or earthenware, and used as soon as possible. Fruit in syrup may be safely left up to 3 days provided it is placed in a refrigerator. Prolonged storage will encourage fermentation and spoil the product. Unsweetened tinned fruit will deteriorate more rapidly.

CONVERSION TABLES

Recipes in this book are given in ounces and pints as well as grammes and litres. For simplicity the ounce is taken as being equivalent to 30 grammes, instead of its true value of 28·35. Since we are dealing with ratios in a recipe, this approximation has no effect upon the balance of the ingredients in the recipe and is small enough for the yield not to be materially affected.

WEIGHTS

Grammes to ounces

28·35 g	1 oz	50 g	1¾ oz
10 g	0·353 oz	100 g	3½ oz
25 g	0·882 oz	150 g	5¼ oz
50 g	1·764 oz	200 g	7 oz
75 g	2·645 oz	250 g	8¾ oz
100 g	3·523 oz	500 g	17⅔ oz
250 g	8·818 oz	1 kg	2 lb 3 oz
500 g	1 lb 1·637 oz	1½ kg	3 lb 5oz
		2 kg	4 lb 6 oz
		2½ kg	5 lb 8 oz
		3 kg	6 lb 10 oz

Ounces to grammes

1 oz	28·35 g		12 oz	340·20 g
2 oz	56·70 g		13 oz	368·55 g
3 oz	85·05 g		14 oz	396·90 g
4 oz	113·40 g		15 oz	425·25 g
5 oz	141·75 g		16 oz	453·60 g
6 oz	170·10 g		17 oz	481·95 g
7 oz	198·45 g		18 oz	510·30 g
8 oz	226·80 g		19 oz	538·65 g
9 oz	255·15 g		20 oz	567·00 g
10 oz	283·50 g		21 oz	595·35 g
11 oz	311·85 g		22 oz	623·70 g

1 cubic centimetre (cc) of water weighs 1 gramme, which can then be converted as above.

CAPACITY

$\frac{1}{2}$ decilitre $= \frac{1}{3}$ gill $= \frac{1}{12}$ pt $= 1\frac{3}{4}$ oz (approx.)
1 decilitre $= \frac{2}{3}$ gill $= \frac{1}{6}$ pt $= 3\frac{1}{3}$ oz (approx.)
$1\frac{1}{2}$ decilitres $= 1$ gill $= \frac{1}{4}$ pt $= 5$ oz (approx.)
3 decilitres $= 2$ gill $= \frac{1}{2}$ pt $= 10$ oz (approx.)
$5\frac{3}{4}$ decilitres $= 4$ gill $= 1$ pt $= 20$ oz (approx.)
7 decilitres $= 5$ gill $= 1\frac{1}{4}$ pt $= 25$ oz (approx.)
9 decilitres $= 6$ gill $= 1\frac{1}{2}$ pt $= 30$ oz (approx.)
10 decilitres $= 1$ litre $= 7$ gill $= 1\frac{3}{4}$ pt $= 35$ oz (approx.)
$11\frac{1}{2}$ decilitres $= 1\frac{1}{7}$ litre $= 8$ gill $= 2$ pt $= 40$ oz (approx.)
2 litres $= 3\frac{1}{2}$ pt $= 70$ oz (approx.)
3·785 litres $= 1$ American gallon
4·546 litres $= 10$ lb distilled water $= 1$ Imperial gallon

LINEAR MEASURE

1 millimetre $= 0·001$ metre $= 0·0394$ in. $= \frac{1}{20}$ in.
10 millimetres $= 1$ centimetre $= 0·3937$ in. $= \frac{3}{8}$ in.
10 centimetres $= 1$ decimetre $= 3·937$ in. $= 4$ in.
10 decimetres $= 1$ metre $= 39·37$ in. $= 39\frac{1}{4}$ in.

TEMPERATURE

To change Celsius (Centigrade) into Fahrenheit:
  Method (i) Multiply by $\frac{9}{5}$ and add 32.
  Method (ii) Add 40, multiply by $\frac{9}{5}$, and subtract 40.

To change Fahrenheit into Celsius:
  Method (i) Subtract 32 and multiply by $\frac{5}{9}$.
  Method (ii) Add 40, multiply by $\frac{5}{9}$, and subtract 40.

Examples

1. Change 5°C into Fahrenheit.

Method (i) $\cancel{5} \times \dfrac{9}{\cancel{5}} = 9$

$9 + 32 = \underline{41°F \text{ Answer.}}$

Method (ii) $5 + 40 = 45$

$\overset{9}{\cancel{45}} \times \dfrac{9}{\cancel{5}} = 81$

$81 - 40 = \underline{41°F \text{ Answer.}}$

2. Change 41°F into Celsius.

Method (i) $41 - 32 = 9$

$\cancel{9} \times \dfrac{5}{\cancel{9}} = \underline{5°C \text{ Answer.}}$

Method (ii) $41 + 40 = 81$

$\overset{9}{\cancel{81}} \times \dfrac{5}{\cancel{9}} = 45$

$45 - 40 = \underline{5°C \text{ Answer.}}$

Note. 'Celsius' and 'Centigrade' degrees are exactly the same thing, but 'Celsius' is the preferred designation. A temperature conversion table appears on page 340.

EQUIVALENTS FOR OVEN TEMPERATURES

Gas mark	Approximate temperature at centre of oven °F	°C	Heat of oven
¼	240	115 ⎫	
½	265	129 ⎬	Very slow or very cool
1	290	143 ⎭	
2	310	154	Slow or cool
3	335	168	Very moderate or warm
4	355	180	Moderate
5	380	193 ⎫	Moderately hot or fairly hot
6	400	204 ⎭	
7	425	218	Hot
8	445	230 ⎫	Very hot
9	470	243 ⎭	
10	500	260	

Note. This Regulo mark for gas is only true for normal town gas. North Sea gas is hotter and for this a different chart would have to be compiled.

2. Short Pastries, Flans, and Tarts

Service of Flans and Tarts

These look attractive when displayed on a doily on a round silver dish. When served, however, it is advisable not to use a doily as it becomes soiled and is likely to stick to the flan.

If the flan or tart is to be served hot, it is advisable to place it on the dish when cold and warm the dish and tart just prior to service. Transferring a hot flan from the oven to the dish very often results in damage.

Scone Flour

For short, flan, or pie pastry, a flour containing a little baking powder is recommended. Because of the difficulty of accurately weighing and distributing small amounts of baking powder, a special scone flour is used. This is made up as follows:

1 *lb* (480 g) *Flour*   1 *oz* (30 g) *Baking Powder*

Sieve together at least 3 times.

Soft Flour

For a short eating pastry, a flour weak in protein content is recommended, such as English or biscuit or a proprietary cake flour.

SHORT PASTRY

There are three methods of making pastry as follows:

Method 1.

(1) Rub the fat, margarine, or butter, into the flour until no lumps are left.

(2) Make a bay and in this place the liquid (egg, milk, or water) and the sugar or salt. These may be previously dissolved in the liquid.

(3) Mix ingredients to a smooth paste.

Method 2.

(1) Cream the sugar and fat together until light.

(2) Add the egg or liquid and beat in.

(3) Stir in the flour and mix ingredients to a smooth paste.

Method 3.

(1) Cream the fat with an equal quantity of flour.

(2) Add the liquid in which has been dissolved the sugar or salt.

(3) Stir in the flour and mix ingredients to a smooth paste.

Note. Method 3 is the only one which guarantees that there is no undissolved sugar and will give the shortest eating paste.

FLANS

The amount of pastry used per person for flans is largely a matter of taste. In some books 1 oz (30 g) flour per person is recommended, whilst in the recipes which follow the minimum of $\frac{1}{2}$ oz (15 g) per person is given. Much depends upon the attitude of the patissier and the preference of his customer. The author believes that the main use of the pastry is to hold the filling and it is in the latter that the customer is really interested. If, however, it is felt that the pastry ranks equal in importance to the filling, the larger quantity of flour will be required and the quantity of pastry per person given would need to be increased.

Flan Pastry—Sweet Pastry—Pâte Sucrée

1 oz (30 g) *scone flour (page 38)*	1 oz (30 g) *sugar*
3 oz (90 g) *soft flour*	1 *teaspoonful lemon juice*
2½ oz (75 g) *butter*	¾ oz (22 g) *eggs (half)*

Short Pastry (for Fruit Pies and Tarts)—Pâte à Foncer

1 oz (30 g) *scone flour (page 38)*	1 oz (30 g) *butter or margarine*
3 oz (90 g) *soft flour*	½ oz (15 g) *sugar*
1 oz (30 g) *lard or cooking fat*	½ oz (15 g) *water*

Method 1 or 3. Mix ingredients to a light short dough.

Short Pastries, Flans, and Tarts

In the above recipe the sugar can be omitted. However, its use will impart a sheen and bloom to pastry which will improve its appearance.

Suet Pastry (for Baked and Steamed Rolls, Puddings, Dumplings, etc.)

2 oz (60 g) *scone flour (page 38)*	2 oz (60 g) *water*
2 oz (60 g) *soft flour*	*A pinch of salt*
2 oz (60 g) *finely chopped suet*	

Method 1. Mix lightly to a stiff paste.
Chopping Suet.
(1) Break into pieces removing all sinew.
(2) Place on a chopping board with some flour.
(3) Chop finely with a large knife.

Figure 1. Baked open flan case prior to filling

Baked Flan Cases

(Yield 8 covers using 8 in. (20 cm) flan ring) (Figure 1).
(1) Make flan paste using 4 oz (120 g) flour (scone and soft flour).
(2) Place an 8-in. (20-cm) flan ring on a clean baking tray (no flour or grease is required).
(3) Make a ball of the paste and then roll out with the rolling pin to approx. 10 in. (25 cm) diameter.
(4) Carefully pick up the pastry by wrapping it around the rolling pin and lay it over the flan ring.
(5) Remove rolling pin and with the fingers gently ease the pastry so that it fills the ring and extends up the sides.
(6) Press pastry firmly against the sides and then trim off surplus by running a knife against the edge of the ring. If done properly there should not be very much pastry to trim off.
(7) The walls or top edge of the flan ring may be crimped either with a pair of metal nippers or with the fingers to give a decorative effect but, if this treatment is contemplated, 6 oz (180 g) flour into paste must be allowed so that the walls are thicker and higher.
(8) Prick the pastry in the base of the flan ring with a knife or docker.
(9) Bake in an oven at 420°F (215°C) until light golden brown in colour.
Note. In many books it is recommended that before baking the flan should be covered with a disc of greaseproof paper and filled with dried peas or beans. If the flan has been made as described, this is unnecessary; but if either more paste is used or the walls are made higher than the ring, then such a precaution is wise, to eliminate risk of the walls of pastry collapsing. If beans or peas have been used, they should be removed before the flan is cooked through and the flan returned to the oven for completion of baking. The flan ring should in any case be removed prior to the finish of the baking, so that the walls of pastry are nicely coloured. These may be egg washed if desired.

Soft and Tinned Fruit

The base of the flan may be first covered with either pastry cream or custard. Drain the fruit well and then arrange it as a pattern on the pastry cream. The quantity of fruit will vary according to type but should never exceed 2 oz (60 g) per head. The flans in the two photographs took only 8 oz (240 g) tinned fruit, i.e. 1 oz (30 g) per head. The following shows how much tinned fruit is approximately equal to 2 oz (60 g).

1 Pineapple Ring	4 Apricots
16 Mandarin Oranges	20 Cherries
1 Peach	1 Pear

Finish off by masking with a glaze (*see* page 302).

Figure 2. Fruit flan: showing
arrangement using
sliced peaches and cherries

Figure 3. Fruit flan: showing arrangement
using mandarin oranges, cherries,
and a pineapple ring

Figure 4. Banana flan

Banana Flan—Flan Aux Bananes (Figure 4)

(Yield 8 covers)

    4 *oz* (120 *g*) *flour into flan pastry*
    ½ *pint* (3 *decilitres*) *pastry cream or thick custard*
    3 *bananas*
    1 *oz* (30 *g*) *apricot jam* (*for glaze*)

(1) Cook flan unfilled and allow to cool.

(2) Make custard or pastry cream and, whilst still hot, pour into flan case. Allow to set.

(3) Peel and slice the bananas evenly and neatly.

(4) Arrange the slices on top so that they overlap each other. Start at the edge first.

(5) Coat with the apricot glaze.

Note. The apricot glaze is made by boiling apricot jam with a little water and passing it through a sieve (*see page* 302).

Fresh Cherry Flan – Flan Aux Cerises (Yield 8 covers)

    4 *oz* (120 *g*) *flour into flan pastry*
    1 *lb* (480 *g*) *cherries*
    4 *oz* (120 *g*) *sugar*
    1 *oz* (30 *g*) *red glaze* (*see page* 302)

(1) Line an 8-in. (20-cm) flan ring with flan paste and prick the bottom.

(2) Remove the stones from the fresh cherries.

(3) Carefully arrange the cherries in the flan case.

(4) Sprinkle on the sugar.

(5) Bake in the oven at 420°F (215°C).

(6) Remove flan ring after 15 minutes baking and return flan to oven for a further 10 minutes approx. or until flan is coloured and cooked.

(7) Cover top with the hot red glaze.

Gooseberry Flan – Flan Aux Groseilles (Yield 8 covers)

    4 *oz* (120 *g*) *flour into flan pastry*
    1 *lb* (480 *g*) *gooseberries* (*washed, topped, and tailed*)
    8 *oz* (240 *g*) *sugar*
    1 *oz* (30 *g*) *apricot glaze*

Same method as for Cherry Flan.

Plum, Apricot, and Rhubarb Flans

Same method and quantities as for Gooseberry Flan. The fruit is first cut into suitable sized pieces. For red plum and rhubarb use the red glaze, and for apricot and yellow plum, the apricot.

Note. The amount of sugar mentioned in the recipes above must be regarded as the maximum and is governed by the type of fruit used, e.g. Morello cherries would require considerably more sugar than eating cherries. Red gooseberry require less than the traditional green gooseberry. Ripe fruit will not require as much sugar as unripe fruit.

High sugar quantities might also cause the pastry at the base of the flan to become soggy and difficult to bake out. Adjustment to the sugar content might have to be made for this reason or alternatively cake crumbs inserted at the base of the flan to absorb the excess juice.

Apple Flan – Flan Aux Pommes (Figure 5) (Yield 8 covers)

> 4 *oz* (120 g) *flour into flan pastry*
> 6 *oz* (180 g) *sugar*
> 2 *lb* (960 g) *cooking apples, fresh*
> 1 *oz* (30 g) *apricot jam (for glaze)*

For tinned apple allow only 1½ lb (720 g) (25% waste in peel and core of fresh apples).

(1) Make the flan pastry and line an 8-in. (20-cm) flan ring. Trim edge and prick base with fork.

(2) Half cook the flan in an oven approx. 400°F (204°C) and allow to cool.

(3) Select two of the best apples and make apple purée with the remainder (*see* next recipe).

(4) Place the cooled apple purée in the flan and spread level.

(5) Peel, core, and then thinly slice the apples selected. Place slices in cold, salt water as they are cut (to prevent discoloration).

(6) Wash slices with fresh water and remove one by one, placing each slice on top of the purée so that they overlap. Start at the edge of the flan and make each slice point to the centre. When a complete circle has been made, it will be necessary to lift up the first slice laid and tuck the last slice under it.

Figure 5. Apple flan

Usually two circles can be formed if the apples are small enough. These circles could run in alternate directions as seen in the photograph. Also the slices of apple may be trimmed to shape and size with either fluted or plain cutters. The flan illustrated has been treated in this way.

(7) Sugar may be sprinkled on top and the flan baked in an oven approx. 400°F (204°C). Since the flan case has already been half baked, it is only necessary to complete the baking and soften the apple slices. If these are thin enough this should be completed in 10 to 15 minutes. Further, because the pastry has been half baked, it is possible to complete the baking without the ring which is removed at the first stage. This allows the flan casing to be baked to a nice golden brown which can be improved by previous egg-washing.

(8) Finally mask the top with the apricot glaze.

Apple Purée – Marmelade de Pommes (Suitable for the flans for 8 covers)

    1 *lb* (480 *g*) *cooking apples*
    4 *oz* (120 *g*) *sugar*
    $\frac{1}{2}$ *oz* (15 *g*) *butter*

Wash, peel, core, and slice the apples. Melt the butter in the saucepan over the fire and add the apples and sugar. Cover with a lid and gently cook until apples are soft. Remove and pass through a sieve.

Notes

1. Take care to see that neither the chopping board, saucepan, knives, or sieve have been contaminated with strong flavoured substances like onions as this will be transferred to the apple and spoil its flavour.

2. The apples should not be cooked for longer than is necessary for them to soften. The action of passing through the sieve will reduce them to a purée even if the slices are still whole.

3. The quantity of sugar can be adjusted to suit the individual taste and also the type of apple used. Some apples require more sweetening than others.

4. If tinned apples are used reduce to $\frac{3}{4}$ lb (360 g). (There is a 25% waste in the peel and core of fresh apples.)

Apple Meringue Pie – Flan Aux Pommes Meringuées (Yield 8 cover)

    4 *oz* (120 *g*) *flour into flan pastry*   2 *egg whites*
    1$\frac{1}{2}$ *lb* (720 *g*) *apples into purée*   4 *oz* (120 *g*) *sugar*

(1) Using an 8-in. (20-cm) flan ring, prepare and cook an apple flan but without the slices. For this purpose the flan case can be completely cooked prior to the purée being added: it need not be replaced in the oven until the meringue has been piped on top.

(2) Using 2 egg whites and 4 oz (120 g) sugar, make a meringue and pipe this in a decorative pattern on top.

(3) Place into an oven approx. 450°F (232°C) for a few minutes until meringue is coloured.

Note. The meringue could be in two colours for a more decorative effect. In some books this is referred to as *Apple Amber*.

Lemon Meringue Pie – Flan Aux Citrons Meringués (Yield 8 covers)

(1) Using an 8-in. (20-cm) flan ring and 4 oz (120 g) flour, make and bake an unfilled flan case.
(2) Make the filling (*see* below) and pour into the baked flan case.
(3) When this has set, make a meringue with 2 egg whites and 4 oz (120 g) sugar and pipe it on top in a decorative fashion.
(4) Place into a hot oven at 450°F (232°C) for a few minutes to colour.

Filling for Lemon Meringue Pie

4 *oz* (120 g) *sugar*
5 *oz* (150 g) *water*
¾ *oz* (22 g) *cornflour*
1 *oz* (30 g) *butter*
2 *egg yolks*
1 *large or* 2 *small lemons or* 2 *oz* (60 g) *lemon juice*

(1) Dissolve sugar in half of the water and bring to the boil.
(2) Add the cornflour mixed with the remaining half of the water and cook mixture until it thickens: stir well.
(3) Add the zest and juice of the lemon and the melted butter.
(4) Lastly whisk in the two yolks.

TARTS

Individual Fruit Tarts (Figure 6) (Yield 12 tarts)

Figure 6. Open fruit tarts: (*left*) peach slices; (*centre*) mandarin oranges; (*right*) pineapple wedges

(1) Use 4 oz (120 g) flour and make into flan pastry.

(2) Roll out pastry $\frac{1}{10}$ in. ($2\frac{1}{2}$ mm) thick.

(3) Cut out with a round cutter and line small patty tins. ⎫ For alternative
(4) Press pastry firmly into the tin and trim off edge.   ⎬ method *see*
                                                           ⎭ Figure 7.

(5) Prick base with a fork and bake in an oven approx. 400°F (204°C) until golden brown.

(6) When cold remove from patty tins and add a suitable piece or pieces of fruit, preferably forming a pattern.

(7) Glaze with either a pectin quick-set jelly or the fruit juice gelled with arrowroot.

Figure 7. Lining patty tins:
     (*a*) Covering with pastry (above left).
     (*b*) Pressing pastry into tins with a piece of scrap pastry (above right).
     (*c*) Passing the rolling pin over to remove excess pastry (below).

Figure 8. Fruit tart: showing method used to notch the edge

Large Fruit Tarts (Yield 8 covers, using an 8-in. (20-cm) pie plate)

(1) Make short pastry using 6 oz (180 g) flour.
(2) Using just over half, make a round ball and pin out sufficient to just cover the plate.
(3) Put in the fruit filling (*see* below).
(4) Pin out remainder of paste to cover the plate.
(5) Brush edges of bottom paste with egg or water and cover the plate with the paste.
(6) Press paste firmly around the edge and trim off with a knife.
(7) Using the thumb and a knife, notch the edge as illustrated in Figure 8.
(8) Make two or three cuts in the top, wash with egg or water, and sprinkle with castor sugar.
(9) Bake in oven at approx. 420°F (215°C).

Fruit Filling for Tarts

Apple, plum, blackberry, bilberry, gooseberry, damson, cherry, red currant, black currant, rhubarb, dates, etc.

The fruit filling should be ¾ to 1 lb (480 g) of which not more than 2 oz (60 g) is juice. Alternatively 8 oz (240 g) of solid fruit and 4 oz (120 g) juice thickened with cornflour could be used.

Dutch Apple Tart (Yield 8 covers)

6 oz (180 g) *flour into shortpastry*	2 oz (60 g) *sultanas*
1 lb (480 g) *cooking apples*	8 oz (240 g) *sugar*

Same method as for Fruit Tarts except for the filling which should be prepared as follows:
(1) Peel, core, and wash the apples.
(2) Partly cook in a saucepan with a little water and the sugar.
(3) Add the cleaned sultanas and allow to cool.

Mincemeat Tart (Yield 8 covers)

> 6 *oz* (180 *g*) *flour into shortpastry*
> 12 *oz* (360 *g*) *mincemeat* (*see page* 237)

Same method as for Fruit Tarts, using mincemeat as the filling.

Jam or Curd Tarts (Figure 9) (Yield 8 covers)

> 6 *oz* (180 *g*) *flour into shortpastry*
> 8 *oz* (240 *g*) *jam or curd* (*e.g. lemon, orange, pineapple, etc.*)

(1) Make shortpastry and line an 8-in. (20-cm) tart plate or flan ring.
(2) Trim and notch the edge and prick the base.
(3) Spread the jam evenly in the tart.
(4) Using the trimmings of pastry, pin out and cut thin strips, either plain or fluted using a jigger wheel.
(5) Lay these over the jam in a criss-cross fashion.
(6) Bake in an oven at 420°F (215°C) until golden brown in colour.
Note. Make sure that the jam is free of lumps. If too stiff it should be reduce slightly with water.
When cold this tart could be decorated or served with fresh whipped cream.

Individual Jam Tarts (Yield 12 tarts)

> 4 *oz* (120 *g*) *flour into shortpastry*   6 *oz* (180 *g*) *jam or curd*

(1) Make shortpastry using 4 oz (120 g) flour.
(2) Roll out pastry to $\frac{1}{10}$ in. ($2\frac{1}{2}$ mm) in thickness.
(3) Cut out with round cutter and line patty pans. (A fluted cutter may be used or the tart may be hand notched with the use of a plain cutter.)
(4) Reduce the jam or curd to the correct consistency with water and pipe it into each tart through either a savoy bag with $\frac{1}{8}$ in. (3 mm) tube or a greaseproof paper bag.
(5) Bake in oven at 420°F (215°C) until pastry is golden brown in colour.
Note. These also may be decorated or served with fresh whipped cream.

Syrup or Treacle Tart (Yield 8 covers)

Same as Jam Tarts but with the following filling:
> 8 *oz* (240 *g*) *syrup or treacle*   1 *teaspoonful* (10 *g*) *lemon juice*
> $1\frac{1}{2}$ *oz* (45 *g*) *white bread-crumbs*

Individual Mince or Fruit Pies (Figure 10) (Yield 8 tarts)

> 4 *oz* (120 *g*) *flour into shortpastry*
> 6 *oz* (180 *g*) *mincemeat* (*see page* 237) *or* 8 *oz* (240 *g*) *fruit*

(1) Make shortpastry using 4 oz (120 g) flour.
(2) Roll out shortpastry $\frac{1}{10}$ in. ($2\frac{1}{2}$ mm) in thickness.
(3) Cut out with round plain cutter and line patty pans.
(4) Place a teaspoonful of mincemeat or fruit filling in the centre of each tart.
(5) Roll out remaining paste very thinly $\frac{1}{16}$ in. ($1\frac{1}{2}$ mm) and cut out with a smaller cutter.
(6) Damp the edges of the tarts with water. (Water may be sprinkled on.)
(7) Lay on the smaller disc of pastry.
(8) Press down with the rolled edge of a smaller cutter so that the top is secured to the bottom.
(9) Prick with a fork or spear with a knife.
(10) Bake in an oven at 420°F (215°C) until a golden colour.
(11) Dredge liberally with icing sugar.
(12) Place on a doily on a silver dish and serve warm with an appropriate sauce, e.g. custard, brandy, etc.

Bakewell Tarts (Yield 8 covers in 8-in. (20-cm) ring)

> 4 oz (120 g) *flour into flan pastry*   2 oz (60 g) *raspberry jam*
> 2 oz (60 g) *icing sugar*

Frangipane Filling

Recipe 1 (*Best Quality*)

> 4 oz (120 g) *castor sugar*
> 4 oz (120 g) *butter or margarine*
> 4 oz (120 g) *eggs*
> 4 oz (120 g) *ground almonds*
> $\frac{1}{4}$ oz (8 g) *flour*

Recipe 2 (*Medium Quality*)

> 4 oz (120 g) *castor sugar*
> 4 oz (120 g) *butter or margarine*
> 4 oz (120 g) *eggs*
> 2 oz (60 g) *ground almonds*
> 4 oz (120 g) *sponge crumbs*
> $\frac{1}{4}$ oz (8 g) *flour*

Figure 9. Jam flan: laying on the trellis prior to baking

Method for Filling. Cream and butter and sugar, beat in the egg, and lastly stir in the dry material.

Method for Tart.

(1) Line flan ring with $\frac{3}{4}$ of the pastry.

(2) Prick the base well with a fork.

(3) Spread on the jam.

(4) Place in the frangipane filling and spread evenly.

(5) Pin out the remaining pastry, cut into strips approx. $\frac{1}{4}$ in. (6 mm) wide and place on top to form a lattice pattern (aˢ for large jam tarts).

(6) Bake in an oven at 36 °F (185°C) for approx. 30 minutes until cooked and golden in colour.

(7) When baked, brush over thin water icing.

Figure 10.   Mince pies:
   (_a_) Showing method of pressing on the tops (above).
   (_b_) Baked and dusted with icing sugar (below).

Fruit Slices (Yield 8 covers)

4 oz (120 g) flour into shortpastry
6 to 8 oz (180 to 240 g) fruit, i.e. date and apple (tinned, fresh, or cooked)
2 oz (60 g) apricot jam

Method for Open Slice.
(1) Pin out the pastry to approx. $\frac{1}{10}$ in. ($2\frac{1}{2}$ mm) thick.
(2) Lift up with the rolling pin and lay the sheet on a baking tray.
(3) Prick well with a fork or docker.
(4) Cut into strips 4 in. (10 cm) wide and bake in oven at 420°F (215°C).
(5) Place on the pieces of fruit.
(6) Cover with apricot glaze.
(7) Cut into slices approx. 2 in. (5 cm) wide.
Note. This is only suitable for fruits which can be cut, e.g. peaches, or whole fruits, e.g. cherries, gooseberries, etc.
Method for Covered Slices.
6 oz (180 g) flour into shortpastry
Other ingredients same as for Fruit Slices.
(1) Repeat (1) to (3).
(2) Cut into strips 4 in. (10 cm) wide.
(3) Place the fruit in the centre leaving about $\frac{1}{2}$ in. (12 mm) along each edge which should be dampened.
(4) Pin out another piece of pastry and cut into strips slightly wider, i.e. $4\frac{1}{2}$ in. ($11\frac{1}{2}$ cm).
(5) Carefully lay this strip over the fruit and seal each edge by pressing down with the fingers. The edge can be notched if required.
(6) Wash top with milk or water, sprinkle on castor sugar, and make cuts with a knife.
(7) Mark into slices approx. 2 in. (5 cm) wide and bake at 420°F (215°C).

Date and Apple Filling (Yield 8 covers)

4 oz (120 g) chopped dates   *4 oz (120 g) castor sugar*
1 lb (480 g) cooking apples

(1) Make a purée with the apples and sugar.
(2) When cold mix in the chopped dates.
Note. The covered fruit slices are suitable for such fruits as fresh gooseberries, cherries, plums, etc., which may be baked into the slice. The tops could be made of puff pastry if desired.

Baked Jam Roll (Yield 8 covers)

Use 3 times the shortpastry recipe,
replacing the flours with:
6 oz (180 g) flour   *5 oz (150 g) jam*
6 oz (180 g) scone flour (see page 38)

(1) Roll out the pastry to approximately 18 in. × 12 in. (45 cm × 30 cm).
(2) Spread with jam to within $\frac{1}{2}$ in. ($1\frac{1}{4}$ cm) of edge.
(3) Roll up Swiss roll fashion starting at the short edge.

(4) Moisten the edge to seal the roll.

(5) Place on a clean baking sheet and bake in an oven at 400°F (204°C) for approx. 30 minutes.

(6) Serve on an oval flat silver dish with jam sauce or custard served separately in a sauce-boat. Cut the slices on the slant.

Other Baked Rolls

1. Mincemeat.
2. Date and Apple – 3 oz (90 g) Diced Apple, 3 oz (90 g) Chopped Dates.
3. Syrup – 4½ oz (135 g) Syrup, 1½ oz (45 g) Bread-crumbs.

Baked Apple Dumpling (Yield 8 covers)

> 8 *small cooking apples* (*approx.* 4 *oz* (120 g) *each*)
> 8 *cloves*
> 4 *oz* (120 g) *sugar*
> 8 *oz* (240 g) *flour into shortpastry*

(1) Roll out the pastry approx. ⅛ in. (3 mm) thick.

(2) Cut into 8 squares, each sufficient to completely cover the apple.

(3) Damp the edges of the squares.

(4) Peel and core the apples and place one in the centre of each square.

(5) Place a clove in each apple.

(6) Fill the centre of the apple with sugar.

(7) Cover the apple with the pastry, making sure that it is completely sealed without the pastry breaking.

(8) From the trimmings, cut out a round using a fancy cutter and place one on each apple.

(9) Egg wash the pastry and place each on a clean baking tray.

(10) Bake in an oven at 380°F (193°C) for approx. 30 minutes.

(11) Serve on a silver dish with a sauce-boat of custard.

Shortbread

4 *oz* (120 g) *butter*	5½ *oz* (165 g) *soft flour*
2¼ *oz* (68 g) *castor sugar*	¼ *oz* (15 g) *ground rice*

(1) Cream the butter and sugar together until light.

(2) Sieve the ground rice and flour together and blend into the butter/sugar cream.

(3) Mix lightly into a smooth paste.

This mixing may now be made into individual biscuits, a large short-bread, or fancy biscuits by means of a wooden block (mould). All three are now described.

Finger Biscuits (Yield 12)

(1) Roll out the paste to ½ in. (1¼ cm) in thickness.

(2) Transfer to a clean baking tray.

(3) Prick all over with a fork or docker.

(4) Trim and cut or mark into slices approx. 1 in. × 2½ in. (2½ cm × 6½ cm).

(5) These slices can be individually baked or the whole piece may be just deeply marked so that it will break into fingers after it is baked.

(6) Bake at 400°F (204°C) until golden brown in colour.

(7) As soon as they are baked and whilst still hot, dredge with fine castor sugar.

Note. These slices may be individually crimped with the fingers or marzipan nippers for decoration.

Large Shortbread (Yield one 9-in. (23-cm) or two 6-in. (15-cm))

(1) Mould into a ball and roll this out to the sizes recommended above.

(2) Prick all over with a fork or docker.

(3) Crimp the edge using either the fingers or a marzipan nipper.

(4) Bake at 380°F (193°C) until golden brown in colour.

(5) When baked and whilst still hot, dredge with fine castor sugar.

Small Moulded Shortbreads (Yield 12)

(1) Divide the paste into approx. 1-oz (30-g) pieces.

(2) Mould round and flatten to approx. size of the impression of the wooden block.

(3) Dust the moulded pieces lightly with rice flour and press this surface into the mould, levelling the base.

(4) Reverse and allow the moulded shortbread to drop onto a papered baking sheet.

(5) Proceed as for fingers.

Notes.

1. As the name suggests, these goods should be very short eating and crisp. To preserve their crispness they should be stored in an airtight tin in a dry atmosphere.

2. Shortbreads, particularly the large ones, may be decorated either with glacé fruits or royal icing. Traditional Scottish messages like 'For Auld Lang Syne' may be piped on in sugar for festive occasions.

3. Puff Pastries

NOTES ON PUFF PASTRY MANUFACTURE

1. Puff Pastry Fat or Margarine

This is a product made specially for puff pastry from oils and fats having a high melting point. It enables puff pastry to be made under warm conditions, i.e. in summer, and will enable the pastry to withstand rough handling. Puff pastry fat does not usually contain moisture, although there are puff pastry emulsions which can be used which contain up to 20% moisture. If this type of margarine is used more must be used in the recipe, e.g. 14 oz (420 g) of margarine equates to 12 oz (360 g) of a 100% fat.

2. Use of Butter

Undoubtedly butter produces the most deliciously flavoured puff pastry and is recommended where first quality goods are demanded. Care must be taken in its handling, however. The paste must be gently rolled and preferably refrigerated between turns. Plenty of rest must also be given and a softer dough made (*see* Note 3). The type of butter should be tough and waxy, Dutch being well recommended.

3. Consistency

The consistency of the dough should equal that of the fat. For a tough puff pastry, fat or margarine, a strong flour made into a tight dough is recommended. Butter or margarine demand a softer dough, preferably one made from a softer flour.

4. Turns

The number of turns normally given is such that about 700 to 1500 layers of fat in the dough should be built up. This may be done in two ways: by rolling out and folding into three, or by folding the ends in first and then folding together like a book (*book turn*). A combination of both methods may also be used. What seems to matter is that the layers should be even and properly insulated. Too many layers (over-rolling) will break down this insulation to render a product more like shortpaste. Too few layers (under-rolling) will result in coarse layers with perhaps uneven lift and the fat running out during baking. Each method has its advocates. The one favoured by the author is the French method in which six half turns are given.

5. Quantity of Fat

Provided there is sufficient fat available to provide the insulation between the dough layers, the quantity of fat is not critical. It can vary between 8 oz

(240 g) and 1 lb ($\frac{1}{2}$ kilo) per lb ($\frac{1}{2}$ kilo) of flour. For the lower quantities, however, less rolling must be given and this will mean slightly less and irregular lift. The lower quantity of fat will also give a harsher tasting pastry. Usually a small quantity of fat is rubbed in to bring about a shortening effect. Three-quarter paste is made with 12 oz (360 g) of fat to the pound ($\frac{1}{2}$ kilo) of flour and this makes an ideal good quality puff pastry.

6. Thickness of Paste

Provided the paste is rolled out sufficiently to enable the operative to fold it and give it the required number of turns, there is no virtue in pinning out the pastry very thinly. Indeed this might damage the structure by breaking the layers. The smaller the quantity of paste the less it needs to be rolled out.

7. Oven Temperature

Puff pastry requires a hot oven. Egg washed varieties, e.g. sausage rolls, should be baked at about 440° to 450°F (232°C), whilst the sugared varieties, because of the nature of the sugar, require a slightly lower temperature, i.e. 420°F (215°C). A low baking temperature will prevent the pastry lifting.

8. Resting

The resting periods between the turns and on the tray prior to baking are essential to ensure even rolling without the risk of the layers breaking down. However, too long a rest just prior to baking will result in a loss of lift even though it aids the perfection of shape.

9. Use of Scrap

Some pastries, e.g. vol-au-vent, require a virgin pastry, whilst others like palmiers require to be made from the pastry scraps. Most items can be made from pastry to which a proportion of scrap is added. The usual method is to turn back the top fold, cover with the scrap, and fold back, so that the cuttings are rolled into the virgin paste. For lift it is essential to use virgin pastry, but where only flakiness is required the use of cuttings is perfectly satisfactory.

Yields for items made from virgin pastry can only be calculated by taking into account the amount of scrap pastry which remains after these items have been cut out.

Whenever puff pastries are being made, the range of items should always include some in which the scrap pastry can be utilized.

10. Storage of Puff Pastry

Puff pastry can be stored indefinitely in the deep freeze. Since it is a time-consuming process to make puff pastry, it is always wise to have some in stock. To de-frost, it should be left in the kitchen for at least 6 hours or removed to the normal refrigerator where it can be left overnight or up to two days.

11. Faults in Puff Pastry

Uneven Lift.

    (*a*) Incorrect rolling technique, e.g. uneven.

    (*b*) Fat not evenly distributed prior to rolling.

    (*c*) Insufficient resting for pastry to recover prior to baking.

    (*d*) Uneven distribution of heat in the oven.

Poor Lift.

    (*a*) Too much rolling, either by giving too many turns or pinning out too thinly.

    (*b*) Either insufficient or too much fat employed.

Excessive Shrinkage. This results in distorting the shape and is the result of insufficient rest prior to baking.

Fat Running Out during Baking. It is inevitable that some fat will run out but this will be excessive if: too cold an oven temperature is used, paste is under-rolled giving too thick fat layers, or too much fat has been used.

Basic Full Paste (English and French Methods)

    8 *oz* (240 g) *flour*

    4–4½ *oz* (120–135 g) *cold water*

    1 *oz* (30 g) *lard, butter, or margarine*

    5–7 *oz* (150–210 g) *butter or margarine (or special fats)*

    2 *teaspoonfuls lemon juice (optional)*

Dough Making

(1) Rub the 1 oz (30 g) lard into the flour.

(2) Add the water and make into a well mixed dough.

Figure 11. Puff pastry: commencing the fold for the English method

English Method.
(1) Roll out the dough to a rectangle approx. 8 in. × 12 in. (20 cm × 30 cm).
(2) Plasticize the butter or margarine and spread it over $\frac{2}{3}$rds of the dough.
(3) Fold the remaining $\frac{1}{3}$rd of dough over the portion spread with the butter or magarine and fold over again so that there are two layers of fat and three layers of dough (Figure 11).
(4) Roll out this piece to about the same size as previously and fold into three. This constitutes a normal *turn*, sometimes referred to as a *half-turn* (Figure 12).
(5) Repeat (4) another five times so that six turns have been given with resting periods between. If two turns are given in succession, it is advisable then to leave the dough to rest for at least 30 minutes.
   Alternatively, four book turns may be given.

French Method.
(1) Mould the dough into a ball, make a knife cut at right angles, and with the rolling pin form a square with the corners rolled extra thinly.
(2) Plasticize the butter or margarine and form it into a square.
(3) Place this diagonally in the centre of the dough and fold over each corner of the dough to meet in the centre, so completely enveloping the fat (Figure 13).
(4) Proceed to give the required turns as in (4) and (5) above. (*See* Figure 14.)

Figure 12. Giving puff pastry a 3-fold turn ($\frac{1}{2}$ turn)

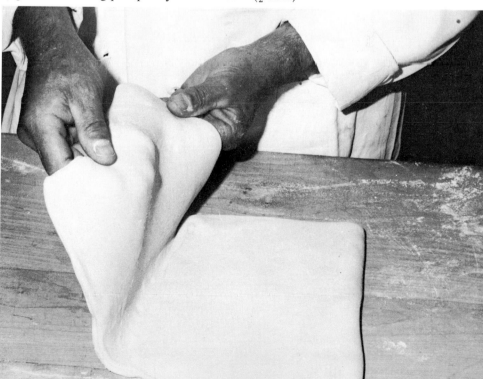

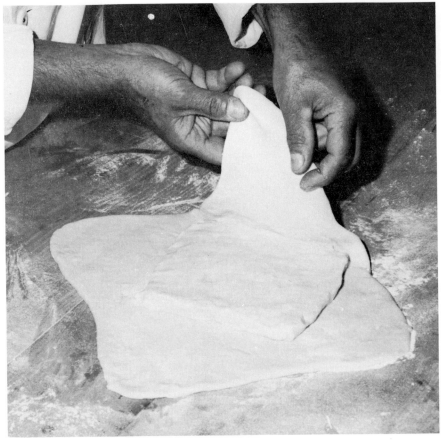

Figure 13. Commencing the French method of making puff pastry

Figure 14. Puff pastry turns (French method): (*a*) half turn; (*b*) book turn

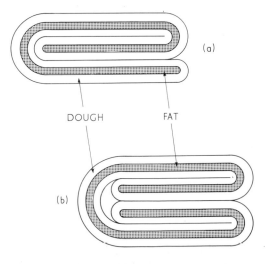

Scotch or Rough Puff

In this method, the butter, margarine, or fat is chopped into cubes approx. 1 in. (2½ cm) and mixed into the dry flour. To this the water is added and a dough made, keeping the cubes of fat intact. Proceed to give turns in any of the conventional ways.

This pastry is suitable only for varieties in which scrap would normally be used, especially for pies.

VARIETIES USING VIRGIN PASTRY

Vol-au-vent (Figure 15)

This is an open baked puff pastry case which is usually filled with a savoury filling. They can be made either large, approx. 6 in. (16 cm), or individual, 2½ in. (6 cm).

Figure 15. Small and large vol-au-vent

Individual Vol-au-vent

Method 1 (Figure 16).

This method produces the best shaped vol-au-vent and is well worth the trouble involved.

(1) Pin out well rested virgin pastry to approx. ⅛ in. (3 mm) thick.
(2) Divide roughly in half and on this piece mark out with a 2½–3-in. (6–8-cm) cutter.
(3) In the centre of these marked circles, cut out a piece using a 1½-in. (4-cm) cutter.
(4) Lightly wash the piece containing the cut out holes, with water.

Figure 16. Vol-au-vents: (a) Laying second sheet over holes

(5) Lay over this the other sheet of pastry (Figure 16(a)) and then reverse both pieces so that the holes can be seen.

(6) Using the 2½–3-in. (6–8-cm) cutter, cut through both layers of pastry with the hole exactly in the centre (Figure 16(b)).

(7) Place the cut out piece on a clean tray and prick the centre with a fork.

(8) Egg wash the top outside edge.

(9) Let pieces rest for 30 minutes to one hour and egg wash a second time if desired.

(10) Bake in a hot oven at 440°F (226°C) until crisp and light brown in colour.

(11) If lids are required, the pieces cut out with the 1½-in. (4-cm) cutter must also be egg washed and baked off separately. (Not on same tray, as these will take less time to bake.)

Method 2.

(1) Pin out the paste to ⅛ in. (3 mm) in thickness and cut out discs, using a 2½–3-in. (6–8-cm) round cutter.

(2) Using a 1½-in. (4-cm) cutter, cut out the centre from half of the discs.

(3) Lay the remaining discs on a clean baking tray and damp tops with water.

(4) Place on the discs cut out in (2).

(5) Egg wash, allow to rest, and bake as in Method 1.

(6) If tops are required, egg wash and bake off the centres also.

Bouchées

Same method as for vol-au-vent but using smaller cutters, i.e. 1¾ and 1 in. (4½ and 2½ cm).

Large Vol-au-vent (Suitable for 4 covers)

For this the paste needs to be slightly thicker, approx. 3/16 in. (½ cm) and cut out with a 6–8-in. (15–20-cm) cutter. Use a cutter approx. 1½ in. (4 cm) smaller for the hole. Bake in a cooler oven at approx. 420°F (215°C).

Yields from 1lb Virgin Pastry

	Scrap over
Large vol-au-vent (1 @ 7 in. (18 cm))	6 oz (180 g)
Individual vol-au-vent (6 @ 3 in. (7½ cm))	7 oz (210 g)
Bouchées (16 @ 1¾ in. (4½ cm))	6 oz (180 g)

(*b*) Cutting out the shapes

Cream Puffs (Figure 17) (Yield 12)

> 10 *oz* (300 g) *puff pastry, leaving 5 oz* (150 g) *scrap*
> ⅓ *pint* (2 *decilitres*) *fresh cream*
> 2 *oz jam*

(1) Roll out the puff pastry to ⅛ in. (3 mm) in thickness and approx. 12 in. × 9 in. (30 cm × 24 cm).

(2) Prick the surface with a docker or fork and cut into twelve squares or circles approx. 3 in. (8 cm).

(3) Before they are baked, dress the surface in one of the following ways:

(*a*) *Puff Royal.* Spread over with royal icing. Pipe a thin line of jam from corner to corner in the form of a cross for additional effect.

(*b*) *Sugar Dressed.* Wash with either water or egg whites and dip into castor sugar.

(*c*) *Egg Washed.* If the top is egg washed the finished piece is left plain.

(*d*) *Dusted.* If the puff is to be dusted with icing sugar after baking, it should be left plain.

(4) Let the pieces rest for at least 30 minutes.

(5) Bake in an oven at 420°F (215°C) for varieties (*a*) and (*b*) and 440°F (226°C) for varieties (*c*) and (*d*).

(6) When baked and cold, split into two and remove the top piece.

(7) Pipe a small bulb of jam onto the bottom piece and then pipe on a bulb of sweetened, whipped fresh cream.

(8) Replace top.

(9) With the (*d*) variety, dust top with icing sugar.

Figure 17. Cream puffs

Slices (Figure 18) (Yield 8)

> 8 *oz* (240 g) *puff pastry, leaving* 2 *oz* (60 g) *scrap*
> (This will make one strip, 4 in. × 12 in. (10 cm × 30 cm) = 8 slices)
> $\frac{1}{4}$ *pint* (1$\frac{1}{2}$ *dl*) *fresh cream*
> 1$\frac{1}{2}$ *oz* (45 g) *jam*

(1) Roll out a piece of well rested virgin puff pastry to $\frac{1}{8}$ in. (3 mm) in thickness and approx. 4 in. × 12 in. (10 cm × 30 cm).

(2) Lay this piece of pastry on a clean baking tray.

(3) Prick well with a fork or docker.

(4) Allow to rest for at least 30 minutes and bake in an oven at 440°F (226°C) until crisp and light golden brown in colour.

(5) When baked turn over and split the pieces in two lengthwise.

(6) Remove the top piece (which was the base) and on the remaining piece spread on a layer of jam followed by a layer of either whipped fresh cream or custard.

(7) Spread the top piece first with boiling apricot purée and then suitably flavoured and coloured warm fondant.

(8) Allow the fondant to set and then cut the piece into slices approx. 1$\frac{1}{2}$ in. (4 cm) wide.

(9) Replace the cut slice on top of the creamed base and finish by cutting through.

Notes.

1. The top or edge could be suitably decorated with coralettes, browned desiccated coconut, etc.

2. The cream sides could also be spread evenly and masked with a suitable dressing, e.g. browned nibbed almonds, etc.

3. Instead of one piece of virgin pastry, the slice could be made from two strips of thinly rolled pastry $\frac{1}{16}$ in. (1$\frac{1}{2}$ mm) in thickness. In this event some scrap pastry could be worked in.

Figure 18. Slices

VARIETIES USING PROPORTION OF SCRAP PASTRY

Sausage Rolls (Figure 19) (Yield 8)

> 6 *oz* (180 g) *puff pastry, leaving* 1 *oz* (30 g) *scrap*
> 4 *oz* (120 g) *sausage meat*

(1) Roll out the pastry to about $\frac{1}{10}$ in. ($2\frac{1}{2}$ mm) in thickness and into a rectangle approx. 10 in. × 6 in. (25 cm × 15 cm).

(2) Cut pastry into two strips 3 in. (8 cm) wide.

(3) Mould the sausage meat into 2 long ropes approx. $\frac{3}{4}$ in. (2 cm) in diameter and lay these in the centre of each strip.

(4) Wash with egg or water between each roll of sausage meat so that the edge of each strip is dampened.

(5) Fold over and press edges together firmly.

(6) Cut lengths of roll into suitable length of approx. $2\frac{1}{2}$ in. (6 cm).

(7) Mark surface with back of a knife.

(8) Wash over with a mixture of egg and water.

(9) Place the individual rolls on a clean baking sheet.

(10) Allow a resting period of at least 30 minutes.

(11) Bake in an oven at approx. 450°F (232°C) until crisp and light golden brown in colour.

Note. The sausage rolls described are dainty enough for a cocktail buffet. If larger rolls are required, the quantities of pastry and sausage meat would have to be increased proportionally.

Figure 19. Sausage rolls: stages in making

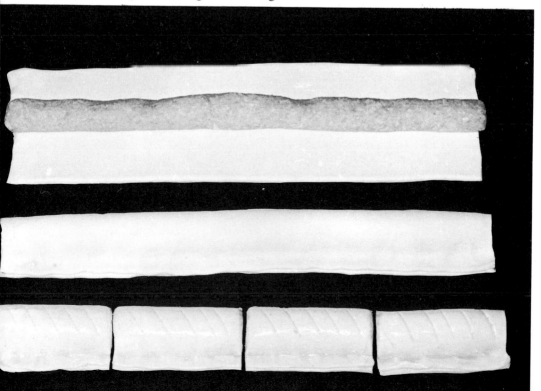

Apple or Jam Turnovers – Chaussons (Yield 8)

12 *oz* (360 g) *pastry, leaving 5 oz (150 g) scrap*
4 *oz* (120 g) *jam*
or
6 *oz* (180 g) *apple*
1 *oz* (30 g) *sugar*

(1) Roll out pastry to $\frac{1}{10}$ in. ($2\frac{1}{2}$ mm) thick.
(2) Cut out with a 4-in. (10-cm) fluted cutter.
(3) With a rolling pin, elongate these discs, keeping the centre thin and the edges thick.
(4) Place in a quantity of jam or sweetened apple.
(5) Damp the edges with egg or water and fold over so that the two meet.
(6) Wash with egg whites or water and dip into castor sugar.
(7) Place on a clean baking tray and leave to rest for at least 30 minutes.
(8) Bake in an oven at 420°F (215°C) until crisp and golden brown in colour.

Eccles (Figure 20) (Yield 8)

12 *oz* (360 g) *pastry, leaving 5 oz (150 g) scrap*
6 *oz* (180 g) *Eccles and Banbury filling*

Filling A	Filling B
3 *oz* (90 g) *currants*	4 *oz* (120 g) *mincemeat*
1 *oz* (30 g) *brown sugar*	2 *oz* (60 g) *cake crumbs*
$\frac{1}{2}$ *oz* (15 g) *golden syrup*	
$1\frac{1}{2}$ *oz* (45 g) *cake crumbs*	Filling C
Pinch mixed spice	1 *oz* (30 g) *butter*
	1 *oz* (30 g) *brown sugar*
	4 *oz* (120 g) *currants*
	Pinch mixed spice

Mix all ingredients together thoroughly.
(1) Roll out the pastry to $\frac{1}{16}$ in. ($1\frac{1}{2}$ mm) in thickness.
(2) Cut out discs using a 4-in. (10-cm) cutter.
(3) Place a tablespoonful of the filling A, B or C in the centre of each piece.
(4) Fold the edges into the centre, sealing in the filling and then turn over.
(5) Either flatten with the palm of the hand or roll out with a rolling pin to approx. 3 in. ($7\frac{1}{2}$ cm) diameter.
(6) Wash the tops with egg white or water and dip into castor sugar.
(7) Place the pieces on a clean baking sheet.
(8) Make two or three slits in the top with a knife so that the filling shows through.
(9) Allow a 30-minute resting period.
(10) Bake at 420°F (215°C) until crisp and golden brown in colour.

Figure 20. (*top*) Banbury cakes; (*bottom*) Eccles cakes

Banburys (Figure 20) (Yield 8)

Ingredients same as for Eccles.

(1) Repeat (1), (2), and (3) as for Eccles.

(4) Fold over the top and bottom edges to meet in the centre but mould it into a boat shape, keeping the filling sealed in.

(5) Flatten with the palm of the hand or rolling pin to approx. 2 in. × 4 in. (5 cm × 10 cm).

(6) Finish off as for Eccles.

Mince Pies (Yield 8)

    1 *lb* (480 g) *puff pastry, leaving* 6 *oz* (180 g) *scrap*

    6 *oz* (180 g) *mincemeat (see page 237)*

    $\frac{1}{2}$ *oz* (15 g) *icing sugar*

(1) Roll out the paste to $\frac{1}{10}$ in. ($2\frac{1}{2}$ mm) thick.

(2) Cut out half the paste with a $2\frac{3}{4}$-in. (7-cm) cutter, either fluted or plain.

(3) Place the pieces on a clean baking sheet.

(4) Damp the edges with water or alternatively splash the whole tray with water.

(5) Place about a teaspoonful of mincemeat in the centre of each cut out piece.

(6) Cover the pieces with discs cut from the remaining half of the paste with a 3-in. (8-cm) cutter, rolling the paste slightly thinner to enable the same number of tops to be cut out.

(7) Using the back rolled rim of a 2-in. (5-cm) cutter, press down the edges to seal in the mincemeat.

(8) Brush over with egg wash and pierce the top with a fork or knife.

(9) Allow to rest for half an hour.

(10) Bake in an oven at 450°F (232°C) until golden brown in colour.

(11) Sprinkle with icing sugar when baked.

(12) Place on a doily on a silver dish and serve warm with an appropriate sauce, e.g. custard or brandy (*see* page 202).

Pithivier (Figure 21) (Yield 1 (suitable for 8 covers))

> 8 *oz* (240 g) *puff pastry, leaving* 1½–2 *oz* (45–60 g) *scrap*
> 1 *oz* (30 g) *apricot jam*
> 6 *oz* (180 g) *frangipane filling* (1½ *oz* (45 g) *butter, etc.*) (*see page* 49)
> ½ *oz* (15 g) *icing sugar*

(1) Roll out a little less than half of the pastry to a thickness of $\frac{1}{16}$ in. (1½ mm) and cut out a disc 9 in. (23 cm) diameter.

(2) Place this piece on a clean baking tray, moisten the edges, and prick it all over with a fork or docker.

(3) Spread over the jam to within 1 in. (2½ cm) from the edge.

(4) Repeat using the frangipane filling.

(5) Roll out the remaining pastry to approx. $\frac{1}{10}$ in. (2½ mm) and cut out a slightly larger disc.

(6) Dampen the edge, turn over and lay this piece carefully on top.

(7) Decorate the edge and with a sharp knife make eight curved slits from the centre to within 1 in. (2½ cm) from the edge in the top layer of pastry (Figure 22).

(8) Brush over with egg wash and allow it to rest for half an hour.

(9) Bake in an oven at 420°F (215°C) until it just begins to colour.

(10) Sprinkle with icing sugar and return to oven to finish cooking and for the sugar to melt and glaze the top.

Figure 21. Gâteau Pithivier

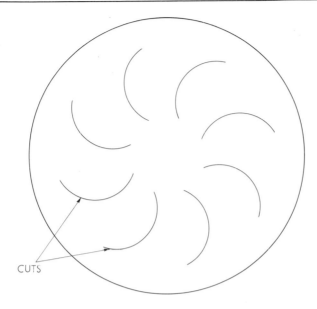

CUTS

Figure 22. Gâteau Pithivier – showing cuts

Jalousie (Figure 23) (Yield same as for Pithivier)

    8 *oz* (240 g) *mincemeat or jam*

or   6 *oz* (180 g) *frangipane* (1½ *oz* (45 g) *butter, etc.*) (*see page* 49)

(1) Roll out a third of the pastry to a thickness of $\frac{1}{16}$ in. (1½ mm) and cut into a strip approx. 10 in. × 4 in. (25 cm × 10 cm).

(2) Place on a clean baking tray, moisten the edges, and prick all over with a fork.

(3) Spread on the filling to within 1 in. (2½ cm) from the edge which should be dampened with water.

(4) Roll out the remaining pastry $\frac{1}{10}$ in. (2½ mm) from the edge which should be dampened with water.

(5) Fold the strip in half lengthwise and cut slits about ¼ in. (6 mm) apart and to within 1 in. (2½ cm) of the edge.

(6) Unfold carefully and place this strip over the other, pressing down the edges to seal.

(7) Trim and decorate the edge.

(8) Brush over with egg wash and allow a half-hour resting period.

(9) Bake in an oven at 420°F (215°C) until it just begins to colour.

(10) Sprinkle on icing sugar, return to the oven, and bake to a golden brown with a sugar glazed top.

Note. Alternatively, castor sugar could be sprinkled on prior to baking instead of using icing sugar.

Figure 23. Jalousie:
        (*a*) Cutting the paste for the top (above).
        (*b*) Laying on the top (below).

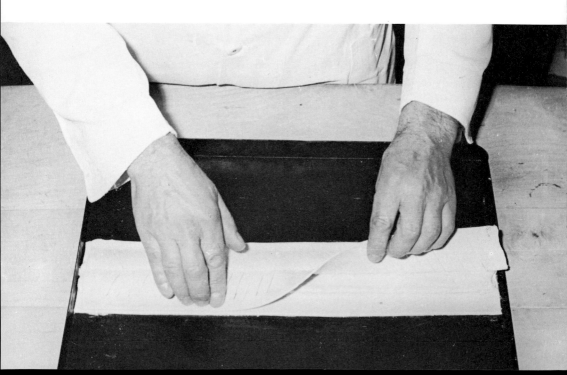

Cream Horns (Figure 24) (Yield 8)

> 8 *oz* (240 g) *puff pastry*   1 *oz* (30 g) *sugar*
> 1 *oz* (30 g) *jam*   ¼ *pt* (1½ *dl*) *fresh cream*

(1) Roll out the puff pastry to $\frac{1}{16}$ in. (1½ mm) in thickness and 24 in. (60 cm) long.

(2) Cut into strips 1 in. (2½ cm) wide.

(3) Dampen with water.

(4) Wrap the strip carefully round a clean cream horn mould so that each strip overlaps half the other. Start at the point and work towards the open end (Figure 25).

(5) Wash top with egg whites or water and dip into castor sugar.

(6) Place on a clean baking tray and allow at least a half-hour resting period.

(7) Bake in an oven at 420°F (215°C) to a golden brown colour.

(8) Remove the moulds whilst the horns are still warm by first giving them a slight twist.

(9) Pipe in a small bulb of jam.

(10) Using a savoy bag with a star tube, fill the horn with suitably flavoured and sweetened whipped fresh cream. Finish neatly with a little rosette and decorate with a cherry.

Figure 24. Cream horns

Figure 25. Cream horns: showing method of wrapping the paste around the tin

Fruit Slice – Bande aux Fruits or Tranche aux Fruits (Yield 8 slices)

> 8 *oz* (240 g) *puff pastry, leaving* 2 *oz* (60 g) *scrap*
> 1 *oz* (30 g) *sugar*
> 8 *oz*–1 *lb* (240–480 g) *fruit*
> 1 *oz* (30 g) *apricot glaze* (*see page* 302)

(1) Roll out the puff pastry $\frac{1}{16}$ in. ($1\frac{1}{2}$ mm) thick and about 14 in. (35 cm) in length.

(2) Cut a strip approx. $4\frac{1}{2}$ in. (12 cm) wide.

(3) Dampen each edge with water and lay on a strip of similar thickness $\frac{3}{4}$ in. (2 cm) wide.

(4) Press these strips down firmly and decorate with the back of a knife.

(5) Prick the base of the slice all over with a fork or docker and let it rest for at least half an hour.

(6) According to the type of fruit used either:

(*a*) Put the fruit, e.g. apple, on the slice and bake together in an oven at 420°F (215°C), or

(*b*) Bake the slice without the fruit in an oven at 440°F (226°C). Afterwards finish off with pastry cream and fruit or just the fruit itself.

(7) Cover with a suitable glaze.

(8) Cut into slices and serve as for flans.

Note. The fruit content is variable depending on the type of fruit used, and whether it is supplemented with pastry cream.

VARIETIES USING ALL SCRAP PASTRY

Palmiers (Figure 26) (Yield 8, sandwiched in pairs)

8 *oz* (240 g) *scrap pastry*	$1\frac{1}{2}$ *oz* (45 g) *castor sugar*
$\frac{1}{4}$ *pt* ($1\frac{1}{2}$ *dl*) *fresh cream*	1 *oz* (30 g) *jam*

Figure 26. Palmiers

(1) Roll out the pastry to $\frac{1}{8}$ in. (3 mm) in thickness and to at least 18 in. (45 cm) in length.

(2) Wash the surface with water and sprinkle liberally with castor sugar.

(3) Starting at each end and folding in three results in six folds altogether, giving a strip approx. $\frac{1}{2}$ in. (12 mm) thick and $2\frac{1}{2}$ in. (6 cm) wide.

(4) Cut this strip into slices $\frac{3}{8}$ in. (1 cm) thick and lay with the folds showing, on a well greased baking tray. Space about 3 in. (8 cm) apart (Figure 27).

(5) Allow to rest for at least half an hour.

(6) Bake in an oven at 450°F (232°C) until just tinged with colour.

(7) Turn over with a palette knife and finish off by baking to a golden brown colour with a glaze of caramelized sugar.

(8) When cold, sandwich two palmiers with a little jam and a bulb of sweetened, whipped, fresh cream.

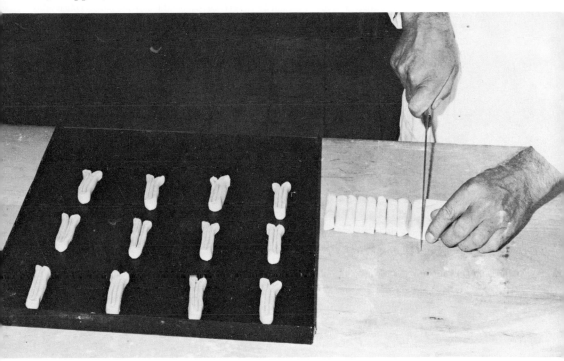

Figure 27. Cutting pastry for palmiers

Cream Slices – Millefeuilles (Figure 28) (Yield 8 covers)

     12 *oz* (360 *g*) *scrap puff pastry*
     2 *oz* (60 *g*) *jam*
     $\frac{1}{2}$ *pt* (3 *dl*) *pastry cream or fresh cream*
     2 *oz* (60 *g*) *fondant or water icing*

(1) Roll out the pastry to $\frac{1}{16}$ in. ($1\frac{1}{2}$ mm) thick.

(2) Transfer the piece of pastry to a clean baking sheet by wrapping around a rolling pin. Prick it all over with a fork or docker.

(3) Allow the piece to rest for at least half an hour and then cut it into three strips 4 in. (10 cm) wide and approx. 16 in. (40 cm) in length.

(4) Bake in an oven at 450°F (232°C) until golden brown in colour.

(5) When cold, select the best slice for the top and sandwich the three strips together with the cream and jam.

(6) Prepare the fondant or water icing by warming and adjusting the consistency with syrup.

(7) Prepare a little of the icing in two colours, e.g. chocolate and pink, and fill a paper cornet with each.

(8) Pour and spread the icing evenly over the top and immediately pipe alternate lines about $\frac{1}{2}$ in. (12 mm) apart of chocolate and pink from the filled paper cornets.

(9) Using the back of a knife and wiping between each stroke, pull the knife across the piped lines at approx. 1 in. ($2\frac{1}{2}$ cm) intervals.

(10) Turn the slice round and repeat, pulling the knife in the opposite direction between the first strokes.

(11) Allow to set and trim off the edge.

(12) Cut into slices prior to service or alternatively serve the whole piece on a doily on a silver dish and cut into slices immediately before serving.

Notes.

1. The operation (9) and (10) is called 'marbling' (*see* Figure 59 on page 125). To get the best results, speed is essential and the icing should not be either too warm or too stiff in consistency.

2. Fresh cream or custard could be used as an alternative variation. Special flavours – fruit, nuts, nougat, etc. – could also be added with advantage, to produce some excellent pastries for use as a sweet.

3. The sides may be masked with cream and roasted nuts if desired.

Figure 28.
Millefeuilles slices

Apple Strudel (German) (Figure 29) (Yield 8 slices)

8 *oz* (240 g) *puff pastry*
1 *lb* (480 g) *apples*
1–2 *oz* (30–60 g) *sultanas* } *Filling*
1½ *oz* (45 g) *sugar*
2–3 *oz* (60–90 g) *strip of sponge*
2 *oz* (60 g) *apricot purée*
2 *oz* (60 g) *water icing*

(1) Roll well-rested puff pastry very thinly to a rectangle 12 in. (30 cm) long and approx. 9 in. (22½ cm) wide.
(2) Cut a strip 4 in. (10 cm) wide and place this on a clean baking tray.
(3) Along the centre of this strip, place a 2 in. (5 cm) wide strip of sponge.
(4) Wash, peel, and core the apples. Chop very finely.
(5) Mix in the sultanas and sugar.
(6) Place this mixing on top of the sponge. It should form a mound about 2 in. (5 cm) in height. Egg wash the edges of the puff pastry.
(7) With the remaining puff pastry, cut a strip about 5 in. (12½ cm) in width. Fold this in half lengthwise and cut slits from the folded edge at ¼ in. (6 mm) intervals, similar to the jalousie in Figure 23.
(8) Keeping this strip folded, carefully lay it over one half of the filling and unfold it over the other half.
(9) Press each side to make a perfect seal.
(10) Egg wash and bake in an oven at 380°F (193°C).
(11) When baked and whilst still hot, brush over with hot apricot purée and then water icing.
(12) When cold, cut into slices approx. 1½ in. (4 cm) in width.
Notes.
1. Instead of fresh apples, stewed or tinned apples may be used. In the latter case only 12 oz (360 g) will be required.
2. The purpose of the sponge strip in the base of these slices is to soak up the juice which will be formed from the mixture. Alternatively, bread or cake crumbs could be added to the filling and the sponge strip omitted
Other varieties. Other fruits, such as cherries, apricots, pears, etc., could be used instead of apples.

Note. For puff pastry bases for various gâteaux *see* Chapter 8.

Figure 29. Apple strudel (German)

4. Sponge Goods

When eggs are beaten or whisked a considerable quantity of air becomes incorporated in the form of bubbles which constitute a foam. The ability of egg to hold air in this way is mainly due to the protein albumen present in the white. When this is agitated, partial coagulation occurs which forms a semi-rigid membrane around each air cell. At the same time as becoming thus aerated, the white also becomes stiffer (which is what one would expect if the egg becomes partially coagulated).

In sponge making, the egg is whisked with sugar until thick and light and the flour carefully incorporated to prevent the light structure from breaking down. Aeration of the sponge is achieved solely by the air trapped by the egg in the beating process.

Detailed Method of Making Sponges

(1) Sterilize the mixing bowl and whisk in boiling water to remove any trace of fat or oil. The presence of fat will interfere with the whisking of the egg and will prevent a perfect sponge from being made.

(2) Weigh the ingredients.

(3) Mix the egg and sugar and warm to approx. 90°F (32°C) by stirring over warm water (*not very hot water* as this might cook the egg). An alternative way to warm the sponge is to place the sugar on a tray and heat it in the oven prior to adding it to the egg.

(4) Whisk the egg/sugar mixture until it becomes thick like the consistency of thick cream. This stage can be accurately judged only by experience. It should be thick enough to leave the marks of the whisk for a few seconds after it is withdrawn.

(5) While the egg and sugar are whisking, prepare the baking pan or sheet, either with paper (as for Swiss rolls) or with grease and flour and sugar for some varieties.

(6) Whisk in any colour, essence, glycerine, or water.

(7) Blend in sieved flour with the hand. This must be done carefully so as not to break down the very light structure which has been built up by the whisking process. It is best to use the hand with fingers outstretched, gently lifting the flour through the sponge and turning the bowl.

(8) Deposit the sponge in the prepared baking pan and bake at the correct time according to the variety made.

Note. Special stabilizers are now on the market which help to keep the sponge from breaking down.

74

VARIETIES

Chocolate and Almond Sponges

The following recipes can be made into either Chocolate or Almond Sponge as follows:

Chocolate – Delete 1 oz (30 g) flour and add 1 oz (30 g) cocoa powder

Almond – Delete 1 oz (30 g) flour and add 1 oz (30 g) gound almonds

Sieve well into flour.

Plain Sponge Sandwich (Figure 30) (Yield 2 × 6 round pans)

5 oz (150 g) eggs (3)
5 oz (150 g) castor sugar
5 oz (150 g) flour (soft)

Figure 30. Sponge sandwich

(1) Prepare sponge mixture as previously described.
(2) Prepare two 6 in. (15 cm) sandwich pans with a coating of fat and dust with flour.
(3) Deposit in the two sandwich pans and bake in an oven at approx. 400°F (204°C) for 25–30 minutes. (To test whether they are done, press the centre of the sponge which should be firm.)
(4) When baked, turn the sponges out of the pans onto a cooling wire.
(5) When cold, sandwich with jam and, if required, cream.
(6) The top may be either dusted with icing sugar or iced with fondant, water icing, or chocolate.

Enriched Sponge Sandwich

As for Plain Sponge Sandwich but with the addition of:
1–1½ *oz* (30–45 g) *egg yolk* (2 *to* 3)
This egg yolk should be added and beaten with the egg.

Enriched sponges are more suitable for gâteaux because the texture is firmer and the sponge slice will not crumble when cut. Also sponge drops and fingers are more satisfactory when made with this mixing.

Sponge Cakes (Frames or Bricks) (Figure 31) (Yield 16)

These are suitable for individual cakes or trifles.

Recipe same as Sponge Sandwich.

(1) Prepare the sponge frames first with a coating of fat, then a dusting of castor sugar, followed by a dusting of flour.
(2) Make the sponge mixing as previously described.
(3) Transfer the sponge mixing to a savoy bag and pipe the mixture to within ½ in. (12 mm) of the top of each cavity in the sponge frame.
(4) Dust the top liberally with castor sugar.
(5) Bake in an oven at 410°F (210°C) for approx. 12 minutes until baked.
(6) Remove from oven and cool on a wire.

Swiss Roll (Yield 3)

10 *oz* (300 g) *eggs*	5 *oz* (150 g) *flour* (*soft*)
7½ *oz* (225 g) *sugar*	½ *oz* (15 g) *glycerine*

For chocolate and almond sponges *see* notes on page 75.
(1) Prepare a baking sheet by lining with greaseproof paper.
(2) Make a sponge as previously described.
(3) Deposit on the lined baking tray and spread level. The area which this amount should cover is approx. 18 in. × 15 in. (45 cm × 38 cm).
(4) Bake in a hot oven at 460°F (238°C) for approx. 4 minutes.
(5) Remove from oven when baked and turn upside down on a clean cloth. It is best if it is placed on several layers of cloth or paper.

Figure 31. Sponge cakes: piping out the sponge mixing into greased and floured sponge frames

(6) Leave with the baking tin on top. The steam should now be trapped in the layers of cloth or paper and eventually moisten the roll.

(7) When absolutely cold, remove the tray and the greaseproof paper.

(8) Spread on a layer of jam, curd, or cream, and with the aid of the cloth roll up (Figure 32).

(9) Cut either into slices or in approx. 6½ in. (17 cm) lengths.

Individual Swiss Rolls (Yield 18)

(1) Proceed as for ordinary Swiss rolls but spread the mixture much more thinly on the tray to cover an area of 18 in. × 19 in. (45 cm × 48 cm).

(2) Spread with jam, curd, or cream.

(3) Cut into squares approx. 3 in. (7½ cm) square.

(4) Roll up each square into a small Swiss roll.

(5) These can be dusted with icing sugar or covered.

Swiss Roll Varieties

1. After spreading the roll sprinkle on a few washed sultanas or chopped cherries, then bake. Finish off in the usual way.

2. Make a raspberry, strawberry, or similar fruit flavoured roll by adding the appropriate flavour and colour to the sponge using the same flavour for the buttercream. This may also contain chopped fruit if desired.

3. Cover the roll first in a layer of boiling purée and then ice with a covering of warmed, appropriately flavoured and coloured fondant. Decorate using cherries, angelica, etc.

4. Cover the roll first with boiling apricot purée. Roll out a sheet of either almond, coconut, or sugar paste, trim to size, and cover the roll. The paste may be textured with a roller prior to covering. Decorate if desired.

5. Cover the roll in buttercream and mask with desiccated coconut or nibbed almonds, either plain or roasted.

Note. Varieties 3, 4, and 5 above, together with a suitable centre, may be cut up into slices and used as afternoon tea fancies (*see* Chapter 11).

Figure 32. Swiss roll: method used to roll up the sponge roll using a sheet of kitchen paper on which the sheet of sponge was placed originally to cool.

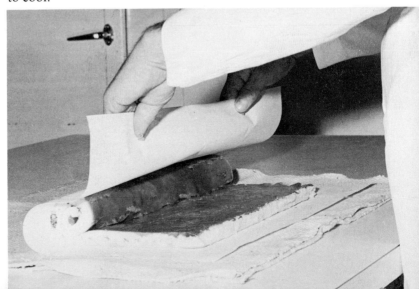

Chocolate Log (Figure 33)

Make a chocolate roll, using a buttercream filling (*see* page 297). After cutting into the required length, the roll may be finished in three ways.
Method 1.
(1) Mask each end with a white buttercream and into this pipe a spiral or circles of chocolate cream to simulate the end grain.
(2) Using a savoy bag fitted with a star tube, pipe lines of chocolate buttercream lengthwise, completely covering the surface. Alternatively a comb scraper may be used.
Method 2.
(1) Cover the roll with boiling apricot jam and chocolate coloured paste. Mark with a fork.
(2) For the ends, roll out a piece of paste into a long strip. Cover with chocolate and, when set, roll up like a Swiss roll. Cut thin slices off this and roll out to cover the ends to which they are attached, using purée.
Method 3.
(1) Cover with chocolate.
(2) Mask each end with either the cream (Method 1) or paste (Method 2).

Figure 33. Chocolate log: this roll is finished with a combination of methods. Buttercream is used to mask the sides and this is spread with a comb scraper. The ends are of almond paste as described under Method 2

Butter Sponge – Genoise

5 *oz* (150 g) *eggs*	5 *oz* (150 g) *flour* (*soft*)
5 *oz* (150 g) *castor sugar*	1 *oz* (30 g) *melted butter*

For chocolate and almond sponges *see* page 75.

(1) Make a sponge of the egg and sugar as previously described.

(2) Add the flour and start to blend it into the sponge. When almost mixed, add the melted butter and finish mixing.

(3) Deposit in greased and floured pans and bake as for sandwiches.

Notes.

1. These are difficult to make successfully because the butter tends to break down the structure of the sponge. For success keep the sponge warm so that the butter does not set before the mixture is deposited in the tin.

2. The proportion of added butter may be increased to 2 oz (60 g), giving a closer crumb structure but better keeping, cutting, and eating qualities. Greater care will be required in the mixing process to prevent a breakdown of the sponge.

Sponge Drops: Sponge Fingers – Biscuits à la Cuillere

(Yield 48 singles, size 3 in. × ½ in. (7½ cm × 1¼ cm) tube)

Use either the plain sandwich or enriched sandwich recipe.

(1) Prepare a baking tray with a sheet of greaseproof paper.

(2) Make the sponge mixing and transfer it to a clean savoy bag fitted with a ½ in. (12 mm) plain tube.

(3) Keeping the size uniform, pipe either fingers or drops onto greaseproof paper on a clean table top (Figure 34). Use separate sheets for the drops and fingers.

(4) When the whole tray has been piped, cover liberally with castor sugar.

(5) Remove excess sugar by picking up the greaseproof sheet on which they have just been piped, holding it vertically, then place it on a baking tray.

(6) Bake immediately in an oven at 450°F (232°C) for approx. 4 minutes. The colour should be a light brown all over.

Figure 34. Sponge fingers: showing method of piping. Notice that the paper on which they are piped is marked with parallel lines to assist in achieving a uniform size

Note. Perfect sponge drops and fingers are difficult to make. The best recipe to use is the enriched sponge since this gives stability to the sponge which is an asset for this type of goods.

The main fault which occurs with these goods is as follows:

Mixture runs flat when piped, giving flat and mis-shapen drops and fingers with cracked surfaces.

Cause.

1. Mixture was overbeaten and broken down when flour was mixed in.
2. Oven temperature too cool.
3. Goods left too long before baking.

Varieties using Sponge Drops and Fingers

1. Sandwich together with jam or cream (buttercream or fresh) and serve in paper cases.
2. Before sandwiching together, dip half the top in chocolate.
3. Sandwich with apricot jam and dip the whole drop or finger in boiling apricot purée. Wipe off surplus with a brush and roll in desiccated coconut either plan or roasted. Instead of apricot, raspberry purée may be used.
4. Charlotte Russe – *see* Chapter 15.
5. Ice-cream dishes – *see* Chapter 22.

Sponge Flans

Use basic or enriched sponge recipe.

Deposit the sponge mixture in greased and floured flan moulds.

When baked these moulds may be filled with various fruit fillings and make quite an acceptable sweet if served with fresh cream.

Figure 35. Othellos

Victoria Sponge Sandwich (Yield 1 sandwich)

Although this is strictly a cake, it is included in this chapter to avoid confusion.

4 oz (120 g) butter	4 oz (120 g) flour (soft)
4 oz (120 g) sugar	⅛ oz (4 g) baking powder
4 oz (120 g) eggs	

(1) Sugar batter method of cake-making (*see* page 93).
(2) Deposit in two greased and floured 6-in. (15-cm) sandwich pans.
(3) Bake at 360°F (182°C) for approx. 25 minutes.
(4) When cool, sandwich together as described under sponge sandwiches (*see* page 75).

Othellos (also Desdemonas, Jagos, and Rosalinds) (Figure 35)
(Yield 12 doubles (24 halves))

A
$\begin{cases} 1\frac{1}{4} \text{ oz (38 g) egg yolks (2}\frac{1}{2}) \\ \frac{1}{2} \text{ oz (15 g) sugar} \\ 1\frac{1}{2} \text{ oz (45 g) flour} \end{cases}$

B
$\begin{cases} 4 \text{ oz (120 g) egg whites (4)} \\ 1\frac{1}{2} \text{ oz (45 g) castor sugar} \end{cases}$

C 1½ oz (45 g) soft flour

For decoration

3 oz (90 g) jam
6 oz (180 g) fondant
6 oz (180 g) lightly beaten buttercream
    or custard
    or ¼ pt (1½ dl) fresh cream

(1) Mix ingredients in A to a smooth paste.
(2) Whisk ingredients in B to a stiff meringue.
(3) Carefully blend the flour C into the meringue and then blend into the paste.
(4) Transfer mixing to a savoy bag fitted with a ½-in. (12-mm) tube.
(5) Pipe small bulbs onto a well-greased and floured baking tray, size 1¼–1½ in. (3–4 cm).
(6) Bake in a hot oven at 460°F (238°C) for approx. 8 minutes.
(7) When cold, scoop out the centre and sandwich together with a good quality cream or custard. Also remove the peak so that they will stand correctly.
(8) Brush over or dip into boiling apricot purée and coat with an appropriately flavoured and coloured fondant.
(9) Finish by piping a spiral of fondant and add a piece of crystallized flower petal, cherry, or nut.

Othellos. This is the name given to the variety which is finished with chocolate custard cream and chocolate fondant.
Desdemonas. These are Othello bases sandwiched with vanilla flavoured whipped dairy cream and finished with white fondant, flavoured with kirsch.
Jagos. The same as Othellos except that coffee flavour is used.
Rosalinds. The same as Desdemonas except that a rose flavoured cream and fondant is used.

5. Meringue Goods

Basic Recipe

    5 *oz* (150 g) *egg whites*   10 *oz* (300 g) *castor sugar*

(1) Scald all utensils with boiling water to eliminate grease.
(2) Whisk egg whites to a stiff snow.
(3) Continue whisking and add $\frac{2}{3}$ of the sugar.
(4) Continue whisking until the meringue is very stiff.
(5) Stir in the remaining sugar with a spatula.
Note. The whisking of meringue is best done on a machine.

Shells (Figure 36) (Yield from basic recipe 30 (15 shells))

(1) Pipe out meringue into oval shells on greaseproof paper using a $\frac{1}{2}$-in. (12-mm) piping tube and savoy bag.
(2) Bake meringue in an oven at 250°F (121°C) for approx. $\frac{1}{2}$ hour leaving door of oven slightly ajar to allow the steam to escape.
(3) The shells should be removed from the oven once they are slightly fawn in colour and set sufficiently to allow them to be removed from the tray.
(4) Remove shells carefully, press in the base with a clean thumb to leave a hollow to receive cream.
(5) Stack shells in a tray and store in a warm, dry place until required.
(6) Finish off with fresh cream, piping it between two shells placed on their sides in a paper case. The cream may be slightly sweetened and flavoured with liqueurs. Also the meringue may be coloured and flavoured if desired.

      (*a*)   (*b*)   (*c*)

Hot Meringue

  5 *oz* (150 *g*) *egg whites*   14 *oz* (420 *g*) *castor sugar*
  Colour and flavour

(1) Place sugar on a papered tray and warm in the oven.
(2) Whisk the whites to a stiff snow.
(3) Add the heated sugar to the whisking whites.
(4) Whisk the meringue until very stiff.
(5) Colour and flavour as desired.

Figure 37. Fancy meringues

Fancy Meringues (Figure 37)

(1) Using a star tube, pipe out a variety of fancy shapes on greaseproof paper. Decorate with glacé fruits, coloured nuts, vermicelli, etc.
(2) Bake as for shells.
(3) Remove from the paper and store in a dry place until required.
Note. Some of these shapes may be dipped in chocolate or have chocolate piped on them prior to serving. These fancy meringues may be served either on their own if they are flavoured or with ice-cream and/or fruit.

igure 36. (*opposite*) Meringue shells:
  (*a*) Finished with star tube for cream.
  (*b*) Finished with a cherry for decoration.
  (*c*) Finished with a few coloured nib almonds.

Meringue Cases with Fruit (Figure 38)

(1) Place meringue shells upside down in a paper case.

(2) Pipe on a bulb of whipped fresh sweetened cream.

(3) Place on pieces of well-drained fruit. In Figure 38 peach, pineapple, and mandarin oranges are used.

Vacherins for 8 Covers (Figures 39 to 44)

    $2\frac{1}{2}$ *oz* (75 g) *egg whites*   5 *oz* (150 g) *castor sugar*

(1) Make up the meringue as described for shells.

(2) Draw shapes with pencil on greaseproof or silicone paper. For round shapes, circle needs to be approx. 7 to 8 in. (20 cm). Other shapes should be of approx. the same area.

(3) Pipe outline using a savoy bag with a $\frac{1}{2}$-in. (12-mm) plain tube. For a base and cover, fill in the outline. For the rings, pipe a few extra lines criss-cross inside the outline for strength.

(4) Bake off as previously described under Shells.

(5) Remove from the paper and thoroughly dry out in a warm atmosphere.

(6) Assemble the meringue rings on the base using a little unbaked meringue to stick the pieces together.

(7) Fill the case either during the construction or afterwards with fresh cream and fruit. Cubes of sponge soaked in liqueur-flavoured syrup may also be used.

(8) The top may be of meringue and piped into a decorative shape (Figure 39) or decorated with cream and small piped meringue shapes with glacé fruits or other decor. Chocolate may also be used as a decorating medium. The sides too may be masked with cream.

Large Vacherin Varieties

Round. (Figure 40). The top may be covered in cream as in this example. Small whirls of cream are first piped around the edge and decorated with cherries. In the centre are laid piped meringue petal shapes which have been sprayed with colour. These are arranged as a flower with a large whirl of cream piped in the centre and adorned with a cherry. Examples of other meringue piped tops which could be used are shown in Figure 39.

Figure 38. Meringue cases with fruit: (*a*) peach; (*b*) pineapple; (*c*) orange

    (*a*)   (*b*)   (*c*)

Figure 39. Vacherins: meringue piped tops for large vacherins

Figure 40. Vacherins: a large round vacherin

Square. (Figure 41). The sides of the vacherin have been coated with cream and spread with a serrated scraper to get the corrugated surface. The bottom edge is masked with browned nib almonds. After filling the case and spreading the cream, level lines of cream are piped on using a $\frac{1}{2}$-in. (12-mm) tube. Over these lines, at right angles, are piped (or spun) melted chocolate, using a paper cornet with a very fine hole cut in the end. Decorate with fruits, either tinned, fresh, or glacé. Alternative piped tops are shown in Figure 39.
Heart. (Figure 42). If the piping of the shapes is accurate, the meringue can be left exposed as in this example. The top here is covered with small piped rosettes and the whole sprayed with colour after assembly.

Individual Vacherins (Figure 44) (Yield from previous recipe: with tops 8, without tops 12)

These are made in the same way as the larger varieties but the size should not exceed 3 in. ($7\frac{1}{2}$ cm) in diameter. Figure 43 shows the rings and bases being piped.

The varieties illustrated in Figure 44 are described as follows:

(*a*) Here the top is a piped meringue dahlia.

(*b*) Mandarin orange segments are arranged as a flower with a cherry for its centre.

(*c*) An apricot is used for the top and on this is placed a chocolate cut out (*see* page 249).

(*d*) The top here is a spiral piped out of meringue.

(*e*) Before baking, one of the rings is dusted with desiccated coconut and this is used for the top. A whirl of cream and a cherry complete the decoration.

(*f*) Another piped meringue shape is used here for the top.

Italian Meringue (Yield for fancy meringues 50)

This meringue is partially cooked and is used in the making of goods which are decorated with meringue flashed off in the oven, e.g. baked Alaska ice-cream. It can also be used for piping fancy shapes, since it is more stable than the other types of meringue.

     5 oz (150 g) egg whites   *3 oz (90 g) water*
     10 oz (300 g) sugar   *Pinch of cream of tartar*

Colour and flavour according to requirements.

(1) Place the sugar, water, and cream of tartar in a copper saucepan and, observing sugar boiling precautions (*see* page 273), heat to 245°F (118°C).

(2) Meanwhile beat the egg whites to a stiff snow.

(3) Keeping the egg whites whisking, add the boiled syrup in a steady stream.

(4) Continue whisking until the meringue is firm.

(5) Lastly, add the colour and flavour according to requirements.

Figure 41. Vacherins: a large square vacherin

Figure 42. Vacherins: a large heart-shaped vacherin

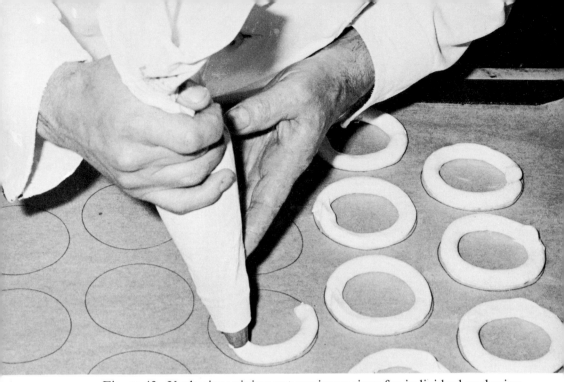

Figure 43. Vacherins: piping out meringue rings for individual vacherins

Figure 44. Individual small vacherins (*see* text)

(*a*)   (*b*)   (*c*)

(*d*)   (*e*)   (*f*)

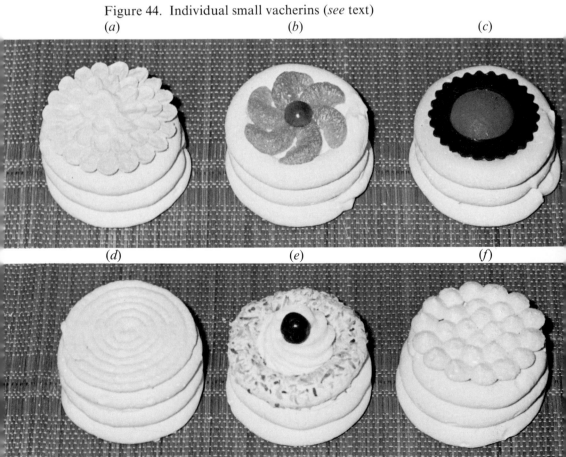

Fruit Meringue

*Add up to 5 oz (150 g) of fruit pulp to the Italian Meringue recipe at
Stage (5).*

The fruit pulp may be apple, raspberry, strawberry, etc.

Piped Meringue Shapes

Meringue is an ideal medium with which to pipe out shapes which can
then be baked crisp and assembled. Animals, flowers, and many other shapes
can be imitated in this way. One of the easiest shapes and one which can
form a suitable decoration in various sweets is mushroom which is described
as follows:

(1) Make a basic meringue.
(2) Pipe out very small bulbs using a $\frac{1}{4}$-in. ($\frac{1}{2}$-cm) tube on greaseproof
paper.
(3) With the same tube, pipe out stems approx. $\frac{3}{4}$ in. ($1\frac{1}{2}$ cm) in length.
(4) Bake off in oven approx. 250°F (121°C).
(5) When dry, remove from the paper.
(6) Using either royal icing or some more meringue mixing, secure the stem
to the underside of the bulbs thus forming a mushroom shape.

Meringue and Ice-cream – Meringue Glacé Chantilly

For each portion allow two half meringue shells (*see* page 82).

Sandwich the two meringue shells with a scoop of ice-cream and decorate
with Chantilly cream.

Note. The ice-cream may be of various flavours and contain fruit. The
decoration could include fruits, nuts, or chocolate pieces (*see* Chapter 22).

6. Cakes

CAKE FAULTS

Before dealing with some basic cake recipes, here is a list of common faults and their diagnoses.

Fault – Cake Sinking in the Centre

Causes.

1. *Too much aeration.* This may be caused by:

(*a*) Too much sugar used in the recipe. This can be detected by excessive crust colour and a sticky seam running in the shape of a U.

(*b*) Too much baking powder. Difficult to detect because it can be confused with (*c*).

(*c*) Overbeating of fat/sugar/egg batter prior to adding flour.

2. *Undercooked.* This can easily be detected by the presence of a wet seam just *below* the surface of the *top* crust.

3. *Knocking in oven prior to cakes being set.* If during cooking when all the ingredients are in a fluid state, a cake gets a knock or disturbance (such as a draught of cold air) some collapse may take place which will result in the centre of the cake caving in.

4. *Too much liquid.* This is easy to detect because, firstly the sides will tend to cave in as well as the top, and if the cake is cut a seam will be discovered immediately *above* the *bottom* crust. Cakes containing too much liquid do not show this fault until they are removed from the oven. During baking, the excess moisture is in the form of steam and actually contributes to the aeration of the cake. On cooling, this steam condenses into water which sinks to the bottom of the cake, collapsing the texture by so doing.

Fault – Peaked Tops

Causes.

1. *Flour used was too strong.* For cakemaking, a weak flour with a low gluten (protein) content is required. If a strong flour is used, the cake will be tough, giving rise to a peaked top which looks unsightly.

2. *Mixing was toughened.* The flour of a cake should be only just mixed in. Overmixing will cause the batter to become tough as the gluten of flour is being developed. Not only will a tough batter produce peaked tops but also a tough and coarse crumb, detracting from its eating qualities.

3. *Too hot an oven with insufficient steam.* The ideal baking condition for a cake is to have a quantity of steam present which will delay the formation of a crust until the cake has become fully aerated and set. If an ovenful of cakes are baked, there is usually sufficient steam generated from the cakes

90

themselves for this purpose, but for small quantities a tray of water should be inserted to get this required steam. A very hot oven will form a crust on the cake too soon and this will in turn cause the cake to rise in the centre only giving the characteristic peak.

Fault – Small Volume with Bound Appearance

Cause. This is caused by insufficient aeration due to:
(*a*) Insufficient beating of the batter.
(*b*) Insufficient sugar used in the recipe.
(*c*) Insufficient baking powder used in the recipe.
Such cakes will have a close crumb structure and be tough to eat.

Fault – Fruit Sinking in Fruit Cakes

Causes.
1. Cake mixing is too soft to carry the weight of fruit. This may be due to:
(*a*) Cake mixing being too light because of overbeating (fat/sugar/egg).
(*b*) Excessive sugar used.
(*c*) Excessive baking powder used.
(*d*) Insufficient toughening of batter.
(*e*) Use of too weak a flour.
Slight toughening of the batter is sometimes necessary to strengthen the crumb and thus make it possible to support the fruit.
2. Fruit was washed and insufficiently dried before being incorporated into the cake batter.
3. Baking temperature was too low. *See* following note on Baking.

BAKING

The general rule is that cakes should be baked as quickly as possible consistent with their being properly cooked through without adverse discoloration of the crust. The following are the factors which affect the baking temperature of cakes.

Steam

As previously mentioned a humid atmosphere is essential in order to achieve a flat top on a cake and to ensure that thorough baking is carried out with a pleasing crust colour. A pan of water inserted in the oven is usually sufficient for this purpose.

Richness

The more sugar a cake contains, the cooler the oven temperature and the longer the cooking time that is required. This is because the richer the cake, the more crust colour is formed.

Shape and Size

The over-riding consideration to be given here is the penetration of heat into the cake mass. It follows from this that the smaller the cake the shorter the baking time, and then the higher the baking temperature. Conversely, large cakes require a lower baking temperature with a longer baking time. However, it is not always appreciated that shape plays an important part. Since it is the penetration of heat that counts, a thin slab of cake cooks very much more rapidly than the same weight but say, double the thickness. The range of temperatures over which cakes may be baked is very wide, ranging from 350°F (177°C) for wedding cakes to 450°F (232°C) for very small fairy cakes.

Additions

Substances like sugar or almonds added to the surface of a cake act as improving the richness of a cake, and baking temperature should be reduced by 10–20°F (5½–11°C) to compensate.

Certain substances like glucose, invert sugar, and honey take on colour at a much lower temperature than sugar. If such substances are added (e.g. for their cake moistening properties), the baking temperature also needs to be lower.

Preparation of Dried Fruit for Fruit Cakes

The moist eating and keeping qualities of cake containing dried fruit depend to a large extent on the amount of moisture retained by the fruit in the cake. To achieve the maximum retention of moisture by the fruit, proper preparation is essential. The fruit should be sorted, washed, and well-drained before use (*see* page 22).

Essences, fruit juices, spirits, etc. may be mixed into the fruit, preferably some time prior to their being used.

The fruit is always added last after the flour has been mixed in.

Choice of Ingredients

Flour. Always use a soft flour but if this is not possible replace a proportion with cornflour.
Fat. Since the aeration of a good quality cake is partly achieved by the trapping of air by the action of beating the fat, one with good creaming qualities is essential. Unfortunately, both butter and normal lard (special processed lards with good creaming qualities are now available) suffer in this respect. In most recipes where butter is used a small quantity of shortening should be incorporated to help overcome this defect.
Sugar. Fine grain castor is best so that it will readily dissolve in the batter.

CAKE MAKING METHODS

To achieve the best possible results, a temperature of approx. 70°F (21°C) should be aimed at and the materials used should be brought to this temperature prior to mixing.

Sugar Batter Method

(1) The fat, margarine, or butter is first beaten to a light foam with the sugar. With fat and margarine, this can be effected in about 4 minutes but butter is difficult to cream and will require at least three times as long. Colour and essences should be added at this stage.

(2) The egg is now added and beaten in. If a machine is employed, the egg can be added in a steady stream over a period of about 2 minutes. If mixing is done by hand, add the egg in about four portions, beating each well in.

(3) Add the flour and carefully mix it into the batter. The aim should be to get a clear smooth batter without lumps and yet not toughened.

(4) Lastly, add any liquid, e.g. milk, fruit, nuts, etc., and blend into the batter carefully to ensure even distribution.

Flour Batter Method

(1) Mix the sugar with the egg and whisk to a half sponge. Add any colour or essence at this stage.

(2) Cream the fat (margarine or butter) with an equal proportion of flour.

(3) Add (1) to (2) in about four portions, blending each portion of the half sponge well into the fat/flour cream.

(4) Blend into the batter the remainder of the flour, so that a smooth mixing free of lumps will result.

(5) Lastly, add any other materials such as milk, fruit, nuts, etc., and blend in carefully to ensure even distribution.

Note. Dry ingredients like cocoa, baking powder, and ground almonds, are always added with the flour.

Fruit Cakes (Yield one 6-in. (15-cm) cake)

3 *oz* (90 g) *butter*	5 *oz* (150 g) *flour*
1 *oz* (30 g) *white cooking fat* (*not lard*)	1 *oz* (30 g) *scone flour* (*see page* 14)
4 *oz* (120 g) *castor sugar*	5 *oz* (150 g) *fruit* (*see below*)
5 *oz* (150 g) *eggs*	$\frac{1}{4}$ *oz* (8 g) *glycerine*

Fruit	Mixed fruit	Sultana	Currant	Cherry
Currants	2 oz (60 g)	—	4 oz (120 g)	—
Sultanas	1½ oz (45 g)	4 oz (120 g)	—	—
Cherries	½ oz (15 g)	—	—	9 oz (270 g)
Peel	1 oz (30 g)	1 oz (30 g)	1 oz (30 g)	—

The above quantities (except Cherry) are for lightly fruited cakes. For medium increase by 50%, and for heavily fruited cakes double these quantities.

(1) Prepare the cake hoops (*see* Note 1 below).
(2) Make the cake on the sugar batter method.
(3) Deposit the above mixing in 6-in. (15-cm) papered hoops (*see* Note 1 below).
(4) Bake at 360°F (182°C) for approx. 1¼ hours until thoroughly cooked. Steam in the oven would be an advantage.
Notes.

1. *Preparation of Cake Hoops.* Cakes baked in hoops need the added protection of paper against the heat of the oven. Several thicknesses of paper should be placed on a tray and covered with greaseproof paper before the hoops are placed upon the tray. The sides of the hoops should also be lined with paper, the final layer being greaseproof. Circles of greaseproof paper can be cut to fit into the bottom of the hoops.

Unless there is plenty of steam in the oven, it is also advisable to cover the top of the cake with a sheet of paper. If the paper sides are extended some way above the level of the cake, this sheet of paper can lie on top without touching the cake.

2. *Size and Weights.* These apply to lightly fruited cakes and madeira cakes. For heavily fruited cakes these weights need to be increased.

Approx. weight of batter	Size of hoops
1 lb 2 oz (540 g)	5½ in. (14 cm)
1 lb 8 oz (720 g)	6 in. (15 cm)
2 lb 4 oz (1080 g)	7 in. (17½ cm)
3 lb 6 oz (1620 g)	8 in. (20 cm)
4 lb 8 oz (2160 g)	9 in. (23 cm)
5 lb 6 oz (2580 g)	10 in. (25½ cm)

Madeira Cakes (Yield one 6-in. (15-cm) cake)

4 *oz* (120 g) *butter*	7½ *oz* (225 g) *eggs*
2 *oz* (60 g) *cooking fat* (*not lard*)	1½ *oz* (45 g) *scone flour* (*see page* 14)
6 *oz* (180 g) *sugar*	7 *oz* (210 g) *soft flour*
½ *oz* (15 g) *glycerine*	*Zest of lemon*

(1) Make using either the sugar or flour batter method.
(2) Proceed as for lightly fruited cakes.
(3) The top may be decorated with a slice of citron peel.
(4) Bake as the lightly fruited cakes.
Note. The butter and fat may be replaced with margarine.

Genoa Cakes (Yield one 6- or 7-in. (15- or 17½-cm) cake)

Use the Fruit Cake recipe with the following amendments:
Fruit

4 *oz* (120 g) *currants*	4 *oz* (120 g) *cherries*
3 *oz* (90 g) *sultanas*	1 *oz* (30 g) *peel*

Add Essences: Almond, Vanilla and Lemon, or Almond and Marachino.
Sprinkle top with flake or strip almonds prior to baking.

Dundee Cakes (Yield one 6- or 7-in. (15- or 17½-cm) cake)

    4 *oz* (120 *g*) *butter*
    1 *oz* (30 *g*) *white cooking fat* (*not lard*)
    5 *oz* (150 *g*) *dark brown soft sugar*
    5 *oz* (150 *g*) *eggs*
    4 *oz* (120 *g*) *flour* (*soft*)
    1 *oz* (30 *g*) *scone flour* (*see page* 14)
    ½ *oz* (15 *g*) *ground almonds*
    2 *oz* (60 *g*) *currants*
    5 *oz* (150 *g*) *sultanas*
    1 *oz* (30 *g*) *cherries*
    1½ *oz* (45 *g*) *mixed peel*
    ½ *oz* (15 *g*) *milk*
    ¼ *oz* (8 *g*) *glycerine*
    Vanilla, almond, and rum essences
    2 *oz* (60 *g*) *split almonds for decoration*

Add Blackjack and egg colour to give a bright golden brown crumb.

Prepare as for fruit cakes, but before baking cover the top with split almonds with the rounded surface facing.

Birthday or Christmas Cakes (Yield one 6- or 7-in. (15–17½-cm) cake)

    3 *oz* (90 *g*) *butter*
    1 *oz* (30 *g*) *white cooking fat* (*not lard*)
    4 *oz* (120 *g*) *dark brown soft sugar*
    5 *oz* (150 *g*) *eggs*
    4 *oz* (120 *g*) *flour*
    1 *oz* (30 *g*) *scone flour* (*see page* 14)
    7 *oz* (210 *g*) *sultanas*
    7 *oz* (210 *g*) *currants*
    2 *oz* (60 *g*) *cut mixed peel*
    ⅛ *oz* (4 *g*) *mixed spice*
    ¼ *oz* (8 *g*) *glycerine*
    Blackjack
    Almond and vanilla essences

(1) Prepare as for fruit cakes.
(2) The size and weights are the same as for wedding cakes (*see* page 97).
Notes.
  1. Christmas cakes may have the addition of rum.
  2. Cherries may be used to replace some of the sultanas if desired.
  3. Blackjack should be added to give the cake a rich dark crumb. If too thick, it should be warmed before adding to the batter.
  4. For finishing refer to wedding cakes (*see* page 97).

Heavy Genoese

    4 *oz* (120 *g*) *butter*
    1 *oz* (30 *g*) *white cooking fat* (*not lard*)

> 5 *oz* (150 g) *eggs*
> 5 *oz* (150 g) *sugar*
> 4 *oz* (120 g) *soft flour*
> 1 *oz* (30 g) *scone flour* (*see page* 14)
> $\frac{1}{4}$ *oz* (8 g) *glycerine*
> *Vanilla essence*

For chocolate. Replace $\frac{1}{2}$ oz (15 g) flour with cocoa powder and add colour.
For almond. Replace $\frac{1}{2}$ oz (15 g) flour with ground almonds.
(1) Make using the sugar batter method.
(2) Spread the mixing to a depth of approx. $\frac{3}{4}$ in. (2 cm) on a deep sided tray lined with greaseproof paper. Make sure the mixing is spread level. This quantity of mixing will produce a sheet approx. 8 in. (20 cm) square.
(3) Bake at 380°F (193°C) for 35–40 minutes.
(4) When cool, keep in a moist place for 24 hours prior to its use.

Boiled Genoese

This genoese is strongly recommended for cutting up into petits fours or afternoon tea fancies because of the stability of its texture and its good keeping qualities.

> 5 *oz* (150 g) *eggs*   ⎫
> 4$\frac{1}{2}$ *oz* (135 g) *sugar* ⎬   A
> 4 *oz* (120 g) *flour*   ⎫
> 4 *oz* (120 g) *butter*   ⎬   Heat
> $\frac{1}{2}$ *oz* (15 g) *glycerine* ⎭

For chocolate. Replace $\frac{1}{2}$ oz (15 g) flour with cocoa powder and add colour.
For almond. Replace $\frac{1}{2}$ oz (15 g) flour with ground almonds.
(1) Heat the egg and sugar (A) to blood heat and whisk to a thick sponge.
(2) Melt the butter in a mixing bowl over heat and stir in the flour and glycerine. Remove from the heat and beat mixture to a smooth paste.
(3) Add the sponge to the fat and flour mixture in three portions. Mix each addition thoroughly but gently to ensure a smooth batter free from lumps.
(4) Pour batter into a four-sided tray for fancies approx. 8 in. (20 cm) square and for petits fours approx. 12 × 9 in. (30 × 22 cm) and spread level.
(5) Bake in an oven at 375°F (191°C) for approx. 40 minutes or until thoroughly baked.
(6) When baked, store in a sealed tin until required. This cake will keep in a moist condition for a month if kept wrapped.
Note. It is usual for the genoese to be cut through the centre and sandwiched either with buttercream or jam. The top and bottom skin should also be trimmed off before the sheet is cut into individual pieces.

Wedding Cakes (Suitable for 2-tier cake of 18 lb (8 kilos) total weight)

> 1 *lb* (480 g) *butter*
> 1 *lb* (480 g) *dark brown sugar*
> 1 *lb* 4 *oz* (600 g) *eggs*
> 1 *lb* (480 g) *flour* (*browned in the oven*)

4 *oz* (120 g) *ground almonds*
2½ *oz* (75 g) *nib almonds* (*roasted*)
3 *lb* (1440 g) *currants*
1 *lb* (480 g) *sultanas*
12 *oz* (360 g) *cut mixed peel*
Zest of 1½ *lemons*
¼ *pt* (1½ *dl*) *rum* (*to rub into baked cake*)

(1) Make cake on the sugar batter process omitting the rum.

The flour as well as the nib almonds are roasted in the oven to enhance the flavour and increase the dark colour. If required, caramel colour can be added to make the cake darker.

(2) Bake the cake in hoops or tins which are well protected from the heat with several layers of paper. A sheet of clean paper can also cover the top during baking, and some steam or water in the oven would be advantageous. When the correct amount of batter has been placed in the hoop it should be flattened into a slight hollow with the back of a wet hand. The temperature should not exceed 350°F (177°C) for a medium sized cake, dropping to 330°F (165°C) for a large one. Some indications of weight of cakes in relation to size of hoops follow:

ROUND CAKES

Hoop size		Cake weight			Board size		Oven time
(in.)	(cm)	(lb	oz)	(grammes to nearest 5 g)	(in.)	(cm)	(hours)
5	13	1	8	680	7	18	2 –2½
6	15	2	4	1020	8	20	2 –2½
7	18	3	0	1360	9	23	2½–3
8	20	4	0	1810	10	25	2½–3
9	23	5	0	2265	12	30	3 –3½
10	25	6	8	2950	13	33	3½
11	28	8	8	3855	14	36	3½
12	30	9	8	4310	15	38	3½

SQUARE CAKES

Frame size		Cake weight			Board size		Oven time
(in.)	(cm)	(lb	oz)	(grammes to nearest 5 g)	(in.)	(cm)	(hours)
5	13	1	15	890	Same as for		Same as for
6	15	2	14	1305	Round Cakes		Round Cakes
7	18	3	13	1730			
8	20	5	1	2295			
9	23	6	5	2865			
10	25	8	4	3740			
11	28	10	13	4905			
12	30	12	1	5470			

The weights above are only approximate and may be varied according to the thickness of cake required.

(3) Store the cakes for at least 6 weeks prior to the reception. Keep wrapped in greaseproof paper in an airtight tin. During this period the rum should be added by pouring onto the surface of the cake and allowing it to soak well in. Apply the rum in two stages, at 14-day and 28-day intervals. The amount stated can be increased to ½ pint (3 decilitres) if a prolonged storage is given. Of course, it can be omitted altogether but the cake will not be so matured nor taste so rich.

(4) After the maturing process, the cake is now ready for marzipanning and icing. The weight of cake should represent 50% of the total, 25% each being for marzipan and royal icing. Before the marzipan is applied, boiling apricot purée is brushed over the top and sides to help the marzipan to adhere to the cake.

(5) Divide the portion of marzipan (for recipe *see* page 251) allocated to the cake into two, for the top and for the sides. For the top, roll the marzipan into a ball and then, using a rolling pin, roll out to the diameter of the cake using icing sugar as the dusting medium. Place the cake upside down on the marzipan disc and, with a palette knife, press the sides of the marzipan, at the same time rotating the cake until the whole top is covered perfectly (Figure 45).

For the sides, make a rope of marzipan three times as long as the cake's width. Flatten with a rolling pin to the cake's thickness. Dust with icing sugar and roll up around the rolling pin or in the hand. Unwind the marzipan, holding the roll upright against the side of the cake, so that it is covered. Trim if necessary with a knife. Place the cake the correct way up (Figure 46).

(6) The next operation can be omitted if desired but is strongly recommended if the finished cake is to be stored for any length of time. Boil some fondant and, with it, completely cover the surface of the marzipan. This seals in the almond oil and prevents it eventually discolouring the royal icing coating.

Figure 45. Covering the top of a cake with almond paste

(7) Mount the cake on a cake board and give it a coating of royal icing as shown in Figure 47 (for recipe *see* page 302). Allow this first coat to dry and harden, i.e. 24 hours, and apply a second coat. If the marzipan has been applied evenly and the cake is symmetrical, two coats should suffice.

(8) Now decorate with a piping tube.

(9) Lastly add the artificial decorations.

(10) Mount the cake on a silver stand at the reception. If it is tiered, mount the tiers on pillars just before the reception. (It is unwise to leave the tiered cake set up with the pillars for a long time prior to the reception because of the risk of accidents.)

SCONES

Notes on Scones

Flour. A medium strength flour should be used. If this is not available, it is recommended that a blend of flour should be used from equal quantities of a strong bread-making flour and a soft cake flour, thoroughly sieved together.

Baking Powder. Most proprietary brands are made from a phosphoric acid derivative with sodium bicarbonate (*see* page 26). Such powders used in the proportions of a scone mixing produce an unpleasant 'bite' or after-taste. Their use has the advantage that the scone mixing can be toughened during the mixing stage to develop a good texture, and then allowed to relax for up to an hour before it is needed to be baked, thus producing a scone with a good appearance.

Figure 46. Coating the sides of a cake with almond paste

Figure 47. Coating a cake with royal icing:
   (*above*) Coating the top using a long-bladed knife.

   (*below*) Coating the sides using a scotch scraper. (A plastic set
   square makes an ideal alternative tool.)

   (*below*) Removing excess sugar from rim with a palette knife. (The
   cake should be turned on the turntable at the same time
   as the blade of the palette knife is pulled towards you.)

For the discriminating customer who is more concerned with flavour and taste, the author strongly recommends the use of a cream of tartar baking powder (*see* page 26), since this leaves no objectionable after-taste. However, if a cream of tartar baking powder is used, the following rules should be observed:

(*a*) Do not toughen the mixing but only mix sufficiently for it to be free of lumps.

(*b*) Bake off as soon as possible after the goods have been egg washed.

Scone Rounds (Yield two rounds (8 scones))

A $\begin{cases} 8 \ oz \ (240 \ g) \ medium \ flour \\ \frac{7}{16} \ oz \ (14 \ g) \ baking \ powder \\ \frac{1}{8} \ oz \ (4 \ g) \ salt \end{cases}$ B $\begin{cases} 1\frac{1}{2} \ oz \ (45 \ g) \ nut \ oil \\ 1\frac{1}{2} \ oz \ (45 \ g) \ sugar \\ 4\frac{1}{2} \ oz \ (135 \ g) \ milk \\ \frac{1}{2} \ oz \ (15 \ g) \ egg \ whites \end{cases}$

(1) Sieve thoroughly the ingredients of A and make a bay (well).
(2) Thoroughly whisk the ingredients of B to make an emulsion.
(3) Pour the emulsion into the bay and mix to a dough.
(4) Add the sultanas which have been previously picked and washed.
(5) Mix to a clear dough free of lumps.
(6) Divide the dough into two and mould round.
(7) Flatten the pieces slightly with a rolling pin and transfer to a clean baking sheet.
(8) With a knife or scraper, cut the piece into four (like a cross).
(9) Separate the four segments on the tray so that there is a gap of approx. $\frac{1}{4}$ in. ($\frac{1}{2}$ cm) between them.
(10) Egg wash the tops of each segment.
(11) Bake in an oven at 450°F (232°C) for approx. 15–20 minutes.

Alternative method of mixing using butter, margarine, or cooking fat instead of oil: Rubbing-in method.
(1) Sieve ingredients of A.
(2) Rub the fat into the flour until it is the consistency of ground almonds with no lumps of fat remaining.
(3) Make a bay (well).
(4) Dissolve the sugar in the liquids and pour into the well.
(5) Mix to a clear dough.
(6) Proceed as for (4) above.

Tea Scones (Yield 18)

8 *oz* (240 *g*) *medium flour*	1$\frac{3}{4}$ *oz* (52 *g*) *sugar*
$\frac{7}{16}$ *oz* (14 *g*) *baking powder*	$\frac{1}{2}$ *oz* (15 *g*) *eggs*
2 *oz* (60 *g*) *butter*	4$\frac{3}{4}$ *oz* (142 *g*) *milk*

Creaming method.
(1) Sieve the flour and baking powder.
(2) Beat the sugar and butter to a light cream.
(3) Add the egg and beat in.

(4) Add half the milk to the creamed butter, etc.
(5) Add the sieved flour and half mix in.
(6) Add the remainder of the milk and mix to a clear and smooth dough.
(7) Roll the dough to approx. $\frac{1}{2}$ in. ($1\frac{1}{4}$ cm) thick.
(8) With a 2-in. (5-cm) round cutter, cut out pieces and place on a clean baking sheet.
(9) Egg wash.
(10) Bake at 440°F (226°C) for approx. 15 minutes.
(11) When baked and cool, these scones may be split and served with butter, fresh cream, and/or jam.

Varieties

Sultana or Currant Scones. Add $2\frac{1}{2}$–3 oz (75–90 g) of the fruit to either of the recipes given.
Fried Scones. Use Scone rounds recipe.
(1) Roll out the dough to $\frac{1}{2}$ in. ($1\frac{1}{4}$ cm) in thickness.
(2) Cut into strips $2\frac{1}{2}$ in. (6 cm) wide, and then into fingers approx. $\frac{1}{2}$ in. ($1\frac{1}{4}$ cm) wide.
(3) Drop into boiling fat. When one side is cooked, turn over to cook the other side.
(4) When cooked, drain and roll in cinnamon flavoured sugar.
(5) The fingers may be split and filled with fresh cream and jam, etc.
   Round and triangular shapes may also be made and finished off in the same way.
Turnover Scones. Use either recipe.
(1) Divide scone mixing into two and mould round.
(2) Roll out the pieces to approx. 8 in. (20 cm) and cut into four.
(3) Place the pieces on a clean baking sheet.
(4) Bake in an oven at 450°F (232°C).
(5) Using a palette knife turn the pieces over as soon as they can be moved without damaging them.
(6) Return to the oven to finish baking.
Farmhouse Scones. Use either recipe.
   Dust heavily with flour instead of egg washing.
Treacle Scones. Use either recipe.
   Replace the sugar with black treacle. Bake at 430°F (221°C).
Wholemeal or Wheatmeal Scones. Use the Tea Scone recipe.
   Replace the white flour with wholemeal or wheatmeal.
   Increase the milk to $5\frac{1}{4}$ oz (158 g).
Hotplate Scones. Use either recipe.
   Bake the scones on a hotplate, turning them over half way through cooking.
Coconut Scones. Use either recipe.
   Add $\frac{1}{2}$ oz (15 g) fine desiccated coconut.
   Proceed as for Turnover Scones (1) and (2) but cut each round into six.

Wash with egg and dip into medium desiccated coconut.

Bake at 430°F (221°C).

Oatmeal Scones. Use either recipe.

Replace half the flour with oatmeal.

Potato Scones. Use Scone Rounds recipe.

Omit the sugar.

Replace up to half of the flour with mashed potatoes.

OTHER SMALL CAKES

Viennese Biscuits (Yield 8)

These may be decorated and served for afternoon tea fancies.

4 *oz* (120 g) *butter*	1¼ *oz* (37 g) *icing sugar*
5 *oz* (150 g) *soft flour*	1 *oz* (30 g) *eggs*

Tarts.

(1) Beat butter and sugar together until light and fluffy.

(2) Beat in the egg.

(3) Add the flour and mix to a smooth paste.

(4) Using a savoy bag and a star tube, pipe the mixture into greaseproof paper cases in the form of a whirl but leaving a shallow depression in the centre.

(5) Bake at 400°F (204°C) until golden brown in colour.

(6) When cold, dust with icing sugar and finish off with a spot of raspberry jam in the centre.

Piped Shapes.

(1) Proceed as (1), (2), and (3) but pipe the mixture into rosettes, fingers, shells, etc. A glacé cherry may be used for decoration.

(2) Bake at the same temperature.

(3) When cold dip half the shape into chocolate or spin it over.

The shapes may be sandwiched with a suitable cream.

Cup Cakes (Yield 18)

4 *oz* (120 g) *butter*

4 *oz* (120 g) *sugar*

6 *oz* (180 g) *eggs*

4 *oz* (120 g) *flour*

2 *oz* (60 g) *scone flour* (*see page* 14)

(1) Prepare a tray of deep custard tart pans in which are placed greaseproof paper cases.

(2) Make on the sugar batter method.

(3) Transfer to a savoy bag with a ½-in. (1¼-cm) tube and pipe a quantity of the mixing into each paper case to within ½ in. (1¼ cm) of the top. For decoration a glacé cherry or sprinkling of currants may be added.

(4) Bake in an oven at 400°F (204°C) for approx. 15–20 minutes.

Note. These can form the bases for afternoon tea fancies by omitting the cherry or currants added as decoration. Suitable finishes for afternoon tea fancies are shown in Figure 90 on page 164.

Queen Cakes (Yield 18)

> 3 *oz* (90 g) *butter*
> 1 *oz* (30 g) *white cooking fat*
> 4¼ *oz* (128 g) *sugar*
> 5 *oz* (150 g) *eggs*
> 5 *oz* (180 g) *flour*
> 1 *oz* (30 g) *scone flour* (*see page* 14)
> 2 *oz* (60 g) *currants* (*optional*)
> *Chopped cherries, flaked almonds, or currants for decoration*

(1) Make on the sugar batter method.
(2) Place batter in a savoy tube with ⅝-in. (1½-cm) plain tube.
(3) Prepare clean queen cake tins with an even coating of grease. Sprinkle in chopped cherries, flaked almonds, and currants to make three varieties.
(4) Pipe the mixture into the tins to within ½ in. (1¼ cm) of the top.
(5) Bake in an oven at 400°F (204°C) for approx. 20 minutes.
(6) When baked, turn out of the tin and present them upside down with the decoration showing.

7. Chou Pastries

Chou paste – Pâté à Choux (Yield eclairs, 16; cream buns, 16; profiteroles, 32)

    2 oz (60 g) butter
    5 oz (150 g) water
    $\frac{1}{8}$ oz (4 g) sugar
    4 oz (120 g) strong flour
    8 oz (240 g) (approx.) eggs

(1) Heat the butter, water, and sugar in a saucepan until boiling.
(2) Remove from the heat.
(3) Using a spatula, stir in the flour.
(4) Re-cook and stir mixture until it leaves the sides of the pan.
(5) Remove from the heat and allow mixture to cool.
(6) Beat in the egg, a little at a time.
(7) The paste should be soft but retain its shape if piped.

Note. The quantity of egg depends upon the strength of the flour: the stronger it is the more eggs are required.

VARIETIES USING CHOU PASTE

Éclairs (Yield 16)

    Chou Paste recipe
    2 oz (60 g) fondant (flavoured and coloured)
    $\frac{1}{2}$ pt (3 dl) whipped cream

(1) Pipe out the chou pastry into finger shapes on a clean baking sheet, approx. 4 in. (10 cm) long using a savoy bag fitted with a $\frac{1}{2}$-in. (1$\frac{1}{4}$-cm) plain tube.
(2) Bake in an oven at 420°F (215°C) for approx. 15 minutes, until brown and set.
(3) When baked and cold, split open with a knife.
(4) Fill with whipped, sweetened fresh dairy cream.
(5) Dip either the top or the base of the eclair in:
    (*a*) Chocolate couverture.
    (*b*) Chocolate flavoured fondant icing.
    (*c*) Chocolate icing (*see* page 249).
(6) Allow to set and then serve.

Note. The base of the éclair is flat and therefore makes an easier surface to coat with icing. Flavours other than chocolate may be used, e.g. coffee–Éclairs au Café.

Cream Buns

Chou Paste recipe
$\frac{1}{2}$ *pt* (3 *dl*) *whipped cream*

(1) Using a savoy bag with a $\frac{1}{2}$-in. (1$\frac{1}{4}$-cm) star tube, pipe out rosettes or bulbs, either in a special cream bun tin or on a baking tray.

(2) The cream bun tin is fitted with a lid in order to prevent steam from escaping from the goods whilst they are being baked. If a baking tray is used, the cream buns will need to be covered with inverted bread tins for the same purpose.

(3) After covering the cream buns, bake in a hot oven at 450°F (232°C) for approx. 20 minutes or until they are brown and set. Since these goods are baked under cover, the covers have to be removed to ascertain whether they are ready to be withdrawn from the oven. *Beware of steam*!

(4) When baked, remove the covers and allow to cool.

(5) Split open with a knife.

(6) Fill with whipped fresh dairy cream which may be sweetened if desired.

(7) Dust with icing sugar and serve.

Petit Cream Buns – Petits Choux à la Crème

These are made for profiteroles, croquembouche, and gâteau St-Honoré. They are made by piping out small bulbs with a savoy bag fitted with a $\frac{3}{8}$-in. (1-cm) tube.

Profiteroles and Chocolate Sauce – Profiteroles au Chocolat (Yield 8 covers)

Chou Paste recipe
$\frac{1}{2}$ *pt* (3 *dl*) *cream chantilly* (*see page* 202)
Chocolate sauce (*see page* 200)

(1) Pipe out petit cream buns about half the size of the ones already described.

(2) After baking, split and fill with sweetened whipped fresh dairy cream.

(3) Dredge with icing sugar and dress neatly on a doily or a flat silver dish.

(4) Serve with a sauceboat of cold chocolate sauce.

Chou Paste Fritters – Beignets Soufflés (Yield 8 covers)

Chou Paste recipe
5 *oz* (150 *g*) *apricot sauce* (*see page* 201)

(1) Using a spoon and finger, break pieces of chou paste about the size of a walnut and drop them into hot fat.

(2) Cook for approx. 10–15 minutes until brown.

(3) Remove, drain well, and sprinkle liberally with icing sugar.

(4) Dress on a doily on a flat silver tray.

(5) Serve separately with a sauceboat of hot apricot sauce.

Savoury Choux Pastries

See Chapter 12.

8. Torten and Gâteaux

TORTEN

On the Continent, especially in Germany and Switzerland, a slice of torten has become a popular after-dinner sweet, as well as a pastry to be eaten with coffee or tea.

There are many interpretations. In some cases any large decorated gâteau is called a torte, but the generally accepted view, is that of a large gâteau already divided into a number of wedge-shaped slices which are individually decorated.

There is a wide variety in the 'make up' of a torte but basically it is made from a sponge, usually soaked with liqueur-flavoured syrup with buttercream and mounted on a disc of either sweetpaste or japonaise.

The sponge may be in three or more layers sandwiched with buttercream or a suitable alternative. If fruit is to be incorporated, two layers with fruit between suffice.

Marzipan, chocolate, nuts, or fruits may all be used, either incorporated in the interior of the torte or used as decoration.

Because the torte is usually sold as a slice, it is important that the interior should look attractive as well as the exterior. If fruits are to be used, these should be put in whole or in slices so that they are clearly visible when the torte is cut. A section of torte should appear as in Figure 48.

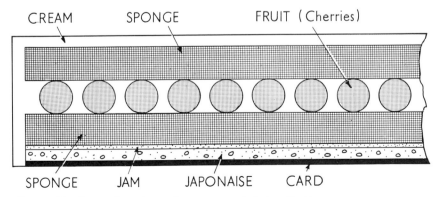

Figure 48. Part of section of a torte containing fruit

Figure 49. Assembly of a torte:
(a) Moistening the sponge base with the flavouring syrup.

(b) Applying the fruit.

(c) Trimming the sides to within $\frac{1}{4}$ in. (3 mm) of the base-board.

(*contd. page* 110)

Quantities of Materials for one 10-in. (25-cm) Torte (16 portions)

1 *sponge base approx.* 12 *oz* (360 *g*) (*see page* 79)
4 *oz* (120 *g*) *raspberry jam*
1 *jap or sweetpaste disc* (*see pages* 157 *or* 148)
1 *A* 2 *tin of fruit*
½ *pt* (300 *g*) *syrup*
2–4 *oz* (60–120 *g*) *liqueur*
1½ *lb* (720 *g*) *buttercream* (*see page* 297)
2 *oz* (60 *g*) *golden syrup* (*to sweeten fruit juice if required*)
2 *oz* (60 *g*) *browned nib or flaked almonds or browned desiccated coconut*

Size of Torte

This is largely at the discretion of the patissier but the height should not exceed 2½ in. (6½ cm). The diameter may vary between 8 and 12 in. (20–30 cm) according to the number of slices required. An 8-in. (20-cm) torte will produce twelve large or sixteen small slices, whilst a 12-in. (30-cm) torte will produce 24 slices.

Method

The following is a step by step method of assembling a torte in accordance with Figure 49.
(1) Select the size of board. A cake board or plate at least 2 in. (5 cm) larger in diameter than the torte on which it should be mounted is needed. A disc of thick waxed card of silvered strawboard the same size as the torte is also necessary.
(2) Place the circle of waxed card on top of the cake board and on this card place a disc of either sweetpaste or japonaise.
(3) On the sweetpaste or japonaise, spread a good quality jam, e.g. raspberry, or cover with chocolate.
(4) Place a disc of sponge on the jammed base and saturate with a suitably flavoured syrup (*see page* 113). This may be done with either a spray or a brush.
(5) Spread this first layer of sponge with good quality, flavoured buttercream and then distribute the fruit evenly.
(6) Spread on another layer of buttercream and then place on the second sponge disc.
(7) Saturate this sponge layer also with the flavoured syrup.
(8) Trim sides with a sharp knife to allow approx. $\frac{3}{16}$ in. ($\frac{1}{2}$ cm) clearance between the edge of the waxed card and sides of the torte. Also gently press the top level with a cake board.
(9) Coat the top and sides with buttercream and finish off as follows:
   (*a*) Side coat. Use a celluloid or plastic scraper (a plastic set square is an ideal tool). Coat the side by holding it against the edge of the waxed card or strawboard, at the same time turning the torte on a turntable. The card acts as a template in this connection and will produce a perfect symmetrical shape.

(*d*) Applying the side coat with a plastic scraper.

(*e*) Showing how the long-bladed knife is used to coat the top.

(*f*) Applying the bottom decoration.

Figure 49 (*contd.*)

(g) Removing the torten marker after marking the top of the torte into 12 divisions.

(h) Using a shield made out of a disc of stiff paper into which has been set a round cutter. Its use enables a circle of coralettes to be placed in the centre of the torte without sprinkling any elsewhere.

(i) Using a savoy bag with a $\frac{1}{4}$ in. (3 mm) tube to pipe plain lines radiating from the centre.

Figure 49 (contd.)

(*b*) Top coat. Using a long-bladed knife, the top is levelled by sweeping the knife from the outside edge to the centre, from about four positions of the turntable. After practice a level and smooth top may be achieved with a clear unbroken edge.

An alternative method is to coat the top first by sweeping over with a knife or straight edge and cutting off with a palette knife as the sides are coated.

If the whole side is to be masked afterwards, less care is required to obtain a perfect edge. In this case the main effort should be directed to obtaining a perfectly smooth and level top coat.

(10) By means of the card under the torte, it may now be picked up and a suitable dressing of nuts or coralettes applied as decoration either to the lower part of the sides or to the complete side.

(11) The top is marked into an appropriate number of divisions by means of a torten marker.

(12) Decoration may now be applied, first by placing coralettes in the centre using a shield, then decorating each segment using buttercream, nuts, fruit, etc.

(13) Store in a cool place, preferably in a refrigerator.

Flavours

Most Continental torten are flavoured with liqueurs in combination with fruit or nuts. The following chart shows some useful combinations:

Fruit, etc.	*Liqueurs*
Apricot	Apricot Brandy
Peach	Peach Brandy
Cherry	Kirsch, Cherry Brandy, Maraschino
Pineapple	Kirsch
Orange	Grand Marnier, Curaçao
Ganache	Rum, Brandy
Chocolate	Rum
Praline	Rum
Coffee	Tia Maria, Rum, Brandy

Figure 50. Pineapple torte

Lemon is so strongly flavoured that it is unnecessary to add any liqueur.

The syrup for such torten should be strongly flavoured with the juice of the fruit itself. If tinned fruit is used, the juice should also be employed for the syrup with which to soak the sponge. However, if a liqueur is used the sweetness may have to be adjusted by adding golden syrup or sugar (icing).

VARIETIES

Pineapple Torte (Figure 50)

Proceed as previously described using either fresh or tinned pineapple pieces in the interior make up and soaking the sponge with a mixture of equal quantities of pineapple juice and syrup. Instead of incorporating whole pieces of pineapple, it may be finely chopped and incorporated in with the buttercream.

Side Decoration. This may be either roasted chopped almonds or coconut.

Top Decoration. Use confiture pineapple (page 261) cut into wedges and placed in a split glacé cherry to form a flower figure. Lines of buttercream are piped on each segment and on these are placed the flower and a piece of angelica cut into a diamond. The centre is filled with chopped roasted nuts, sieved japonaise crumbs, or roasted desiccated coconut.

Orange Torte (Figure 51)

Proceed as previously described using tinned oranges or peeled and skinned segments of fresh oranges in the interior make up. Flavour the syrup with the orange juice (from tinned oranges) and the appropriate liqueur. Also add sufficient liqueur to the buttercream to flavour.

Side Decoration. As previous torte.

Top decoration. Pipe a rosette of buttercream on each segment and on this place a glazed segment of orange. The glazing is done by dipping the orange segments into boiling apricot purée. The centre is finished off as in the previous torte.

Figure 51. Orange torte

Praline Torte (Figure 52)

Proceed as previously described using rum flavoured syrup with which to soak the sponge, and a praline and rum flavoured buttercream. Since no fruit is to be placed inside this torte, three layers of sponge should be used.
Note. Praline is made from croquant (page 265) crushed and milled into a smooth paste. Unless it is added to buttercream carefully, lumps can be formed. The praline should be first broken down to a smooth semi-fluid paste with a little of the buttercream and then added to the rest. If it is very hard, heat should be applied to soften it first.
Side Decoration. Roasted almonds either crushed, nibbed, or flaked should be used.
Top Decoration. On a piped line of white buttercream (without the addition of praline) place an unblanched almond. The centre is covered with roasted almond nibs and a few of these are sprinkled lightly on the top.

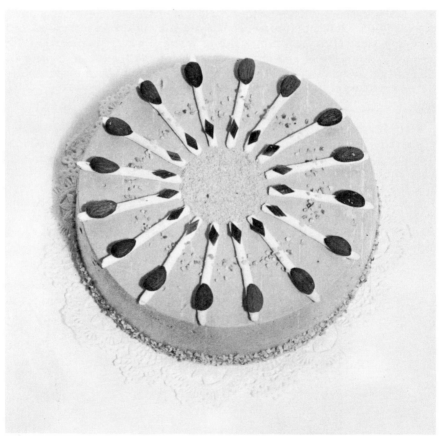

Figure 52. Praline torte

Chocolate Ganache Torte (Figure 53)

Proceed as previously described using a mixture of buttercream and ganache flavoured with rum. The syrup used to soak the sponge is also flavoured with rum. Use three layers of sponge as in the previous torte.

Side Decoration. Use chocolate coralettes or a mixture of chocolate coralettes and green almond decor.

Top Decoration. On each segment, pipe a rosette of white buttercream and place on filigree chocolate flowers (*see* Chapter 18). In the centre place a truffle ball made from cake crumbs bound with a little apricot purée, dipped into melted chocolate and coralettes. Dust this ball with icing sugar first and set if off with a surround of angelica diamonds.

Figure 53. Ganache torte. A comb scraper has been used for the coating of the torte.

Fresh Cream Torte (Figure 54)

Fresh cream torten make delicious sweets. The fruit used may be fresh or tinned but the fresh cream used should be *double*. The following is a step by step description of the making of an orange fresh cream torte.

1 sponge 10 in. (250 cm) diameter, approx. 8 oz (240 g)

1 japonaise or sweetpaste disc (same size) (see pages 157 or 148)

Oranges extracted from two 10-oz (300-g) or one A2 tin of mandarin oranges

Juice of one 10-oz (300-g) tin or half one A2 tin

4 oz (120 g) Grand Marnier liqueur

2 oz (60 g) golden syrup (to sweeten fruit juice)

½ pt (3 dl) double fresh cream

4 oz (120 g) raspberry jam

1 oz (30 g) sugar

1 oz (30 g) coralettes or roasted nuts

(1) Coat a disc of japonaise or sweetpaste with raspberry jam and mount it on a card base.

(2) Place the sponge on the jammed base.

(3) Soak this sponge with half the syrup into which 2 oz (60 g) of liqueur has been mixed.

(4) Select twelve orange segments for the top and neatly arrange the remainder of the fruit in a layer on top of the sponge.

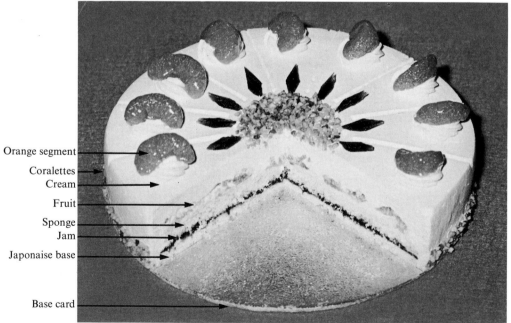

Orange segment
Coralettes
Cream
Fruit
Sponge
Jam
Japonaise base
Base card

Figure 54. Fresh cream torte

(5) Trim the sides and base to within $\frac{1}{4}$ in. (6 mm) of the card edge.

(6) Whisk the double cream with the remaining 2 oz (60 g) liqueur and a little sugar to sweeten.

(7) Completely cover the torte, neatly coating the top and sides with the cream, leaving just sufficient for twelve rosettes to be piped on the top.

(8) Mark the twelve divisions of the torte using a torten marker.

(9) Using a shield, dust desiccated coconut or coralettes into the centre.

(10) Pipe a rosette of cream on each segment.

(11) Dip the orange segments in boiling apricot purée and when set place upon each rosette.

(12) Lastly dip the bottom edge in coralettes.

Wine Cream Torte

Same ingredients as Fresh Cream Torte except that Wine Cream (*see* page 300) is used instead of Fresh.

(1) Same as (1)–(4) in Fresh Cream Torte.

(2) After the fruit has been added, place on a hoop the same size as the torte.

(3) Pour into the hoop the wine cream before it sets; fill to the appropriate depth sufficient to cover the fruit.

(4) Mask the sides with roasted almonds.

(5) Mark the top into the desired number of portions.

(6) Decorate each portion with the fruit covered with an appropriate glaze.

Fruit Torte (Alternative method)

The torte previously described contains fruit but it is totally enclosed by the buttercream or fresh fruit filling. Some fruits, such as fresh strawberries, look so attractive that the whole of the top of the torte may be covered with them, suitably glazed. The method for such a torte is as follows.

Fresh Strawberry Torte

(1) Prepare a base of japonaise or sweetpaste and sponge $\frac{1}{2}$–$\frac{3}{4}$ in. (1$\frac{1}{4}$–2 cm) thick as already described.

(2) Sprinkle the sponge with liqueur syrup, i.e. Kirsch or Maraschino.

(3) Spread on a layer of good quality buttercream flavoured with liqueur.

(4) Select strawberries of uniform size, remove the stalks, and place them upside down on top of the cream layer to cover it completely.

(5) Brush over a red glaze.

(6) Finish by masking the sides with cream and roasted flake almonds.

A variety of fruit torte may be made in this way with fruits used either on their own or mixed. With the latter many attractive decorative patterns may be made, not unlike fruit flans.

Swiss Pineapple Torte (Figure 55)

Proceed as for Pineapple Torte but without coating the top and sides with buttercream. Decorate as follows:

(1) Make petit Swiss rolls and cut up into slices approx. $\frac{1}{4}$ in. (6 mm) thick.

(2) Place these flat to cover the top layer of sponge.

(3) Completely cover the torte in a pectin glaze applied as follows:

(*a*) Stir a measured amount of acid into the pectin syrup and spread it on a sheet of greaseproof paper before it sets.

(*b*) When set reverse the greaseproof paper and lay it pectin side down on the torte.

(*c*) Wash the back of the greaseproof paper with water and gently peel it away from the pectin jelly layer which should now completely enrobe the torte.

Figure 55. Swiss pineapple torte

(4) Trim the bottom edge free of any jelly and place the torte on a round dish.

(5) Pipe rosettes of fresh whipped cream around the bottom edge. Pipe eight rosettes on top and decorate with wedges of confiture pineapple.

Kirsch Torte (Figure 56)

This is a classical dish from Switzerland. It is prepared as follows:

2 *japonaise discs* 10 *in.* (25 *cm*) *in diameter* (*see page* 157)
1 *sponge base approx.* 1 *in.* (2½ *cm*) *thick* (*see page* 79)
8 *oz* (240 *g*) *buttercream*
2 *oz* (60 *g*) *roasted almonds*
1 *oz* (30 *g*) *icing sugar*
4 *oz* (120 *g*) *kirsch liqueur*
6 *oz* (180 *g*) *stock syrup* (*see page* 265)

(1) Make two japonaise discs approx. 10 in. (25 cm) in diameter.
(2) Make one sponge base of the same size.
(3) Flavour the buttercream with 1 oz (30 g) of kirsch and spread a layer on one of the jap discs.
(4) Place the disc of sponge in a shallow dish with the syrup in which the rest of the kirsch has been added. Leave until all the syrup has been absorbed by the sponge.

Figure 56. Kirsch torte

(5) Place the soaked sponge on the cream covered jap base.
(6) Spread more cream over the soaked sponge.
(7) Cover with the second disc of jap. Now there is a disc of sponge sandwiched between two japonaise discs.
(8) Mask the sides with the cream and roasted almonds.
(9) Dust the surface with icing sugar and, with the back of a knife, mark with a diamond pattern.

Dairy Cream Cheese Torte

    1 *sponge 9 in. (23 cm) by $\frac{3}{4}$ in. (2 cm) thick*
    8 *oz (240 g) cheese curd (cream cheese)*
    2 *oz (60 g) sugar*
    7 *oz (210 g) lemon curd*   Filling
    $\frac{3}{4}$ *oz (22 g) gelatine (leaf)*
    $\frac{1}{2}$ *pt (3 dl) whipped cream*
    3 *oz (90 g) sultanas (soaked in rum)*
    1 *oz (30 g) rum*
    2 *oz (60 g) syrup*
    1 *oz (30 g) icing sugar (for decoration)*
    1 *oz (30 g) whipped cream (for decoration)*
    Roasted nib almonds (for decoration)

(1) Split the sponge into two discs one $\frac{1}{2}$ in. (12 mm) and the other $\frac{1}{4}$ in. (6 mm) thick.
(2) Place the $\frac{1}{2}$ in. (2 mm) thick sponge in a 9-in. (23-cm) torten ring.
(3) Sprinkle the sponge liberally with rum syrup. (First soak the sultanas in rum, drain, and mix the remainder of the rum with the syrup.)
(4) Spread on top of the sponge the cheese filling which is made as follows:
    (*a*) Soak the gelatine in water until pliable and then melt over heat.
    (*b*) Mix the cheese, lemon curd, and sugar, add the gelatine, and mix in.
    (*c*) Lastly fold in the whipped cream and sultanas.
(5) Refrigerate.
(6) Cut the $\frac{1}{4}$ in. (6 mm) thick sponge into eight (or the desired number) of segments and dust liberally with icing sugar.
(7) Carefully arrange these segments on top of the torte.
(8) Pipe a rosette of cream on each segment and sprinkle with roasted nib almonds.
Notes.

    1. As decribed, this torte is cut into eight typically large German portions. If smaller portions are required, it is suggested that the torte be cut into twelve.

    2. The torte should be kept in a refrigerator and served cold.

Dobos Torte (Yield 8 in. (20 cm) torte suitable for cutting into 8 or 12 portions)

    3 *oz (90 g) egg yolks (4)*
    5 *oz (150 g) egg whites (4)*
    4 *oz (120 g) castor sugar*
    4 *oz (120 g) butter*
    3 *oz (90 g) flour*
    3 *oz (90 g) sugar for caramel*
    1 *pt (6 dl) caramel dairy cream*

(1) Cream the butter and 2 oz (60 g) of sugar into a light batter.
(2) Gradually add the yolks, continuing to beat well.

(3) Whisk the egg whites and remaining sugar (2 oz) to a stiff meringue.
(4) Blend the meringue into the batter.
(5) Carefully blend in the flour and mix to a smooth batter without toughening.
(6) Grease and flour a baking tray and on this spread the mixture ⅛ in. (3 mm) thick, into four 8-in. (20-cm) rings to form four discs.
(7) Bake at 420°F (215°C) until discs are baked a golden brown colour and are crisp.
(8) Remove from the tray and allow to cool.
(9) Select the best baked disc for the caramel top and liberally sandwich the others with caramel cream.
(10) Ice the top disc with caramel (*see* below) and cut into the desired number of segments.
(11) Coat the top layer with cream and arrange the segments on top.
(12) Mask the sides with cream and roasted nuts.

To make and use the caramel.
(1) Place the sugar in a copper pan with a little lemon juice and heat to first melt the sugar and then to bring it to the caramel degree (*not too dark*) (*see page* 272).
(2) When the sugar is coloured sufficiently, stir in a small knob of butter, ¼ oz (7 g).
(3) Pour the hot caramel onto the baked disc and with a palette knife quickly spread it evenly to cover.
(4) Allow the sugar to set and then, using a knife with a saw-like action, cut into the desired number of segments.
Making the caramel cream.
    1 *pt* (6 *dl*) *fresh dairy double cream*
    6 *oz* (180 *g*) *sugar*
    A drop of lemon juice
(1) Weigh the sugar into a copper saucepan, add a drop of lemon juice, and place on the heat to melt.
(2) Once melted, raise the temperature until the sugar boils and then turns to an amber colour (*not too dark*).
(3) Remove from the heat and add a little water (*beware of steam*) to bring the sugar to a syrup which, when cold, has the consistency of golden syrup.
(4) Start whisking the fresh double dairy cream, add the cold caramel syrup to flavour and sweeten, and continue whisking until thick.
Note. Dobos may also be made into slices by baking the mixture in the form of strips and then sandwiching together.

    The preceding examples should show the reader how any particular torte can be made. For example, if apricots are used, these would not only feature inside but also appear glazed on top as illustrated for the orange torte. A torte may also be finished off by covering the top with the fruit laid out in a decorative pattern as in fruit flans. Indeed many examples of these types of finish may be seen in the Continental shops.

In exhibitions, one finds the most elaborate interior designs exquisitely decorated; but whilst appearance is important, the eating characteristics and flavour are paramount particularly to the customer who chooses such a delicacy as a sweet course.

GÂTEAUX

The dividing line between gâteaux and torten is very fine and, in fact, in some cases, one is indistinguishable from the other. Each means a large decorated cake, the name gâteaux being the French term and the word torte being the German. In Switzerland especially, the name of torte is given to many types of large decorated cakes which are not divided into slices (*see* Kirsch Torte and Fruit Torte). The definition that a torte should be divided into portions in the decoration is the accepted British interpretation; but if classical cakes like Kirsch Torte are being sold it is best to retain the descriptive name of the country of its origin.

Except for specialities, the make up of most gâteaux is similar to torten. It usually consists of an enriched sponge or butter sponge (page 79) sandwiched with buttercream, fresh cream, ganache, curd, jam, with or without fruit, liqueur, chocolate, nuts, etc. Buttercream, fresh cream, fondant, or other suitable icing is then used to cover the sponge which may be masked in nuts and suitably decorated. Gâteaux may be named according to the type of mixings and the flavours used. For example, if meringue is used, this could be named with the fruit or flavour used, e.g. Strawberry Meringue Gâteaux. Usually, however, the gâteau is named according to the main flavour used, whether it is fruit, liqueur, chocolate, praline, coffee, etc. They are usually placed on a doily on a flat silver dish for service.

The following description is of a typical chocolate gâteau but, by altering the basic flavour (in this case chocolate) and applying an appropriate decoration, it can form the basis of a great number of gâteaux.

Figure 57. Chocolate gâteau

Chocolate Gâteau (Figure 57) (Suitable for cutting into 8 portions)

1 *sponge approx. 7 in. (18 cm) diameter by 2 in. (5 cm)*
or two 1 in. (2½ cm) thick
6 *oz* (180 *g*) *buttercream vanilla* (*see page* 297)
6 *oz* (180 *g*) *ganache* (*see page* 250)
1 *oz* (30 *g*) *chocolate coralettes*
⅓ *pt* (2 *dl*) *rum syrup* (*optional*)
Decorative sugar or chocolate pieces

(1) Split the sponge base into three.
(2) Sprinkle on the rum syrup.
(3) Keep about 2 oz (60 g) of the vanilla buttercream for decoration. Mix the rest with the ganache.
(4) Sandwich the sponge layers with the ganache buttercream.
(5) Coat the top and texture it with the end of a palette knife as follows:
  Using a turntable, start at the centre and whilst turning the turntable, pull the palette knife towards the edge so that a spiral pattern is created.
(6) Coat the sides and mask with chocolate coralettes.
(7) The decoration is made as follows:
  Colour half the white buttercream green and pipe a few lines resembling leaf stems. To these attach a few green sugar paste cut out leaves and white cut out flowers. The flower centres may be either crystallized mimosa or piped yellow sugar balls. With the rest of the white buttercream, pipe out the inscription.
Variations.
  1. Instead of ganache, 10 oz (300 g) buttercream may be flavoured with the addition of 2 oz (60 g) melted chocolate.
  2. Various alternative decorative treatments may be made using chocolate cut-outs or piped pieces (*see* Chapter 18) and with a buttercream piped border.
  3. Instead of buttercream, the top could be coated with chocolate fondant or another type of chocolate icing.

Gâteau Millefeuilles – Gâteau of a Thousand Leaves (Figure 58)
(Yield 8 in. (20 cm) suitable for cutting into 8 portions)

12 *oz* (360 *g*) *puff pastry trimmings*
2 *oz* (60 *g*) *jam*
½ *pt* (3 *dl*) *pastrycream or fresh cream*
4 *oz* (120 *g*) *fondant or water icing*
1 *oz* (30 *g*) *browned almonds*

(1) Roll out the paste very thinly and cut three discs of approx. 9 in. (23 cm) diameter. This will shrink to approx. 8 in. (20 cm) in baking.
(2) Prick each piece all over with a fork or a docker and allow to rest for at least half an hour.
(3) Bake in a hot oven at 450°F (232°C) until crisp and brown in colour.

(4) When cold, trim each piece to a perfect round shape and select the best for the top.

(5) Sandwich the pieces together with the cream and jam. Place the top disc on upside down to present a good surface.

(6) Prepare the fondant with syrup to a thin spreading consistency.

(7) Prepare a little of the icing in two colours, e.g. chocolate and pink, and fill a paper cornet with each.

(8) Pour and spread on the icing evenly over the top and immediately pipe alternate lines about $\frac{1}{2}$ in. (12 mm) apart of chocolate and pink fondant from the paper cornets.

(9) Using the back of a knife and wiping between each stroke, pull the knife across the piped lines at approx. 1 in. ($2\frac{1}{2}$ cm) intervals (Figure 59).

(10) Turn the gâteau round and repeat pulling the knife in the opposite direction between the first strokes.

(11) Allow to set and trim off the edge.

(12) Coat the edge with cream and mask with the browned almonds.

Note. The operation described under (8)–(10) is called marbling or feathering and is illustrated in Figure 59. To get the best results, speed is essential and the icing should not be either too warm or too stiff in consistency.

Figure 58. Millefeuilles gâteau

Nougat Gâteau (Yield 8 in. (20 cm) suitable for cutting into 8 portions)

12 oz (360 g) puff pastry trimmings
2 oz (60 g) icing sugar
½ pt (3 dl) whipped fresh cream
6 oz (180 g) nougat nibs (see page 265)

(1) Roll out the paste very thinly and cut three discs of approx. 9 in. (23 cm) diameter. These will shrink to about 8 in. (20 cm) in the baking.
(2) Prick each piece with a fork or docker and allow to rest approx. half an hour.
(3) Dust each piece liberally with icing sugar.
(4) Bake in a hot oven at 450°F (232°C) until brown and crisp. (Some of the sugar will caramelize into a brown glaze.)
(5) Keep a little of the whipped cream aside to coat the sides. Mix the remainder with 4 oz (120 g) of crushed nougat nibs.
(6) Trim the puff pastry discs all to the same size and an even round shape and select the best for the top.
(7) Sandwich together using the nougat cream, placing the selected disc upside down on top.
(8) Mask the sides with the whipped cream reserved for this purpose and also the rest of the nougat nibs.
(9) Dust the top liberally with icing sugar and mark on a diamond pattern with the back of a knife. Finish is similar to Kirsch Torte (Figure 56).

Figure 59. Marbling a gâteau top

Gâteau Pithiviers ⎫
              ⎬   *see* Chapter 3 on Puff Pastry, pages 66 and 67.
Gâteau Jalousie ⎭

Gâteau Tom Pouce (Yield 8 in. (20 cm) suitable for cutting into 8 portions)

     8 *oz* (240 *g*) *puff pastry trimmings*
     2 *oz* (60 *g*) *apricot jam*
     $\frac{1}{4}$ *pt* (1$\frac{1}{2}$ *dl*) *cream into bavarois* (*see page* 208)
     4 *oz* (120 *g*) *fondant or water icing*

(1) Roll out the paste very thinly and cut into two discs of approx. 9 in. (23 cm) diameter. In the baking this will shrink to approx. 8 in. (20 cm).
(2) Prick each piece all over with a fork or docker and allow to rest for at least half an hour.
(3) Bake in a hot oven at 450°F (232°C) until crisp and brown in colour.
(4) When cold, trim each piece to a perfect round to just fit into a hoop. Select the best disc for the top.
(5) Spread the jam on the base and place it inside a paper-lined hoop.
(6) Make the bavarois mixing and pour it onto the base inside the hoop.
(7) Chill, and when set remove the hoop and paper lining.
(8) Cover the top disc with 'feathered' icing (*see* (6)–(10) of Gâteau Mille Feuilles, page 124).
(9) When the icing has set this may now be placed on top of the bavarois layer. To facilitate cutting into portions, this feathered-iced top may be first cut into eight segments and each placed on the bavarois.
Note. Although chocolate bavarois is generally recommended for this gâteau, any flavour may be used. This gâteau may also be made as a strip and cut into slices.

Gâteau Macmahon (Figure 60) (Yield 8 covers)

     5 *oz* (150 *g*) *flour into almond sweetpaste* (*see page* 148)
     $\frac{1}{4}$ *pt* (1$\frac{1}{2}$*dl*) *cream into strawberry bavarois* (*see page* 208)
     2 *oz* (60 *g*) *red glaze or piping jelly*
     1 *oz* (30 *g*) *icing sugar*
     2 *oz* (60 *g*) *apricot or strawberry jam*

(1) Divide the sweetpaste into two pieces and roll them out into two thin discs of 8 in. (20 cm) diameter.
(2) Prick the discs well with a fork or docker and cut or mark one of them into eight segments.
(3) Bake until crisp and brown in an oven at 380°F (193°C).
(4) Spread jam on the base disc and place it inside a paper-lined 8-in. (20-cm) hoop.
(5) Make the strawberry bavarois and pour it into the prepared hoop.
(6) Chill, and when set remove the hoop and lining.
(7) Separate the segments of the top disc, coating four with red glaze. Dredge the other four liberally with icing sugar.
(8) Arrange the segments on top alternately red and white.
Note. This gâteau may also be made as a strip and cut into slices.

Figure 60. Gâteau MacMahon

Gâteau St-Honoré (Figure 61) (Yield suitable for cutting into 8 portions)

    Short pastry or puff pastry (see pages 39 and 56)
    Chou paste (see page 105)
    Crème St-Honoré (see page 301)
      or
    Crème chantilly (see page 202)
    Boiled sugar (see page 273)
    Crystallized violets, cherries, pineapples
    Nibbed pistachio nuts or green nib almonds
    Genoese cubes (see page 95)

(1) Roll out either short paste or puff paste to approx. ⅛ in. (3 mm) thick. For puff pastry, use well rested trimmings.
(2) Cut out a disc about 9 in. (23 cm) and prick or dock over well.
(3) Transfer to a clean water splashed baking sheet. For puff pastry allow to rest for at least 1 hour.
(4) Wash the outer edge of these discs with egg.
(5) Prepare chou paste.
(6) Using a savoy bag with ½-in. (12-mm) tube, pipe a ring of the chou paste on the pastry edge.
(7) Using a soft brush, wash the chou paste ring with egg, making sure that the shape is not spoilt.
(8) Bake at 400°F (204°C) until the chou paste ring is dry and brown.
(9) Make sixteen petits choux.
(10) Proceed with the preparation of the base by first filling with small cubes of pink and white genoese soaked in a liqueur syrup.

(11) Top up with cream Chantilly or cream St-Honoré.

(12) Fill the petits choux with the cream and then dip the tops of each into sugar syrup boiled to the crack degree 280°F (138°C) and then immediately into four of any of the following:

(*a*) broken crystallized violet petals

(*b*) chopped glacé cherries

(*c*) chopped glacé pineapple

(*d*) nibbed green almonds or pistachio nuts

(*e*) broken crystallized rose petals

(*f*) browned nib almonds.

(13) Arrange these alternately around the top edge of the base.

(14) Brush the outside edge with apricot purée and cover with pale roasted flaked almonds.

(15) Cover with spun sugar (*see* page 273) immediately prior to service.

Note. There are many variations of this traditional dish. Besides cream Chantilly and cream St-Honoré, a mixture of pastrycream and fresh cream is often used to fill the centre, and in some recipes no genoese is used. Glacé and sometimes fresh fruits dipped in boiling sugar are also used to decorate the top prior to service.

Figure 61. Gâteau St-Honoré. Note the spun sugar.

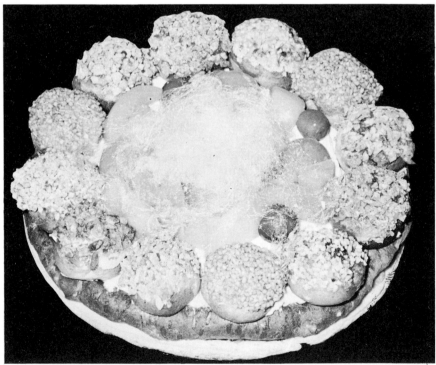

Croquembouche (Figure 62)

> *Chou paste* (*see page* 105)
> *Nougat* (*see page* 265)
> *Boiled and spun sugar* (*see page* 273)
> *Crème bavarois* (*see page* 208)
> *Crème chantilly* (*see page* 202)

Figure 62. Gâteau Croquembouche: assembling petits choux

(1) Prepare a number of petit cream buns. Vary the size a little so that some are very small and others larger. Thoroughly bake, allow to cool, and fill with crème Chantilly.

(2) Meanwhile prepare a conical mould of the size required. This may be made of tin but a temporary one may be made of cardboard. Grease the mould evenly and stand on a greased tin.

(3) Boil a sugar syrup to the hard crack degree 310°F (154°C). Remove, plunge pan into cold water to arrest the rise in temperature, and dip each petit cream bun.

(4) Place the cream buns side by side against the base of the papered mould. Once a ring is formed, start on another ring and so on until a pyramid of cream buns has been built up. Use the smallest cream buns for the top and the largest for the base.

(5) Once set, turn upside down and remove the mould and paper lining.

(6) The centre of the croquembouche can be filled in a variety of ways:

(*a*) cubes of genoese soaked in liqueur-flavoured syrup and cream Chantilly and sometimes fruit.

(*b*) alternate layers of bavarois and fruit.

(7) Mount the croquembouche on a decorative base made of nougat.

(8) Finish off the top with a ball of spun sugar or some figure.

9. Petits Fours Secs

The term 'petits fours' means 'small fancy biscuits' but there is often confusion as to the meaning of the word 'small', since it is relative to something larger. The author's interpretation is cakes or biscuits which may be consumed in one or at the most two mouthfuls. Their size, therefore, should be only about 1 in. (2½ cm) wide.

Sometimes the petits fours are glazed with icing, in which case we call them Petits Fours Glacés. Very small fondant dipped fancies are in this category, but so are many varieties of small biscuits which may also be glazed.

When the petits fours are left plain, they are called Petits Fours Secs, i.e. dry. Many of these are made from almonds and are sometimes referred to as Almond Dessert Biscuits.

Petits fours may be served as follows:

(*a*) With coffee at a luncheon, dinner, or banquet.

(*b*) At a buffet or special party.

Almost any cake or sweetmeat may be called a petit four, provided it is small enough to fit into our category.

Parisian Rout Biscuits (Figure 63) (Yield 24–30)

    4 *oz* (120 g) *ground almonds*
    4 *oz* (120 g) *icing sugar*
    1¼ *oz* (38 g) *egg whites* (1 *large egg*)

(1) Mix all ingredients together to a smooth stiff paste.

(2) Prepare a tray with a dusting of ground rice and rice paper.

(3) Place mixing in a savoy bag fitted with an appropriate tube and pipe out fancy shapes.

(4) Decorate with cherries, angelica, glacé pineapple and nuts.

(5) Let biscuits lie for at least 6 hours or overnight.

(6) Place in a hot oven at 480°F (249°C) for a few minutes to obtain a brown tinge at the edges.

(7) On removal from the oven, wash biscuits over immediately with a solution of gum arabic to obtain the glaze.

Gum Arabic Solution

    ¾ *oz* (22 g) *powdered gum arabic*
    4 *oz* (120 g) *water*

Bring to the boil to dissolve.

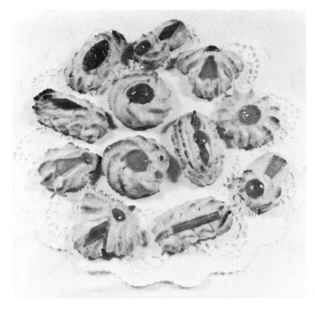

Figure 63. Parisian rout biscuits

Dutch Macaroons (Figure 64) (Yield 24 or 48 halves)

2½ oz (75 g) ground almonds
½ oz (15 g) castor sugar
5½ oz (165 g) icing sugar
2 oz (60 g) egg whites

(1) Mix all ingredients together to a smooth paste and warm.
(2) Prepare a clean tray with a sheet of greaseproof paper.
(3) Pipe the warm mixture into oval shapes on the greaseproof paper using a savoy bag fitted with ¼-in. (6-mm) tube. The mixture should flow quite flat.
(4) Let the biscuits lie for at least 6 hours or overnight.
(5) Using a razor blade, cut the surface of each shape lengthwise (Figure 65(*a*)).
(6) Bake in a cool oven at 350°F (177°C) until golden brown in colour.
(7) Remove from the greaseproof paper by washing the back with water.
(8) Join the biscuits together with either jam or jelly.

Variations of Dutch Macaroons. This macaroon mixing may be varied by:

(*a*) Adding colour and flavour to the mixing.
(*b*) Piping out into round shapes and cutting the surface with a razor blade in the following ways:
(*i*) In the form of a cross (Figures 65(*b*) and 71(*a*)).
(*ii*) Using a small round cutter as shown in Figures 65(*c*) and 71(*c*).

Figure 64. Dutch macaroons

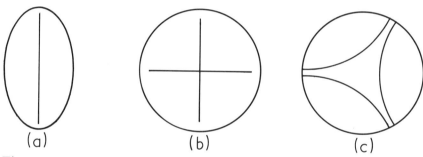

(a) (b) (c)

Figure 65. Dutch macaroons showing different cuts:
    (a) Piped oval and cut lengthwise.
    (b) Piped round and cut in a cross.
    (c) Piped oval and three cuts made with a small cutter.

Figure 66. Italian macaroons

Almond Boulée (Yield 24–30)

    4 *oz* (120 g) *ground almonds*
    4 *oz* (120 g) *castor sugar*
    1 *oz* (30 g) *icing sugar*
    1 *oz* (30 g) *egg whites*

(1) Mix all ingredients together to a smooth paste: do not overwork.
(2) Prepare a tray with grease and dust with flour.
(3) Divide and make into small balls.
(4) Dip balls in soft royal icing (*see* below), drain, and roll into the following mediums:
    (*a*) Nib almonds.
    (*b*) Flaked almonds.
    (*c*) Strip almonds.
    (*d*) Coloured nib almonds.
    (*e*) Desiccated coconut.
(5) Place on the greased and floured tray.
(6) Let balls lie for a least 6 hours or overnight.
(7) Bake in an oven at 350°F (177°C) until golden brown in colour.
Note. This mixture may be flavoured and appropriately coloured to give a wider variety.
Royal Icing for Dipping.
    4 *oz* (120 g) *icing sugar*
    1 *oz* (30 g) *egg whites*
Beat together.

Fancy Macaroons (Yield 48)

    4 *oz* (120 g) *ground almonds*
    8 *oz* (240 g) *castor sugar*
    ¾ *oz* (22 g) *ground rice*
    2½ *oz* (75 g) *egg whites*

(1) Mix all ingredients together to a smooth paste.
(2) Prepare a tray with ground rice covered with rice paper.
(3) Pipe out biscuits of 1 in. (2½ cm) diameter, using a savoy bag with ⅜ in. (9 mm) tube.
(4) Decorate using a wide variety of nuts as follows:
    (*a*) Split almonds.
    (*b*) Strip almonds.
    (*c*) Nib almonds.
    (*d*) Coloured nib almonds.
    (*e*) Pistachio nuts.
    (*f*) Walnuts.
    (*g*) Hazelnuts.
    (*h*) Cashew nuts.
(5) Bake in an oven at 350°F (177°C) until golden brown in colour.

Walnut Macaroons (Figure 71(*d*))

These are the same as Fancy Macaroons, except for the following:
1. Add walnut essence to the macaroon mixture.
2. Decorate with a large half walnut.

Italian Macaroons (Figure 66) (Yield 48)

Ingredients as for Fancy Macaroons.
Repeat (1), (2), and (3) of Fancy Macaroons.
(4) Dust surface with granulated sugar or desiccated coconut.
(5) Remove surplus sugar or coconut by lifting up the sheet, and make a depression with a clean index finger in the centre of the biscuit.
(6) Bake in oven at 350°F (177°C) until golden brown in colour.
(7) When cold, fill depression with a bulb of suitably flavoured and coloured fondant or jelly.
Note. This macaroon mixing may be flavoured and coloured to give a wider variety.

English Routs (Figure 67) (Yield 36)

> 5 *oz* (150 g) *ground almonds*
> 3 *oz* (90 g) *castor sugar*
> 2 *oz* (60 g) *icing sugar*
> 1½ *oz* (45 g) *egg yolks* (3)

(1) Mix to a smooth paste.
(2) Make into any of the varieties described opposite.
(3) Brush over with egg.
(4) Leave for at least 6 hours or overnight.
(5) Bake in a hot oven at 480°F (249°C) until tinged golden brown in colour.

Figure 67. English
rout biscu

Varieties.

1. Roll out paste approx. $\frac{1}{2}$ in. (12 mm) thick and cut out with $\frac{3}{4}$–1 in. (18–25 mm) plain or fluted cutter. After egg washing, decorate the top with cherry, walnut, disc of angelica, or confiture pineapple (for the latter two, cut out with $\frac{1}{2}$-in. (12-mm) cutter or metal savoy tube).

2. Roll out paste to approx. $\frac{1}{4}$ in. (6 mm) in thickness, mark position of a round $1\frac{1}{4}$-in. (3-cm) fluted cutter, and cut out either (*a*) three small $\frac{1}{4}$-in. (6-mm) holes or (*b*) one $\frac{1}{2}$-in. (12-mm) hole within this circle. Lay this piece on top of a plain sheet approx. $\frac{1}{4}$ in. (6 mm) thick and cut through both layers with the $1\frac{1}{4}$-in. (3-cm) fluted cutter at the positions already marked. After baking, fill these holes with coloured jelly or jam.

3. Mould two balls, one twice the size of the other. Flatten slightly, place the small ball on top of the larger one, and with a pointed stick or modelling tool, make an impression in the centre to make a cottage loaf shape. Cut the sides before egg washing.

4. Mould into a ball, flatten slightly and, with a knife, mark a cross on the top to form a Coburg loaf shape.

5. Roll out paste $\frac{1}{8}$ in. (3 mm) in thickness and cut out a disc 1 in. ($2\frac{1}{2}$ cm) in diameter. On this place a ball shape moulded like an apple. After egg washing, place on a piece of angelica to represent the stalk.

6. Cut out a 1-in. ($2\frac{1}{2}$-cm) disc as in 5 and wrap it around a pear shape. Use angelica for the stalk.

7. Roll out the paste thinly to approx. $\frac{1}{8}$ in. (3 mm) and cut it into strips $\frac{1}{8}$ in. (3 mm) wide. Trim these to approx. $1\frac{1}{4}$ in. (3 cm) in length and assemble some of them as a bundle, using one strip to tie them together.

Modelling Nut Paste (Almond, Coconut, and Hazelnut)
(Yield 36; small cut-outs 48)

> $6\frac{1}{2}$ *oz (195 g) granulated sugar*
> 1 *oz (30 g) confectioner's glucose (corn syrup)*
> 2 *oz (60 g) water*
> 1 *oz (30 g) egg yolks or whites*
> 4 *oz (120 g) ground almonds, coconut, or hazelnuts*

(1) Boil sugar, glucose, and water to 245°F (118°C).
(2) Stir in ground almonds or coconut.
(3) Quickly stir in the egg as follows:
   Yolks – For yellow paste.
   Whites – For white paste (for coloured paste).
(4) Turn out onto a slab and work down into a pliable paste.
(5) Keep paste in airtight container or plastic bag to prevent paste from skinning.
(6) Make into the varieties described below.

Note. The coconut paste is very short and difficult to handle except for cut-out shapes. For economy purposes, the paste may be made by substituting the hazelnuts or almonds for coconut. The hazelnut paste is naturally brown in colour and is unsuitable for colouring for which white paste (using egg whites) is required. This paste is deliberately made stiff for modelling but may be softened by using more egg yolks or whites.

Varieties for Modelling (Figure 68)

Method.

(1) Colour the paste approximately as follows:
    Green – apples and pears
    Yellow – bananas, lemons, and peaches
    Orange – oranges.

(2) Mould the paste into the required shape using modelling tools where necessary. The rough surface of the orange and lemon is obtained by rolling the shape on a cheese grater.

(3) Allow the shapes to lie overnight to set firm.

Finishing.

Apples. With a fine brush, paint on streaks of red and yellow colour. When set, rub on a little melted cocoa butter or cooking fat to imitate the wax-like surface of the apple. For the stems, use either brown marzipan, stalk of maidenhair fern, or a thin strip of angelica coloured brown.

Pears. Using a toothbrush and wire, scatter chocolate colour all over until required depth of colour is achieved. Use the same materials already described for the stem.

Figure 68. Marzipan fruits: (*left to right*) oranges, lemons, pears, bananas, apples, peaches

Bananas. Paint on chocolate brown marks using a fine brush. Use a little green at each end of the banana shape. When dry, rub on a little melted cocoa butter or cooking fat.

Lemons. With a brush, colour each end of the lemon shape with green colour. Glaze with confectioner's varnish or a solution of gum arabic.

Peaches. Brush on each side orange and red colour. When dry, powder with a little cornflour to imitate the bloom.

Oranges. Fill a small impression in the top of the orange with chocolate coloured marzipan to imitate the flower end. Glaze with confectioner's varnish or a solution of gum arabic.

Note. The aerograph spray may be used to colour the fruits (*see* Figure 69).

Cut-outs and Slices (Figure 70)

(1) Roll out paste $\frac{1}{2}$ in. (12 mm) in thickness and cut out various shapes using different cutters.

(2) Roll out paste $\frac{5}{8}$ in. (1$\frac{1}{2}$ cm) thick in various colours. Sandwich two coloured layers together with egg whites. Cut into strips $\frac{1}{2}$ in. (12 mm) wide and lay over on cut side. Using the fancy cutters, cut out so that one colour is on one side and the other colour opposite. The scraps may be coloured chocolate for other varieties.

(3) Roll out paste $\frac{1}{2}$ in. (12 mm) thick in various colours. Sandwich two sheets together using egg whites. Cut into strips $\frac{1}{2}$ in. (12 mm) wide. Reverse each alternate strip and sandwich two strips together so that the colours alternate, making a strip 1 in. (2$\frac{1}{2}$ cm) square, comprising four strips of two colours. Cut this composite strip into $\frac{1}{2}$-in. (12-mm) slices and lay flat so that the check pattern is presented to view.

(4) Roll out paste in various colours $\frac{1}{4}$ in. (6 mm) in thickness. Sandwich four of these sheets together using egg whites, alternating the colours. Cut into strips $\frac{1}{4}$ in. (6 mm) thick, reverse each alternate strip, and sandwich

Figure 69. Using the aerograph spray to colour marzipan pears

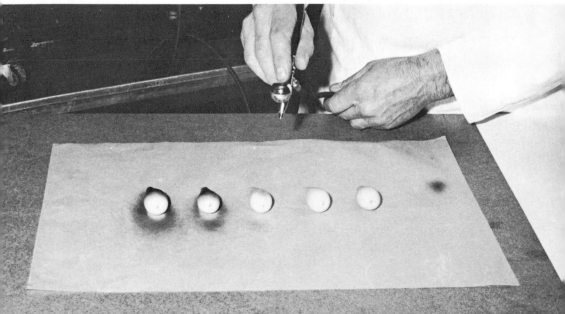

together four strips to make a chequerboard pattern endwise. This makes a composite strip 1 in. (2½ cm) thick. This is then wrapped in another thin sheet before being cut into ½-in. (12-mm) slices and laid flat for presentation.

Chraebeli – Aniseed Biscuits (Figures 71(*b*) and 72) (Yield 24)

> 5 *oz* (150 g) *castor sugar*
> 6 *oz* (180 g) *soft flour*
> 1½ *oz* (45 g) *eggs*
> ½ *oz* (15 g) *water*
> ⅕ *oz* (6 g) *aniseed*
> *A pinch of VOL* (*Ammonium bicarbonate*)

(1) Place sugar, eggs, and water in a pan and warm slightly.
(2) Whisk to a foam.
(3) Sieve the flour and VOL.
(4) Add the sugar/egg mixture and aniseed.
(5) Mix into a stiff dough.
(6) Cover the dough to prevent drying and allow it to stand for about an hour.
(7) Divide the dough into 24 pieces and mould first round and then into a pear shape.
(8) Make three incisions into this shape as shown in Figure 72.
(9) Place the pieces, slightly curved, on a greased tray.
(10) Allow to stand overnight or for at least 4 hours to dry.
(11) Bake in an oven at 350°F (177°C) until the base just begins to colour.

Figure 70. Variety of marzipan cut-outs

Milan Biscuits (Yield 144)

    4 *oz* (120 g) *soft flour*
    1 *oz* (30 g) *scone flour* (*see page* 38)
    3 *oz* (90 g) *butter*
    3 *oz* (90 g) *icing sugar*
    1 *egg yolk*

(1) Make into a smooth paste.
(2) Roll out to ⅛ in. (3 mm) in thickness.
(3) Cut out a variety of shapes using small fancy cutters.
(4) Lay out the shapes on a clean baking tray.
(5) Egg wash.
(6) Bake in an oven at 400°F (204°C) until golden brown in colour.

Note. Make sure that the biscuits are of all the same thickness and size to ensure uniform baking.

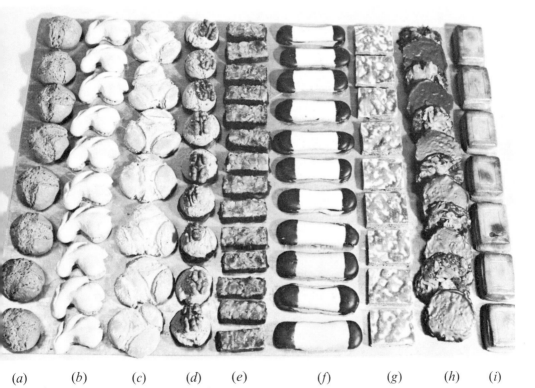

(a)   (b)   (c)   (d)   (e)   (f)   (g)   (h)   (i)

Figure 71. Selection of petits fours secs:
    (a) Chocolate Dutch macaroons (2nd variety).
    (b) Chraebeli.
    (c) Dutch macaroons (3rd variety).
    (d) Walnut macaroons.
    (e) Toscaner.
    (f) Langue du chat biscuits (Marquis).
    (g) Basel leckerli.
    (h) Petites florentines.
    (i) Zurich leckerli.

Dutch Biscuits (Figure 73) (Yield approx. 60)

     8 *oz* (240 *g*) *soft flour*
     2 *oz* (60 *g*) *scone flour* (*see page* 38)
     6 *oz* (180 *g*) *butter*
     3 *oz* (90 *g*) *icing sugar*
     1 *oz* (30 *g*) *egg yolks* (2)
     Chocolate colour

(1) Cream the butter and icing sugar together.
(2) Beat in the egg yolks.
(3) Sieve together the two flours and add.
(4) Make into a smooth paste.
(5) Add chocolate colour to one quarter of the paste.

Description of Varieties shown in Figure 73

     Variety (*a*).
(1) Roll out the white paste to approx. $\frac{3}{4}$ in. (2 cm) in thickness.
(2) Sprinkle with chopped or strip almonds.
(3) Continue rolling to reduce the paste to $\frac{1}{2}$ in. (12 mm) in thickness thereby rolling the almonds into the surface.
(4) Cut the sheet into rectangles approx. $1\frac{1}{4}$ in. × $\frac{1}{2}$ in. (3 cm × 12 mm).
(5) Lay the pieces on a clean baking tray with the almonds on top.
(6) Bake at 400°F (204°C).
     Variety (*b*).
(1) Roll out the two differently coloured pastes approx. $\frac{1}{8}$ in. (3 mm) in thickness and 3 in. ($7\frac{1}{2}$ cm) wide.
(2) Damp the surface of one and lay the other on top.
(3) Damp the top surface and roll up the strip Swiss roll fashion.
(4) Cut the roll into slices approx. $\frac{3}{8}$ in. (1 cm) thick and lay each slice flat on a clean baking sheet.
(5) Bake in an oven at 400°F (204°C).
     Variety (*c*).
(1) Roll out some of the white paste into ropes approx. $\frac{3}{8}$ in. (1 cm) in diameter.
(2) Cut into lengths of approx. 3 in. ($7\frac{1}{2}$ cm).
(3) Wash over the surface with water.
(4) Dip the washed surface into castor sugar and arrange as a horseshoe on a clean baking tray with the sugared surface showing.

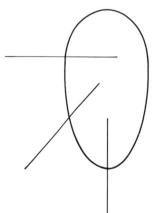

Figure 72. Chraebeli: showing position of cuts

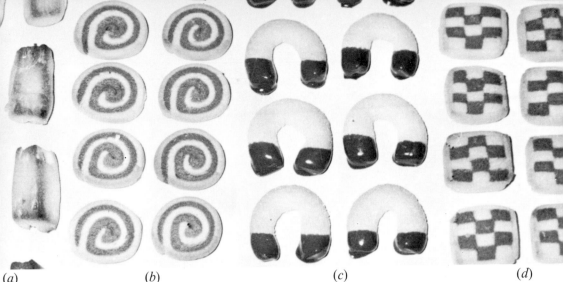

(a) (b) (c) (d)

igure 73. Dutch biscuits (*see* text)

(5) Bake at 400°F (204°C).
(6) When cold, dip the ends into tempered chocolate couverture (page 244).

Variety (*d*).

(1) Roll out the two differently coloured pastes approx. $\frac{1}{4}$ in. (6 mm) thick.
(2) Damp the top of the white piece and lay on the chocolate piece.
(3) Cut in two, dampen the surface of one piece and lay the other on top to give four layers of alternate colours.
(4) Cut strips $\frac{3}{8}$ in. (1 cm) wide and join three of these together using water to dampen the surfaces so that white is against chocolate and vice versa.
(5) Roll out a piece of white paste $\frac{1}{16}$ in. (1$\frac{1}{2}$ mm) thick, dampen the surface, and wrap up the composite strip.
(6) Cut the strip into slices approx. $\frac{3}{8}$ in. (1 cm) thick and lay them flat on a clean baking tray.
(7) Bake at 400°F (204°C).

Almond Slices (Figure 74) (Yield 72)

> 5 oz (150 g) *soft brown sugar*
> 2$\frac{1}{2}$ oz (75 g) *butter*
> 4 oz (120 g) *soft flour*
> 1 oz (30 g) *scone flour* (*see page* 38)
> 2 oz (60 g) *nib almonds*
> *Cinnamon spice*
> $\frac{1}{2}$ oz (15 g) *egg yolks* (1)

(1) Make into a paste.
(2) Divide the paste into two and form from each piece a length of dough of approx. 8 in. (20 cm) in a square and a round.
(3) Place these in a refrigerator, preferably in the deep freeze compartment to set for approx. 1 hour.
(4) Cut the hardened lengths of dough into slices approx. $\frac{1}{6}$ in. (4 mm) thick and lay them flat on a clean baking tray.
(5) Bake in an oven at approx. 380°F (193°C) until crisp.

Toscaner (Figure 71(*e*)) (Yield 20)

> 1 *oz* (30 g) *butter*
> 2 *oz* (60 g) *ground almonds*
> 2 *oz* (60 g) *castor sugar*
> 2½ *oz* (75 g) *eggs*
> ½ *oz* (15 g) *flour*

(1) Beat butter, sugar, and ground almonds.
(2) Add egg a little at a time and beat in well.
(3) Lastly stir in the flour.
(4) Spread the mixing level on a greaseproof lined baking tray to a depth of ⅓ in. (8 mm).
(5) Bake in an oven at 380°F (193°C).
(6) When baked turn upside down and remove the paper.
(7) Spread on top the following mixture whilst still hot.

Topping.

> 1 *oz* (30 g) *butter*
> 1 *oz* (30 g) *sugar*
> 1 *oz* (30 g) *confectioners' glucose*
> 1½ *oz* (45 g) *fine flaked almonds*
> ½ *oz* (15 g) *water*

(8) Cook together for a few minutes.
(9) Return the sheet to a very hot oven at 500°F (260°C) for a few minutes to colour the topping to a golden brown.
(10) When baked, turn the slab upside down and cut into rectangles approx. 1 × ¾ in. (25 × 20 mm).
(11) Dip the pieces in chocolate to cover the base and sides, leaving the topping to show.

Figure 74. Almond slices

Basel Leckerli (Figure 71(*g*)) (Yield 36)

    4 *oz* (120 g) *honey*
    2 *oz* (60 g) *castor sugar*
    ½ *oz* (15 g) *water*
    2½ *oz* (75 g) *nib almonds*
    1½ *oz* (45 g) *orange and lemon peel*
    ½ *oz* (15 g) *milk*
    6 *oz* (180 g) *soft flour*
    1½ *oz* (45 g) *scone flour* (*see page* 38)
    ¼ *oz* (7 g) *mixed spice*
    ½ *oz* (15 g) *kirsch* (*or increase milk to* 1 *oz*)

(1) Warm honey, sugar, and water to dissolve the sugar.
(2) Mix in the other materials to make a smooth paste.
(3) Roll out the dough approx. ¼ in. (6 mm) and place on a baking tray.
(4) Prick it all over with a fork or docker.
(5) Bake in an oven at approx. 420°F (215°C).
(6) Whilst the baked sheet is still hot, brush over the following icing until it grains.

Icing.

    6 *oz* (180 g) *sugar*
    2 *oz* (60 g) *water*
  Boil to 225°F (107°C).

(7) Cut the sheet into approx. 1-in. (2½-cm) squares.

Zurich Leckerli (Figure 71(*i*)) (Yield 32 halves = 16 sandwiched biscuits)

    5 *oz* (150 g) *ground almonds*
    6 *oz* (180 g) *icing sugar*
    1½ *oz* (45 g) *egg whites*

(1) Mix into a smooth dough.
(2) Roll out the dough approx. ¼ in. (6 mm) thick and, using a little sugar for dusting, cut into rectangles approx. 1 × 1½ in. (2½ × 3¾ cm).
(3) Transfer these to a clean baking tray and allow to dry out overnight.
(4) Place in an oven at 500°F (260°C) for a few minutes to colour a golden brown.
(5) After baking glaze with gum arabic.
(6) Two of these biscuits may be sandwiched with an almond paste thinned with either a spirit or water.

Note. The traditional Zurich Leckerli should be moulded using special wooden moulds.

Langue du Chat Biscuits – Cat's Tongues (Figure 71(*f*))
(Yield for biscuits approx. 1½ in. (4 cm) long piped with a ¼-in. (6-mm) tube = 160)

    These biscuits may be made in different sizes and in either a finger or round shape. They have several uses as follows:

1. As a decoration for gâteaux, torten, ice bombs, etc.
2. They may be served with ice-cream dishes.
3. Sandwiched with an appropriate buttercream or ganache, they may be made into either afternoon fancies (large shapes) or petits fours secs (small shapes), then either partly dipped into chocolate or left plain.

> 4 *oz* (120 *g*) *butter*
> 4 *oz* (120 *g*) *sugar*
> 3 *oz* (90 *g*) *egg whites*
> 4½ *oz* (135 *g*) *soft flour*

(1) Prepare a baking tray with a coating of grease.
(2) Make the biscuit mixing on the sugar batter method.
(3) Transfer mixing to a savoy bag fitted with a ¼-in. (6-mm) tube.
(4) Pipe out shapes to the size required. As these biscuits flow during baking, allow sufficient space on the tray.
(5) Bake in an oven at 420°F (215°C) until the edges of the biscuit are tinged a light golden brown colour.
(6) Remove from the baking tray whilst still warm.
Notes.
   1. If the biscuits are removed from the tray as soon as they are baked they are flexible enough to be twisted or curled round a round stick. These curled biscuits are especially attractive to serve with ice-cream dishes.
   2. They may also be half dipped into chocolate as an added decoration.

Marquis

> *Langue du Chat Biscuit recipe (see above)*
> *Ganache recipe (see page 250)*
> *Praline (ground nougat) recipe (see page 265)*
> *Chocolate.*

(1) Sandwich two langue du chat biscuits with the following filling:
   3 parts ganache and 1 part crushed nougat or praline paste.
(2) Either write the word 'Marquis' in chocolate on the top biscuit or dip each end in chocolate couverture.

Rum Balls

These are made from sponge or genoese crumbs in the following way.
(1) Mix good quality sponge or cake crumbs with just sufficient boiled apricot purée to bind the crumbs together.
(2) Add sufficient rum or an alternative spirit or liqueur to taste.
(3) Mould into small balls about the size of a large cherry.
(4) Dip into thin warm fondant or melted chocolate and roll in a suitable dressing as follows:
   (*a*) Dip into chocolate and roll in chocolate corals or vermicelli – two varieties, milk and plain.
   (*b*) Dip into chocolate and roll in toasted almonds or coconut.
   (*c*) Dip into fondant and roll in coloured vermicelli (sugar or almonds) or white desiccated coconut or nib almonds.
(5) Serve in small petit four cases.

Sable à la Poche (Yield 48 petits fours or 24 afternoon tea fancies)

  8 *oz* (240 g) *soft flour*
  6 *oz* (180 g) *butter*
  4 *oz* (120 g) *castor sugar*
  1½ *oz* (45 g) *egg yolks* (3)

(1) Beat the butter and sugar to a cream.
(2) Add the egg yolk and beat into the cream.
(3) Add the flour and mix to a smooth paste.
(4) Transfer to a clean savoy bag fitted with a star tube.
(5) Pipe the mixing into rosettes (Figure 75).
(6) Decorate with half a cherry.
(7) Bake in an oven at 380°F (193°C) until tinged a golden brown colour.

 Other mixings from which petits fours varieties may be made can be found in the following Chapters:
2. *Shortpastry, Flans, and Tarts;* 5. *Meringue Goods;* 6. *Cakes;* 11. *Afternoon Tea Fancies;* 20. *Sugar Work.*

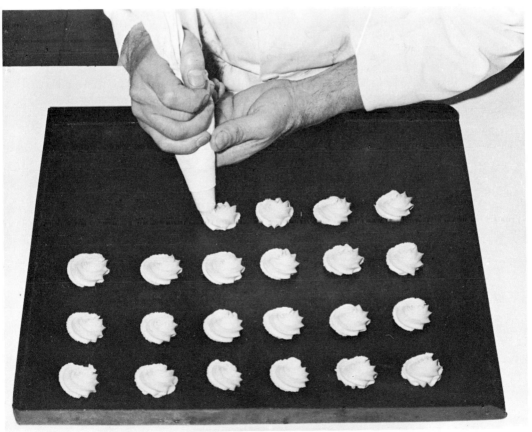

Figure 75. Piping out: sable à la poche

10. Petits Fours Glacés

Genoese Base (Yield 96 squares (less for shapes))
See Genoese recipes (pages 95 and 96).

VARIETIES

Fondant Dips (Figure 76)

(1) Cut cake in half and sandwich with a suitable filling, i.e. jam, curd, ganache, buttercream, etc.

(2) Cover the sheet of genoese with a thin layer of marzipan, using hot apricot purée with which to stick it to the cake.

(3) Cut this sheet into a variety of different shapes using the knife and assorted cutters. The shapes should be approx. $\frac{3}{4}$ in. (2 cm) square in area.

(4) Dip each shape into hot apricot purée and place approx. $\frac{3}{4}$ in. (2 cm) apart on a wire tray resting on a drip tray.

(5) Using a bain marie, warm and reduce fondant with stock syrup to the correct consistency and temperature (approx. 100°F (38°C)).

(6) Place the fondant in a savoy bag fitted with a $\frac{1}{4}$-in. (6-mm) tube and pipe it over the shapes so that they are completely covered. The surplus fondant in the drip tray can be used again.

(7) When the fondant has set, remove the shapes from the tray and place them in paper cups.

Figure 76. Fondant dipped genoese

(8) Decorate using cherries, angelica, chocolate coloured fondant, coloured jelly, or prefabricated decorations.

Note. The variety may be increased further by placing a piece of marzipan or piping a small bulb of buttercream, ganache, etc., on the shape prior to enrobing it with fondant. The use of flavours and colours for the genoese cake, fillings, and fondant, produces an even wider variety.

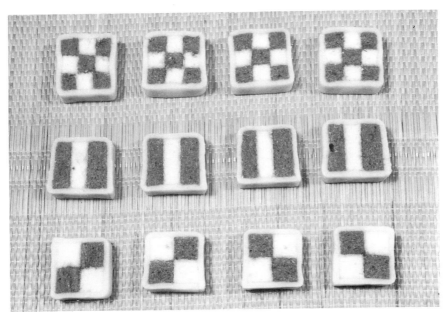

Figure 77. Battenburg slices

Battenburg Slices (Figure 77)

Bake the genoese in two or more colours, e.g. chocolate and yellow.

Four Square.

(1) Cut two differently coloured sheets into slices $\frac{1}{2}$ in. (12 mm) thick.

(2) Using a liberal amount of boiling apricot purée, sandwich two different coloured layers together.

(3) Cut the laminated sheet into strips $\frac{1}{2}$ in. (12 mm) wide.

(4) Place these strips on their side, spread with purée, and stick together so that the coloured strips are opposite each other, i.e. chocolate adjacent to yellow.

(5) Roll out a piece of marzipan, cover with purée, and wrap up the composite strip of genoese.

(6) Cut the strip into slices approx. $\frac{1}{2}$ in. (12 mm) thick and lay flat in paper cases.

(7) Glaze top by spreading over pectin jelly or hot apricot purée.

Tricolour.
(1) Cut three differently coloured sheets into slices approx. $\frac{1}{3}$ in. (8 mm) thick.
(2) Using a liberal amount of purée, sandwich the three different coloured layers together.
(3) Cut sheet into strips 1 in. ($2\frac{1}{2}$ cm) wide.
(4) Repeat processes (5) and (7) of Four Square.
Nine Square.
(1) Cut strips of genoese $\frac{1}{3}$ in. (8 mm) square of at least two different colours.
(2) Stick these together with boiled apricot jam to form a composite strip of nine squares in which the colours alternate.
(3) Repeat processes (5) and (7) of Four Square.
   The transparent glaze which is spread over the top may be of any jelly or purée but pectin quick-setting jelly gives a non-sticky surface. The glazed surface not only adds to the appearance of the goods but also seals the moisture in the genoese, improving their keeping properties.

Almond Sweetpaste Biscuit Paste (Yield for various petits fours 144)

>   10 *oz* (300 g) *flour*
>   6 *oz* (180 g) *butter*
>   4 *oz* (120 g) *icing sugar*
>   3 *oz* (90 g) *ground almonds*
>   1$\frac{1}{2}$ *oz* (45 g) *eggs*
>   *One teaspoonful lemon juice*

Sweetpaste Biscuit Paste – Pâte Sucrée (Yield 120)

>   10 *oz* (300 g) *flour*
>   5$\frac{1}{2}$ *oz* (165 g) *butter*
>   4 *oz* (120 g) *icing sugar*
>   1$\frac{1}{2}$ *oz* (45 g) *eggs*
>   *One teaspoonful lemon juice*

(1) Cream the butter and sugar.
(2) Add egg and beat in well.
(3) Add lemon juice.
(4) Add dry ingredients and mix to a smooth paste.

Fruits Glacés with Biscuit (Almond or Sweetpaste)

(1) Roll paste out to approx. $\frac{1}{8}$ in. (3 mm) thick and cut into a variety of shapes using cutters and knife. The average size of these should be 1 in. ($2\frac{1}{2}$ cm) square.
(2) Line a number of different shaped barquette moulds thinly with the paste.
(3) Bake in an oven at 380°F (193°C) until crisp and golden brown in colour.
(4) Spread, on each biscuit or mould, a suitably flavoured and coloured buttercream and finish in the varieties below.
(5) Glaze either by pouring on or dipping decorated shapes in warm,

Figure 78. Fruits glacés on biscuit base (*see* text)

thinned fondant. The fondant should not be heated above blood temperature at approx. 100°F (38°C) and should be reduced to pouring consistency with syrup. Fruit juice and/or liqueurs may also be added instead of syrup.

Varieties on Biscuit Base (Figure 78)

Shape.
(*a*) Wedge – Pieces of fresh, tinned, or confiture pineapple.
(*b*) Crescent or half circle – Mandarin orange, slice of peach, apricot or pear.
(*c*) Circle – Half grapes, black or green, fresh strawberry, or slice of banana.
(*d*) Rectangle – Two cherries (stoned) or any of the fruits in (*b*) or (*c*) above.

The particular varieties shown in Figure 78 are (*left to right*) pineapple wedge; dates; small grapes; cherries; large grapes; and mandarin orange.

Varieties in Barquette Moulds (Figure 79)

(1) Spread some suitably flavoured and coloured buttercream in each mould and fill with either individual small fruits, i.e. cherries, grapes, mandarin oranges, etc., or various other fillings.
(2) Glaze with fondant.

The varieties illustrated in Figure 79 are (*left to right*) grapes; raisins; mandarin orange and cherry; chopped cherries; chopped dates; and chopped pineapple.

Figure 79. Fruits glacés in barquette moulds (*see* text)

Varieties without Fruit (Figure 80)

Both the barquette and biscuit bases may be finished with a variety of fillings, before being glazed. Many of these fillings are derived from basic recipes which are used to decorate and flavour afternoon tea fancies. In fact, most of these petits fours glacés could pass for tea fancies if made slightly larger in size.

Other Varieties

Pipe a bulb or scroll of the filling on top of a biscuit base prior to glazing with fondant. Decorate suitably if desired.

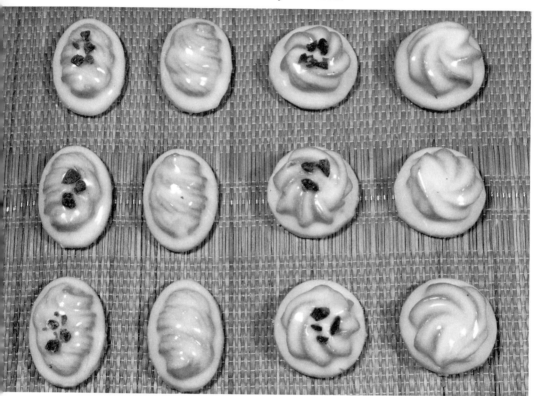

Figure 80. Varieties without fruit on biscuit base

Fruits Glacés

      8 *oz* (240 *g*) *cube or gran. sugar*

      $2\frac{1}{2}$ *oz* (75 *g*) *water*

(1) Boil ingredients to 310°F (154°C) (hard crack) washing down sides of pan with water to prevent crystallization (*see* notes on sugar boiling, page 268).

(2) Dip the fruit into the boiling syrup and quickly transfer it onto an oiled slab to set.

The following fruits may be used for this purpose:

Dates and Prunes – Usually stuffed with marzipan.

Grapes – Cut with scissors but leave on stalk with which to handle fruit. If large, glaze individually but if small, in pairs.

Cherries – Keep in pairs with stalks attached.

Mandarin Oranges – If tinned, make sure fruit is dried.

Strawberries – Make sure fruit is dry and keep on stalk for handling the fruit.

Many of the fruits may be stuffed with marzipan, for example:

Cherries or a petit four made from marzipan and nuts may be used.

Two walnut halves with marzipan sandwiched between.

Two halves of glacé cherry with marzipan sandwiched between.

Because of the hygroscopic nature of boiled sugar, it is essential to store these glacé fruits in a warm dry place. Moist conditions will dissolve the sugar, making the fruits sticky and eventually washing away the sugar from the fruit. It is advisable for these glacé fruits to be made at the last moment before being presented at the function.

Fondants

Glacé Fruits *See* Chapter 20 on Sugar Work, page 258.

Nougat

11. Afternoon Tea Fancies

Almost any small variety of cake may be served with afternoon tea and thus be termed an afternoon tea fancy. The range is so enormous and decoration so wide that a tome could be written on this aspect of patisserie alone. The author has endeavoured to give a cross-section of decorated fancies which may be produced from a very limited range of cake bases.

Frangipane Fancies (Yield 36 tarts) (Figures 81–83)
>   10 *oz* (300 g) *flour into sweetpaste* (*see page* 148)
>   *Frangipane filling* (*see page* 49)
>   *Decorating materials* (*buttercream, chocolate, nuts, etc.*)

(1) Make the sweetpaste.
(2) Roll out the paste to $\frac{1}{16}$ in. ($1\frac{1}{2}$ mm) thick.
(3) Cut out with a suitable size cutter and line clean patty pans, pressing the paste into the pan with the thumb. Trim off excess with a small knife. (*See* Figure 7, page 46, for alternative method.)
(4) Into the 36 lined patty tins, pipe some jam, curd, or other filling, such as crushed fruit, sultanas, glacé fruit, or fruit-cream.
(5) Pipe the frangipane mixing into the pan and fill to within $\frac{1}{4}$ in. (6 mm) from the top.
(6) Bake in an oven at 365°F (185°C) until golden brown in colour.
(7) Decorate in a variety of ways, some of which are shown in Figure 82, and explained as follows:

(*a*) Cut through the top of the cake, remove, and cut in half. Pipe a scroll of buttercream each side, replace the two halves 'butterfly' fashion and dust with icing sugar.

(*b*) Cut top almost through, raise, and pipe in a scroll of buttercream; lower the top so that it rests on the cream. Coat top with boiling, red purée and sprinkle on some green almond decor (almond nibs coloured green).

(*c*) Colour and flavour some buttercream by adding and stirring in some melted chocolate. Using a small star piping, pipe lines from the edge to the centre until the whole top is covered. Finish by placing on a small piece of almond paste to resemble the stalk of this mushroom decorated fancy.

(*d*) Remove a disc of the frangipane cake from the centre with a small cutter. Fill the hole with buttercream and dust top with icing sugar. Replace the piece previously removed after its top has been coated with red purée.

(*e*) Roll out a piece of almond or sugar paste very thinly. With a fluted cutter, cut out a disc and in this cut three holes. Coat the top of the tart with apricot purée and lay on the disc. Fill the holes with coloured jelly or jam.

(*f*) On top of the tart lay a ring of glacé or confiture pineapple. Fill the centre hole with red jelly or jam.

152

Figure 81. Frangipane fancies: (*left*) filled cases; (*right*) empty baked cases

Figure 82. Frangipane fancies (*see* text)

(*a*)	(*b*)	(*c*)	(*d*)

(*e*)	(*f*)	(*g*)	(*h*)

(*g*) Chop some glacé fruits, e.g. cherries, angelica, pineapple. Add some apricot purée and spread mixture on top of the tart.

(*h*) Roll out some almond or sugar paste very thinly. Cut out a disc with a fluted cutter and cut a cross in the centre. Pipe a bulb of buttercream in the centre of the tart. Place the cut out disc over so that the buttercream shows through the cross.

Note. Red purée can be made by sieving apricot jam and boiling it with a little sugar and red colour, or by sieving raspberry jam and boiling this with a little sugar.

Boat-shaped Fancies

Figure 83 shows boat-shaped frangipane fancies, the decoration of which is explained as follows:

(*a*) Pipe on each edge a line of buttercream using a small star tube. Fill the centre with either melted chocolate or warm fondant. Sprinkle on some crystallized violets.

(*b*) Using the small star piping tube, cover the top of the tart with a zig-zag pattern. Spin over liquid chocolate in a criss-cross design. (To spin chocolate, place the liquid chocolate in a greaseproof paper cornet with a very small hole at its point: apply pressure so that the chocolate emerges from the paper cornet in a steady stream, and cover the area as rapidly as possible, moving the bag to and fro according to the direction of the chocolate lines.) Finish the decoration of this variety with a piece of crystallized rose petal or similar.

(*c*) Cover top with a thin layer of boiled apricot purée. Pipe on three rosettes with buttercream and on these place chocolate buttons. The chocolate buttons are made previously by piping out bulbs of liquid chocolate onto greaseproof paper.

(*a*)   (*b*)   (*c*)   (*d*)

Figure 83. Frangipane
fancies (*see* tex

(*e*)   (*f*)   (*g*)   (*h*)

(*d*) Cover with either chocolate fondant (fondant coloured and flavoured with melted chocolate) or melted chocolate. Decorate with three silver dragees or crystallized mimosa balls.

(*e*) Chop some glacé fruits and mix with a little apricot purée. Cover the top of the tart with this mixture and then coat with thin hot fondant.

(*f*) Coat top of tart first with boiling apricot purée and then dip into warm fondant (100°F (38°C)). Before fondant sets, mask sides in browned coconut. Sprinkle on pieces of crystallized rose petals or coloured almond decor.

(*g*) Spread over the top some boiled apricot purée. Cover with half cherries and glaze with purée.

(*h*) Coat top of tart with boiling apricot purée and dip in warm fondant. Decorate with half cherry and two diamonds of angelica.

Ganache Fancies (Figure 84) (Yield 36)

> 8 *oz* (240 *g*) *flour into sweetpaste* (*see page* 148)
> 12 *oz* (360 *g*) *ganache* (*see page* 250)
> 6 *oz* (180 *g*) *sultanas*
> *Stock syrup*
> *Rum*
> *Icing sugar*

The following is a description of the fancies in Figure 84.

(1) Roll out the sweetpaste to $\frac{1}{16}$ in. (1½ mm) and cut out, using a round cutter. Line patty pans with the paste, trim, and bake off at 380°F (193°C). *See* Figure 7 for alternative method.

(2) Soak the sultanas in a mixture of stock syrup and rum for at least 24 hours.

(3) Drain the sultanas and place a few in the bottom of the baked unfilled pastry cases.

(4) Top up with the ganache and spread level.

(5) Decorate with icing sugar, using paper as a mask to get the three different patterns shown.

(6) Finish with a small rosette of ganache and either a crystallized mimosa ball or silver dragee.

Note. Instead of sultanas other fruits may be used, e.g. cherries soaked in a little Kirsch or Cherry Brandy make a delicious variation.

Sponge Slices (Figure 85) (Yield 24)

> *Basic Swiss roll mixing* (*see page* 76)
> 12 *oz* (360 *g*) *buttercream*
> 4 *oz* (120 *g*) *glacé fruits*
> 6 *oz* (180 *g*) *almond paste*
> 2 *oz* (60 *g*) *roasted flaked almonds*

(1) Make a basic Swiss roll.

(2) When baked, turn upside down onto a dry cloth and some layers of kitchen paper.

(3) Remove the paper carefully from the back of the sheet of sponge.

Figure 84. Ganache fancies

Figure 85. Sponge slices

(4) Place a rope of coloured almond or coconut paste at the long edge of the sheet.

(5) Spread sheet with a good quality buttercream into which has been mixed one of the following:

(*a*) Chopped glacé cherries.

(*b*) Chopped glacé pineapple.

(*c*) Any other glacé fruits.

(6) Starting at the edge with the almond paste rope, roll up into a roll, using the cloth or paper (*see* page 77).

(7) Place the roll in a refrigerator to chill and to make the buttercream inside firm.

(8) Remove, coat sides with buttercream, and cover with roasted almonds or other nuts.

(9) Cut into slices with a sharp knife and lay pieces on the tray so that the interior decoration shows.

Note. Alternative treatments may be made by covering the roll with almond paste or chocolate before cutting into slices.

Japonaise (Figure 86) (Yield 36–40 individual biscuits = 18–20 fancies)

> 5 *oz* (150 *g*) *egg whites* }
> 5 *oz* (150 *g*) *castor sugar* }   Meringue
> 5 *oz* (150 *g*) *ground almonds*
> 1 *oz* (30 *g*) *cornflour*
> 1½ *oz* (45 *g*) *castor sugar*
> *Buttercream or ganache*
> *Decorating materials*

(1) Prepare some trays by brushing on a thick film of vegetable fat and dusting with flour.

(2) Whisk the egg whites with 5 oz (150 g) castor sugar to a meringue.

(3) Mix and sieve the almonds, cornflour, and 1½ oz (45 g) castor sugar.

(4) Carefully stir these dry ingredients into the meringue.

(5) Place the japonaise mixing into a savoy bag with ⅜ in. (1 cm) tube and pipe out the shapes as follows:

(*a*) Pipe a spiral to make a flat biscuit approx. 2 in. (5 cm) diameter. A cutter may be used to mark out the size on the tray prior to piping.

(*b*) Using a larger tube approx. ½–⅝ in. (1½ cm) pipe out a ring approx. 2 in. (5 cm) diameter.

(*c*) Using a ½-in. (12-mm) tube, pipe out fingers or ovals.

(6) Bake in an oven at 350°F (177°C) for approx. 15 minutes until biscuits are light fawn in colour.

(7) Using buttercream or ganache, decorate as follows.

Flat Biscuits. First trim the flat and ring biscuits with the 2-in. (5-cm) cutter. Pipe on a bulb of cream, place on another biscuit upside down and press down slightly. Do a number of these and place them in the refrigerator to set the cream firm. Remove, mask the sides with cream, and roll in either nibbed browned almonds, roasted desiccated coconut, or japonaise crumbs.

The top may be decorated as follows:
(1) Coat all over with cream and cover with either of the dressings described.
(2) Cover with fondant icing or chocolate.
(3) Place on a 2-in. (5-cm) disc of marzipan which may be marked with a knife or similarly patterned.

Rings. The ring is sandwiched to the jap base with cream and the sides masked in the manner already described for the flat biscuits. The biscuit may be left showing or decorated with criss-cross lines of chocolate. The centre is then filled with either chopped glacé fruit or a suitable jelly.

Fingers and Ovals. Sandwich together with cream piped from a star tube. Lines of chocolate may also be used for a decorative effect (spinning chocolate).

Other Varieties. Using either the round or oval base, pipe on a bulb or rosette of well-beaten ganache cream. Chill and coat with chocolate.

In Figure 86 the varieties are explained as follows:

(*a*) Flat biscuit, completely coated with ganache or buttercream and masked with sieved jap crumbs.

(*b*) Two finger biscuits sandwiched and decorated by spinning on liquid chocolate.

(*c*) A ring sandwiched to a flat biscuit with ganache or cream. Sides masked with cream and nibbed brown almonds. Centre filled with red jelly.

(*d*) A ring sandwiched to a flat biscuit. Sides masked with cream and jap crumbs. Top is decorated with melted chocolate spun first one way and then at right angles. Centre is then filled with chopped glacé pineapple.

(*e*) Two finger biscuits sandwiched with ganache piped as a scroll using a star tube.

(*f*) Flat biscuits, topped with a cut-out disc of textured marzipan (marked with the back of a knife) and decorated with a piece of crystallized violet.

Figure 86. Japonaise fancies (*see* text)

Fancy Genoese Tea Fancies (Figure 87)
(Yield from basic ingredients 30 including slices)

> *Genoese (5 oz (150 g) egg) (see pages 95 and 96)*
> *Decorating materials*

In Figure 87 the varieties are as follows:

(*a*)
(1) Trim and cut the genoese sheet into circles using a cutter of approx. $1\frac{1}{2}$ in. (4 cm) diameter.
(2) Roll out some green almond paste to approx. $\frac{1}{10}$ in. ($2\frac{1}{2}$ mm) thick. Cut out some discs using a $1\frac{1}{4}$-in. (3-cm) cutter.
(3) Spread some cream or jam around the sides of the genoese and attach the almond paste discs so that they overlap.
(4) Finish off by piping small stars of buttercream all over the top. This variety should resemble a cauliflower.

(*b*)
(1) Roll out coloured almond paste to approx. $\frac{1}{10}$ in. ($2\frac{1}{2}$ mm) thick.
(2) Using a jigger wheel, cut into strips approx. $1\frac{1}{4}$ in. (3 cm) wide.
(3) Coat sides of genoese piece with jam or cream and wrap around it the strip of almond paste with the crinkled edge uppermost. Cut off surplus.
(4) Fill centre with jelly or chocolate and decorate with coloured nib almonds.

(*c*)
(1) Repeat (*b*) but this time cut almond paste into strips with a knife, instead of using a jigger wheel. Fill centre with white fondant and decorate with a split almond.

(*d*)
(1) Spread some melted chocolate on a sheet of greaseproof paper. When just set, cut into squares of approx. $1\frac{1}{2}$ in. (4 cm). Allow chocolate to harden and then remove (*see* Chapter 18, page 244).
(2) Coat sides of a square of genoese with cream and attach the squares of chocolate to form a box.
(3) Pipe a scroll of buttercream on top and place on another square of chocolate.

(*e*)
(1) Roll out some coloured almond paste, approx. $\frac{1}{10}$ in. ($2\frac{1}{2}$ mm) thick and cut into strips approx. $1\frac{1}{4}$ in. (3 cm) wide.
(2) Coat sides of a square of genoese with cream or jam.
(3) Wrap round the strip of almond paste, removing surplus with a knife.
(4) Fill centre with chocolate or jelly and decorate with a piece of crystallized violet.

(*f*)
(1) Repeat (*e*) but use a jigger cutter for the strips of almond paste.
(2) Fill the centre with coloured fondant.
(3) Decorate with a cherry and diamond of angelica.

Figure 87. Genoese fancies (*see* text)

(*g*)

(1) Mask the sides of a square of genoese with buttercream and roasted crushed flaked almonds.

(2) Pipe a zig-zag pattern on top using a star tube.

(3) Decorate, spinning melted chocolate over the top and split almond, dipped in chocolate.

(*h*)

(1) Dip top and sides into boiled raspberry purée (raspberry jam boiled and passed through a sieve).

(2) Mask sides in brown desiccated coconut.

(3) Pipe a rosette of buttercream on the top and decorate with a chocolate button.

(*i*)

(1) Coat top and sides of a genoese square with buttercream and mask with browned flaked almonds.

(2) Cut through about $\frac{1}{8}$ in. (3 mm) from top.

(3) Lift up top and fill with a scroll of buttercream.

(*j*)

(1) Dip top and sides of a circle of genoese in boiled raspberry purée.

(2) Mask sides with browned desiccated coconut.

(3) Decorate with a rosette of cream and piece of crystallized rose petal.

(*k*)

Same as (*j*) except a square of genoese is used and a scroll used for decoration.

(*l*)

Similar to (*j*) but top consists of a piped ring of buttercream filled with red jelly.

Genoese Slices (Figure 88)

Top Row. For these varieties a strip of genoese approx. $2\frac{1}{2}$ in. ($6\frac{1}{2}$ cm) is sandwiched with ganache, buttercream, or jam, and after decorating is cut into slices approx. 1 in. ($2\frac{1}{2}$ cm) wide.

(*a*)

(1) Place on a number of ropes of coloured almond paste.

(2) Cover with coloured and flavoured fondant reduced to the correct consistency with stock syrup and temperature 100°F (38°C).

(3) Decorate with crushed crystallized rose petals.

(*b*)

Similar to (*a*) but ropes of different sizes are used.

(*c*)

(1) A rope of almond paste is placed on each edge.

(2) The centre is filled with chocolate or jelly.

(3) Decorate with coloured nib almonds.

Bottom Row. In these varieties, glacé fruits, e.g. cherries or pineapple, are used in the sandwiching medium. When the strips are cut into slices the glacé fruits show through and add to the decoration of the slice as a whole.

(*d*)

(1) Roll out coloured almond paste, spread with jam, and cover the genoese strip, top and sides. This may be marked or textured if desired.

(*e*)

(1) Coat sides with buttercream and mask with browned desiccated coconut.

(2) Pipe a scroll of buttercream along each edge of the strip.

(3) Fill in the centre with chocolate or jelly.

(4) Decorate with coloured almond nibs.

(*f*)

(1) Similar to (*e*) but use fondant.

(2) Decorate with browned nib almonds.

(*a*)   (*b*)   (*c*)

(*d*)   (*e*)   (*f*)

Figure 88. Genoese slices (*see* text)

Marshmallow Fancies (Figure 89) (Yield 18)

    5 *oz* (150 *g*) *flour into sweetpaste* (*see page* 148)

    4 *oz* (120 *g*) *sugar into marshmallow* (*see page* 297)

    2 *oz* (60 *g*) *chocolate couverture* (*for decoration*)

    2 *oz* (60 *g*) *coconut*

(1) Roll out the sweetpaste to $\frac{1}{8}$ in. (3 mm) thick and cut out a variety of shapes from round and oval cutters as shown in Figure 89(*b*).

(2) Bake these shapes in an oven approx. 380°F (193°C) until they are baked to a delicate shade of golden brown.

(3) Make up the marshmallow and when it begins to stiffen, fill a savoy bag. For the plain oval or round shapes a $\frac{1}{2}$-in. (1$\frac{1}{4}$-cm) tube will be necessary

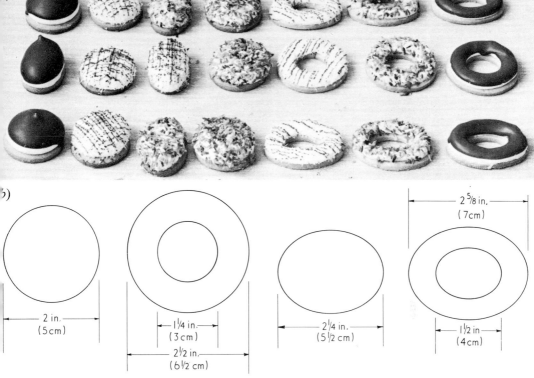

Figure 89. Marshmallow fancies: (*a*) finished fancies: (*b*) size and shapes

and for the other ring shapes a $\frac{3}{8}$-in. (1-cm) tube is required. Pipe a bulb of marshmallow on the plain shapes and a ring on the others.

(4) Cover them immediately with the desiccated coconut, either plain or toasted.

(5) Decorate, using chocolate, to coat the marshmallow either completely or half way. Alternatively chocolate may be spun across. In Figure 89 each of these treatments is given on the four bases originally described.

Marshmallow Snowballs

(1) Spread on a tray some desiccated coconut.

(2) On this pipe bulbs of marshmallow.

(3) Cover immediately with coconut.

(4) Remove, slightly flatten, and place on greaseproof paper. Serve in paper cups.

Note. The marshmallow recipe previously referred to will make 16 snowballs in addition to the 18 marshmallow fancies.

Cup Cakes

> *Cup Cake bases (see page* 103)
> *Buttercream*
> *Fondant*
> *Icing Sugar*
> *Glacé Cherries*

Varieties. (Figure 90)

   (*a*)
(1) Cut top off the cup cake and divide in half.
(2) Pipe a scroll of buttercream on each side of the base.
(3) Replace the two halves of the top to rest on the buttercream at an angle.
(4) Dust with icing sugar.

   (*b*)
(1) Remove a disc of cake from the base with a circular cutter.
(2) Fill the hole so formed with buttercream.
(3) Replace the disc of cake.
(4) Dust with icing sugar.

   (*c*)
(1) Brush over with hot apricot purée.
(2) Dip the top into warmed fondant.
(3) Decorate with a cherry.

Notes.
   1. Instead of fondant, chocolate may be used.
   2. The edge of the fondant or chocolate icing may be covered in roasted desiccated coconut.

Florentines (Figure 71(*h*)) (Yield 48 petits fours)
              (Figure 91) (Yield 24 afternoon tea fancies)

    3 *oz* (90 *g*) *butter*
    3¼ *oz* (97 *g*) *sugar*
    1 *oz* (30 *g*) *chopped cherries*
    1 *oz* (30 *g*) *chopped peel*
    2 *oz* (60 *g*) *sultanas or other crushed fruit, e.g. pineapple, ginger, etc.*
    4½ *oz* (135 *g*) *flaked or nibbed almonds*
    1 *oz* (30 *g*) *fresh cream*
    Chocolate couverture (for decoration)

Figure 90. Decorated cup cakes (*see* text)
   (*a*)   (*b*)   (*c*)

(1) Melt the butter in a saucepan.
(2) Add the sugar and bring to the boil. Remove from the heat.
(3) Add the fruit, then the almonds and stir well.
(4) Lastly stir in the cream.
(5) Deposit the mixture with the aid of a spoon, in small heaps on either:
    (*a*) A well-greased and floured baking tray.
    (*b*) A silicone papered tray.
    Allow plenty of space between the heaps for spreading during baking.
(6) Flatten the heaps as much as possible before baking.
(7) Bake in an oven at 360°F (182°C) until they are baked a light golden colour.
(8) As soon as they are removed from the oven and whilst still hot, pull the edges of the baked mixing inwards with a circular cutter to form the florentine into a perfect circle (Figure 91(*a*)).
(9) Leave to get quite cold and crisp before removing from the tray.
(10) Coat the flat underside of the florentine with tempered chocolate couverture (*see* page 244).
Coating Florentines with Chocolate.
(1) Temper the chocolate and spread it out in a thin sheet on greaseproof paper.
(2) Before the chocolate sets, lay the florentines flat upside down on the liquid chocolate.
(3) When the chocolate has set, trim the florentines round with an appropriately sized cutter.
(4) Remove from the greaseproof paper.
(5) Spread some more chocolate on the already coated side of the florentine and, just before it sets, use a comb scraper to mark on wavy lines (Figure 91(*b*)).
(6) Display the florentines alternately showing the nut side as well as the chocolate side (Figure 91(*c*)).

Notes.
    1. An alternative method of giving the florentine its first coating of chocolate, is to spread some chocolate on its underside and place coated side down on greaseproof paper. The only disadvantage in this method is that if the florentine has any holes in its surface, the chocolate will pass through to the nut side and so spoil its appearance.
    2. The florentine mixing may be spread, baked in sheets, and cut into squares.
    3. It may also be baked in rings and cut into segments to form a top decoration of a torte.
    4. For an afternoon tea fancy the usual size is approx. 3 in. (7½ cm).
    5. For petits fours, the size should be 1½ in. (4 cm). When making these the fruit and the nuts need to be much more finely chopped.
    6. The pieces of florentine left in the chocolate remaining on the greaseproof paper, may be removed by melting the chocolate and passing it through a fine sieve.

Figure 91. Florentines:
>   (*a*) Pulling into a round shape with a cutter (*above*).
>   (*b*) Spreading the second coat of chocolate with a comb scraper (*below*).
>   (*c*) Finished florentines (*opposite*).

Brandy Snaps (Figure 92) (Yield 36–40)

$4\frac{1}{2}$ *oz* (135 g) *butter*
8 *oz* (240 g) *castor sugar*
4 *oz* (120 g) *soft flour*
4 *oz* (120 g) *golden syrup*
$\frac{1}{8}$ *oz* (4 g) *ground ginger*

(1) Mix all the ingredients to a smooth paste.
(2) Prepare a baking tin by thoroughly cleaning and giving it a liberal dressing of fat.
(3) Roll out the paste into a long rope and, with a knife, chop off small pieces of equal size (approx. $\frac{1}{2}$ oz (15 g)).
(4) Place these about 5 in. (13 cm) apart on the greased tray and flatten them with the hand or a fork.
(5) Bake at 340°F (171°C) until they are golden in colour. During baking the paste flows out flat with a holey surface.
(6) Once they are baked allow them to cool slightly and then lift them off with a palette knife.

Figure 92. Brandy snaps

(7) Whilst still warm, they may be moulded into a shape; but once cold they are very brittle and easily snap.

(8) The brandy snap may be rolled round a wooden or a metal cream horn tin (with the top surface showing).

(9) These shapes may then be filled with fresh whipped cream.

Notes.

1. Brandy snaps, moulded into shapes, may be used as decorative pieces. For example, each segment of a torte could be decorated with a cornet shape filled with cream.

2. If the brandy snaps have become too cold to mould into shape, warm the tray and they will once again become soft enough to mould.

12. Savoury Goods

Cold Savoury Paste

> 14 *oz* (420 *g*) *flour*
> 6 *oz* (180 *g*) *lard*
> $\frac{1}{4}$ *oz* (8 *g*) *salt*
> $3\frac{3}{4}$ *oz* (112 *g*) *cold water*

(1) Mix all the fat with half the flour and cream well together.
(2) Add remaining flour and salt dissolved in the water.
(3) Mix to a clear paste.

Hot Savoury Paste (Yield 2 pork pies at approx. 1 lb (480 g) each)

> 10 *oz* (300 *g*) *flour*
> 5 *oz* (150 *g*) *lard*
> $\frac{1}{8}$ *oz* (4 *g*) *salt*
> $2\frac{1}{2}$ *oz* (75 *g*) *boiling water*

Method 1.
(1) Rub lard into the flour.
(2) Add the boiling water.
(3) Partially mix flour and water until cooler.
(4) Finish off to a clear paste by mixing lightly with the hands.
Method 2.
(1) Rub half the fat into the flour.
(2) Melt remainder in the water.
(3) Proceed as (3) and (4) above.
Note. Do not use this paste until it is *cold*.

Boiled Savoury Paste

> *Use previous recipe.*

(1) Boil water, salt, and lard.
(2) Add flour to the boiling mixture.
(3) Mix to a clear smooth paste.
(4) Use immediately whilst still hot.

Hand Raised Pork Pies

> *Use a boiled or hot paste.*

To shape a pork pie case successfully, we need a block of approx. 4 in. (10 cm) diameter. Special wooden blocks are available for this purpose but, if not available, the bottom of a large jar may be used.
(1) Use approx. 6 oz (180 g) of paste and form a ball.
(2) With the heel of the hand, form a cup shape.
(3) Reverse and press onto the block.

169

(4) Pressing firmly, rotate the block to raise the paste up its side. Aim at producing a slightly thicker paste at the base with the sides tapering off to the top.

(5) Allow paste to set and remove from the block.

(6) Fill with approx. 11 oz (330 g) of meat (*see* below). Flatten the meat and make sure that there are no air spaces left.

(7) Roll out the remaining 2 oz (60 g) of pastry for the lid and cut out to the required size.

(8) Wash the top inside edge with egg or water.

(9) Place on the lid and press firmly into the sides. Pinch with fingers or nippers to seal.

(10) Wash sides and top with egg and apply top decoration, i.e. diamonds of paste or shaped as leaves.

(11) Bake at 400°F (204°C) for approx. 1 hour.

(12) After baking and whilst still hot, puncture the top crust and insert a good stock to which 1 oz (30 g) of gelatine per pint (6 decilitres) has been added.

Meat Filling. (Yield sufficient for two 1-lb (480-g) pies)

  11 *oz (330 g) lean pork*
  5½ *oz (165 g) fat pork*
  2 *oz (60 g) rusk or bread*
  3¾ *oz (112 g) water*
  ½ *oz (15 g) seasoning No. 2.*

Seasoning.

Recipe 1.

  2 *of salt*
  1 *of pepper*

Recipe 2.

  1 *lb (480 g) salt*
  ½ *lb (240 g) pepper*
  ¼ *oz (8 g) ground nutmeg*
  ¼ *oz (8 g) ground mace*

Seasoning used at the rate of ½ oz per 1 lb (15 g per 480 g) of meat gives a spicy flavour that may be too pronounced for some palates. This, of course, may be adjusted to suit individual tastes.

Steak and Kidney Pie

Paste.

  4 *oz (120 g) cold savoury paste* (*see page* 169)

Filling.

  1 *lb (480 g) lean steak*
  ¼ *lb (120 g) kidney*
  1½ *oz (45 g) flour*
  Seasoning to taste
  Pinch of thyme
  A little water

(1) Cut meat into small cubes.
(2) Cover with water and place in oven in a pie dish.
(3) When cooked, mix flour with a little water and stir in.
(4) Season and then allow to cool.
(5) Cover with the paste, making sure that it sticks securely to the top edge of the pie dish, using a little egg wash.
(6) Egg wash the top and bake at approx. 425°F (218°C) for approx. 25 minutes.

Veal and Ham Pie

Use boiled savoury paste and proceed as for the making of pork pies.
Filling.
 8 *oz* (240 g) *chopped veal*
 11 *oz* (330 g) *chopped pork*
 ½ *oz* (15 g) *seasoning No. 2*
 2 *oz* (60 g) *water*

Meat and Potato Pie

Paste.
 4 *oz* (120 g) *cold savoury paste* (*see page* 169)
Filling.
 10 *oz* (300 g) *potatoes*
 2 *oz* (60 g) *onions*
 4 *oz* (120 g) *lean beef*
 2½ *oz* (75 g) *water*
 ⅛ *oz* (4 g) *seasoning No. 1*
(1) Cut the meat into cubes and dice the onion.
(2) Cover with water, add the seasoning, and place in a pie dish.
(3) When cooked, thicken with the flour.
(4) Partially cook the potatoes and add.
(5) Proceed as for steak and kidney pies.

Cornish Pasties

 ½ *lb* (240 g) *savoury paste* (*see page* 169)
 4 *oz* (120 g) *steak* (*minced or finely chopped*)
 4 *oz* (120 g) *potatoes* (*minced or finely chopped*)
 2 *oz* (60 g) *onions* (*minced or finely chopped*)
 Salt
 Pepper
(1) Divide the paste into four and pin each piece to a diameter of approx. 5 in. (13 cm).
(2) Mix the steak, potatoes, and onions together with a little water and season.
(3) Place the filling in the centre of the pastry discs.
(4) Wash the edges of the pastry with either water or egg.

(5) Draw up each side of the pastry to the centre to cover the filling, pinching them firmly together.

(6) Notch the seam with the thumb and finger. Finish moulding it into a boat shape with the fluted seam on top.

(7) Egg wash.

(8) Bake in an oven at 400°F (204°C) for approx. 30 minutes until the filling is thoroughly cooked.

Note. Other pasties may be made in a similar way using different fillings such as veal, ham, potatoes, and carrots.

Pizza (Yield one 8-in. (20-cm) plate)

Dough.

　　4 *oz* (120 g) *bread roll dough* (*see page* 185)
　　½ *oz* (15 g) *butter*
　Mix well together.

Filling.

　　Finely chopped garlic
　　Tomato (*cut in slices*)
　　Salt, pepper, and sweet marjoram
　　Anchovy fillets
　　Black olives (*stoned*)
　　Oil

(1) Divide the dough into two 4-oz (120-g) portions.

(2) Mould round and then roll out to cover an 8-in. (20-cm) metal plate.

(3) Allow the paste to rise slightly.

(4) Sprinkle with finely chopped garlic.

(5) Cover with the slices of tomato, overlapping.

(6) Sprinkle on salt, pepper, and sweet marjoram.

(7) Decorate with strips of anchovy and stoned black olives. A criss-cross or star pattern may be formed.

(8) Sprinkle with olive or cooking oil.

(9) Leave to rise for approx. ½ hour.

(10) Bake in an oven of 390°F (199°C) until baked.

SHORT PASTE SAVOURIES

A very wide variety of savouries, both hot and cold, may be made from tartlets lined with the savoury short paste and either baked with a savoury filling or baked blind and a savoury filling inserted afterwards.

Flans may also be made in this way and cut into portions afterwards (*see* Quiche Lorraine).

Quiche Lorraine (Yield 1 large flan suitable for 8 covers)

> 8 *oz* (240 g) *savoury short paste*
> ¾ *pt* (4½ *dl*) *milk*
> 2 *oz* (60 g) *Gruyère cheese*
> 3 *eggs*
> 6 *oz* (180 g) *bacon*
> *Salt and cayenne pepper*

(1) Roll out the pastry and line a large flan ring.
(2) Prick the base with a fork.
(3) Place on strips of bacon.
(4) Place on thin slices of Gruyère cheese.
(5) Whisk the eggs and milk together to form a custard, add the seasoning, and pour this over the cheese and bacon.
(6) Place into an oven at 400°F (204°C) until set and brown.
Note. The milk may be replaced with single cream to improve quality.

SAVOURIES FROM CHOU PASTE

Cheese Fritters

> *Add to the basic chou paste recipe* (*see page* 105):
> 8 *oz* (240 g) *grated Cheddar cheese*

(1) Using a spoon and finger, break off pieces of the savoury chou paste and drop into hot fat.
(2) Cook until brown.
(3) Remove, drain well, and serve immediately.
Note. Instead of a spoon, the mixture may be piped into the hot fat by means of a savoy bag fitted with a ⅛-in. (3-mm) plain tube. A pair of oiled scissors can be used to cut off appropriately sized pieces as it emerges from the tube.

Cheese Éclairs or Cream Buns

> *Basic chou paste recipe* (*see page* 105).

(1) Pipe out as for small éclairs or cream buns, but before baking sprinkle on grated parmesan cheese.
(2) Bake in the usual way.
(3) When cold, split open and pipe in the cheese filling (*see* page 174).

Béchamel (Yield 1 quart (12 decilitres))

> 1 *qt* 40 *oz* (12 *dl*) *milk*
> 4½ *oz* (135 g) *margarine*
> 4 *oz* (120 g) *flour*
> 1 *small onion studded with* 2 *cloves*

(1) Add the studded onion to the milk and bring to the boil.
(2) Melt the margarine in a saucepan.
(3) Add the flour and gently cook the mixture (roux) for a few minutes.

(4) Add the warmed milk gradually, thoroughly stirring in each addition to make a smooth sauce.

(5) Simmer the sauce gently for 30 minutes to 1 hour.

(6) Remove the onion and pass the Béchamel through a conical strainer.

Cheese Fillings

Recipe 1.

> 4 *oz* (120 g) *powdered or finely grated cheese*
> 4 *oz* (120 g) *butter*
> 4 *oz* (120 g) *water*

(1) Beat the cheese and butter together to a light cream.

(2) Add the water gradually beating in each addition.

Recipe 2.

> 2½ *oz* (75 g) *Béchamel*
> 1½ *oz* (45 g) *egg yolks* (3)
> 2 *oz* (60 g) *butter*
> 4 *oz* (120 g) *grated cheese*
> 2 *oz* (60 g) *cream*
> *Salt*
> *Cayenne pepper*

(1) Using hot Béchamel, add first the butter, and when this has been mixed in follow with the egg yolks, cheese, and lastly the cream, mixing in each addition before adding the next ingredient.

(2) Season with salt and cayenne.

SAVOURIES FROM PUFF PASTE

Vol-au-Vents and Bouchées

Various fillings may be used including chicken, ham, cheese, mushrooms, shrimps, salmon, etc.

(1) Prepare the puff pastry cases as described in Chapter 3 on Puff Pastry (*see* pages 59 and 60).

(2) Dice the chicken, ham, mushrooms, or salmon. The cheese should be grated and the shrimps left whole.

(3) Mix with either Béchamel sauce or Velouté (*see* below) and a small quantity of fresh double cream.

(4) Deposit in the baked cases. Replace the puff pastry top or, alternatively, omit and use an appropriate garnish instead.

Velouté. This is made in the same way as the Béchamel sauce but instead of milk, an appropriate stock is used, e.g. chicken stock for chicken, fish stock for shrimps.

Cheese Straws – Paillettes au Fromage

    4 *oz* (120 g) *well-rested puff pastry*
    2 *oz* (60 g) *grated cheese*
    Cayenne pepper

(1) Roll out the pastry to about 6 in. × 18 in. (15 cm × 45 cm).
(2) Cover two-thirds with the grated cheese and sprinkle with cayenne.
(3) Fold the uncovered one-third portion into the centre of the covered portion and complete as if a single turn is given (English method).
(4) Roll out to ⅛ in. (3 mm).
(5) Cut out four or five discs with a 2-in. (5-cm) cutter and remove the centre with a 1½-in. (4-cm) cutter to form rings.
(6) Cut up the remainder of the puff pastry into strips approx. 3 in. × ¼ in. (7½ cm × 6 mm) wide.
(7) Twist each of these and place upon a lightly greased baking tray together with the rings.
(8) Bake at 450°F (232°C) for approx. 10 minutes, until they are golden brown in colour.
(9) Place a bundle of straws inside each circle and serve.

Parmesanes

Base.
    Puff pastry
    Gruyère or Parmesan cheese (grated)
Filling (Garniture à Parmesanes).
    10 *oz* (3 dl) *milk*
    1 *oz* (30 g) *cornflour*
    2 *egg yolks*
    3 *oz* (90 g) *butter*
    3 *oz* (90 g) *grated Parmesan or Gruyère cheese*
Method for Making Filling.
(1) Mix the cornflour with about ¼ of the milk.
(2) Add the egg yolks and grated cheese and mix.
(3) Boil the remainder of the milk.
(4) Pour the boiling milk onto the cornflour mixture and stir well to prevent formation of lumps.
(5) Return to the heat and allow to boil for a few minutes.
(6) Lastly, add the butter and remove from the heat.
(7) Store in a cold place until required.
Method for Making Parmesanes
(1) Roll out virgin puff paste to ⅛ in. (3 mm) in thickness, cut out rounds of approx. 4 in. (10 cm) diameter.
(2) Place them on moistened clean baking tins.
(3) Place in the centre of each, a small quantity of grated Gruyère cheese.
(4) Allow a short resting period and bake off in a hot oven at 480°F (249°C).

(5) After they are cooked, split in half, place in some of the filling in the bottom half, and replace the top.

Other Varieties

Many other varieties of puff paste savouries may be made as follows:
(1) Roll out the puff paste to approx. ¼ in. (½ cm) thick and cut out with a 3½-in. (9-cm) fluted cutter.
(2) Extend these with a rolling pin to form an oval shape keeping the edges thicker than the centre.
(3) Wash with egg and place in the centre a quantity of filling (*see* below).
(4) Fold over to enclose the filling and seal edge.
(5) Wash with egg and bake at 390°F (199°C).
Fillings. Cheese, cooked minced meats, vegetables, cooked chicken, scampi, etc.

CANAPÉS

These are very small round, square, rectangular, or oval shapes, approx. ⅛ in. (3 mm) thick made from either bread or biscuit. The bread may be wholemeal, rye, or white, and either left plain, fried, or toasted, the last being the most popular. The individual pieces are first buttered or spread with a savoury filling, suitably garnished, and glazed in aspic. For ease of handling, cocktail sticks may be inserted, so that the consumers need not soil their hands. The stages in making canapés are thus:
(1) Make a number of small bases from either bread or biscuit.
(2) Spread on a butter mixture.
(3) Cover with the combination of savouries (*see* below).
(4) Decorate with a suitable garnish.
(5) Glaze with warm aspic.

Some Ideas for Varieties

Liver.
 1. A slice of goose liver, garnished with a disc of truffle in the centre.
 2. Liver paste garnished with a small slice of raw carrot.
Egg.
 1. Three overlapping slices of hard boiled egg. Garnish the yolk with a slice of gherkin.
 2. Finely chopped hard boiled egg, mixed with a little cream. Garnish with a slice of tomato.
 3. Pass hard boiled eggs through a sieve and mix with mayonnaise, seasoned with mustard. Garnish with a small sprig of watercress.
Ham.
 1. Meat paste covered with a slice of ham. Garnish with a small rosette of mashed potatoes and a cooked pea.

2. Make a small roll of the ham slice. Garnish with a small wedge of pineapple.

Tongue. Slice of tongue. Garnish with a rosette of mashed potatoes and piece of pickled walnut.

Salami. A slice of salami wrapped around a piece of gherkin.

Smoked Salmon.

1. A slice of smoked salmon rolled into a cone and filled with mashed potato. Garnish with a piece of tomato.

2. A slice of smoked salmon laid flat and garnished with a small piece of lemon.

Shrimp. Select six small shrimps and arrange head to tail in the form of a rose. Pipe a rosette of butter in the centre.

Sardine. Small sardine, lightly dusted with paprika.

Tomato. Slice of tomato on which is sprinkled finely grated cheese. Garnish with a caper.

Cheese. Slice of cheese garnished with a piece of apple.

Chicken. Finely chopped chicken mixed with mayonnaise. Garnish with paprika and then pieces of green and red pepper.

Method of Applying Aspic

Place the canapés on a wire with a drip tray underneath. Use a dropping funnel and stick (page 265) to deposit sufficient aspic on each canapé to completely cover them. The surplus should run into the tray underneath.

Use the aspic warm so that it completely covers the canapé before it sets.

The varieties of canapés are endless and offer unlimited scope to the imaginative patissier. However, care is required to ensure that the items chosen complement each other in taste and colour.

PASTA

Pasta is the general term for macaroni, spaghetti, vermicelli, noodles, etc., which include any specific shape. It originates in Italy.

There are two types of pasta namely, dry and fresh. The dry pastas are Macaroni, Spaghetti, Vermicelli, and Lasagne. The fresh pastas are Nouilles, Ravioli, and Gnocchi. The patissier is only concerned with the making of these last three.

Noodles – Nouilles

4 *oz* (120 g) *strong flour*
2 *oz* (60 g) *eggs*
½ *oz* (15 g) *olive oil*
A pinch of salt

(1) Sieve the flour and salt.
(2) Add the oil and egg.
(3) Thoroughly mix into a well-developed, smooth dough.
(4) Cover and let the dough rest for 2 hours or more.
(5) Roll out very thinly into pieces approx. 3 in. (7½ cm) wide and leave to dry.
(6) Cut these pieces into thin strips approx. ¼ in. (6 mm) wide and leave to dry.

Notes.

1. For dusting purposes use either a strong flour or semolina.

2. Noodles are cooked in the same way as spaghetti and served in the same way as for any spaghetti recipe.

3. It may be served mixed with fresh hot cream.

4. The paste may be mixed with tomato or spinach purée for further varieties.

5. Noodles may also be used as a garnish, e.g. with braised beef.

Ravioli

> 8 *oz* (240 g) *strong flour*
> 1¼ *oz* (38 g) *olive oil*
> 3¾ *oz* (112 g) *water*
> *A pinch of salt*

(1) Sieve the flour and salt.
(2) Add the oil and water.
(3) Thoroughly mix into a well-developed, smooth dough.
(4) Allow the dough to rest for at least 30 minutes.
(5) Roll out the dough very thinly to approx. 12 in. × 18 in. (30 cm × 45 cm).
(6) Cut into two and egg wash one half.
(7) Fill a savoy bag with a large plain tube, with the ravioli filling (*see* below).
(8) Pipe out small pieces of the filling about the size of a cherry approx. 1½ in. (3½ cm) apart on the egg-washed piece of paste.
(9) Cover with the other half of paste and press down between each pile of filling to seal, taking care not to trap any air.
(10) Using a serrated pastry wheel, cut the pastry between the lines of filling or cut into 1¼-in. (3-cm) circles with a cutter.
(11) Separate and place on a floured tray.
(12) Place in gently boiling water to poach for 8–10 minutes.
(13) Drain well and arrange in layers in a buttered gratin dish.
(14) Pour over about ½ pint (3 decilitres) of jus-lie, demi-glace, or tomato sauce.
(15) Sprinkle with about 2 oz (60 g) grated cheese.
(16) Brown under the salamander.
(17) Place dish on a flat and serve immediately.

Note. There are several different fillings for ravioli. These would normally be made for the patissier by the chef but a suitable filling is included here:

Ravioli Filling.

    8 *oz* (240 *g*) *beef or veal* (*braised or boiled*)
    2 *oz* (60 *g*) *chopped onion or shallot*
    ½ *oz* (15 *g*) *fat*
    1 *lb* (480 *g*) *spinach*
    1 *clove of garlic*
    A pinch of salt
    Pepper
    1 *egg yolk*

(1) Mince the meat.
(2) Cook and mince the spinach.
(3) Cook the onions or shallots in the fat without colouring.
(4) Mix the ingredients with the egg yolk to bind the mixture and season.

Gnocchi

These are small dumplings and may be made from:

    (*a*) *Chou paste – Gnocchi à la parisienne.*
    (*b*) *Semolina – Gnocchi à la romaine.*
    (*c*) *Potato and flour – Gnocchi à la piedmontaise.*

Gnocchi à la Parisienne (Yield 8 covers)

    10 *oz* (300 *g*) *water into chou paste* (*see page* 105)
    4 *oz* (120 *g*) *grated cheese*
    1 *pt* (6 *dl*) *Béchamel sauce* (*see page* 173)

(1) Make the chou paste.
(2) Add 2 oz (60 g) of the grated cheese.
(3) Place in a savoy bag fitted with a plain tube.
(4) Pipe out and cut with an oiled palette knife into suitable lengths ½–1 in.
(1¼–2½ cm) into a shallow pan containing boiling salted water.
(5) Slowly poach for 10 minutes.
(6) Drain well and arrange in a buttered fireproof dish.
(7) Cover with the Béchamel sauce
(8) Sprinkle over the remaining cheese.
(9) Brown under the salamander.
(10) Serve immediately on a flat silver dish.

Gnocchi à la Romaine (Yield 8 covers)

    2 *pt* (12 *dl*) *milk*
    12 *oz* (360 *g*) *semolina*
    3 *oz* (90 *g*) *butter*
    3 *oz* (90 *g*) *grated cheese*
    3 *egg yolks*
    Seasoning
    Grated nutmeg

(1) Boil the milk.
(2) Sprinkle in the semolina, stirring continuously.

(3) Allow to simmer for 5–10 minutes.
(4) Season and add the nutmeg.
(5) Add the egg yolk, cheese, and butter and mix in.
(6) Pour onto a greased tray to a depth of approx. $\frac{1}{2}$ in. ($1\frac{1}{4}$ cm).
(7) When cold, cut out pieces with a 2-in. (5-cm) round cutter or into crescent shapes.
(8) Place the scraps of the cutting in an earthenware dish.
(9) Arrange the rounds or crescents neatly on top.
(10) Sprinkle on melted butter and the grated cheese.
(11) Place under the salamander to brown.
(12) Serve on a flat silver dish.

Gnocchi à la Piedmontaise (Yield 8 covers)

> $1\frac{1}{2}$ *lb* (720 g) *mashed potatoes*
> 8 *oz* (240 g) *flour*
> 2 *oz* (60 g) *butter*
> 6 *egg yolks*
> *Seasoning*
> *Grated nutmeg*
> 1 *pt* (6 *dl*) *tomato sauce*

(1) Boil or steam the potatoes.
(2) Pass through a sieve and keep as dry as possible.
(3) Whilst still hot, mix in the flour, butter, seasoning, and egg.
(4) Mould into small balls about the size of a walnut.
(5) Dust well with flour and flatten slightly with a fork.
(6) Place into boiling water and poach for 5 minutes.
(7) Drain carefully and place on a clean cloth to dry.
(8) Arrange in a buttered fire-proof dish and cover with the tomato sauce.
(9) Sprinkle with grated cheese and place under the salamander to brown.
(10) Serve immediately on a flat silver dish.

13. Fermented Goods

YEAST FERMENTATION

Before dealing with the various goods which are aerated by the fermentation of yeast, the principles of fermentation are outlined here so that the patissier will have a better understanding of what happens when yeast ferments.

Yeast is a living micro-organism existing as a cell, having a diameter of $\frac{1}{2500}$ to $\frac{1}{4000}$ in. ($\frac{1}{100}$ to $\frac{1}{160}$ mm) invisible to the naked eye but easily discernable under the microscope.

When this organism is introduced to warmth, food, and moisture, it ferments, i.e. it produces carbon dioxide gas and ethyl alcohol, at the same time reproducing itself. When we introduce yeast into our goods, we provide the food material and moisture and to a certain extent control the temperature, so that the yeast ferments under the best conditions to generate carbon dioxide which we need for the goods to become aerated. (The brewer or distiller requires the other by-product of fermentation, ethyl alcohol.)

However, the process of yeast fermentation is complicated and there are many factors which affect it. The best way to understand these factors is to elaborate upon each.

Food Material

Yeast requires Dextrose Sugar (Glucose) before it can ferment, but because it contains enzymes which are capable of changing both Cane Sugar (Sucrose) and Malt Sugar (Maltose) into Dextrose, almost any sweet material (except Milk Sugar) will act as a source of food material. Wheat flour already contains 2·5% of these sugars so that any mixture of flour and water will readily ferment without the addition of any extra sugar.

What is important, however, is the concentration of sugar which the yeast is expected to ferment. The optimum is approx. $12\frac{1}{2}\%$ and concentrations above this have a retarding effect. This must be remembered when doughs are made which are very rich in sugar. The yeast content must be increased considerably to compensate for this effect.

Temperature

Yeast is dormant at 32°F (0°C) but as the temperature increases so too does the activity of the yeast until, at 120°F (49°C), it becomes killed. The best working temperatures are between 70°–85°F (21°–29°C). Without understanding this, it is easy to be tempted to ferment yeast at too high a temperature. Even 85°F (29°C) feels comparatively cool to the touch. Too high a temperature causes dough skinning and the encouragement of other

181

undesirable characteristics and it should be tolerated only for the final proof stage. It is a mistake to believe that warm water must always be used. In summer the use of water straight from the tap is recommended to achieve the right dough temperature.

Method of Determining Water Temperature for a Dough.
1. Determine the temperature of the flour to be used.
2. Subtract the value from *twice* the required dough temperature.
3. The result will be the required water temperature. It can be expressed thus:

Water temperature = (Required dough temperature × 2) − Flour temperature.

Salt

This commodity is invariably used in all yeast goods for the enhancement of flavour, although it has other side effects, namely:
(*a*) Strengthens the gluten of the flour and so stabilizes the dough.
(*b*) Produces a whiter crumb and colour and bloom to the crust.
(*c*) Reduces staling.
(*d*) Retards fermentation.

It is this last effect which we have to consider carefully. Bringing yeast into direct contact with salt will soon kill it or at least dangerously retard its activity. The concentration of salt usually used in a dough is tolerable by the yeast provided that at the mixing stage it is kept in a sufficiently dilute solution.

Spices

These too retard fermentation. In heavily spiced goods (e.g. hot cross buns), more yeast needs to be used to compensate for this retarding effect.

Fats

These also have a retarding effect.

Time

So far we have only considered one effect of using yeast, i.e. to aerate. If this were the only aspect in which we were interested, there would be no purpose in allowing a dough to lie in bulk for a given time before proceeding to scale, mould, and prove.

When yeast starts to ferment, a very complicated series of enzyme changes take place, not only causing the production of carbon dioxide and alcohol but also causing the protein gluten network of the dough to become softened and more elastic. This function enables the gluten to stretch more and retain more gas. A perfect dough is one in which this function has been allowed to reach the optimum, i.e. the time allowed for the dough to lie in bulk has been correct for the temperature chosen and quantity of yeast used. Below the optimum, the dough is said to be *under-ripe*; over this optimum, the dough is said to be *over-ripe*.

It follows from this that, for a perfect dough to be made, there must be perfect correlation between dough temperature and dough time for any given yeast quantity. If the temperature is reduced, the yeast quantity must be increased and vice versa.

Definitions

Bulk Fermentation Time (B.F.T.). This is the period of time from when the dough is made until when it is taken for weighing into the correctly sized pieces ready for moulding, proving, and baking.

Scaling. Dividing the dough into pieces by weight.

Moulding. Shaping the dough pieces into the appropriate shape for the purpose required.

Proving. Allowing the dough pieces to lie and grow in size before being baked. This is usually done in a cabinet in which warmth and steam are applied so that the goods are prevented from developing a skin and so grow uniform in shape. The correct degree of proof can only be learned by experience and varies with each type of goods; but, approximately, the dough pieces should at least double their size prior to being placed in the oven.

Baking. All fermented goods require a hot oven at between 400°F (204°C) and 450°F (232°C). Goods rich in sugar and fat require the lower temperature whilst goods such as dinner rolls, lean in sugar and fat, require the higher temperature. For the best possible baking conditions some steam should be present in the oven. When an oven is full, there is sufficient steam being generated by the goods themselves; but if the oven is only a quarter to half full, it is an advantage to place in some water. This is to create a humid atmosphere and prevent the skin of the goods from setting until they have had the chance to grow slightly. Furthermore, the presence of steam will help to create moist eating goods and the production of a bloom on the crust.

FAULTS

The two main faults which occur in fermented goods may be attributed to under-ripeness or over-ripeness.

Under-ripeness

This is detected by all or any of the following characteristics:

(*a*) High crust colour.

(*b*) Small volume and bound buns, rolls, etc.

(*c*) Poor shapes split at the sides or top.
(*d*) Tough close textured crumb.
Under-ripeness is caused by insufficient fermentation and may be due to:
1. Insufficient yeast.
2. Too cool a dough temperature.
3. Too much sugar/salt/spice/fat/etc.
4. Yeast coming into contact with salt at the mixing stage.
5. Insufficient dough time.
Note. Faults (*b*) and (*c*) may also be due to insufficient proof.

Over-ripeness

This is indicated by:
(*a*) Anaemic crust colour.
(*b*) Flat shapes with no stability.
(*c*) Loose, woolly crumb.
Over-ripeness is caused by too much fermentation and may be due to:
1. Excessive amount of yeast.
2. Too high a dough temperature.
3. Omission of salt or the sugar in a bun dough.
4. Too prolonged a dough time.
Note. Fault (*b*) may also be due to excessive proof.

Method of Mixing Fermented Doughs by Hand

(1) Sieve flour.
(2) Rub into the flour the required fat quantity.
(3) Make a bay with the flour/fat mixture.
(4) Calculate the water temperature (i.e. required dough temperature $\times 2 -$ flour temperature).
(5) Measure the required amount of water at the required temperature.
(6) Mix a small quantity with the yeast and the remainder with the other soluble ingredients, i.e. salt and sugar.
(7) Pour the solutions into the bay and lightly mix until every particle of flour is wetted.
(8) Now knead the dough, stretching and pulling until it is a clear, elastic mass free of stickiness and lumps.
(9) Place it aside under a cover to prevent skinning for its required bulk fermentation time.
Note. Some text books still state that the sugar and yeast should be creamed together. This is *bad* practice and results in a loss of yeast activity owing to the retarding effect of a high concentration of sugar.
Water Quantity. This varies with the required consistency and with the strength of flour used. All fermented goods require a strong flour, but even the water absorption capacity of a strong flour can vary. Therefore, the quantity of water given in each recipe may have to be adjusted to suit individual circumstances.

Bread Rolls (Yield approx. 16 rolls)

1 *lb* 4 *oz* (600 g) *strong flour*
$\frac{1}{2}$ *oz* (15 g) *milk powder*
$\frac{3}{8}$ *oz* (11 g) *salt*
$\frac{1}{2}$ *oz* (15 g) *sugar*
$\frac{1}{2}$ *oz* (15 g) *fat*
$\frac{7}{8}$ *oz* (26 g) *yeast*
11$\frac{1}{2}$ *oz* (345 g) *water*

Dough B.F.T. 1 hour @ 76°F (24°C).
(1) Mix dough as previously described.
(2) Allow to rest under a cover for 1 hour.
(3) Divide dough into 2-oz (60-g) pieces.
(4) Mould round.
(5) Place on baking trays.
(6) Prove in a little steam to prevent skinning.
(7) Bake in an oven at approx. 450°F (232°C) for 12–15 minutes.

Basic Bun Dough (Yield approx. 16 buns)

1 *lb* 4 *oz* (600 g) *strong flour*
$\frac{1}{2}$ *oz* (15 g) *milk powder*
2$\frac{1}{2}$ *oz* (75 g) *sugar*
$\frac{1}{4}$ *oz* (7$\frac{1}{2}$ g) *salt*
2 *oz* (60 g) *fat*
1 *oz* (30 g) *egg*
1$\frac{1}{4}$ *oz* (37$\frac{1}{2}$ g) *yeast*
10 *oz* (300 g) *water*

Dough B.F.T. 1 hour @ 76°F (24°C).
(1) Mix dough as previously described.
(2) Proceed as for Bread Rolls.

VARIETIES FROM BASIC BUN DOUGH

Cream Buns (Devon Splits) (Figure 93(*b*))

(1) When the buns are cold, cut $\frac{3}{4}$ through the top.
(2) Pipe in a bulb of raspberry jam.
(3) Pipe in a bulb of whipped fresh cream.
(4) Dust liberally with icing sugar.

Iced Buns (Swiss) (Figure 93(*a*))

(1) Mould dough pieces into finger shapes and proceed as for bread rolls.
(2) When cold, dip the tops in a water icing which may be flavoured and coloured as desired (*see* recipe, page 301).

Currant Buns (Figure 94(*b*)) (Yield 18 buns)

Basic Bun Dough recipe
6 *oz* (180 g) *currants*

(1) Proceed as for Cream Buns.

(2) When the buns have been baked and whilst still hot, brush over with a glaze made of either syrup (equal parts sugar and water) or egg custard. The syrup will give a sticky sweet glaze, whilst the custard will give a less sweet glaze but remain dry.

Chelsea Buns (Figure 95(*a*)) (Yield 18 buns)

> *Basic Bun Dough recipe.*
> 8 *oz* (240 *g*) *currants*
> 1 *oz* (30 *g*) *brown sugar*
> $\frac{1}{8}$ *oz* (4 *g*) *mixed spice*
> 1 *oz* (30 *g*) *cooking oil*

(1) Proceed as for Cream Buns but, instead of moulding, roll out to cover an area approx. 15 in. (38 cm) square.

(2) Spread over a mixture of the brown sugar and spice and then sprinkle over the currants.

(3) Roll up Swiss roll fashion.

(4) Cover the surface with the oil.

(5) Cut into eighteen slices.

(6) Place each slice flat side down on a well-greased or buttered tray almost touching.

(7) Prove to double the size.

(8) Bake at 440°F (226°C) for approx. 12–15 minutes.

(9) When baked and whilst still hot, liberally cover with stock syrup and dust with castor sugar.

Figure 93. Fermented buns: (*a*) swiss buns; (*b*) cream buns (Devon splits)

(a)   *(b)*

Figure 94. Fermented buns: (*a*) doughnuts; (*b*) currant buns

Figure 95. Fermented buns: (*a*) Chelsea buns; (*b*) Bath buns

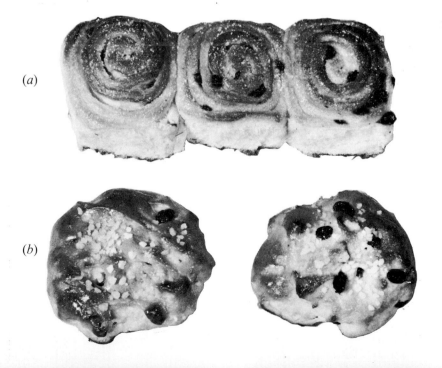

Bath Buns (Figure 95(*b*)) (Yield 18 buns)

Basic Bun Dough recipe.

6 *oz* (180 g) *sultanas* ⎱
1 *oz* (30 g) *peel* ⎬ For the dough
2 *oz* (60 g) *sugar nibs* ⎰

½ *oz* (15 g) *sugar nibs*   For top decoration

(1) Make up the basic bun dough with the above ingredients.
(2) Divide the dough into approx. 2-oz (60-g) pieces and leave in a rough shape on the baking tray.
(3) Prove and, before they are placed in the oven, sprinkle with ½ oz (15 g) sugar nibs.
(4) Bake at 440°F (226°C) for approx. 12–15 minutes.
(5) On removal from the oven and whilst still hot, glaze as for currant buns.

Doughnuts (Figure 94(*a*)) (Yield 18)

(1) Proceed as for Cream Buns.
(2) When moulded insert the thumb and fill the impression with raspberry jam, sealing afterwards.
(3) Prove on an oiled tray.
(4) When fully proved, drop the pieces into hot fat approx. 380°F (193°C).
(5) The pieces will float. When one half is sufficiently browned, turn over to cook the other half.
(6) Remove, drain off excess oil, and roll in castor sugar. A little cinnamon spice may be added.

Special Bath Bun Recipe (Yield 24 buns)

Ferment (½ hour at 76°F (24°C)).

5 *oz* (150 g) *egg* ⎱
5 *oz* (150 g) *water* ⎮
½ *oz* (15 g) *sugar* ⎬ (*A*)
1 *oz* (30 g) *flour* ⎮
1 *oz* (30 g) *yeast* ⎰

Dough (1 hour at 76°F (24°C)).

1 *lb* (480 g) *flour* ⎱
$\frac{1}{16}$ *oz* (2 g) *salt* ⎮
8 *oz* (240 g) *butter* ⎬ (*B*)
5 *oz* (150 g) *sultanas* ⎮
1 *oz* (30 g) *mixed peel* ⎰

8 *oz* (240 g) *nib sugar* (*C*)

2 *oz* (60 g) *nib sugar* (*D*)

(1) Mix together the ingredients of (*A*) and allow to ferment for ½ hour.
(2) After this time add the ingredients of (*B*) and make into a smooth dough.
(3) Leave dough to ferment for 1 hour and then mix in the nib sugar (*C*).

(4) Allow to recover for 15 minutes, during which time prepare a clean baking tin by greasing with butter.

(5) Divide into pieces and lay out on the buttered tray. The appearance should be as rocky as possible.

(6) Wash with egg.

(7) Allow to prove *in the cold* until approx. double their original size.

(8) Sprinkle some nib sugar on each piece (*D*).

(9) Bake in an oven at 430°F (221°C) for approx. 15 minutes.

(10) Wash the pieces lightly with bun wash on removal from the oven.

Danish Pastry (Yield 16–18 depending on varieties made)

 9 *oz* (270 *g*) *medium strength flour*
 1¼ *oz* (38 *g*) *yeast*
 5 *oz* (150 *g*) *chilled milk*
 2 *oz* (60 *g*) *egg*
 6 *oz* (180 *g*) *tough butter or mixture of margarine*
 ⅛ *oz* (4 *g*) *cardomon spice*

Mixture of Margarine.

 2 *oz* (60 *g*) *pastry margarine*
 4 *oz* (120 *g*) *cake margarine*

 Blend well together.

Fillings.

 1. Mincemeat. *See* page 237.

 2. Almond Cream. Equal quantities of ground almonds, sugar, and butter.

 3. Cinnamon Cream. Equal quantities of butter and castor sugar flavoured with cinnamon spice.

 4. Custard. *See* page 199.

 5. Dried Fruit. Currants, sultanas, glacé cherries.

Toppings.

 1. Water Icing. *See* page 301.

 2. Apricot Glaze. *See* page 302.

 3. Sugar and Almond Nibs. Mix equal quantities.

 4. Almond Nibs.

(1) Sieve the flour and make a bay.

(2) Mix the yeast with the egg and milk and pour into the bay.

(3) Mix the dough *lightly. Do not toughen.*

(4) Roll out the dough to approx. 8 in. × 15 in. (20 cm × 37½ cm) and cover two-thirds with the margarine or butter.

(5) Fold the remaining one-third into the centre and fold the whole into three (as English method of making Puff Pastry).

(6) Proceed to give it three half-turns and lastly one fold over. If the dough is not tough, this should be accomplished with about 10 minutes rest between turns.

(7) Allow the dough to rest about 20 minutes and, using the fillings, make various varieties as described.

(8) Once the varieties have been made, give them the maximum proof in a slightly humid prover *but not hot*.

(9) Bake in a hot oven approx. 460°F (238°C).

(10) When baked and whilst still hot, brush over with rum-flavoured apricot glaze and water icing.

Note. The secret of making good Danish Pastry is to keep all the ingredients cool. To achieve this it is a good idea to store the flour etc. in the refrigerator prior to use.

Unlike puff pastry, the paste should not be too tough. It should be worked off as soon as possible, very well proved, and baked in a very hot oven. Only by observing these rules will a tender and flaky article be made.

Varieties. A great number of varieties of Danish Pastries may be made according to the imagination and ingenuity of the patissier, but a useful selection is shown in Figure 96. Here the pastries are as they should appear before being baked. For the purposes of the photographs, all these 12 varieties are placed on one baking tray but in practice only varieties of the same type should be baked together, i.e. 1, 2, 3, and 4, as in Figure 97. Some varieties, such as those dressed in nib almonds, require an oven about 20°F (11°C) cooler than that recommended; otherwise the almonds will take on too much colour.

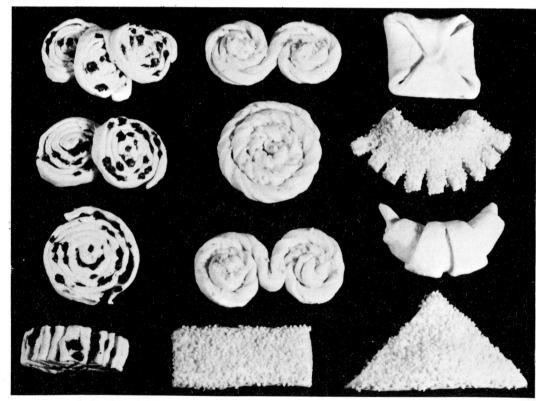

Figure 96. Varieties of Danish pastries prior to baking (*see* text)

1	5	9
2	6	10
3	7	11
4	8	12

Figure 97. Danish pastries: varieties 1–4 finished

Explanation of Varieties.
   Variety 1.
(1) Roll out the dough to approx. $\frac{3}{16}$ in. (4 mm) thick in a strip approx. 10 in. (25 cm) wide.
(2) Spread on some cinnamon cream and cover with currants.
(3) Roll up like a Swiss roll.
(4) Cut pieces approx. $\frac{3}{4}$ in. (2 cm) wide and make two cuts with the knife almost severing the roll into three pieces.
(5) Arrange the three pieces like a fan and lay them flat on the baking tray.
   Variety 2.
(1) Proceed as (1), (2), and (3) for Variety 1.
(2) Cut pieces approx. $\frac{3}{4}$ in. (2 cm) wide and make one cut with the knife almost severing the roll in two pieces.
(3) Arrange the two pieces like a fan and lay them flat on the baking tray.
   Variety 3.
(1) Proceed as (1), (2), and (3) for Variety 1, but pin out the dough into a wider strip of approx. 12 in. (30 cm).
(2) Cut into slices approx. $\frac{1}{2}$ in. ($1\frac{1}{4}$ cm) in thickness and lay them flat on the baking tray.
   Variety 4.
(1) Proceed as (1), (2), and (3) for Variety 1.
(2) Cut the rolled piece in half lengthwise.
(3) Cut this into slices approx. $\frac{3}{4}$ in. (2 cm) wide.
(4) Lay pieces on the tray with the cut surface showing.

Variety 5.

(1) Roll out the dough to approx. $\frac{1}{4}$ in. (6 mm) thick.

(2) Spread half with a thin layer of the almond cream and fold over to form a sandwich.

(3) Roll out this piece to a width of approx. 15 in. (37$\frac{1}{2}$ cm) at an approx. thickness of $\frac{1}{4}$ in. (6 mm).

(4) Cut this into strips of approx. $\frac{3}{8}$ in. (1 cm).

(5) Starting at each end of the strip and moving the hands in alternate directions, give a twist to the strip.

(6) Form the twisted strip into a figure S.

(7) Dress the top with a sprinkling of almond and sugar nib mixture.

Variety 6. Proceed as for the previous variety but forming the twisted strip into a circle.

Variety 7. Proceed as for the previous two varieties but forming the twisted strip into the shape illustrated.

Variety 8.

(1) Roll out the dough to approx. $\frac{1}{4}$ in. (6 mm) thick and into a strip approx. 3 in. (7$\frac{1}{2}$ cm) wide.

(2) Place some filling down the centre of the strip.

(3) Egg wash one edge, fold the other edge into the centre, and fold over the washed edge to overlap.

(4) Turn the whole strip over so that the seal is underneath.

(5) Cut into pieces approx. 3 in. (7$\frac{1}{2}$ cm) long.

(6) Egg wash and dip the pieces into nib almonds.

Variety 9.

(1) Roll out the dough to approx. $\frac{1}{4}$ in. (6 mm) and cut into squares approx. 4 in. (10 cm).

(2) Place a portion of custard filling in the centre of each square and fold the corners into the centre to form a cushion.

(3) Egg wash and place on the baking tray.

(4) When baked and glazed, a bulb of custard may be piped into the centre; alternatively a bulb of custard may be piped into the centre prior to baking.

Variety 10.

(1) Proceed as (1) and (2) for Variety 8.

(2) Egg wash one edge and fold over to enclose the filling.

(3) Press the edge well to thoroughly seal.

(4) With the end of a knife, make a series of cuts along the sealed edge at about $\frac{3}{8}$-in. (1-cm) intervals. Cut into 3 in. (7$\frac{1}{2}$ cm) lengths.

(5) Egg wash and dip into nibbed almonds.

(6) Arrange the piece like a crescent with the cut edges on the outside.

Variety 11.

(1) Roll out the dough approx. $\frac{3}{16}$ in. (4 mm) thick into a strip approx. 7 in. (18 cm) wide.

(2) Cut this strip into triangles with a base of approx. 3$\frac{1}{2}$ in. (9 cm).

(3) Cut a slit approx. 1$\frac{1}{2}$ in. (4 cm) long near the apex (point) end of the triangle and place some filling at the base end.

(4) Starting at the base end, roll up the triangle.
(5) Form a crescent by giving the piece a twist and place on the baking tray.
(6) Egg wash.
   Variety 12.
(1) Roll out the dough to a thickness of approx. $\frac{3}{16}$ in. (4 mm).
(2) Cut into squares of approx. 3 in. ($7\frac{1}{2}$ cm) sides.
(3) Place a portion of filling in the centre of each.
(4) Egg wash two edges and fold over to form a triangle. Press edges to seal.
(5) Egg wash and dip into nib almonds before placing on tray.

Brioche (Figure 98) (Yield 16–18)

> 9 *oz* (270 *g*) *strong flour*
> $\frac{1}{4}$ *oz* (7 *g*) *salt*
> 1 *oz* (30 *g*) *sugar*
> 5 *oz* (150 *g*) *eggs*   (*A*)
> 1 *oz* (30 *g*) *milk*
> 1 *oz* (30 *g*) *yeast*

    $2\frac{1}{2}$ *oz* (75 *g*) *butter* (*B*)
  B.T.F. 1 hour at 76°F (24°C).
(1) Disperse the yeast with the milk and make the ingredients of (*A*) into a well-beaten dough.
(2) Add the butter and beat well to form a silky, smooth toughened dough.
(3) Allow to ferment for 1 hour.
(4) Lightly grease some fluted patty pans.
(5) After the hour, divide the brioche dough into approx. 1-oz (30-g) pieces.
(6) Mould first round and then to a dumbell shape with the small end about half the size of the other.
(7) Place the longer bulbous end of the piece in the pan (Figure 98(*a*)).
(8) Keeping the small bulb suspended make a hole in the centre of the large bulb with the finger.
(9) Allow the small bulb to rest in this impression so that the shape now resembles a cottage loaf.
(10) Carefully wash over with egg.
(11) Allow to prove to double their size in a humid place (not too warm).
(12) Bake at approx. 460°F (238°C) for 10 minutes.
(13) Remove from the pan whilst still hot and transfer to cooling wires.

Croissants (Figure 99) (Yield 20)

> 10 *oz* (300 *g*) *flour*
> $\frac{1}{2}$ *oz* (15 *g*) *yeast*
> $\frac{1}{4}$ *oz* (8 *g*) *salt*   (*A*)
> 1 *oz* (30 *g*) *sugar*
> 7–8 *oz* (240 *g*) *milk*

    $4\frac{1}{2}$ *oz* (135 *g*) *tough butter or pastry margarine* (*B*)

Figure 98. Brioche: (*a*) placing the shaped pieces in the tins (*above*);
(*b*) finished brioche (*below*)

(1) Make the ingredients of (*A*) into a well-toughened dough.

(2) After allowing 30 minutes rest, roll out the dough to a rectangle approx. $\frac{1}{4}$ in. (6 mm) thick.

(3) Cover two-thirds of the dough with the butter and fold as in the English method of making puff pastry (*see* page 57).

(4) Proceed to give three half-turns allowing a rest period between each turn.

(5) Roll out the paste to approx. $\frac{1}{10}$ in. (2 mm) in thickness and cut into two strips 8–9 in. (20–23 cm) wide.

(6) Cut these into triangles as follows having a base of approx. 4–4$\frac{1}{2}$ in. (10–11 cm) (Figure 99(*b*)).

(7) Starting at the base, lightly shape the triangle into a crescent and lay on a clean baking sheet. Use up the paste shown in the shaded areas by adding a little to the centre of each croissant as it is being rolled.

(8) Egg wash thoroughly.

(9) Prove in a humid atmosphere to about double their original volume (not too warm).

(10) Bake at approx. 460°F (238°C) for approx. 10 minutes.

Note. This is a typical French pastry which is served with coffee for breakfast in many Continental countries.

Figure 99. Parisian croissants: (*a*) finished croissants (*above*); (*b*) showing how paste should be cut (*overleaf*)

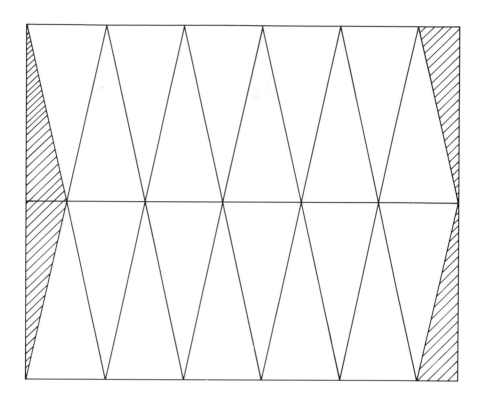

Savarins (Figure 100) (Yield two—each suitable for 8 covers in 7 in. or 18 cm mould)

Dough

    4 *oz* (120 *g*) *strong flour*

    3 *oz* (90 *g*) *eggs*

    $\frac{3}{8}$ *oz* (11 *g*) *yeast*

    $\frac{1}{2}$ *oz* (15 *g*) *water*

    $\frac{1}{8}$ *oz* (4 *g*) *sugar*

    2 *oz* (60 *g*) *melted butter*

Syrup

    4 *oz* (120 *g*) *sugar*

    8 *oz* (240 *g*) *water* (1 *oz water may be replaced by* 1 *oz liqueur. Other flavours and/or fruit juices may be used, e.g. lemon, orange, and cinnamon*)

(1) Make a dough at about 80°F (27°C) of all the ingredients except the butter. Beat well into a smooth and elastic dough.

(2) Allow the dough to lie for 30 minutes in a warm place (keep covered).

(3) Beat in the 2 oz (60 g) of melted butter, small quantities at a time.

(4) Grease or butter a savarin mould and into this pipe the savarin dough.

(5) Prove fully – to the top of the savarin mould.

(6) Bake at 450°F (232°C) for 20–25 minutes.

(7) Remove from the mould whilst still warm.

(8) When cold saturate with the syrup. If the savarin has been properly made it should absorb all this syrup. One recommended method is to pour the syrup into the savarin mould and replace the savarin. Leave until all the syrup has been absorbed, remove, and turn upside down onto a draining wire.

(9) Glaze with boiling apricot glaze.

(10) Fill centre with fruit.

(11) Decorate with fresh, sweetened cream (crème Chantilly).

(12) Serve on a flat dish.

Rum Baba – Baba au Rhum

Recipe same as for Savarins except that rum is used as the liqueur, and add:

    2 *oz* (60 g) *currants*

(1) Proceed as for savarins.

(2) When dough is ready, half fill eight greased dariole moulds and prove.

(3) Continue as for savarins.

(4) Serve without fruit but with crème Chantilly.

Croûtes (Yield 8 covers)

The base of croûtes is savarin which has been allowed to stale slightly. Since even slices of savarin are required, it is best to bake the savarin in a special round, circular tin or a charlotte mould.

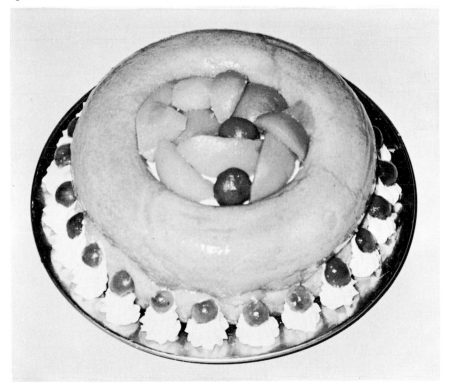

Figure 100. Savarin aux fruits

Fruit Croûtes – Croûtes aux Fruits

1 savarin cut into 8 slices
1 lb 6 oz (660 g) stewed assorted fruit
3½ oz (105 g) muscatel raisins (stoned)
8 oz (240 g) thick apricot sauce. (This may be flavoured with rum or kirsch)
Icing sugar

(1) Cut the savarin into eight slices approx. ½ in. (1¼ cm) thick and place on a clean baking tray.
(2) Dust the slices liberally with icing sugar and glaze in a very hot oven.
(3) Arrange the slices on a round, flat dish with every slice overlapping the other so as to form a crown.
(4) Add the fruit to the apricot sauce and fill the centre of the dish.
(5) Serve either hot or cold.

Pineapple Croûtes – Croûtes à l'Ananas (Yield 8 covers)

8 slices of savarin
8 slices of pineapple (large)
8 red cherries
3 oz (90 g) butter
½ pt (3 dl) apricot sauce (flavoured with kirsch)

(1) Fry the slices of savarin lightly in butter.
(2) Place a slice of cored pineapple on each and a red cherry in the centre of each.
(3) Arrange them as a crown on a flat round dish.
(4) Cover with hot apricot sauce.
(5) Serve hot or cold.

Apricot Croûtes – Croûtes aux Abricots

As for pineapple croûtes but using two apricot halves instead of one slice of pineapple. A red cherry is placed in the hollow of each apricot.

Croûtes Parisienne

As for Croûtes aux Fruits but using fruit salad instead. May be served hot or cold but, if served cold, it is usual to decorate it with fresh whipped cream.

14. Sweet Sauces

Custard (Yield ½ pint (3 decilitres) = 4–8 covers)

½ pt (3 dl) milk
½ oz (15 g) custard powder
1 oz (30 g) sugar
Vanilla essence

(1) Mix the custard powder with a little milk in a basin.
(2) Boil the remainder of the milk in a saucepan.
(3) Pour onto the custard powder continuously whisking.
(4) Return to the saucepan and bring to the boil stirring continuously. Flavour with vanilla.
(5) Lastly add the sugar.

Almond

½ pt (3 dl) milk
½ oz (15 g) cornflour
1 oz (30 g) sugar
½ oz (15 g) ground almonds or almond essence

(1) Mix the cornflour with a little milk.
(2) Boil the remainder of the milk in a saucepan.
(3) Pour onto the cornflour continuously whisking.
(4) Return to the saucepan and bring to the boil. If almonds are used, add at this stage.
(5) Boil for a few minutes.
(6) Lastly add the sugar.
(7) If a very smooth sauce is required pass it through a sieve.

Cold Custard Cream

3 egg yolks
2 oz (60 g) castor sugar
¼ pt (1½ dl) milk
¼ pt (1½ dl) cream
Vanilla essence

(1) Whisk the egg yolks with the sugar.
(2) Boil the milk and strain.
(3) Whisk onto the yolks and sugar.
(4) Stir over gentle heat until it is thick enough to coat the back of a spoon (*do not boil*). Add vanilla essence.
(5) Cool and fold in half whipped cream.

Chocolate – Chocolat

Recipe 1. Mix 2 oz (60 g) cocoa powder into a thin paste with water and add to the cold custard cream.

Recipe 2. Melt 4 oz (120 g) couverture and add to the custard whilst still warm and before the cream is folded in.

Recipe 3. Make a ganache with chocolate couverture and cream but add more cream until the desired consistency is reached (*see* page 250).

Recipe 4. Make an icing from chocolate and syrup recipe but thin it down to the desired consistency with cream (*see* page 249). If too sweet, adjust by replacing some or all of the couverture with unsweetened chocolate.

Recipe 5.

$\frac{1}{2}$ *pt* (3 *dl*) *milk*
1$\frac{1}{2}$ *oz* (45 *g*) *sugar*
$\frac{1}{4}$ *oz* (8 *g*) *butter*
$\frac{1}{2}$ *oz* (15 *g*) *cornflour*
1 *oz* (30 *g*) *unsweetened chocolate or* $\frac{1}{2}$ *oz* (15 *g*) *cocoa*

(1) Mix the cornflour with a little milk. If cocoa is used also add it here.
(2) Boil the rest of the milk and strain.
(3) Stir into the cornflour.
(4) Return to the saucepan and bring to the boil.
(5) Mix in the sugar and butter. If chocolate is used, shred and add it at this stage.

Coffee

Recipe 1. Mix 1 oz (30 g) soluble coffee powder to the cold custard cream.

Recipe 2. Replace the chocolate in Chocolate Sauce recipe 5 above with 1 oz (30 g) soluble coffee powder.

Fresh Egg Custard – Crème Anglaise

$\frac{1}{2}$ *pt* (3 *dl*) *milk*
2 *egg yolks*
1 *oz* (30 *g*) *castor sugar*
Vanilla essence

(1) Whisk the sugar and yolks in a basin.
(2) Boil the milk and stir it in.
(3) Return to the saucepan and place on low heat.
(4) Stir until it coats the back of a spoon (*do not boil*).
(5) Pass mixture through a fine strainer and add the vanilla essence.

Jam

Recipe 1.

8 *oz* (240 *g*) *jam*
3–4 *oz* (90–120 *g*) *water* (*according to consistency of jam*)

Boil the jam and water together and then strain. This mixture may be thickened with a little cornflour if desired.

Recipe 2.
      8 *oz* (240 *g*) *fruit pulp*
      8 *oz* (240 *g*) *sugar*
      2 *oz* (60 *g*) *glucose*
      2 *oz* (60 *g*) *water*
Bring to the boil and allow to simmer until correct consistency is reached.

Apricot

Same as for Jam Sauce using either apricot jam or pulped apricots. This sauce may be flavoured by the addition of kirsch, cognac, or rum.

Lemon

Recipe 1. Add the zest and juice of 1 lemon to the cold custard cream recipe (*see* page 199).
Recipe 2.
      ½ *pt* (3 *dl*) *water*
      2 *oz* (60 *g*) *sugar*
      ½ *oz* (15 *g*) *cornflour*
      1 *lemon* (*zest and juice*)
(1) Dilute the cornflour with a little water.
(2) Boil the rest of the water with the sugar.
(3) Add the diluted cornflour and stir continuously whilst it boils.
(4) Strain and add the zest and juice of the lemon.

Orange

Recipe 1. Add the zest and juice of 1 orange to the cold custard cream recipe (*see* page 199).
Recipe 2. Replace the lemon with orange in Lemon Sauce recipe 2 above.

Syrup

      8 *oz* (240 *g*) *golden syrup*
      ½ *pt* (3 *dl*) *water*
      ½ *oz* (15 *g*) *cornflour or arrowroot*
      1 *lemon* (*juice only*)
(1) Mix the cornflour with a little of the water.
(2) Boil the rest of the water with the syrup and lemon juice.
(3) Add the diluted cornflour, stir, and boil for a few minutes until it thickens.

Caramel

Add 4 oz caramel syrup (*see* page 121) to the cold custard cream. To facilitate perfect blending it may be necessary to warm the caramel with a little water first if the caramel is too thick.

Brandy or Rum

This is a special cold butter sauce to accompany Christmas pudding, etc.
Recipe 1.

> 9 *oz* (270 g) *butter*
> 5 *oz* (150 g) *icing sugar*
> 3½ *oz* (105 g) *brandy or rum*
> *A few drops of lemon juice*

(1) Cream together the butter and icing sugar until light and fluffy.
(2) Gradually beat in the spirit and lastly the lemon juice.
Recipe 2.

> ½ *pt* (3 *dl*) *milk*
> ½ *oz* (15 g) *butter*
> 1 *oz* (30 g) *sugar*
> ¾ *oz* (22 g) *cornflour*
> *Brandy or rum*

(1) Mix the cornflour with a little milk in a basin.
(2) Boil the remainder of the milk in a saucepan.
(3) Pour the boiling milk onto the diluted cornflour and stir until it thickens.
(4) Return to the heat and allow to boil for a few minutes.
(5) Stir in the sugar and butter.
(6) Remove from the heat and add the spirit to taste.

Liqueur

Any liqueur flavoured sauce can be made by adding an appropriate
quantity of liqueur to the cold custard cream recipe. For example, Maraschino
Sauce – Maraschino liqueur added to the cold custard sauce (*see* page 199).

Thickened Syrups

The juice of stewed fruits or tins of fruit may be made into an acceptable
sauce by thickening it with a little cornflour or arrowroot. Liqueur or spirits
may also be added to improve the taste. Colour may also be added to
enhance the appearance.

Chantilly

> 1 *pt* (6 *dl*) *fresh cream*
> 2 *oz* (60 g) *castor sugar*
> *Flavouring*

(1) Keep the cream cold.
(2) Whisk with the sugar to the correct consistency (*do not over-beat*).
Notes.

1. *See* details on fresh cream (page 18).
2. For sauces, only half whip the cream so that there is a degree of flow
remaining.
3. For decoration, whisk until stiff enough to be piped.

Melba

Recipe 1.

    1 *lb* (480 g) *raspberry jam*
    $\frac{1}{4}$ *pt* (1$\frac{1}{2}$ *dl*) *water*

Boil together and strain. Add red colour if necessary.

Recipe 2.

    1 *lb* (480 g) *raspberry pulp or sieved fresh raspberries*
    $\frac{1}{2}$ *lb* (240 g) *icing sugar*
    Half a lemon (*juice only*)

Mix well together. Add red colour if necessary.

Recipe 3.

    $\frac{1}{2}$ *lb* (240 g) *raspberry pulp*
    $\frac{1}{2}$ *lb* (240 g) *strawberry pulp*
    $\frac{1}{2}$ *lb* (240 g) *red currant pulp*
    1 *lemon* (*juice only*)
    Stock syrup

Mix the pulps and lemon juice together. Add stock syrup (*see* page 265) until correct consistency is reached. Add red colour if necessary.

Cardinal Sauce

Same as Melba Sauce.

Mousseline

    5 *oz* (150 g) *sugar*
    4 *oz* (120 g) *water*
    6 *egg yolks*
    1 *pt* (6 *dl*) *cream*
    Vanilla essence

(1) Boil the sugar and water, skim, and strain.

(2) Pour over the egg yolks.

(3) Transfer to a bain-marie and, continually stirring, gently heat until mixture becomes like thick cream (scrape sides constantly). Add vanilla essence.

(4) Remove from heat and vigorously whisk until cold.

(5) Partly whip the cream and blend in.

Liqueur Mousseline

Add liqueur to taste. The mousseline sauce may now take the name of the added liqueur, e.g. Sauce Mousseline au Kirsch, etc.

Wine Mousseline

Use $\frac{1}{4}$ pint (1$\frac{1}{2}$ decilitres) wine instead of water. For very dry wines like Burgundy an extra 1 oz (30 g) of sugar should be added.

Fruit Mousseline

Add 4 oz (120 g) of the designated fruit pulp, e.g. raspberry, strawberry, etc. A little lemon juice should also be used.

Lemon Mousseline

Add ¼ pint (1½ decilitres) lemon juice instead of water and. the zest of one lemon. Increase the sugar to 8 oz (240 g).

Orange Mousseline

Add ¼ pint (1½ decilitres) orange juice instead of water and the zest of one orange.

Praline Mousseline

Add 4 oz (120 g) praline paste.

Sabayon

> 6 *oz* (180 *g*) *castor sugar*
> 6 *egg yolks*
> ½ *pt* (3 *dl*) *white wine*
> ½ *lemon* (*juice only*)

(1) Mix the ingredients together.
(2) Whisk in a bain-marie over gentle heat until a thick creamy consistency is reached (*do not boil*).
Note. The sabayon may be named after the type of wine used, e.g. Sabayon Marsala.

Liqueur Sabayon

Increase egg yolks to 8 and add 2 oz (60 g) of the desired liqueur.

Lemon Sabayon

Increase egg yolks to 8 and add ¼ pint (1½ decilitres) of lemon juice (instead of juice of ½ lemon) and the grated zest of one lemon.

Orange Sabayon

Same as Lemon Sabayon substituting oranges.

15. Bavarois and Jelly Sweets

Charlotte Russe (Figures 101 and 102) (Yield 1 for 8 covers)

Half Bavarois Recipe (see page 208).
24 (approx.) sponge fingers (see page 79)
(1) Line a charlotte mould with sponge fingers, trimming them where necessary to make a flower-like design on the base, and a number set vertically for the sides, with the sugar-coated side of the finger against the metal.
(2) Make a bavarois and fill to the level of the mould.
(3) Set aside in a cool place to set.
(4) Trim the edge and turn the mould out into a silver flat dish from which it is served.

Charlotte Royal (Figures 101 and 103) (Yield 1 for 8 covers)

Half Bavarois Recipe (see page 208)
6 small Swiss rolls (see page 76)
(1) Line a charlotte mould with small Swiss rolls cut into thin slices $\frac{3}{8}$ in. (1 cm) thick. Arrange the slices neatly so that the complete tin is lined.
(2) Make a bavarois and fill to the level of the mould.
(3) Set aside in a cool place to set.
(4) Trim the edge and turn out onto a silver flat dish from which it is served.
Note. An alternative method, giving the charlotte a glazed finish, is often favoured by practising patissiers.

The mould is first lined with jelly on which the Swiss rolls are set. These rolls may be dipped into jelly and applied to the sides of the mould for speedy commercial finishes. To remove the charlotte the mould would need to be momentarily placed into hot water and then it may be turned out onto pre-set jelly on a silver dish.

Charlotte de Fraises à la Royale

Same as Charlotte Royal except that the bavarois has the addition of strawberries and the charlotte is served with fresh strawberries and whipped fresh cream.

Charlotte de Fraises à la Mode

Same as Charlotte Russe, except that a liqueur jelly is used to line the bottom of the mould. Strawberries and whipped fresh cream are also served.

Charlotte Andalouse

Same as Charlotte Russe, except that an orange bavarois is used and served with glazed oranges and whipped fresh cream.

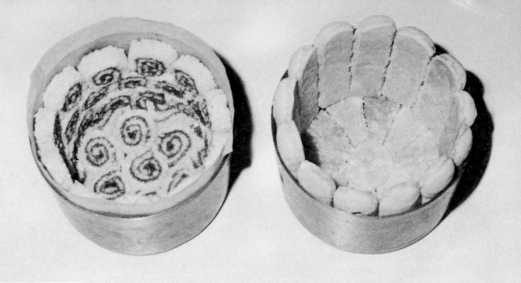

Figure 101. Charlottes lined ready for the bavarois filling: (*left*) Charlotte
Royale; (*right*) Charlotte Russe

Charlotte Muscovite

Same as Charlotte de Fraises à la Mode, except that a vanilla bavarois
and a raspberry jelly are used to line the bottom of the mould.

Other Varieties

Other Charlottes may be made by using other fruits and jellies for the
top instead of sponge fingers.

Lemon Jelly – Gelée Citron (Yield 8 covers)

> 1 *qt* (12 *dl*) *water*
> 4 *oz* (120 *g*) *sugar*
> 2 *oz* (60 *g*) *gelatine*
> 2 *oz* (60 *g*) *egg whites*
> *Zest and juice of* 2 *lemons*

Figure 102. Charlotte Russe

(1) Place all the ingredients in a saucepan and bring to the boil.
(2) Once it starts to boil, remove and allow to rest for $\frac{1}{2}$ hour in a hot place, keeping it well covered.
(3) Strain through a fine cloth or filter.
(4) Fill into moulds.
(5) When jelly has set turn out of mould by first placing it momentarily in hot water.
Note. Any fruit jelly may be prepared in the same way as lemon jelly, replacing the lemon with the fruit required. This may be an extract with the addition of colouring matter.

Liqueur Jelly – Gelée Liqueurs

Add to the jelly the required liqueur and colour appropriately.

Russian Jelly – Gelée Moscovite

Beat cold jelly to a white froth and immediately fill the mould.

Ribboned Jelly – Gelée Rubanée

Lemon Jelly
Orange Jelly
Russian Jelly

(1) Prepare each of the above jellies.
(2) One-third fill the mould with Russian jelly.
(3) When this has set fill to two-thirds with the orange jelly and allow to set.
(4) Lastly add the lemon jelly.
(5) When cold and set it is ready to serve.

Figure 103. Charlotte Royal

Bavarois (Yield sufficient to fill one 1-quart charlotte mould (8 covers) or two 1-quart Charlotte Russe, etc.)

    8 *oz* (240 *g*) *milk*
    2 *oz* (60 *g*) *eggs*
    ½ *oz* (15 *g*) *gelatine sheets* (*approx.* 3)
    1¾ *oz* (52 *g*) *sugar*
    8 *oz* (240 *g*) *cream*

(1) Cream the egg yolks with the sugar.
(2) Boil the milk and whisk into the egg and sugar cream.
(3) Replace on low heat and stir till it thickens (*do not boil*).
(4) Remove from the heat and stir in the gelatine which has been previously soaked in cold water. Continue to stir until the gelatine has dissolved.
(5) Strain and cool the mixture until it reaches the consistency of half whipped cream (almost setting).
(6) Half whip the cream and fold it into the custard until clear.
(7) Beat the whites to a stiff snow and carefully fold in.
(8) Fill the mould, which may be slightly greased, and then chill.
(9) Remove from mould by shaking and serve on a flat silver dish. The bavarois may be served with cream Chantilly.

Vanilla Bavarois – Bavarois Vanillé

To the basic recipe add either vanilla essence or extract or immerse a vanilla pod in the boiling custard. Decorate with vanilla flavoured cream.

Chocolate Bavarois – Bavarois au Chocolat

Add 2 oz (60 g) melted chocolate to the basic recipe, blending it into the custard. Use chocolate pieces or vermicelli in the decoration.

Coffee Bavarois – Bavarois au Café

Essence, extract, or instant coffee is added to the basic recipe to taste.

Orange Bavarois – Bavarois à l'Orange

To the basic recipe add orange flavour and colour. Decorate with orange zest, orange segments, and cream Chantilly.

Strawberry Bavarois – Bavarois aux Fraises

Raspberry Bavarois – Bavarois aux Framboises

To the basic recipe add 8 oz (240 g) washed, picked, and sieved fruit (purée). Reduce milk content to 6 oz (180 g).

The fruit purée should be added when the custard is nearly cool and before the cream is blended in. Decorate, using whole fruit and cream Chantilly.

Junket (Yield 8 covers)

> *2 pt (12 dl) milk*
> *1 oz (30 g) sugar*
> *2 teaspoonsful rennet*
> *Grated nutmeg*
> *Colour and flavour*

(1) Warm the milk with the sugar to blood heat.
(2) Add any desired flavour and colour.
(3) Add the rennet and stir gently.
(4) Pour into individual dishes or serving dish.
(5) Leave in a warm room to set.
(6) Sprinkle with grated nutmeg.
(7) Serve on a doily on a flat silver dish.
  These may be decorated with a whirl of whipped, fresh cream if desired.

16. Fruit and Other Sweets

Fruit Sherry Trifle (Yield 8 covers)

Half of basic recipe for sponge or Swiss roll (see page 76)
12 oz (360 g) tinned fruit (or one E.1 tin)
1 oz (30 g) jam
1 oz (30 g) cooking sherry
1 pt (6 dl) custard (see page 199)

(1) If a plain sponge has been used, sandwich with jam.
(2) Cut into 1-in. ($2\frac{1}{2}$-cm) cubes and place half of these in the bottom of a glass bowl.
(3) Soak this sponge with the fruit juice to which the sherry has been added. It is best to add the sherry to about half the juice from the tin of fruit, initially. If more soaking is necessary, the rest of the juice may be used. If fresh fruit is used, e.g. strawberries, use a flavoured syrup for soaking purposes.
(4) Dice the fruit and lay half the quantity prescribed on the sponge layer.
(5) Repeat operations (2), (3) and (4).
(6) Make the custard and pour onto the layers of sponge and fruit.
(7) When the custard is cold, whip the sweetened cream and cover the custard.
(8) Put the remaining cream into a savoy bag with a star tube and decorate the top.
(9) Finish the decoration with cherries, angelica, or chocolate pieces.

Fresh Fruit Salad

Before fresh fruit salad is prepared, make sure that the equipment used (knives, chopping board, etc.) is absolutely free from any odours left by vegetables (especially onions) which have been prepared previously using the same equipment. The chopping board must be especially clean and free from odour. It is very difficult to eradicate odours from wood even after repeated cleaning and these are easily picked up by the fruit. The best solution is to keep a chopping board exclusively for the purpose of chopping fruit and not allow its use for anything else.

Any fresh fruit may be used in a fruit salad but usually a selection from the following list is made: oranges, bananas, dessert pears, dessert apples, melon, grapes, peaches, apricots, pineapple, cherries, strawberries, and raspberries.

Approximately $\frac{1}{4}$ lb (120 g) of unprepared fruit should be allowed per portion.

Basic quantities for 8 covers

2 *bananas*	4 *oz* (120 *g*) *cherries*
2 *oranges*	4 *oz* (120 *g*) *grapes*
2 *dessert pears*	*Juice of* 1 *lemon* (*omit if liqueur is used*)
2 *dessert apples*	4 *oz* (120 *g*) *sugar*

4 *oz* (120 *g*) *fruit liqueur or sherry* (*optional*)
or 4 *oz* (120 *g*) *water or fruit juice*

(1) Boil the water with the sugar and add the lemon juice. Place aside to cool preferably in the refrigerator.

(2) Prepare the fruit by removing peel, stones, pips, core, etc., and cut up into either slices (Salade des Fruits) or dices (Macédoine des Fruits). Start preparing the hard fruits such as apples first so that they have a chance to soften in the syrup. Prepare bananas last so that the risk of browning is kept to the minimum.

(3) Carefully mix the fruit with the syrup.

(4) Chill in the refrigerator.

(5) Place mixture in a bowl on a flat silver dish with a doily to serve.

Alternative Method

(1) As operation (2) above.

(2) Place the fruit in layers in the bowl and sprinkle each layer with sugar and liqueur.

(3) As operations (4) and (5) above.

Note. If liqueur or sherry is used, it is best to use the alternative method. In this case the lemon juice should be omitted as its use would mask the flavour of the liqueur or sherry used.

FRUIT CONDÉ

A condé consists of poached or tinned fruit placed on a bed of a rice pudding mixture and glazed. Many different types of fruits could be used but the most popular are pears, bananas, pineapple, peaches, and apricots. The following recipe is for pears.

Pear Condé – Poire Condé (Yield 8 covers)

2 *pt* (12 *dl*) *milk into rice condé* (*see page* 227)
4 *dessert pears*
8 *oz* (240 *g*) *apricot glaze*
Cherries (*for decoration*)
Angelica (*for decoration*)

(1) Make a rice condé mixture.

(2) Allow the rice to cool and place neatly in a bowl or silver flat dish or in individual coupes. The rice may be moulded and shaped if desired.

(3) If fresh pears are used, peel, core, halve, and poach, and then leave to cool before using.

(4) Drain the pears of juice and carefully arrange them on top of the rice.
(5) Coat with apricot glaze.
(6) Decorate with cherries and angelica.

Poached Fruits – Compote de Fruits

Preparation of Fruit.
Apples and pears. Peel, remove core, and cut into quarters or halves.
Stoned Fruits, Gooseberries, Black Currants, and Red Currants. Wash the fruit and remove stalks and blemishes. Add extra sugar if necessary.
Rhubarb. Cut off the stalk and leaf and wash. Cut into $1\frac{1}{2}$-in. (4-cm) lengths. Add extra sugar if necessary.
Dried Fruits. These should be washed and allowed to soak in cold water overnight. Cook the fruit gently in its own liquor adding sufficient sugar to taste. Some lemon juice may be added for additional flavour.
Soft Fruits (strawberries, loganberries, raspberries).
(1) Pick and wash the fruit.
(2) Transfer to a glass bowl.
(3) Pour over a hot syrup.
(4) Cool and serve as previously described.
Note. Compotes may be served with various sauces, e.g. custard, mousseline, or ice-cream. They may also be flavoured with liqueurs, etc.

Compote de Fruits (Yield 8 covers)

> 2 *lb* (960 g) *fruit*
> 1 *pt* (6 *dl*) *stock syrup* (*see below*)
> *Added sugar to taste*
> *Lemon juice*

(1) Place the fruit in a shallow dish with the syrup. The size of the dish should be such that the syrup just covers the fruit.
(2) Add a few drops of lemon juice.
(3) Cover with a sheet of greaseproof paper.
(4) Place in a cool oven to simmer slowly until fruit is soft.
(5) Transfer fruit and juice into a glass bowl and serve on a doily on a flat silver dish.

Note. The amount of sugar used in the stock syrup will depend upon the sweetness of the fruit used but for dessert fruit this will rarely need to exceed 50 per cent.

Fruit Fool (Yield 8 covers)

A. (Apple, Plum, Rhubárb, Gooseberry, Banana, etc.).

> 2 *lb* (960 g) *fruit* ⎫
> 8 *oz* (240 g) *sugar* ⎬ Purée
> $\frac{1}{4}$ *pt* ($1\frac{1}{2}$ *dl*) *water* ⎭
> 1 *pt* (6 *dl*) *milk*
> 2 *oz* (60 g) *sugar*
> 2 *oz* (60 g) *cornflour*

(1) Cook the fruit, water, and sugar to a pulp and pass it through a sieve to form a purée.
(2) Add a little milk to the cornflour and sugar.
(3) Boil the remainder of the milk.
(4) Pour boiling milk onto diluted cornflour and stir well.
(5) Return mixture to the saucepan and, on a low heat, stir until it boils.
(6) Mix this with the fruit purée.
(7) Pour mixture into eight coupés and allow to set.
(8) Using sweetened fresh cream, decorate with a rosette and serve.

B. *(Strawberries, Loganberries, Raspberries, and Bananas)*.
   2 lb (960 g) fruit
   8 oz (240 g) sugar
   1 pt (6 dl) whipped fresh cream
(1) Wash the fruit and pass it through a sieve to make a purée.
(2) Add the sugar and the whipped cream.
(3) Transfer to eight coupés and serve.

Baked Apple – Pomme Bonne Femme (Yield 8 covers)

   8 medium-sized apples
   4 oz (120 g) sugar
   2 oz (60 g) butter
   8 cloves
   $\frac{1}{4}$ *pt* $(1\frac{1}{2}$ *dl) water*

(1) Wash and core the apples and make an incision about $\frac{1}{16}$ in. $(1\frac{1}{2}$ mm) round the apple about one-third of the way down.
(2) Place apples in a roasting tin.
(3) Fill the core hole with sugar, add a clove and a $\frac{1}{4}$ oz (8 g) knob of butter.
(4) Add the water.
(5) Bake in an oven at approx. 350°F (177°C) until soft. Time of baking will depend upon the size of apple but it should take about 30–40 minutes. The apples may first be placed into the oven upside down without the sugar. After 20 minutes cooking they may be turned over, the sugar added, and baking completed.
(6) Serve on a hot, flat silver dish with a little of the syrup and an appropriate sauce served separately. The sauce may be custard, honey, or cream.

Stuffed Baked Apple

As for Baked Apple except that the centre is filled with washed sultanas.

Apple Meringues

These are baked apples which have been covered with Italian meringue, flashed off in a hot oven, and served on either a bed of rice, a sheet of genoese, or puff pastry.
(1) Bake the apples as described above.
(2) Meanwhile prepare a suitable base.

(3) Once cooked, transfer the apples to the prepared base on a flat silver dish.

(4) Cover the apples with Italian meringue with the aid of a savoy tube fitted with a star tube.

(5) Return to a very hot oven to colour.

(6) Serve with an appropriate sauce.

Apple Charlotte – Charlotte aux Pommes (Yield 8 covers)

> 2 *lb* (960 *g*) *stale bread*
> 2 *lb* (960 *g*) *apples* (*preferably dessert*)
> 6 *oz* (180 *g*) *sugar*
> 8 *oz* (240 *g*) *butter or margarine*
> *Grated rind of lemon or a clove*

(1) Recipe will fill either two small charlottes or eight dariole moulds.

(2) Peel, core, and wash the apples. Cut into fairly thick slices and place in the pan with about ¾ oz (22 g) butter, the sugar, and the lemon rind or clove.

(3) Do not add any water. Simmer apples gently until barely cooked.

(4) Cut the bread into slices approx. ¼ in. (6 mm) thick and remove the crusts.

(5) Cut out circles of bread, one to fit the top and one to fit the bottom of the moulds.

(6) Melt the butter or margarine and dip one side of the rounds which have been cut for the base. Place these rounds fat-side down in the moulds.

(7) Cut the remaining bread slices into fingers 1–1½ in. (2½–3½ cm) wide. Dip each in the melted fat and place them vertically around the inside of the mould, so that they overlap without leaving any gaps.

(8) Fill the centre of the mould with the cooked apple, after removing any lemon rind or cloves which have been added.

(9) Cover with the round of bread cut for the top.

(10) Bake in an oven at approx. 450°F (232°C) for 35–45 minutes, until the bread lining is brown and crisp.

(11) Allow to cool slightly before turning out.

(12) Carefully turn out onto a hot, flat silver dish and serve with a sauce-boat of apricot sauce.

Notes.

1. Dessert apples will produce a more stable purée than that obtained from cooking apples. If the apples used make a thin purée when cooked, it may be stiffened by adding bread-crumbs.

2. The base may be cut into the required portions before being placed in the mould.

3. One common fault with this sweet is that it readily collapses. The main cause of this is that the bread case is not firm enough to withstand the pressure exerted upon it by the apple filling. To overcome this fault observe the following:

(*a*) Use small moulds, i.e. two small charlotte moulds rather than one large.

(*b*) Bake the bread very crisp.

(*c*) Do not overcook the apple filling and keep it as stiff as possible by not adding water and if necessary adding some bread-crumbs. Also use dessert apples.

Apple Snow (Yield 8 covers)

>| | |
>|---|---|
>| 2 *lb* (960 *g*) *apples* | 2 *oz* (60 *g*) *water* |
>| 4 *oz* (120 *g*) *sugar* | 4 *whites of eggs* |
>| *Lemon rind* | 8 *savoy fingers* (*see page* 79) |

(1) Peel, core, and slice the apples.

(2) Rinse and place in a pan with a strip of lemon rind, water, and sugar.

(3) Cook until soft and then pass through a sieve to make a purée.

(4) Whip the egg white until stiff and gradually add them to the purée. Continue whisking till white and stiff. It may be coloured if desired.

(5) Fill into champagne glasses (old-fashioned saucer type). Chill and serve with a savoy finger.

Alternative Variety.

>*Sponge cakes* (*see page* 76)
>1 *pt* (6 *dl*) *milk into custard* (*see page* 199)
>*Cherries and angelica* (*for decoration*)

(1) Place sponge cakes in the bottom of a deep dish.

(2) Make up the custard and whilst hot pour over the sponges.

(3) Make up the apple snow and pour it over the custard.

(4) Decorate with cherries and angelica.

(5) Serve cold.

Note. Sponge cakes may be soaked in fruit juice or a flavoured syrup before placing them into the dish.

FLAMBÉ FRUITS

Only hard fruits such as pears, apricots, peaches, pineapple, bananas, etc., can be used for this process. Tinned fruit may be used. Fresh fruits such as pears need to be poached in syrup first to soften them.

Peaches or Pears Flambé – Pêches/Poires Flambées   (Yield 8 covers)

>8 *half peaches or pears*
>3 *oz* (90 *g*) *stock syrup* (50 *per cent sugar*)
>2 *oz* (60 *g*) *liqueur or spirit* (*Kirsch, Benedictine, rum, etc.*)
>*Icing sugar*
>8 *oz* (240 *g*) *apricot or strawberry purée* (*for sauce added to liquor*) (*optional*)

(1) In the dining room place a copper pan on a flambé réchaud. Pour in the syrup and allow to boil.

(2) Heat the fruit in this syrup for a few minutes.
(3) Sprinkle on a little icing sugar.
(4) Warm the liqueur, pour over, and ignite.
(5) Serve immediately with the liquor.

Bananas Flambé – Bananes Flambées (Yield 8 covers)

> 8 *bananas*
> 1 *orange (juice only)*
> 2 *oz (60 g) butter*
> 3 *oz (90 g) sugar*
> 3 *oz (90 g) rum*
> 8 *oz (240 g) apricot purée*
> 1½ *oz (45 g) nibbed roast almonds (for decoration)*

(1) Split the bananas lengthwise on a serviette.
(2) Put the orange juice, butter, and purée in the pan and bring to the boil.
(3) Proceed the same as for Peaches Flambé.

This sweet may take the name of the liqueur used; thus with Pêches Flambées à la Benedictine, Benedictine has been used.

FRUIT SWEETS WITH ICE-CREAM

A very wide variety of fruit sweets may be made in combination with ice-cream, sometimes using a tampion of sponge (thin base, round or shaped) and covering with an appropriate sauce, e.g. Melba, mousseline, Chantilly cream, etc.

The basic method of preparation is as follows:
(1) Place a slice of ice-cream on the plate.
(2) Cover with the fruit (which could be flambé).
(3) Mask with a suitable sauce.
(4) Decorate using glacé fruit, violets, nuts with or without Chantilly cream.
Variations to the method described above are described on page 219.

These sweets may either be individually prepared on plates, etc. or more usually several portions, e.g. eight, are assembled in a large dish or timbale and suitably decorated.

Yields

Fruit. Allow ½ pear, peach, etc., or ¼ lb (120 g) raspberries, strawberries, etc., per portion.
Ice-cream. Allow 1½ pints (9 decilitres) for eight portions.
Sauce. Allow ¾ pint (4½ decilitres) for eight portions.

Names of Sweets

A summary of the names of some of these sweets is given here. The name of the fruit follows the name of the sweet. For example, if peaches are served under the name Hélène, the sweet becomes known as Pêches Hélène.

Name	*Ice-cream*	*Sauce*	*Decoration*
Adeline	Chocolate	Mousseline	Whipped cream, langues du chat, and violets
Aïda	Strawberry	—	Whipped cream and crystallized violets
Alma	Vanilla	Port mousseline	Grated chocolate
Almina	Coffee	Noyeau flavoured apricot	Chantilly mixed with praline paste
Alphonse	Pistachio	Mousseline	Whipped cream and strawberries
Arlésienne	Vanilla	Kirsch flavoured apricot	Whipped cream, cherries, and angelica
Balmoral	Hazelnut	Chocolate	Chantilly
Beatrice	Hazelnut	Melba	Shredded walnuts
Beauregard	Pistachio	Maraschino flavoured apricot	Whipped cream and violets
Bohémienne	Chocolate	—	Chantilly cream and pistachio nuts
Calvé	Strawberry	Kirsch mousseline	Crystallized roses
Demi Deuil	Vanilla	Chocolate and Chantilly	Whipped cream
Donna Sol	Vanilla	Orange mousseline	Crystallized violets
Edna	Chocolate	Apricot	Whipped cream and pistachio nuts
Ethel	Vanilla	Pistachio mousseline	Red currant jelly and crystallized violets
Fémina	Orange	Grand Marnier liqueur	—
Frascati	Almond	Strawberry	Shredded walnuts. Serve cream separately
Frou-frou	Pistachio	Apricot	Whipped cream and almond finger biscuits

Name	Ice-cream	Sauce	Decoration
Grand-maison	Vanilla	Raspberry mousseline	Glacé pineapple, grated chocolate, and praline nuts
Hélène	Vanilla	Hot chocolate sauce served separately	Whipped cream
Herman	Raspberry	Kirsch flavoured Chantilly	Red currant jelly and crystallized violets
Hilda	Raspberry	Kirsch mousseline	Strawberries
Hortancier	Vanilla	Apricot	Whipped cream and strawberries
Ilka	Apricot	Chantilly	Chocolate shavings and pistachio nuts
Madeleine	Orange	Curaçao mousseline	Orange quarters
Margaret	Lemon	Raspberry mousseline	Whipped cream and strawberries
Marquise	Apricot	Chantilly	Chocolate shavings
Mauresque	Chocolate	Chocolate	Petit chou
Melba	Vanilla	Melba	Whipped cream
Mezerdoff	Vanilla	Raspberry	Whipped cream
Mireille	Raspberry	Melba	Whipped cream and cherries
Montpensier	Coffee	Raspberry	Whipped cream and crystallized roses
Niçoise	Orange	Curaçao mousseline	Strawberries and orange quarters
Niniche	Praline	Maraschino Chantilly	Whipped cream and petit chou
Ninon	Raspberry	Chantilly	Crystallized violets
Orientale	Vanilla	Melba	Whipped cream and spun sugar
Orléans	Vanilla	Red currant	Kirsch Chantilly and broken marron glacé
Parisienne	Praline	Strawberry mousseline	Whipped cream and crystallized violets
Petit Duc	Lemon	Red currant	Whipped cream
Pompadour	Vanilla	Pistachio mousseline	Whipped cream and violets
Princesse Louise	Pineapple	Apricot	Whipped cream and roasted nib almonds

Name	Ice-cream	Sauce	Decoration
Princesse Olga	Apricot	Kummel mousseline	Whipped cream and crystallized violets
Printanière	Vanilla	Pistachio mousseline	Whipped cream, strawberries, and crystallized violets
Régence	Apricot	Kirsch flavoured Chantilly	Whipped cream and grated chocolate
Sarah Bernhardt	Pineapple	Curaçao mousseline	Whipped cream and crystallized violets
Savoy	Coffee praline	Anisette mousseline	Crystallized violets
Stanley	Vanilla	Chantilly	Whipped cream and grated chocolate
Sultane	Pistachio	Maraschino apricot	Glacé pineapple
Tetrazzini	Pineapple	Kirsch flavoured apricot mousseline	Whipped cream flavoured praline
Toscane	Coffee praline	Chantilly	Meringue mushroom and chocolate shavings

Other Varieties

Chantecler. Place fruit on a piece of sponge sprinkled with kirsch. Cover with kirsch-flavoured apricot sauce and then portions of vanilla ice-cream. Decorate with whipped cream and crystallized violets.

Diplomate. Place fruit on a piece of sponge. Cover with brandy mousseline. Add portions of vanilla ice-cream. Decorate with orange quarters and violets.

Rivièra. Place fruit in a dish or timbale and cover with Melba sauce. Add portions of vanilla ice-cream. Decorate with crystallized violets.

Tyrolienne. Place vanilla ice-cream on chocolate sponge. Place fruit and cover with vanilla mousseline. Decorate with whipped cream glacé.

USE OF PEEL

The peel or outside shell of some fruits may be used with advantage in the preparation of some sweets. These fruits are: lemons, oranges, grapefruit, melon, and pineapple.

Grapefruit Florida – Pamplemousse Florida (Yield 8 covers)

   4 *large grapefruit*
   3 *oranges*
   6 *oz* (180 *g*) *stoned cherries*
   6 *oz* (180 *g*) *small strawberries or diced pineapple*
   3 *oz* (90 *g*) *cooking sherry*
   4 *oz* (120 *g*) *sugar*
   Glacé cherries (for decoration)
(1) Cut the grapefruit into two, horizontally.
(2) Cut out the segments, remove the skin, and mix with the skinned orange segments and other fruit.
(3) Macerate the mixed fruit in sugar and sherry and chill.
(4) Fill the grapefruit shells.
(5) Decorate with a glacé cherry.
(6) Serve very cold.
   This is served as an hors d'oeuvre.

Frosted Lemons (Yield 8 covers)

   8 *lemons*
   1½ *pt* (9 *dl*) *lemon ice (see page* 308)
   Angelica (for decoration)
(1) Cut the lemon lengthwise about one-third of the way down.
(2) Carefully remove the pulp and clean out the lemon shells.
(3) Use part of the lemon pulp to make lemon ice.
(4) Fill the larger shells with the ice and place the other shells on top.
(5) Sprinkle with water and allow to freeze so that a frost appears.
(6) Decorate with a piece of angelica and serve immediately.

Frosted Oranges

   Same as above, substituting oranges for lemons.

Orange or Tangerine Surprise (Yield 8 covers)

   8 *large oranges*
   1 *pt* (6 *dl*) *orange ice (see page* 308)
   8 *oz* (240 *g*) *Italian meringue (see page* 86)
(1) Cut off the top of the orange about one-quarter of the way down to form a top.
(2) Carefully remove all the pulp and clean the inside of the shell.
(3) Use part of the orange pulp to make the orange ice.
(4) Place the larger shells on crushed ice and fill with the orange ice.
(5) Mask with Italian meringue and flash off in a hot oven at 480°F (250°C) to colour.

(6) Dress on a napkin and serve immediately.

Other varieties may be made with different flavoured ice-creams with diced orange segments and masked with Chantilly cream.

Melon Majestic (Yield 8 covers)

> 1 *ripe cantaloup melon*
> 1¼ *lb (600 g) small strawberries*
> ¼ *pt (1½ dl) Chantilly cream*
> 2 *oz (60 g) Kirsch liqueur*
> *Chocolate curls or rolls (for decoration)*

(1) Cut the melon a quarter of the way from the top.

(2) Remove the centre seeds and liquid.

(3) Carefully scoop out the flesh without damaging the shell.

(4) Make the flesh into water ice (page 308, but substituting melon).

(5) Macerate the strawberries in a little sugar and the kirsch liqueur and chill.

(6) Place the larger shell of the melon in a dish of crushed ice.

(7) Fill with the melon ice.

(8) Arrange the strawberries on top.

(9) Decorate with Chantilly cream and chocolate rolls. Lightly dust with icing sugar.

Pineapple à la Ninon – Ananas à la Ninon (Yield 8 covers)

> 1 *large pineapple*
> 18 *oz (540 g) wild strawberries*
> 4 *bananas*
> ½ *pt (3 dl) whipped cream*
> ¾ *pt (4½ dl) raspberry sauce (Melba, see page 203)*
> 8 *boats made from almond sweetpaste (see page 148)*

(1) Cut off the top of the pineapple.

(2) With a knife, cut out the flesh of the pineapple without damaging the shell and keeping the flesh in a whole piece.

(3) Cut the flesh into thin slices and remove the centre core with an apple corer.

(4) Macerate the pineapple slices in sugar and kirsch and likewise the strawberries and sliced banana. Chill well.

(5) Place the pineapple shell on a round dish and half fill with the strawberries and sliced banana.

(6) Place the pineapple slices on top, each overlapping.

(7) Fill up with whipped cream using a savoy bag with a star tube.

(8) Replace the top containing the green leaves.

(9) Fill the pastry boats with whipped cream, small pieces of pineapple, and strawberries, and arrange them around the filled pineapple shell.

(10) Serve raspberry sauce separately.

Rice Empress Style – Riz à l'Impératrice (Yield 2×8 covers)

> 2 pt (12 dl) milk into rice condé mixing (see page 227)
> Vanilla bavarois mixing (see page 208)
> 4 oz (120 g) diced glacé fruits (cherries, angelica, pineapple, etc.)
> ½ pt (3 dl) red jelly (see page 207)
> 2 oz (60 g) Kirsch liqueur (optional)

(1) Make the rice condé mixing.
(2) Prepare the red jelly and pour into the bottom of dariole or charlotte moulds to about ¼ in. (½ cm) in thickness.
(3) Make the bavarois mixing.
(4) Mix the condé and bavarois together before they have set.
(5) Mix in the crystallized fruits. If used the fruit should first be macerated in the liqueur.
(6) Fill the prepared moulds.
(7) Allow to set in a refrigerator.
(8) Serve on a flat silver dish.

Variations

Tangerine Rice – Riz à la Mandarine.
  Instead of the crystallized fruits, add the zest of six tangerines. After the mould has been turned out decorate with tangerine segments macerated in curaçao liqueur.
Singapore Rice – Riz Singapour.
  Instead of crystallized fruits, mix in 8 oz (240 g) diced pineapple macerated in maraschino. Serve with cold apricot sauce, flavoured with the maraschino in which the pineapple was macerated.
Rice Trauttmansdorf – Riz Trauttmansdorf.
  Instead of crystallized fruits, mix in 4 oz (120 g) diced fresh fruit in season and the maraschino liqueur in which the fruit should be macerated. Serve with ½ pint (3 decilitres) purée of fresh raspberries or strawberries.

Snow Eggs – Oeufs à la Neige

(Yield: using a tablespoon, 24 egg shapes may be made, allowing 3 each = 8 covers)

> 8 medium eggs
> 12 oz (360 g) sugar
> 2 pt (12 dl) milk
> Vanilla essence

(1) Divide the yolks from the whites.
(2) Beat the whites to a stiff snow and carefully fold in 8 oz (240 g) of sugar.
(3) Boil the milk.
(4) Keeping the milk hot but not boiling, spoon the meringue in shape of an egg into the hot milk.
(5) Allow them to poach for about 3 minutes on each side.
(6) When firm enough, remove with a skimmer and allow to drain on a cloth.

(7) Prepare a custard sauce from the egg yolks, milk, and rest of the sugar (*see* page 199). Flavour, strain, and cool.

(8) Place the snow eggs in the bottom of a dish and cover with the custard sauce.

(9) Chill and serve very cold.

Snow Eggs with Chocolate Sauce – Oeufs Religieuse

Make only half the quantity of custard sauce and add 4 oz (120 g) chocolate. Coat the snow eggs with the chocolate sauce and sprinkle on 2 oz (60 g) crushed praline.

PANCAKES – CRÊPES

Basic Batter (Yield 8 covers)

> 8 *oz (240 g) flour*
> 3 *oz (90 g) eggs (2)*
> 1 *oz (30 g) butter*
> *A pinch of salt*
> 1 *pt (6 dl) milk*
> 4 *oz (120 g) lard*

(1) Whisk the egg, salt, and milk together.

(2) Add the sieved flour a little at a time, whisking each portion into the liquid to make a smooth batter.

(3) Mix in the melted butter.

(4) Place a small quantity of lard in a clean small frying pan and heat to smoking point.

(5) Pour in sufficient batter to just cover the base of the pan very thinly.

(6) Cook until it is a light golden brown.

(7) Turn the pancake over and cook this side to the same colour.

(8) The pancake is now ready for serving in any of the following varieties.

Lemon Pancakes – Crêpes au Citron

> *Basic pancake batter*
> 3–4 *oz (90–120 g) castor sugar*
> 2 *lemons*

(1) Prepare pancakes.

(2) Turn the pancakes onto a plate.

(3) Sprinkle with sugar.

(4) Fold into four.

(5) Serve hot with quarters of lemon, free of pips, two per person.

If several are to be served, dress the folded pancakes neatly overlapping on a flat silver dish. Instead of fresh lemons, lemon juice could be substituted.

Jam Pancakes – Crêpes à la Confiture

Basic pancake batter
2 oz (60 g) castor sugar
4 oz (120 g) jam

(1) Prepare pancakes.
(2) Spread a spoonful of jam on each.
(3) Roll up the pancakes.
(4) Sprinkle with sugar and serve.

Apple Pancakes – Crêpes Normande

Basic pancake batter
4 apples
4 oz (120 g) castor sugar

Method 1.
(1) Prepare pancakes.
(2) Spread on a purée made from the apples.
(3) Roll up the pancakes.
(4) Sprinkle with sugar and serve.
Method 2.
(1) Dice some cooked apple and sprinkle it into the greased pan.
(2) Pour on the pancake mixture on top and cook both sides in the usual way.
(3) Turn out onto a plate and sprinkle with sugar.
(4) Roll up and serve.

Orange Pancakes – Crêpes à l'Orange

As for lemon pancakes but using oranges instead.

Crêpes Suzette

These pancakes are finished at the table in the dining room by the head waiter. The patissier prepares the pancakes *very* thinly and places the number required on top of each other on a silver dish. The head waiter prepares the dish in front of the customer on a spirit stove.

16 small pancakes (2 each person)
2 oz (60 g) butter
2 oz (60 g) sugar
Zest and juice of 1 orange
1 oz (30 g) Grand Marnier
1 oz (30 g) Cognac

(1) Obtain the zest and juice of the orange.
(2) Add the sugar and liqueur and stir to dissolve.
(3) Place the butter in the hot pan and when melted add the liquor.
(4) Place the pancakes in the pan, one at a time, covering them with the sauce.
(5) Fold the pancakes into four.

(6) Pour over the brandy and light by holding the pan sideways over the flame.

(7) Serve immediately with the sauce.

Note. It is only practicable to cook four pancakes at the same time so that, for eight persons having two pancakes each, the procedure would have to be repeated four times, using $\frac{1}{4}$ of the quantities quoted.

Crêpes Soufflés

> 1 *egg*
> 1 *oz (30 g) castor sugar*
> $\frac{1}{4}$ *oz (8 g) butter*
> $\frac{1}{2}$ *oz (15 g) apricot jam*
> 2 *oz (60 g) whipped cream*
> 2 *oz (60 g) tinned or fresh fruit*
> $\frac{1}{2}$ *oz (15 g) icing sugar*

(1) Separate the yolks from the whites.

(2) Cream the sugar and yolks.

(3) Whisk the whites to a stiff foam.

(4) Carefully fold the whites into the yolk and sugar cream.

(5) Heat the butter in an omelette pan.

(6) Pour in the mixture.

(7) Allow it to cook for about $\frac{1}{4}$ minute to set the base.

(8) Transfer pan to a hot oven (approx. 450°F (232°C)) for about 3–5 minutes until golden brown.

(9) Turn pancake out onto a clean cloth sprinkled with icing sugar.

(10) When cold, spread half of the pancake with apricot jam.

(11) Place on some fruit and whipped cream.

(12) Fold the other half of the pancake over the fruit and cream.

(13) Dust with icing sugar.

(14) Serve cold.

FRITTERS – BEIGNETS

Basic Batter (Yield 8 covers)

> 8 *oz (240 g) flour*
> 2 *oz (60 g) olive or salad oil*
> $\frac{1}{2}$ *pt (3 dl) water or milk*
> 2 *oz (60 g) egg white (2) (stiffly beaten)*
> *A pinch of salt*

(1) Sieve the flour and gradually add to the water or milk, whisking well to make a smooth batter.

(2) Gradually beat in the oil and add the salt.

(3) Allow to rest before using.

(4) Just prior to use, add and carefully fold in the egg whites.

Apple Fritters – Beignets de Pommes

Basic fritter batter
1½ *lb* (720 g) *cooking apples*
½ *pt* (3 *dl*) *apricot sauce* (*see page* 201)
2 *oz* (60 g) *flour*
4 *oz* (120 g) *icing sugar*

(1) Peel and core the apples.
(2) Cut into ¼-in. (6-mm) rings.
(3) Dip into flour and shake off any surplus.
(4) Dip them into the frying batter.
(5) Lift out with the fingers or a long skewer and gently drop them into fairly hot fat (smoking slightly).
(6) Cook until both sides are a golden brown colour, approx. 6–8 minutes.
(7) Drain well, dust liberally with icing sugar, and put under a salamander to glaze.
(8) Serve on a doily on a hot flat dish.
(9) Serve a sauceboat of hot apricot sauce, separately.

In place of apple, other fruits are also suitable for fritters and may be served in the same way.

Banana Fritters – Beignets de Bananes

Basic fritter batter
8 *bananas*

Split in half lengthwise and cut in half across, each banana making four pieces.

Pineapple Fritters – Beignets d'Ananas

Basic fritter batter
8 *pineapple rings*

If the rings are large they may be cut in two.

Apricot Fritters – Beignets d'Abricot

Basic fritter batter
16 *apricot halves*

17. Puddings

MILK PUDDING

Rice Pudding (Yield 8 covers)

    2 pt (12 dl) milk
    3 oz (90 g) rice
    1 oz (30 g) butter
    4 oz (120 g) sugar
    Vanilla
    Grated nutmeg

Method 1.

(1) Wash the rice and place in a greased pie dish.
(2) Add the sugar, milk, and flavouring and stir well.
(3) Bake in an oven at a moderate heat 350°F (177°C) until the milk starts simmering. Stir.
(4) Sprinkle on the nutmeg and add a few knobs of butter.
(5) Reduce the heat to approx. 300°F (149°C) and cook for a total time of approx. $1\frac{1}{2}$ to 2 hours.

Method 2.

(1) Boil the milk in a saucepan.
(2) Wash the rice and sprinkle it into the milk.
(3) Stir until the milk starts to boil, then simmer slowly, stirring frequently until the rice is cooked.
(4) Stir in the sugar and flavouring, then transfer to a pie dish.
(5) Place on a few knobs of butter and sprinkle on the grated nutmeg.
(6) Either place in a hot oven until brown on top, or brown lightly under a salamander.
(7) Serve on a doily on a silver dish.

Rice Mould or Condé (Yield 8 covers)

    2 pt (12 dl) milk
    6 oz (180 g) rice (whole grain)
    4 oz (120 g) sugar
    4 egg yolks
    1 oz (30 g) butter
    Vanilla essence

(1) Boil the milk, add the rice, and simmer gently until the rice is cooked.
(2) Mix in the sugar, butter, flavouring, and egg yolks.
(3) Pour into a damp mould or eight small dariole moulds.
(4) Leave to become cold and set.
(5) Turn out and serve with a jam sauce or with poached fruit.

Cornflour Mould (Yield 8 covers)

> 2 pt (12 dl) milk
> 3 oz (90 g) cornflour
> 4 oz (120 g) sugar
> 1 oz (30 g) butter
> Vanilla essence

(1) Blend the cornflour with a little of the milk in a basin.
(2) Place the remainder of the milk in a saucepan and bring to the boil.
(3) Add the boiling milk to the diluted cornflour stirring all the time.
(4) Return it to the heat and allow to simmer for a few minutes, whisking all the time.
(5) Mix in the butter and sugar.
(6) Pour into a damp mould or eight dariole moulds.
(7) Leave until it becomes cold.
(8) Easing the mixture away from the sides of the mould, turn it out onto a flat silver dish.
(9) Serve the mould surrounded with a cold jam sauce.

Variations

Chocolate.
　(*a*) Add 2 oz (60 g) cocoa powder (mix with the cornflour and form a thin paste with milk). Add extra 1 oz (30 g) sugar.
　(*b*) Use 2 oz (60 g) melted chocolate.
Coffee.
　(*a*) Use 2 pints (12 decilitres) white coffee instead of milk.
　(*b*) Add instant coffee to desired flavour.
Neapolitain Blancmange.
(1) Divide the cornflour mixture into three equal parts.
(2) Colour and flavour as follows:

White	Vanilla
Pink	Strawberry
Green	Almond

(3) Pour the pink mixing into a damp mould and leave for a few minutes to set. Keep the other mixings warm.
(4) When the pink is set, pour on the white, and when this is set pour on the green.
(5) Leave to cool in a refrigerator.
(6) Easing the mixture away from the sides of the mould with the fingers, turn out into a flat silver dish.
(7) Serve with a cold jam sauce, separately.

Semolina Pudding (Yield 8 covers)

> 2 pt (12 dl) milk
> 3 oz (90 g) semolina

4 *oz* (120 *g*) *sugar*
1 *oz* (30 *g*) *butter*
Lemon juice or essence

(1) Heat the milk in a saucepan.
(2) When nearly boiling, sprinkle in the semolina, stirring well.
(3) Allow to simmer for 15–20 minutes, stirring continuously until the semolina is cooked.
(4) Pour into a pie dish.
(5) Either bake in a moderate oven until brown, or brown under a salamander.
(6) Serve on a doily on a flat silver dish.

Semolina Mould

To the pudding recipe *add* 4 egg yolks; *increase* semolina to 4 oz (120 g).
(1) Proceed as for semolina pudding.
(2) When mixture is made, pour into damp mould and proceed as for a cornflour mould.

Sago, Tapioca, Ground Rice, Puddings

These are made in the same way as semolina pudding using vanilla instead of lemon flavouring.

Baked Egg Custard (Yield 8 covers)

2 *pt* (12 *dl*) *milk*
4 *oz* (120 *g*) *sugar*
9 *oz* (270 *g*) *eggs* (6)
Vanilla
Grated nutmeg

(1) Whisk the eggs, sugar, and vanilla flavour in a bowl.
(2) Slightly warm the milk and whisk it into the eggs and sugar.
(3) Pour the mixture through a sieve into a clean greased pie dish.
(4) Sprinkle on a little grated nutmeg.
(5) Wipe the edges of the pie dish and stand in a baking tin, half filled with water (bain-marie).
(6) Cook slowly in an oven at 350°F (177°C) for approx. 45 minutes to 1 hour.
(7) Clean the edge of the dish and serve on a doily on a flat silver dish.
Note. Never allow the water in the tin in which egg custard sweets are cooked to boil. This might curdle the custard.

Cream Caramel Custards – Crème Caramel (Yield 8 covers)

Custard.
1½ *pt* (9 *dl*) *milk*
3 *oz* (90 *g*) *sugar*
9 *oz* (270 *g*) *eggs* (6)
Vanilla

Caramel.

  6 *oz* (180 *g*) *sugar*

  $3\frac{1}{2}$ *oz* (105 *g*) *water*

(1) Make the caramel by mixing 3 oz (90 g) of the water with the sugar in a pan (preferably copper) and observing sugar boiling precautions (*see* page 273), heating it until it turns to an amber colour.

(2) Add the remaining water (*beware of steam*) and re-boil until the sugar and water are thoroughly mixed.

(3) Pour the caramel into eight dariole moulds and allow it to set.

(4) Prepare the custard in the same way as baked custard.

(5) Pass through a strainer into eight greased dariole moulds.

(6) Place moulds in a baking tin half full of water.

(7) Cook in a moderately hot oven at 380°F (193°C) until custard is set (approx. 30–40 minutes).

(8) When thoroughly cold, gently loosen the edges of the cream caramels, shake to loosen, and turn out onto a flat silver dish.

(9) Any caramel remaining in the moulds should be poured over the creams.

Bread and Butter Pudding (Yield 8 covers)

  2 *pt* (12 *dl*) *milk into baked egg custard* (*see page* 229)

  6 *thin slices buttered bread*

  2 *oz* (60 *g*) *sultanas*

  1 *oz* (30 *g*) *castor sugar*

(1) Remove the crusts from the buttered bread slices and cut into four triangles.

(2) Arrange in the bottom of the pie dish with the slices neatly overlapping.

(3) Sprinkle over the sultanas and cover with the rest of the bread slices.

(4) Make an egg custard.

(5) Pour half of the custard over the bread and allow to stand for half an hour so that the bread is prevented from floating to the surface.

(6) Add the rest of the custard, dredge with castor sugar, and sprinkle on the nutmeg.

(7) Bake and serve as baked egg custard.

Cabinet Pudding – Pouding Cabinet (Yield 8 covers)

  Cream caramel custard (*see page* 229)

  6 *oz* (180 *g*) *sponge cake or fingers* (*see page* 76)

  $1\frac{1}{2}$ *oz* (45 *g*) *glacé cherries*

  $\frac{3}{4}$ *oz* (22 *g*) *sultanas*

  $\frac{3}{4}$ *oz* (22 *g*) *currants*

(1) Grease and sugar dariole or charlotte moulds. The base of these may be decorated with cherries and angelica if desired.

(2) Dice the sponge into $\frac{1}{4}$-in. (6-mm) cubes and mix with the chopped cherries, sultanas, and currants.

(3) Fill the moulds half way with the mixed fruit and sponge.
(4) Prepare the egg custard and pour the mixture to almost fill the moulds. Allow to stand for ½ hour.
(5) Proceed as for Cream Caramels. The time of cooking will depend upon the size of mould but should be 30–45 minutes. To test whether it is set, insert a knife. If it is cooked it should come out clean, without any trace of custard adhering.
(6) When cooked, leave to stand for a few minutes and then turn out onto a flat silver dish.
(7) Serve with an egg custard sauce or hot apricot sauce, separately.
Notes.
  1. This pudding may also be steamed.
  2. The diced fruit may be soaked in rum.
  3. This pudding may also be served with a rum-flavoured sabayon sauce.

Diplomat Pudding – Pouding Diplomate

Proceed as for Cabinet Pudding but serve cold. Fresh fruit may be used instead of dried fruit. Serve with jam or sabayon sauce.

Queen of Puddings (Yield 8 covers)
  1½ *pt (9 dl) milk*
  3 *oz (90 g) butter*
  3 *oz (90 g) castor sugar*
  6 *oz (180 g) cake or bread-crumbs*
  1½ *oz (45 g) jam*
  5 *oz (150 g) eggs (3)*
  3 *oz (90 g) castor sugar (for meringue)*
  Grated rind of 1 lemon
(1) Bring the milk and butter to the boil.
(2) Mix the yolks of the eggs and sugar and pour on the hot milk and butter mixture.
(3) Place the crumbs in a buttered pie dish.
(4) Pass the custard through a strainer over the crumbs. Allow to soak for ½ hour.
(5) Bake in an oven at 380°F (193°C) in a bain-marie for approx. 30 minutes until it is set.
(6) Allow to cool.
(7) Make a meringue with the egg whites and sugar.
(8) Spread warm jam over the top of the baked mixture.
(9) Using a savoy bag and star tube, pipe on the meringue.
(10) Place into a hot oven at 450°F (232°C) for the meringue to become tinged a brown colour (flashing).
(11) Serve on a doily on a flat silver dish.

SUET PUDDINGS

Steamed Fruit Pudding (Yield 8 covers)

> 8 *oz* (240 *g*) *flour into suet paste* (*see page* 39)
> 2 *lb* (960 *g*) *fruit*
> 6–8 *oz* (180–240 *g*) *approx. sugar* (*according to type of fruit used*)
> *Water* (*according to type of fruit used*)

(1) Using approx. three-quarters of the paste, line a slightly greased basin.
(2) Add prepared and washed fruit, sugar, and water (see below). If apples are used, add two cloves.
(3) Brush the edge of the paste with water.
(4) Cover with the remaining paste and seal firmly.
(5) Cover with a pudding cloth or greased greaseproof paper.
(6) Steam for approx. 1½ hours.
(7) Clean the basin and wrap around it a folded napkin.
(8) Serve in the basin on a flat silver dish with a separate sauceboat of custard.
Notes.

1. Fruits suitable for such sweets are plums, rhubarb, apple, apple and black currant, gooseberry, etc. Sharp fruits like rhubarb require more sugar than apple.

2. Soft fruits like rhubarb will not require any water added, but for dry fruits like plums up to 3 oz (90 g) may be used.

Steamed Rolls (Yield 8 covers)

Recipe and quantity of ingredients same as Baked Jam Roll recipe (page 51), using suet pastry instead of shortpastry.
(1) Make the same as baked jam roll.
(2) Place the roll into a pudding cloth and secure both ends.
(3) Steam for approx. 2 hours.
(4) Serve as for baked jam roll.
Varieties. Jam, marmalade, mincemeat, date and apple, syrup.

Steamed Currant Roll (Yield 8 covers)

> 8 *oz* (240 *g*) *flour*
> ½ *oz* (15 *g*) *baking powder*
> 2½ *oz* (75 *g*) *sugar*
> 4 *oz* (120 *g*) *chopped suet*
> 4 *oz* (120 *g*) *prepared currants*
> ¼ *pt* (1½ *dl*) *milk*
> *A pinch of salt*

(1) Sieve the flour with the baking powder and salt into a bowl.
(2) Add the suet and mix in.
(3) Mix in the sugar and currants.
(4) Add the milk and mix to a dough.
(5) Proceed as for steamed jam roll.

STEAMED SUET PUDDINGS

Basic Recipe (Yield 8 covers)

  6 *oz* (180 g) *suet*
  6 *oz* (180 g) *soft flour*
  6 *oz* (180 g) *bread-crumbs*
  ¼ *oz* (8 g) *baking powder*
  A pinch of salt
  8–10 *oz* (240–300 g) *milk or water (see operation* (3) *below)*

(1) Sieve the flour, baking powder, and salt.
(2) Add the bread-crumbs and chopped suet and mix.
(3) Add sufficient milk or water to make a soft dough which will drop easily from a spoon. The strength of flour used and the dryness of the bread-crumbs will affect the quantity of water needed to achieve this consistency.
(4) Place in well-greased basins or moulds (sleeves).
(5) Cover with greased greaseproof paper.
(6) Steam for 2–2½ hours according to size.
(7) Turn out onto a hot dish and serve with a custard or a jam sauce.

VARIETIES

Fruit Pudding

  Add to basic suet pudding recipe:
  4–6 *oz* (120–180 g) *selected and washed dried fruit*
  2–4 *oz* (60–120 g) *sugar*
  Serve custard sauce separately.
Note. Fruit may include currants, sultanas, raisins, figs, dates, cherries, etc.

Golden or Syrup Pudding

  Add to basic suet pudding recipe:
  6 *oz* (180 g) *golden syrup (for layering)*
(1) Prepare basic recipe.
(2) Use only basins, not sleeves.
(3) Deposit a layer of syrup in the bottom of a well-greased basin and then place a layer of the basic mixing on top.
(4) Repeat this process to finish with a layer of the basic mixing on top.
(5) Serve a syrup sauce separately.

Marmalade Pudding

  Add to basic suet pudding recipe:
  2 *oz* (60 g) *sugar*
  4–6 *oz* (120–180 g) *marmalade (for layering)*
(1) Proceed as for Golden Pudding, substituting marmalade for syrup.
(2) Serve marmalade or custard sauce separately.

Jam Layer Pudding

Add to basic suet pudding recipe:
   4–6 *oz* (120–180 *g*) *jam* (*for layering*)
(1) Proceed as for Golden Pudding, substituting jam for syrup.
(2) Serve jam sauce separately.

STEAMED SPONGE PUDDINGS

Basic Recipe (Yield 8 covers)
   8 *oz* (240 *g*) *soft flour*
   ½ *oz* (15 *g*) *baking powder*
   5 *oz* (150 *g*) *castor sugar*
   5 *oz* (150 *g*) *margarine*
   5 *oz* (150 *g*) *eggs* (*approx.* 3)
   2 *oz* (60 *g*) *milk*
(1) Make mixing on the sugar batter method (*see* page 93).
(2) Deposit mixture into a well-greased pudding basin.
(3) Securely cover with greased greaseproof paper.
(4) Steam for approx. 1½ hours.
(5) Turn out onto a hot flat silver dish and serve with an appropriate sauce.

Varieties

Vanilla. Add vanilla essence to the basic mixture. Serve with a vanilla-flavoured sauce.
Chocolate. Substitute 1½ oz (45 g) flour in the basic mixture for cocoa powder. Serve with a chocolate sauce (*see* page 200).
Fruit (*currants, sultanas, raisins*). Add 4 oz (120 g) of selected, washed, and well-dried fruit to the basic mixture. Serve with a custard sauce.
Cherry. Add 4 oz (120 g) of chopped or quartered glacé cherries to the basic mixture. Serve with almond or custard sauce.
Lemon. Add to the basic mixture the zest of 2 lemons and lemon essence to taste. Serve with a lemon sauce.
Orange. Proceed as for Lemon Sponge Pudding but using oranges instead. Serve with an orange sauce.
Ginger. Add ½ teaspoonful powdered ginger and 1½ oz (45 g) finely diced preserved ginger. Serve with a custard sauce.
Harlequin.
(1) Divide the basic mixture into three.
(2) Flavour one portion vanilla, another chocolate, and the third strawberry or raspberry with sufficient colouring to make it pink.
(3) Deposit into well-greased basins to form alternating layers of white, pink, and chocolate.
(4) Serve with a custard or jam sauce.

Eve's Pudding

    Basic Steamed Sponge Pudding recipe (*opposite*).
    Jam
    Apple purée (*see page* 44)

(1) Spread a little jam in the bottom of a greased pie dish.
(2) Cover with a thick layer of apple purée.
(3) Spread on sufficient sponge mixture to completely cover the apple purée and fill the dish.
(4) Bake in an oven at 400°F (204°C) for approx. 10 minutes and then reduce heat to approx. 365°F (185°C) and allow a further 30 minutes to finish cooking.
(5) Serve with a custard sauce.

Christmas Puddings (Yield 1 pudding at 4 lb (1,920 g) sufficient for 16–20 covers)

Recipe 1		*Recipe 2*
6 oz (180 g)		10 oz (300 g) suet
2 oz (60 g)	(A)	4 oz (120 g) flour
		1½ oz (45 g) ground almonds
12 oz (360 g)	(B)	6 oz (180 g) bread-crumbs
8 oz (240 g)		8 oz (240 g) sultanas
4 oz (120 g)		8 oz (240 g) raisins (stoned)
8 oz (240 g)		10 oz (300 g) currants
4 oz (120 g)		2 oz (60 g) chopped peel
8 oz (240 g)	(C)	6 oz (180 g) brown sugar
1 oz (30 g)		1½ oz (45 g) syrup
	(D)	2 oz (60 g) figs $\Big\}$ (optional) 1 oz (30 g) water
¼ oz (8 g)		¼ oz (8 g) mixed spice
⅛ oz (4 g)		⅛ oz (4 g) salt
8 oz (240 g)	(E)	5 oz (150 g) eggs
2 (zest only)		Zest and juice of 1 lemon
		Zest and juice of 1 orange
		2½ oz (75 g) old ale
		1 oz (30 g) milk

(1) Chop the ingredients of (A) finely together or, if already shredded suet is used, just blend together.
(2) Add the bread-crumbs and mix well (B).
(3) Blend in the ingredients listed under (C) and make a bay.
(4) Mix together all the ingredients listed under (E).

(5) If No. 2 recipe is being used chop or mince the figs (*D*), mix with the water, and bring to the boil. Add the thick syrup so made to the other liquids of (*E*).

(6) Add the mixed liquids of (*E*) and (*D*) pouring them into the bay made in the dry materials. Stir until a homogeneous mixture is formed. This may be left a day before filling.

(7) Fill the mixture to the top of clean, well-greased pudding basins. Make sure the mixture is filled to the top.

(8) Cover each basin with two discs of greaseproof paper cut to size.

(9) Lay a square of clean cloth over each basin, tie this under the rim with string, and knot the opposite ends of the cloth together over the top of the basin.

(10) Either boil or preferably steam as follows:

    1-lb pudding   4 hours
    2-lb pudding   6 hours
    4-lb pudding   8 hours.

Once started the puddings must not be allowed to go off the boil.

(11) When finished the puddings should be removed at once from the boiling water or steamer.

(12) Untie the knot in the cloth and leave extended to dry thoroughly.

(13) When the puddings have cooled, remove the cloth leaving the greaseproof discs untouched.

(14) Clean the outside of the basin with a clean cloth and tie up the top again using a clean cloth.

(15) Store puddings in a cool *dry* place.

(16) When required for service, another hour's steaming (2 hours for the larger puddings) is required.

(17) Serve on a silver flat with a sprig of holly and with rum or brandy sauce.

Notes.

    1. For better effect, warm some brandy in a spoon, set it alight, and pour it over the pudding prior to bringing it to the table.

    2. Christmas puddings improve if kept for a year.

Mouldy Puddings. This is a common fault and is caused by damp conditions either in storage or the pudding itself. This may be due to several causes as follows:

    1. Mixture was too soft initially.

    2. Basins not filled to the top, thus letting water seep in during cooking.

    3. Cloth insufficiently tied so that water seeps in during cooking.

    4. Allowing water to go off the boil (if boiling).

    5. Insufficient cooking.

    6. Leaving knots of cloth untied immediately after cooking.

    7. Failing to remove puddings from the steamer or boiler immediately they have been cooked.

    8. Leaving pudding for too long in a steamy atmosphere.

    9. Damp storage conditions.

Mincemeat

8 *oz* (240 *g*) *finely chopped suet* (*A*)

8 *oz* (240 *g*) *apples* (*B*)

8 *oz* (240 *g*) *sultanas*
8 *oz* (240 *g*) *currants*
8 *oz* (240 *g*) *raisins* $\Big\}$ (*C*)
4 *oz* (120 *g*) *chopped peel*
Juice and zest of 1 *lemon*

8 *oz* (240 *g*) *sugar* (*D*)

$\frac{1}{4}$ *oz* (8 *g*) *mixed spice* $\Big\}$ (*E*)
1 *oz* (30 *g*) *ground almonds*

$\frac{1}{4}$ *pt* (1$\frac{1}{2}$ *dl*) *rum, brandy, or stock syrup* (*F*)

(1) Finely chop the suet (*A*).
(2) Peel and core the apples (*B*) and finely chop. Add to (*A*).
(3) Chop the raisins and peel. Mix all the ingredients of (*C*) together and then add to the suet and apples.
(4) Stir in the sugar (*D*).
(5) Add the ingredients of (*E*).
(6) Lastly stir in (*F*) and mix all the ingredients thoroughly together.
(7) Keep for at least two days before transferring to jars.
(8) Fill the jars, cover with greaseproof paper, and tie down.
(9) Store in a cool, dry place until required.
Notes.
1. Mincemeat should never be used freshly made. It matures and improves on storage and should not be used until it is at least 14 days old.
2. Cool, dry storage is essential if mincemeat is to be kept for any time. Damp and warm conditions will encourage the development of mould and wild yeasts which will bring about undesirable fermentation.

SWEET OMELETTES

Basic Recipe per Person
2–3 *eggs*
1 *oz* (30 *g*) *approx. filling*
$\frac{1}{4}$ *oz* (8 *g*) *butter*
$\frac{1}{4}$ *oz* (8 *g*) *sugar*
Pre-preparation. Firstly make sure that the omelette pan is well proved. Pans for omelettes should be thick-bottomed and reserved solely for this purpose. They should never be washed but only wiped with kitchen paper.

To clean the pan, make it very hot, rub the inside with salt, and wipe it with kitchen paper.

Ensure that, before starting to make the omelette, everything is ready, i.e. the garnish, filling, and hot serving dish.

Once made, the omelette must be served immediately or it will become tough.

(1) Break the eggs into a basin and beat the yolks and whites thoroughly together.

(2) Place the butter in the pan and heat it until it is quite hot (*do not allow the butter to brown*).

(3) Pour the eggs into the hot pan and stir with a fork, slowly at first and then faster as the eggs begin to set.

(4) Keep a good heat but not too fierce so that a golden brown colour is achieved.

(5) Place in the filling.

(6) Remove from the heat and fold the edges of the omelette over to enclose the filling.

(7) Shape the omelette into an oval cushion shape by tapping the handle of the pan to turn over the omelette.

(8) Turn out immediately onto an oval fireproof dish or silver flat.

(9) Serve immediately.

Note. The omelette should not take longer than 5 minutes to make.

Varieties of Fillings

Jam – Omelette à la Confiture.

The jam should be warmed before folding into the omelette. To finish, dust liberally with icing sugar and, with a red hot poker, mark the top with a criss-cross pattern. Alternatively, glaze quickly under a salamander.

Fruit Purée.

Any sweet fruit purée may be used instead of jam.

Mincemeat.

This may also be appropriately called a 'Christmas' omelette. Sprinkle with sugar, pour over warm rum, and ignite when served.

Rum or other Spirits (*Cognac, Kirsch, etc.*) *– Omelette au Rhum, etc.*

Prepare omelette without filling. Sprinkle with sugar, pour spirit into a heated spoon, ignite, and pour over the omelette just prior to service.

Soufflé Omelette

There is often confusion between this and Crêpe Soufflé because the same basic recipe is used. The following method is the one recognized for this sweet.

Basic recipe per person:

    1 *egg*

    1 *oz* (30 g) *sugar*

(1) Separate the yolks from the whites.

(2) Cream the yolks with the sugar.

(3) Whisk the whites to a stiff foam.

(4) Carefully fold the whites into the yolk and sugar cream.

(5) Butter and sugar a long oval mould or dish and fill with the soufflé mixture.

(6) Dust with sugar and bake in an oven at 400°F (204°C) for approx. 15–18 minutes depending upon size.

(7) When baked, place on a doily on a flat silver dish and serve at once.

Note. It is usual for this to be made for a number of covers, e.g. 4, and not individually.

SWEET SOUFFLES – SOUFFLÉS D'ENTREMETS

The basic preparation up to and including the yolks may be made well in advance of the time the soufflé is required, provided it is kept in a cool place.

The stiffly beaten egg whites should be added at the last moment just before the soufflé is placed in the oven.

The beaten egg whites should be stirred into the mixing very carefully to ensure that the entrapped air is not broken down. If this does happen the soufflé will not rise.

Large soufflés should be baked in an oven 325–350°F (163–177°C) for 20–25 minutes.

Small soufflés should be baked in an oven at 400°F (204°C) for approx. 7–9 minutes.

Too hot an oven will form a crust on top too quickly and thus prevent the soufflé from rising properly. It may also cause collapsing of the soufflé when taken from the oven.

The soufflé dish should be three-quarters filled, and when baked the soufflé should rise to 1–1½ in. (2½–4 cm) above the top of the mould. A slight collapse after baking is normal.

Soufflés should always be served immediately.

Basic Mixture (Yield 2 soufflés of 4 portions each)

1 *oz* (30 *g*) *flour*
1 *oz* (30 *g*) *cornflour*
2 *oz* (60 *g*) *butter*
2 *oz* (60 *g*) *castor sugar*
½ *pt* (3 *dl*) *milk*
5 *egg whites*
5 *egg yolks*
Flavouring

Method 1.

(1) Grease the soufflé or cocotte dishes with clarified butter and dress with sugar.

(2) Boil the milk in a saucepan.

(3) Beat the butter to a cream, add the sugar, and beat well.

(4) Add the flour and gently mix it into the butter/sugar mixture.

(5) Pour on the boiling milk slowly, stirring vigorously to produce a perfectly smooth mixture (*panada*).

(6) Return to the pan and, continuing to stir, cook the panada for a few minutes.

(7) Remove from the heat and allow it to cool slightly.

(8) Add the egg yolks individually, beating each well into the mixture.

At this stage the mixture may be left until required for finishing.

(9) Whisk whites to a stiff snow, blend some into the mixture first to soften it, and then very carefully fold in the remainder. *Do not over-mix.*

(10) Fill the moulds to three-quarters full.

(11) Place in an oven at 400°F (204°C) to bake for 20–25 minutes.

(12) One minute before they are cooked, sprinkle on icing sugar and return to the oven to glaze.

(13) Serve at once in the soufflé dish, either on a doily or folded table napkin on a flat silver dish.

(14) Serve with an appropriate sauce.

Method 2.

(1) Prepare the soufflé or cocotte dishes.

(2) Make a white roux by melting the butter in a thick-bottomed pan and adding the flour.

(3) Heat the milk and add it gradually to the roux stirring continuously to form a perfectly smooth mixture.

(4) Cook the mixture gently, stirring continually until it thickens.

(5) Add the sugar.

(6) Proceed as for operations (7) to (14) in Method 1.

Varieties

Chocolate – Soufflé au Chocolat.

Using the basic recipe, add 2 oz (60 g) of grated chocolate to the hot milk, allowing it to melt before proceeding. Serve a custard or chocolate sauce separately.

Coffee – Soufflé au Café.

Using the basic recipe, add 2 oz (60 g) liquid coffee or $\frac{1}{2}$ oz (15 g) instant coffee to the milk or use white coffee instead of milk. Serve with a custard sauce.

Lemon – Soufflé au Citron.

Add the zest of 2 lemons to the mixture prior to adding the yolks. Add the juice to the accompanying sauce.

Orange – Soufflé a l'Orange or Soufflé Maltaise.

Add the zest of 2 oranges to the mixture prior to adding the yolks. Part of the milk may be replaced by orange juice. Add the juice to the accompanying sauce.

Hazelnut – Soufflé Noisettine.
  Using the basic recipe, add 4 oz (120 g) ground hazelnuts to the milk.
Serve with a hazelnut sauce.
Almond – Soufflé Amandines.
  Using the basic recipe, add 4 oz (120 g) ground almonds to the milk.
Serve with an almond sauce.
Soufflé Regence.
(1) Line a charlotte mould with caramel (*see* page 230).
(2) Fill with the basic soufflé mixing.
(3) Serve with a custard sauce to which crushed caramel has been added.
Soufflé Montmorency.
  Soak 3 oz (90 g) candied cherries in a little kirsch and add to the mixture
after the egg yolks are added. Serve with a sabayon sauce.
Soufflé Ananas.
  Same as above but using diced pineapple.
Soufflé Rothschild.
  Soak 3 oz (90 g) of mixed candied fruit in kirsch or brandy and add to
the mixture after the egg yolks are added. Also add vanilla flavour. Serve
with a sabayon sauce.
Note. Many other varieties of soufflés may be made from this basic recipe
with different flavourings.

SOUFFLÉ PUDDINGS

Basic Recipe (Yield 2 soufflés of 4 portions each)
  2 oz (60 g) flour
  2 oz (60 g) cornflour
  4 oz (120 g) butter
  4 oz (120 g) sugar
  5 oz (150 g) egg yolks
  5 oz (150 g) egg whites
  ½ pt (3 dl) milk
  Flavouring
(1) Grease the mould with butter and dress with sugar.
(2) Separate the whites from the yolks.
(3) Cream the butter and flours.
(4) Boil the milk in a saucepan with the sugar and other flavourings.
(5) Add and whisk in the creamed butter/flour and cook until the mixture
thickens.
(6) Allow to cool slightly and whisk in the yolks one or two at a time.
(7) Whip the whites to a stiff snow, stir a little into the mixing to soften,
and carefully fold in the remainder.
(8) Fill the mould three-quarters full.
(9) Place the filled moulds in a bain-marie on the stove and simmer until
the mixture reaches the top of the mould.

(10) Transfer to an oven at 400°F (204°C) and bake for 20–25 minutes.
(11) Turn out onto a hot flat silver dish.
(12) Serve with a vanilla sauce.
Note. These soufflés have more of a pudding consistency and are able to stand a while in a bain-marie prior to service without collapsing.

Varieties

Chocolate, Coffee, Lemon, Orange, Hazelnut, Almond.
    Proceed in the same way as for the other types of soufflé described on page 240.
Pouding Soufflé à l'Indienne.
    Using the basic pudding mixture add 2 oz (60 g) crystallized preserved ginger to the mixture after the egg yolks are added. Serve with a custard sauce flavoured ginger.
Pouding Soufflé Montmorency.
    Same as Soufflé Montmorency (*see* page 241).
Pouding Soufflé Maltaise.
    Same as Orange Soufflé Pudding.
Pouding Soufflé Vésuvius.
    Cook the soufflé pudding mixture in a prepared savarin mould. When baked fill the centre with raisins in an apricot sauce. Flambé with brandy.
Pouding Soufflé à la Royale.
    Butter a charlotte mould and line bottom and sides with thin slices of apricot Swiss roll (*see* page 76). Fill with the pudding mixture and bake in the usual way. Serve with custard flavoured with kirsch or apricot sauce flavoured with Madeira or Muscatel wine.
Pouding Soufflé au Grand Marnier.
    Using the basic pudding mixture, add the zest of one orange to the milk. Add some diced macaroon biscuits soaked in grand marnier.
Pouding Soufflé aux Marrons.
    Add chestnut purée and piece of marron glacé. Serve with an apricot sauce.
Pouding Soufflé Saxon.
    Vanilla flavoured, served with a custard sauce.
Pouding Soufflé à la Reine.
    Cook the pudding mixture in a savarin mould. When baked, fill the centre with candied fruit soaked in kirsch. Serve with an apricot sauce.
Pouding Soufflé Sans Souci.
    Add currants and diced cooked apples.

Cold Lemon Soufflé – Soufflé Milanaise (Yield 8 covers)

$\frac{1}{2}$ *pt* (3 *dl*) *cream*
2 *lemons*
$\frac{1}{2}$ *oz* (15 *g*) *gelatine*
$\frac{1}{2}$ *lb* (240 *g*) *sugar*
5 *oz* (150 *g*) *eggs* (3)
1 *oz* (30 *g*) *roasted almond nibs or green almond decor*

(1) Prepare a soufflé mould by tying a band of greaseproof paper around the side so that it is extended about $1\frac{1}{2}$ in. ($3\frac{1}{2}$ cm) beyond the top.
(2) Add the gelatine to the juice of the lemons and warm to dissolve.
(3) Whisk the egg yolks and sugar to a thick cream.
(4) Add the dissolved gelatine solution.
(5) Whip the cream and fold carefully into the mixture.
(6) Whisk the whites to a stiff foam and carefully blend this into the mixture.
(7) Pour into the prepared soufflé mould and allow to set.
(8) Finish by removing the paper band and decorating the edge with toasted almonds or green decor. It may be further decorated with whipped cream.

Other Cold Soufflés

Other varieties may be made, using the same flavouring agents as used for the hot soufflé.

18. Chocolate Work

Cooking Chocolate

Although the uses described in this chapter refer to Chocolate Couverture, many of the techniques can be applied to Cooking Chocolate. The results will not be as good however, the chocolate lacking the flavour, gloss, and snap of couverture. Its advantage is the ease with which it can be used since no tempering is necessary. All one has to do is warm it to approx. 100–110°F (38–43°C) and use.

Tempering of Chocolate Couverture

Before chocolate can be successfully used it must be free from contamination by moisture and must be tempered. This process can be explained as follows:

Cocoa butter can be regarded as being a mixture of two fats – A with a low melting point and latent heat, and B with a high melting point and latent heat. The A type has crystals of fat which are soft and feel greasy, whilst the B type crystals of fat impart the gloss and snap required in well-tempered chocolate.

To eliminate the A type crystals, the couverture should be completely melted, then cooled to the setting point of the A crystals, when B crystals are produced as well. The mass is now heated to the temperature at which only the A crystals will melt, leaving some B crystals. On setting, the whole mass will crystallize out in the B crystal form. (This process is known as 'seeding'.)

There are several techniques used to temper chocolate:

(*a*) A double-jacketed pan known as a 'bain-marie' or 'porringer' is used. It consists of a small pan in which the chocolate is contained and a larger pan which is filled with warm water. The small pan is placed inside the larger one and heat is transferred by the water. To melt the chocolate this water must not exceed 120°F (49°C).

When all the chocolate has melted, transfer the small pan into another large one containing very cold water (some *ice* may be used). Stir continually until some of the chocolate sets on the bottom. Transfer again to the pan of hot water where it remains until the solid chocolate just begins to melt. Remove and stir until all the solid chocolate has melted and been dispersed. The temperature at this stage should be cool, approx. 84°F (29°C) for Milk and 86°F (30°C) for Plain.

(*b*) Melt chocolate in bain-marie. Remove from heat and stir in flakes of solid chocolate, shredded from a block of well-tempered chocolate. The proportion depends on the amount of liquid chocolate and its temperature which should be sufficient to only *just* melt the shreds of solid chocolate being stirred in.

(*c*) Once a quantity of liquid tempered chocolate has been obtained, it can be used to *seed* fresh batches of untempered chocolate. The usual procedure is to have a large bowl of liquid chocolate available and, as the tempered chocolate is used, it is replaced by the liquid untempered variety. This is how chocolate is tempered for large scale use in a factory.

Moulding (Figure 104)

When tempered chocolate sets, it contracts and this action makes it easy for all types of figures to be moulded. Moulds may be either metal, usually tinned, or plastic, the latter having the advantage of being flexible and so aiding release of the figure from the mould. The temperature of setting is important. Although it needs to be cool, it is a mistake to place the mould in a refrigerator. This will cause uneven contraction and result in a cracked figure.

Detailed Method of Moulding Eggs and Figures.

(1) Make sure that the moulds are clean, dry, and polished by rubbing cotton wool on the surface.
(2) Temper the chocolate couverture as previously described.
(3) Fill the figure or mould to the brim with the liquid chocolate.
(4) Turn upside down and empty mould of chocolate (Figure 104(*a*)).
(5) Wipe the brim free of surplus chocolate and place brim downwards on greaseproof paper.
(6) Place in a cool room and allow chocolate to set in the mould.
(7) Repeat the operation if the coating of chocolate is too thin. Except for very small moulds, most require two thicknesses of chocolate for strength.
(8) Leave the moulds in a cool room until the chocolate has contracted sufficiently for the chocolate shape to be removed from the mould. This may take as long as two hours. The release of the chocolate from the mould is easier from plastic moulds than from tin.
(9) To finish off Easter eggs, the two halves have to be joined with chocolate. This is best done by heating a clean tray and placing the rim of one half of the chocolate egg on the heated tray for a few seconds so that the chocolate melts. When this happens the two halves can be secured by placing the two edges together.
(10) The Easter eggs can be decorated by piping stiffened chocolate in a shell pattern around the join. Also marzipan flowers and inscriptions may be piped on.

Dipping

Chocolate may be used for sweets by dipping various centres, e.g. fondants. It must be well-tempered and at such a temperature that the first one has started to set whilst the sixth is being dipped.

Several varieties of pastries, marzipan shapes, and animals, are enhanced by having a part dipped in chocolate. Wholly enrobed cakes and biscuits will keep fresh and moist for very much longer periods.

Figure 104.
Chocolate goods:

(a) Moulding in chocolate: the rabbit mould in this figure has been filled and is being held to enable surplus chocolate to run back into the pan. During this time, the plastic mould is being tapped with the wooden spoon to eliminate any air bubbles which might form. Two filled egg moulds and other shapes are shown in the foreground.

(b) Chocolate moulded figures and Easter eggs. The rabbit and egg on the left are made from milk chocolate, the others from plain. The milk chocolate egg has chocolate piped in a shell pattern over the seal.

Piping (Figure 105)

When a liquid is added to chocolate, it thickens and in this state it can be piped. Piping chocolate loses its characteristic gloss and some of its snap and is not, therefore, recommended for piped off-pieces. Substances which may be added to thicken chocolate are as follows:

1. Water or milk – Not recommended.
2. Glycerine – Recommended – helps to maintain gloss.
3. Piping jelly – Recommended – helps to maintain gloss.
4. Gelatine jelly – Recommended – helps to maintain gloss.
5. Spirits and liqueurs – Recommended – adds to flavour.

Thinning

To make chocolate thinner we must add cocoa butter. This is useful if a very thin covering is required.

Flavouring

Chocolate or block cocoa may be used to flavour icings and creams and the crumb of cakes. Block cocoa (lacking in sugar) is especially useful to flavour very sweet mediums such as fondant. Although the chocolate is used mostly in the liquid state, solid flakes may be scattered or mixed in mediums like fresh cream.

Carving

The very nature of chocolate makes it an ideal medium in which figures may be carved. All that is needed is a flair for this type of sculpture work and a sharp knife. In the first instance, a sufficiently large block of chocolate has to be provided and it may be necessary for the chocolate to be first melted, tempered, and then poured into a suitably sized frame or mould.

Figure 105. Chocolate work: piping chocolate into filigree shapes suitable for decorative purposes. Piped outline of flower has crystallized mimosa placed in the centre

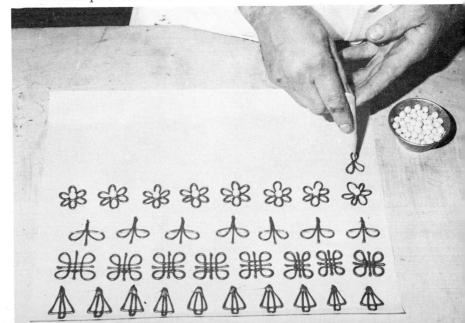

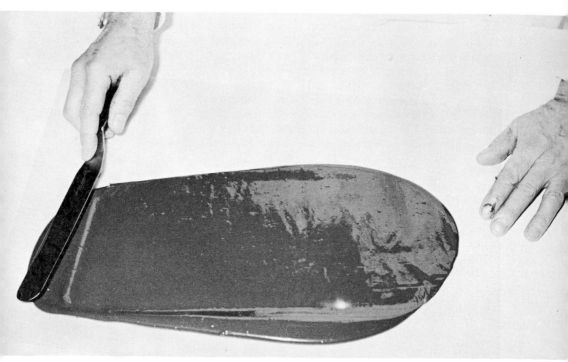

Figure 106. Chocolate work: spreading liquid chocolate onto a sheet of greaseproof paper in preparation for the production of cut-outs

Figure 107. Chocolate work: making chocolate curls

Decoration

(*a*) Shapes may be piped out onto greaseproof paper from drawn designs. When set, these shapes may be used to decorate gâteaux, torten, fancies, ice bombs, and special sweets.

(*b*) Chocolate may be spread out on greaseproof paper and, when nearly set, a cutter or knife can cut out shapes which, when set, can be removed from the sheet and used for decoration (Figure 106).

(*c*) Spread chocolate out on marzipan or sugar paste and, as it is setting, spread with a serrated scraper to obtain a corrugated effect. Cut out shapes with a cutter or knife when chocolate has set and use shapes for decoration.

(*d*) Spread chocolate on marzipan or sugar paste and, before it sets, sprinkle on a variety of dressings, e.g. nibbed almonds, coloured decor, coconut (white and browned), violet petals, rose petals, etc. Cut out shapes as in (*c*).

(*e*) Texture marzipan or sugar paste with rollers. Place melted chocolate in a greaseproof bag with a fine aperture. Pipe lines of chocolate at speed (*spinning*) over the textured paste, in different directions. Cut out shapes as in (*c*).

(*f*) Curls (Figure 107). Pour some chocolate onto a marble, metal, or melamine slab and spread backwards and forwards until it just sets. With a sharp knife, cut the chocolate off the slab using a shearing action. The chocolate will form long curls, the thickness depending upon the length of the shearing action. *Flakes* may be done in the same way, but the chocolate has to be more firmly set.

Plastic Chocolate

If confectioners' glucose and couverture are blended homogeneously together, they will form a plastic paste which may be modelled into roses etc. The proportions should be approximately two of chocolate to one of glucose, both warmed to about 90°F (32°C) before being blended together.

Faults

(*a*) *Fat Bloom*. This manifests itself with white streaks on the chocolate and is the result of using chocolate too warm.

(*b*) *Sugar Bloom*. This is a white bloom which appears on the surface of the chocolate and results from the use of chocolate at too low a temperature.

RECIPES

Chocolate Icing (or Sauce) (Suitable for imitation ganache as well)

    8 *oz* (240 *g*) *chocolate couverture*
    3 *oz* (90 *g*) *stock syrup* (*see page* 265)

(1) Melt chocolate in bain-marie.
(2) Warm solution of stock syrup to approx. 120°F (49°C).
(3) Add the syrup to the melted couverture, a little at a time, stirring each

addition well in. At first the mixture will thicken and become similar to toffee but as the syrup is increased the mixture will become thinner and approach the consistency of fondant.

(4) The consistency may be slightly adjusted by the use of more syrup if necessary. It is used like fondant for covering purposes. When set, it forms a skin but the icing remains soft.

Ganache

$\frac{1}{2}$ *pt* (3 *dl*) *fresh cream*
1 *lb* (480 *g*) *chocolate couverture* (*milk or plain*)

(1) Melt the chocolate in a bain-marie.

(2) Place cream in a clean saucepan and bring to the boil.

(3) Remove from the heat and stir in the melted chocolate. Whisk until completely mixed and smooth.

Notes.

1. This mixing can be flavoured by the addition of spirits and liqueurs and its consistency varied by altering the ratio of cream/chocolate. For a thinner mixture, increase the cream and for a thicker one increase the chocolate.

2. Ganache can be used in four ways:

(*a*) Used hot, it may be poured over a sponge (or similar base) like fondant when it will set into a thin, soft eating coating.

(*b*) If refrigerated, it sets to a firm paste, which may be moulded into chocolate centres and sweets.

(*c*) It may be whisked when slightly warm to produce a light cream which may be piped into a variety of patterns like buttercream.

(*d*) As a filling, either on its own or mixed with other fillings.

Imitation Ganache

Several concoctions can be made from chocolate and liquids to give a filling having similar properties to ganache (except flavour). The Chocolate Icing recipe, once cold, makes a passable imitation.

The best imitation is to use either artificial cream or evaporated milk instead of fresh cream.

19. Almond and Other Pastes

Almond Paste

Recipe 1.

4 oz (120 g) *ground almonds* } (*A*)
4 oz (120 g) *icing sugar*

4 oz (120 g) *castor sugar* } (*B*)
1½ oz (45 g) *whole egg* (1)

(1) Sieve the ingredients of (*A*) thoroughly together and make a bay.
(2) Place the ingredients of (*B*) in a saucepan and warm to approx. 120°F (49°C).
(3) Transfer contents of saucepan to the bay.
(4) Mix into a smooth paste.

Recipe 2.

1 *lb* (480 g) *sugar*
2 oz (60 g) *confectioners' glucose* } (*A*)
¼ pt (1½ dl) *water*

10 oz (300 g) *ground almonds* (*B*)

1½ oz (45 g) *egg yolks* (3) (*C*)

(1) Place ingredients of (*A*) in a clean copper saucepan and boil to 240°F (115°C). Observe sugar boiling precautions (*see* page 273).
(2) Allow the boiling syrup to cool slightly, then add the ground almonds (*B*).
(3) Lastly stir in the egg yolks (*C*) and work to a smooth paste.
Notes.
  1. Extra colour may be applied as desired.
  2. Consistency may be adjusted by altering the egg quantity.

Modelling Nut Paste

See Chapter 9 on Petits Fours Secs (page 135).

Sugar Paste

Recipe 1.

4 oz (120 g) *marshmallow*
4 oz (120 g) *icing sugar*
½ oz (15 g) *cornflour*
1/16 oz (2 g) *gum tragacanth*

(1) Mix all the ingredients together and knead into a smooth paste.
(2) Keep wrapped in polythene bag or covered with a damp cloth to prevent drying and skinning.

Recipe 2.

$\frac{1}{2}$ *oz (15 g) water*
2 *oz (60 g) sugar* $\Big\}$ *(A)*
1$\frac{1}{2}$ *oz (45 g) glucose*

$\frac{1}{4}$ *oz (7 g) gelatine*
1$\frac{1}{2}$ *oz (45 g) royal icing*
11 *oz (330 g) icing sugar*

(1) Bring the ingredients of (*A*) to the boil.
(2) Stir in the gelatine until it dissolves.
(3) Stir in the royal icing.
(4) Add the icing sugar and knead the mixture to a firm paste.
(5) Wrap in polythene bag or cover with a damp cloth.

Note. If paste is too stiff for any particular purpose, it will become more pliable if it is warmed.

Uses of Sugar Paste.

1. Covering for all types of gâteaux and fancies. It may be coloured and flavoured. It can also be used to cover cake surfaces which have to be coated in icings or chocolate. A thin coating of sugar paste will give a flat, smooth surface which forms a good base to obtain a perfect coating of icing. This is especially useful when icing is required for the top and sides of a gâteau.

2. Rolling out the paste thinly and cutting out shapes, either with a knife or special cutters. These shapes may be flowers, leaves, animals, or shapes like diamonds or hearts. They are very useful for decorating all types of fancies, gâteaux, and sweets.

3. Sugar paste may be used in the same way as gum paste for making various models, caskets, and table pieces. It may also be modelled into flowers, animals, figures, etc., in the same way as marzipan.

Gum Paste (for Pastillage)

1$\frac{1}{4}$ *lb (600 g) icing sugar*
2$\frac{1}{2}$ *oz (75 g) cornflour* $\Big\}$ *(A)*
$\frac{1}{4}$ *oz (7 g) gum tragacanth*

2$\frac{1}{2}$ *oz (75 g) cold water* *(B)*

(1) Mix the ingredients of (*A*) thoroughly together and make a bay.
(2) Add the water (*B*) and mix to a clear smooth paste.

Notes.

1. This paste should be left for an hour or so and re-mixed prior to using, to enable the gum tragacanth to become thoroughly dissolved in the paste.

2. Always keep covered with a wet cloth. When exposed to the atmosphere, it rapidly dries and hardens.

CASKETS

Gum paste, sugar paste, or almond paste may be used to make caskets. The latter, however, will need the addition of gum tragacanth at the rate of $\frac{1}{4}$ oz (7 g) per lb (480 g).

Caskets may be of any size or shape, the most popular being square, rectangular, round, or heart-shaped. They are usually filled with petits fours or sweets and are placed upon the banqueting table. Caskets may be made in coloured pastes and suitably decorated with royal icing, etc.

Making a Square Casket

First a full scale drawing has to be made of the top and base and of the sides as shown in Figure 108(*a*).

The slabs of paste may be accurately cut to shape and size by the following method:

(1) Extend the sides of the square and rectangular shapes which represent the top, base, and sides on the drawing.

(2) Transfer this drawing to a flat board and cover with a piece of waxed or greaseproof paper so that the drawing shows through.

(3) Roll out the paste to sufficient thickness (about $\frac{1}{8}$ in. (3 mm)) and lay this on the paper covering the drawing.

(4) Now, although the actual plan of the top, etc. is obscured, the extended lines are not and it is an easy matter to cut the paste to the accurate size and shape as shown in Figure 108(*b*).

(5) Now the paper containing the accurately cut slab of paste may be transferred to another flat board to dry. The slab of paste will not become distorted in shape if kept on the paper on which it was cut.

(6) After an hour or so, when the sugar piece has crusted over, lay on a sheet of clean tissue or greaseproof paper, and then lay on another board. Pressing the two boards together, turn upside down and then remove the first board which is now on top. Peel away the paper from the underside of the sugar slabs and allow this side to crust over also.

(7) From time to time, keep reversing the drying out position as previously described to make sure that even drying out occurs. If this is not done, then distorted shapes will result.

Once the sugar slabs are set, they may be joined together with royal icing and then suitably decorated as shown in Figure 108(*c*).

Heart-shaped Caskets

For this we need a mould round which the sides may be placed to set. A heart-shaped casket has to be made in five pieces: the base, two sides, and the top which is divided into two halves. If finding a heart-shaped mould proves difficult, a slab of 2 in. thick polystyrene may be easily cut into a heart shape by a carpenter with a band saw. Besides this we need a template made from stiff cardboard and cut into a heart-shape larger than the mould on

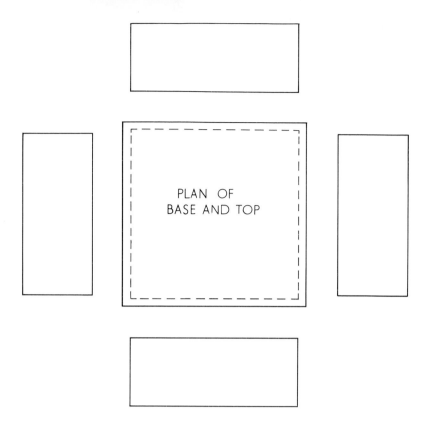

Figure 108. Square casket:

      (a) Diagram showing top, base, and sides of a square casket. Dotted lines show the position of the sides when fixed to the base. Notice two sides are shorter than the others to allow for the thickness when joined (*above*).

      (b) Showing how the paste may be accurately cut to the drawing with its lines extended (*below left*).

      (c) Casket assembled ready for filling and decorating (*below right*).

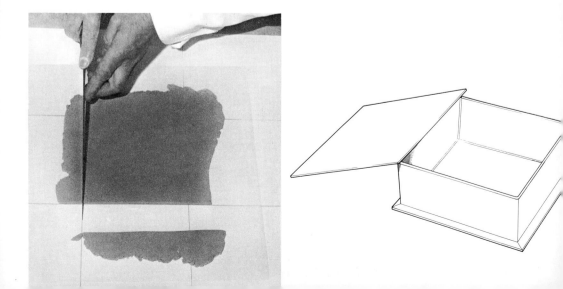

which the sides are shaped. In Figure 109(*a*) we see the sugar pieces which, when assembled, will make the heart casket, together with the mould and template used. The finished casket is shown in Figure 109(*b*).

Round Caskets

Here the techniques are very similar to the heart-shaped casket. If size is not critical, it is easy to get a round tin of appropriate size to use as the mould. The sides in this case would be made from a strip of paste, wrapped round. When this has set it is easy to slip out the mould and cement the side onto a circular base which has been cut from the template. The top may be left in one piece or cut in half as in the heart-shaped casket.

Figure 109. Heart-shaped casket:
       (*a*) 1. Cardboard template used for cutting out shape.
          2. Base.
          3. Top, cut in half.
          4. The sides made in two pieces and shown here placed around a heart-shaped mould to set.

(*b*) This casket has been filled with petits fours marzipan fruits.

Modelling Roses

Many types of flowers may be modelled from sugar or almond paste but the most popular is undoubtedly the rose. These may be used to decorate torten and gâteaux and also sugar or marzipan caskets.

The paste used for this purpose has to be smooth and pliable but stiff enough to stand up. Some gum tragacanth, at the rate of $\frac{1}{4}$ oz (7 g) per lb (480 g), improves the pliability of the almond paste and its ability to stand.

Figure 110 shows the stage by stage assembly of a rose and is explained as follows:

(1) Take a ball of paste and from it fashion a shape like a rose but with a pinnacle. Leave sufficient paste attached to form a base.

(2) From a ball of paste, make a petal by pressing the edges to paper thickness, keeping the centre thicker for rigidity. The very fine edge may be made by tapping the paste with the middle finger on the table, making sure that there is sufficient icing sugar dust underneath to prevent sticking. Damp the centre of the inside of the petal and wrap it around the pinnacle, leaving one edge furled back.

(3) Repeat and put on the other petal with one edge tucked into the first petal.

(4) Make a larger petal and apply it to the outside. Furl the outside edge before applying.

(5) Repeat (4).

(*a*)　　　　(*b*)　　　　(*c*)　　　　(*d*)　　　　(*e*)

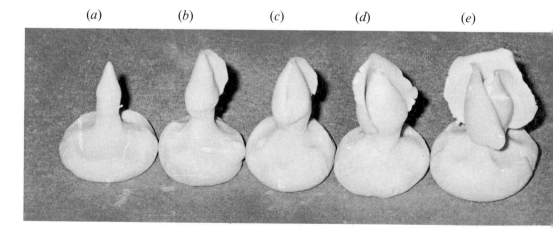

Figure 110. Marzipan rose: stages in making a marzipan rose:
(*a*) Pinnacle for the base.
(*b*) One petal assembled (rosebud).
(*c*) Two petals assembled (rosebud).
(*d*) The third petal assembled (rosebud).
(*e*) The fourth petal assembled (rose).

Figure 111. Marzipan rose: fully blown

Figure 111 shows a completed rose made in two colours. This is done by inlaying paste of another colour into the petal before final shaping.
Hints.

1. The number of petals on a rose is neither constant nor important to get a good effect. Usually five petals are sufficient, two for the centre bud and three surrounding it.

2. The petals are put on haphazardly, there being no regular pattern: nor are they necessarily tucked into each other.

3. For vividly coloured roses, e.g. carmine, powdered colours may be used to colour the marzipan and also applied by brush on the finished dried rose afterwards. To do this, the rose should first be dampened by holding it in steam.

Assembly. The roses are first removed from the base with a knife. Leaves, stems, etc., may be made from green paste, but maidenhair and dried asparagus fern may also be employed with good effect.

20. Sugar Work

SUGAR SYRUPS

For many types of patisserie goods, e.g. ice-cream, confiture fruits, etc., a sugar syrup of a definite density is required. This is ascertained by the use of an instrument called a 'saccharometer'. This is a hydrometer which may be calibrated in either Brix or Baumé degrees. The instrument is a hollow glass tube sealed at each end. At one end it is weighted with lead shot so that when it is placed in a solution it floats upright. The scale marked in either Brix or Baumé indicates the depth at which the tube floats. This is influenced by the density of the sugar which in turn is controlled by the ratio of sugar to water used for the solution. By the use of this instrument we can thus measure the amount of sugar in solution.

Use of Saccharometer

(1) Make sure that the solution to be tested is at 20°C (68°F). As the density changes with temperature, the Brix or Baumé tables have been standardized at this temperature.

(2) Pour the solution to be tested into a tall cylinder (a 500 cc glass cylinder is ideal).

(3) Insert the hydrometer and take the reading with the eye looking horizontally.

(4) To adjust the density of the sugar solution, add a syrup with a high concentration of sugar but at the same temperature of 20°C (68°F).

The following table is adapted from the Canners' Bulletin No. 2. issued from the Campden Research Station. Although only the Baumé scale will be used in this book, reference to this table will quickly give the reader the alternative Brix scale if required. To obtain the weights of sugar used per gallon of water, multiply the weights given by ten. For practical purposes, ounces should be brought to the nearest eighth (0·125) and grammes to the nearest whole number for the small quantities given in this chart.

Degrees Brix (per cent sugar by weight @ 20°C (68°F))	Degrees Baumé 20°C (68°F)	Weight of sugar to be added to each pound of water (approximately)	
		(ounces)	(grammes) (oz × 28·3)
10	5·6	1·8	50·9
11	6·1	2·0	56·6
12	6·7	2·2	62·3
13	7·2	2·4	67·9
14	7·8	2·6	73·6

Degrees Brix *(per cent sugar by weight @ 20°C (68°F))*	Degrees Baumé *20°C (68°F)*	Weight of sugar to be added to each pound of water (approximately)	
		(ounces)	*(grammes) (oz × 28·3)*
15	8·3	2·8	78·2
16	8·9	3·0	84·9
17	9·5	3·3	93·4
18	10·0	3·5	99·0
19	10·6	3·7	104·7
20	11·1	4·0	113·2
21	11·7	4·3	121·7
22	12·2	4·5	127·4
23	12·7	4·8	135·8
24	13·3	5·1	144·3
25	13·8	5·3	150·0
26	14·4	5·6	158·5
27	14·9	5·9	167·0
28	15·5	6·2	175·5
29	16·0	6·6	186·8
30	16·6	6·9	195·3
31	17·1	7·2	203·8
32	17·7	7·5	212·3
33	18·2	7·9	223·7
34	18·7	8·3	234·9
35	19·3	8·6	241·4
36	19·8	9·0	254·7
37	20·4	9·4	266·0
38	20·9	9·8	277·3
39	21·4	10·3	291·5
40	22·0	10·7	302·8
41	22·5	11·2	317·0
42	23·0	11·6	328·3
43	23·6	12·1	352·4
44	24·1	12·6	356·6
45	24·6	13·1	370·7
46	25·2	13·7	387·7
47	25·7	14·2	401·9
48	26·2	14·8	418·8
49	26·8	15·5	438·7
50	27·3	16·0	452·8
51	27·8	16·7	462·6
52	28·3	17·4	482·4
53	28·9	18·1	512·2
54	29·4	18·8	532·0

Degrees Brix (*per cent sugar by weight @ 20°C (68°F)*)	Degrees Baumé 20°C (68°F)	Weight of sugar to be added to each pound of water (*approximately*)	
		(ounces)	(grammes) (oz × 28·3)
55	29·9	19·6	554·7
56	30·4	20·4	577·3
57	30·9	21·3	602·8
58	31·5	22·2	628·3
59	32·0	23·1	653·7
60	32·5	24·1	682·0
61	33·0	25·1	710·3
62	33·5	26·2	741·5
63	34·0	27·3	772·6
64	34·5	28·5	806·6
65	35·0	29·8	843·3
66	35·5	31·2	883·0
67	36·1	32·6	917·6
68	36·6	34·1	965·0
69	37·1	35·7	1010·3
70	37·6	37·4	1058·4

Making of Confiture Fruit

This process is only suitable for hard or semi-hard fruits such as pears, apples, peaches, apricots, plums, cherries, or pineapple.

(1) Select perfect near-ripe fruit. Remove skins and if large cut into suitably sized pieces.

(2) Make sufficient sugar syrup with a density of 18°B to cover the fruit.

(3) Place the fruit in this syrup and bring to the boil.

(4) Remove from the heat and leave for 24 hours.

(5) On the second day carefully remove the fruit. Add sugar or heavy syrup to bring the syrup to a density of 20°B.

(6) Replace the fruit, bring to the boil, remove from the heat, and leave for 24 hours.

(7) On each successive day, repeat (5) and (6) above, increasing the density of sugar by 2°B each day, until the 6th day, when the density should be 28°B.

(8) At this stage of 28°B, add confectioners' glucose to bring the density up to 30°B.

(9) Repeat the process for the following 3 days, adding glucose until on the 9th day the syrup is 34°B.

(10) On the tenth day remove the fruit and store in a clean airtight tin until required.

Note. If the fruit is required to be candied, add sugar at operation (8) instead of glucose. The fruit will then crystallize out when stored.

Confiture Using Tinned Fruit (e.g. Pineapple)

> One $A2\frac{1}{2}$ *tin fruit* $(1\frac{3}{4}$ *lb*)
> 12 *oz* (360 *g*) *sugar*
> $\frac{1}{16}$ *oz* (2 *g*) *citric acid*
> 1 *pt* (6 *dl*) *water* (*including juice of fruit*)

(1) Pour off the juice of the tinned fruit into a measure and make this up to 1 pint (6 decilitres) with water.
(2) Add the sugar and acid and bring to a clear syrup with heat.
(3) Immerse the fruit and bring to the boil.
(4) Remove from the heat and leave for 24 hours.
(5) On the second day replace over the heat and re-boil.
(6) Remove from heat and leave for 24 hours.
(7) Repeat operations (5) and (6) for 5 more days, making 7 days intermittent boiling in all.
(8) At the end of the process, remove the fruit and store for future use.
Note. The syrup may be used as stock syrup.

Petits Fours

Wedge-shaped pieces of confiture pineapple make ideal petits fours and should be prepared as follows.
(1) Cut the rings of confiture pineapple into wedges.
(2) Heat some white fondant to approx. 140°F (60°C) and dip the wedges two-thirds of the way starting at the broadest end. Set these upright on oiled greaseproof paper.
(3) When the fondant has set, dip the one-third of the base in tempered chocolate couverture and replace the wedges to set.

When finished the piece of confiture pineapple should look as depicted in Figure 112.

Figure 112. Pineapple wedges for petits fours

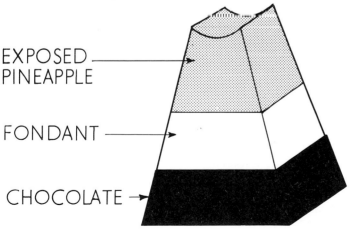

Fondant

Recipe 1.	*Recipe 2.*
14 *oz* (420 *g*) *sugar*	1 *lb* (480 *g*) *sugar*
2 *oz* (60 *g*) *confectioners' glucose*	¼ *pt* (1½ *dl*) *water*
¼ *pt* (1½ *dl*) *water*	1/16 *oz* (2 *g*) *cream of tartar*

Note. To weigh such a small amount as 1/16 oz (2 g), weigh ¼ oz (8 g) and use a quarter of this quantity.

(1) Bring the sugar and water to a clear syrup with a gentle heat.

(2) Raise the temperature so that it boils vigorously. Add the glucose or acid. Observe the sugar boiling precautions (*see* page 273).

(3) Boil to the feather degree of 240°F (115°C).

(4) Pour out onto an oiled slab between toffee bars (heavy sticks of metal) or into a tray with sides.

(5) Splash surface with water to prevent skinning and leave until temperature drops to approx. 100°F (38°C).

(6) Now agitate with a spatula. The mass will first become creamy and, as agitation continues, it also becomes thicker and whiter in colour.

(7) When the mass is too stiff to work with a spatula, continue by hand, working it down to a smooth pliable white mass.

(8) Store in an airtight tin with a little water covering the surface to prevent skinning.

Note. Hand made fondant is never as white or as smooth as the product which is manufactured for sale to the Confectionery Industry; it is therefore preferable to purchase and use the proprietary product whenever possible.

USES OF FONDANT

Fondant Icing

(1) Place some lumps of fondant in a bain-marie and apply gentle heat.

(2) Add stock syrup to bring the fondant to the correct consistency for icings.

Notes.

1. The icing should not be used above 100°F (38°C) and only sufficient stock syrup should be added to adjust to the consistency required at this temperature. The fondant icing should set with a pleasing gloss, but in order to achieve this it is imperative that at no stage should the fondant be over-heated. This will cause the minute crystals to grow in size and so reduce their light reflecting properties which cause the white appearance and gloss of this type of icing. The surface of the medium which is to be iced is also worthy of consideration. If the fondant icing is poured onto an absorbent surface like a sponge, the moisture quickly migrates from the fondant to the sponge, resulting in a drying out of the icing with a loss of gloss. To prevent this, cake surfaces should be coated either with a layer of marzipan or boiled apricot purée.

2. Several things may be added to fondant to improve its gloss and flavour.

(*a*) *To improve gloss*   *Quantity*
* Gelatine   1 oz (30 g) gelatine solution per lb
* Piping jelly   Up to 2 oz (60 g) per lb
  Marshmallow   2 oz (60 g) per lb
* Egg whites   Up to 1 egg white per lb

(*b*) *To improve flavour*   *Quantity*

Unsweetened couverture (block chocolate)	Up to 3 oz (90 g) per lb
Instant coffee	Up to $\frac{1}{2}$ oz (15 g) per lb
Liquid coffee concentrate	Up to 1 oz (30 g) per lb
Fruit, chocolate, or coffee Combined colour and flavour (combienne) Essences Essential oils Fruit juice concentrates or purée	To required taste according to strength of concentrate
Juice of tinned fruit or citrus fruit	Use as syrup for reducing fondant to required consistency

3. A product is available which is fondant in powder form and is reconstituted by adding a certain quantity of water. By replacing this water with fruit juice, a deliciously flavoured icing may be made.

Fudge Icings

By adding butter or fat to fondant, a soft fudge-like icing may be made. A recipe for a typical fudge icing is as follows.

$4\frac{1}{2}$ *oz (135 g) butter*
8 *oz (240 g) fondant*   (*A*)
$\frac{1}{2}$ *oz (15 g) evaporated milk*

1 *oz (30 g) evaporated milk*   (*B*)

(1) Warm and blend together ingredients (*A*) above.
(2) Add (*B*) and blend to a smooth icing.
Note. When warm (100°F (38°C)), it may be used as fondant. When cold it may be beaten and used as a buttercream.

Fondant Sweets (Yield approx. 30 sweets)

These may be used for petits fours secs.
1 *lb (480 g) fondant*
$2\frac{1}{2}$ *oz (75 g) condensed milk*
$\frac{1}{2}$ *oz (15 g) yeast water (see over)*
Flavour and colour

* These additives will affect the consistency and must be taken into account when the syrup is added.

Yeast Water.

> 1 *oz* (30 *g*) *yeast*
> 3 *oz* (90 *g*) *water*

Method 1. (For fondant drops.)

(1) Heat the fondant mixture to 150°F (65°C).

(2) Transfer the fondant to a greaseproof paper cornet or savoy bag and pipe out bulbs onto silicone paper or a tray, well-floured with cornflour.

(3) When set, remove the drops and store in a dry place for use as petits fours.

Method 2. (For shapes and chocolate centres.)

(1) For this a tray approx. 1½ in. (4 cm) deep is required to be filled with corn starch.

(2) In this starch impressions are made by pressing in a series of mould shapes. As an alternative one can use a special rubber mould which already has the impressions and is flexible to enable the fondants to be removed easily.

(3) Fill a dropping funnel (with stick) (Figure 113) with fondant and fill the impressions left in the starch.

(4) When set, carefully remove the fondant shapes brushing off any starch which adheres.

(5) Keep these shapes in a dry place until required.

There are usually two uses for these shapes as follows.

Crystallized Fondants

Crystallizing Syrup.

> 1 *lb* 6 *oz* (660 *g*) *sugar*
> ½ *pt* (3 *dl*) *water*

Boil to 224°F (106°C).

Dissolve the sugar before boiling point is reached. Boil rapidly and strictly observe sugar boiling precautions. Cool at room temperature and check with saccharometer: it should be 33° Baumé. Store without any disturbance in a cool place.

(1) Remove all traces of starch from the fondants. Place them on a draining wire and rest the wire in a shallow tray.

(2) Gently pour the crystallizing syrup over the fondants, until they are completely covered.

(3) Leave undisturbed for at least 6 hours, during which time a uniform layer of crystals will have formed around each fondant.

(4) When the fondants are sufficiently covered with crystals, remove them from the wire and allow to drain for at least 4 hours.

(5) Remove to a dry place and allow a further 12–16 hours for them to dry thoroughly.

Chocolate Centres

(1) Temper the chocolate (*see* page 244).

(2) With a fork dip each centre into the chocolate, wipe off the surplus

adhering to the bottom, and place on waxed or greaseproof paper to set.
(3) Decorate using chocolate or crystallized fruits, etc.

Stock Syrup (for reducing fondant, etc.)

> 1 *pt* (6 *dl*) *water*
> 1½ *lb* (720 *g*) *sugar*

Bring the water and sugar to the boil, remove any scum, and store in a clean jar for future use.

Figure 113. Fondant centres: method used to deposit warm fondant in cornflour moulds

Nougat (Croquant)

Recipe 1.

> ¾ *lb* (360 *g*) *sugar*
> ¼ *lb* (120 *g*) *confectioners' glucose*
> ¾ *lb* (360 *g*) *nibbed almonds*

(1) Stir the sugar and glucose over gentle heat until all sugar has dissolved and melted.

(2) Raise the temperature and cook until pale amber in colour.

(3) Warm and then stir in the almonds and remove mixture from the heat.

(4) Turn out onto a greased or oiled slab and keep turning it over with a palette knife until cool enough to mould.

Recipe 2.

> 1 *lb* (480 *g*) *sugar*
> *Juice of* ½ *lemon*
> ¾ *lb* (360 *g*) *nibbed almonds*

(1) Stir the sugar and lemon juice over gentle heat until all the sugar has dissolved and melted.

(2) Proceed as for Recipe 1.

Note. For the best decorative effect, the sugar should be amber in colour before the almonds are added so that there is a contrast between the dark colour of the sugar and the white of the almonds. However, the almonds may be added slightly earlier and cooked with the sugar to the desired colour when the almonds will also become browned. Alternatively, browned nibbed almonds may be added.

Uses of Nougat

Moulding. For moulding purposes the nougat must not be allowed to go cold, otherwise it will set and become brittle. As soon as it is cool enough to handle, it should be shaped or rolled or cut out into the required pieces. Oil should be used to prevent the nougat from sticking to the slab, rolling pin, or knife. If it becomes hard and brittle before the final shaping or cutting has been done, it may be softened by placing it in a hot oven. To cement the pieces together for making a basket, etc., hot boiled sugar should be used or alternatively chocolate or royal icing.

Nougat baskets or centrepieces may be decorated either with pulled sugar (flowers, leaves, ribbon, etc.) or with royal icing. They make an attractive centrepiece for a table and provide a base on which to display petits fours, etc.

Decorative Shapes. Gâteaux and torten may be decorated using shapes cut out from a sheet of nougat.

Masking. When set, nougat is easily crushed with a rolling pin. This should then be placed first in a coarse sieve to remove the very large particles (which need re-crushing) and then through a medium sieve to retain an even-sized number of nougat nibs. These are used as a dressing for masking the sides of gâteaux or torten.

Ingredients. The fine particles and dust may be mixed into fresh cream, buttercream, or ice-cream for flavouring purposes.

Paste. By putting this crushed nougat through a mill, a fine paste may be made which may also be used for flavouring purposes (praline).

Nougat Montelimart

14 *oz (420 g) sugar*
4 *oz (120 g) water*
4 *oz (120 g) honey*
4 *oz (120 g) confectioners' glucose*
1½ *oz (45 g) egg whites*
2 *oz (60 g) chopped cherries*
2 *oz (60 g) pistachio nuts or green nib almonds*
1 *oz (30 g) nibbed almonds* ⎫
1 *oz (30 g) flaked almonds* ⎬ *or hazelnuts*
⎭

(1) Boil the sugar and water rapidly to 225°F (107°C).
(2) Add the honey and glucose and continue to boil as rapidly as possible to 275°F (135°C).
(3) Whip the egg whites to a stiff snow and then beat in the hot syrup. Continue beating until the mixture becomes firm in consistency. This operation is best done on a machine.
(4) Warm the cherries and nuts and blend into the mixture.
(5) Pour this mixture into a wafer paper-lined tray or frame, spread level, and cover the surface also with wafer paper.
(6) Press down the surface with a weighted flat board and leave until perfectly cold, preferably overnight.
(7) Cut into suitable sized pieces with a damp hot knife.
Petits Fours. Small pieces of nougat montelimart make ideal petits fours. They should be cut into small rectangles, turned over so that the cut surface shows, and then the base and sides dipped into chocolate.

Rock Sugar

This is used for decorative effect on Christmas cakes, etc.

1 *lb (480 g) sugar*
6 *oz (180 g) water*
¾ *oz (22 g) royal icing (well beaten)*

(1) Boil the sugar and water to 280°F (138°C) observing the sugar boiling precautions (*see* page 273).
(2) Take the saucepan off the heat and remove surface heat by plunging the base into cold water.
(3) Add the well beaten royal icing and mix quickly and thoroughly.
(4) Pour quickly into a well greased bowl. When the royal icing is introduced into the boiling sugar syrup, there is considerable frothing and when it is transferred to the bowl, the mixture will rise rapidly, puffing out steam and looking much like an active stream of lava from a volcano. When it is set firm and is cool, it may be broken into pieces.
Note. For coloured rock sugar, use coloured royal icing.

SUGAR BOILING

The art of sugar boiling is usually acquired by patissiers through experience but is often little understood, and when faults are experienced the knowledge to ensure their correction is sometimes lacking. Therefore, before dealing with recipes and methods, some technical detail is given.

Equipment Required for Sugar Boiling

Copper saucepans
Sugar-boiling thermometer
Scissors
Snippers
Spirit lamp
Fast table fan
Infra-red lamp
Fine sieve
Canvas
Blowing tubes, different sizes, with puffing bellows
Copper tube of $\frac{1}{8}$ in. (3 mm) bore
Rolling pins, large and small
Modelling tools
Bunch of wire for spun sugar
Dipping forks for petits fours
Palette knife for turning sugar
Chisel scraper for turning sugar
Marble slab
Sugar nippers to hold sugar for warming
Knife for warming and cutting sugar
Some of this equipment is shown in Figure 114.

Some Uses of Boiled Sugar

Fondant
Fudge, toffees
Boiled and other sweets
Dipping and glazing petits fours
Pulled sugar work
Spun sugar
Blown sugar work
Sugar models
Cast sugar
Marshmallow
Italian meringue
Nougat
Rock sugar

Theory of Sugar Boiling

The sugar used for this purpose is commonly known as cane sugar. It can exist in many crystalline forms (*see* page 16) but because it can easily become contaminated with dust from the atmosphere, preserving or lump sugar is preferred as this is sugar in its purest state. Whether cane sugar exists as a powder or a cube it is the same chemical substance called *sucrose*.

If a solution of sugar receives prolonged boiling, the sucrose undergoes a chemical change. First another molecule of water is added, and then the chemical structure is broken down into two simpler sugar molecules.

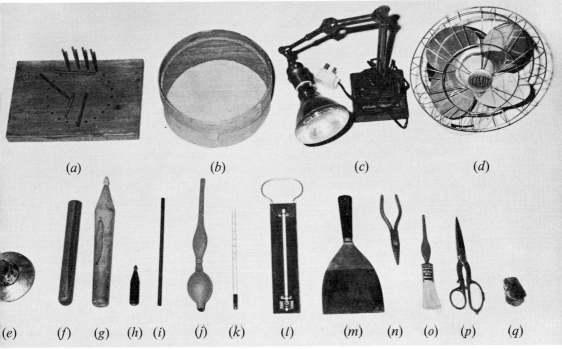

(a)   (b)   (c)   (d)

(e)   (f)   (g)   (h) (i)   (j)   (k)   (l)   (m)   (n)   (o)   (p)   (q)

Figure 114. Some equipment used in sugar boiling:
(*a*) Base board and loose pegs for use in the making of a basket; (*b*) Sieve on which stock of pulled sugar is kept during the making of various shapes; (*c*) Infra red lamp under which the sieve containing the stock of pulled sugar should be kept during the manipulating operations; (*d*) Electric fan used for cooling the sugar; (*e*) Spirit lamp; (*f*) Rolling pin; (*g*) Large nozzle for blown sugar work; (*h*) Small nozzle for blown sugar work; (*i*) Metal tube for blowing sugar with the mouth; (*j*) Hand pump or bellows; (*k*) Saccharometer; (*l*) Sugar boiling thermometer; (*m*) Large chisel scraper; (*n*) Bull-nosed pliers for making mould out of strip metal; (*o*) Washbrush for washing sides of sugar boiling pan; (*p*) Scissors for cutting pulled sugar; (*q*) Pincers for holding hot pulled sugar.

These are *dextrose* and *levulose*. Combined they form *invert* sugar, and it is largely the properties of this mixture which affects the characteristics of boiled sugar. We call this change '*inversion*'.

The change from sucrose to invert sugar by boiling is increased by the presence of an acid which acts as a catalyst. This is the reason that lemon juice or tartaric or citric acid is often used. The rate of boiling also has an effect upon the amount of inversion which takes place. The slower the boil the more invert sugar will be produced.

Crystallization

Another vital factor to be given the utmost consideration in sugar boiling is that of crystallization. To produce a saturated solution of sugar, we require approximately twice as much sugar as water but, because sugar can *melt* as well as dissolve, it is possible to get into solution by boiling three parts of sugar to one part of water. Such a solution is termed *super-saturated* and has certain properties.

If agitated, a super-saturated solution will crystallize out and give a mass of coarse grained crystals. We call this process '*graining*'. We can control the size of the crystals formed in this process in two ways: by adding sugar of a certain granular size, or by carefully controlling the rate of inversion. Since invert sugar does not readily crystallize, it follows that the more sucrose that can be 'inverted', the less sugar will remain to be crystallized. In fact, crystallization can be completely inhibited by inversion, particularly in the presence of acid. Examples of how we use these theories in practice may be given thus:

(*a*) In fondant making, we agitate a super-saturated solution of sugar which has been boiled to 240°F (115°C) in order to produce a white thick mass which is in reality millions of minute light reflecting crystals of sugar.

(*b*) When making fudge and cast sugar, a proportion of fondant is stirred into the mixture in order to bring about the production of fine crystals.

(*c*) In pulled sugar, great care is required *not* to over-agitate and so induce premature crystallization.

Another substance used by sugar confectioners to modify or inhibit crystallization of the sugar syrup, is *confectioners' glucose*. This is a manufactured product, being a thick white viscous syrup containing a high percentage of dextrose along with other sugars and the gum dextrin. Many confectioners use this substance in preference to acid which can tend to carry the inversion too far. The recipes available vary in the quantities of glucose used. The glucose itself varies in its constituents and therefore the amount can vary according to its quality.

The Boiling Process

Besides the chemical changes which take place, there is also a very apparent physical change which occurs. As boiling of the sugar syrup proceeds, some of the water evaporates and the resulting syrup becomes more viscous, resulting in the syrup setting firm when cold. As the syrup becomes thicker, so its boiling temperature progressively increases and so we can determine its temperature by its physical state. Indeed many experienced sugar confectioners and patissiers test their sugar by its physical state (as outlined below) instead of using a thermometer.

Hand Tests for Sugar Boiling.

Temperature		Name of degree	How to test
°F	°C		
220	104·5	Boiling	Effervescence
225	107	Thread Degree	Touch the surface of the boiling sugar with a dry finger. Join the thumb and this finger together and separate them. An elastic thread of sugar will be formed
230	110	Pearl Degree	Repeat the foregoing. The sugar will form a pearl-like bead at the ends of the thread as it breaks
235	113	Blow	When a loop of wire is inserted into the syrup and removed, a thin film will be produced which can be gently blown
240	115	Feather	At this stage the film of sugar syrup can be blown into feather-like pieces

Up to this stage, the syrup is still fairly thin although it is becoming noticeably thicker. To test the next few stages, it is necessary to take out some of the syrup and shock-cool it by plunging it into cold water to test its characteristics. This is done with the fingers by first immersing them in cold water, then plunging them into the syrup for just as long as it takes to collect a little of the syrup, then quickly putting them back into cold water again. The syrup will set and can be worked with the fingers.

245	118	Soft Ball	The syrup at this stage sets into a very plastic ball when manipulated with the fingers
250	121	Hard Ball	A very much firmer ball is now formed. At this stage the syrup is becoming really thick and the temperature rises rapidly
270–280	132–138	Soft Crack	The ball of sugar which is formed at this temperature forms a thin skin which will crack slightly
280–310	138–154	Hard Crack	The ball of sugar now sets with a very thick skin which requires considerable pressure before it is shattered (Many patissiers crunch this ball of sugar with their teeth to ascertain the correct degree)

Beyond this stage, the syrup begins to turn to a pale and then a dark amber colour emitting acrid fumes, until eventually a very dark, almost black, mass is formed.

Temperature		Name of degree	How to test
°F	°C		
310–	154–	Caramel	Very dark amber colour
350	177		

Notes.

1. If glucose or acid is used, this should be added at 220°F (104°C).

2. The above sugar boiling degrees are only approximate and there are of course differences which can be detected between the extremes of 250–270°F and 310–350°F. Only a sugar boiling thermometer can give an accurate indication of the true temperature and its use is to be strongly recommended. In the final stages, the temperature at which the sugar syrup finally boils or colours is also modified by the percentage of inversion which has taken place and the percentage of confectioners' glucose or invert sugar (e.g. honey) used in the initial syrup. This is because invert sugar and dextrose colour at a much lower temperature than sucrose.

Storage of Boiled Sugar

Boiled sugar is very hygroscopic, i.e. it takes up moisture from the air. If left for a length of time, particularly in a damp atmosphere, it will first become sticky and then lose its shape. Under extreme conditions the boiled sugar will actually make a syrup with the water it absorbs and run away. This is particularly prevalent in dipped fruits and spun sugar. (The hygroscopic nature of pulled sugar varies with the percentage of glucose or invert sugar present.)

To keep spoilage due to this cause to the minimum, goods like sugar dipped fruits (petits fours glacés) and spun sugar should not be done until just prior to service. Pulled sugar baskets, flowers, fruits, and blown sugar pieces should be kept under cover with a dehydrating agent present such as slaked lime or calcium chloride. Alternatively, they may be sprayed with confectioners' varnish or another non-toxic varnish. Under ideal storage conditions sugar work has a very long life although there is always the possibility of pulled sugar, etc., graining in time.

Faults Which Occur in Boiled Sugar Work

Fault 1. Sugar sets too hard so that it is difficult to work and readily breaks.
Cause: (*a*) Insufficient glucose used; (*b*) Boiled to too high a temperature.
Fault 2. Sugar appears greasy and will stick to the hands and table. Finished goods will soon disintegrate.
Cause: (*a*) Too much glucose used; (*b*) Boiled to too low a temperature.
Fault 3. Sugar grains.
Cause: (*a*) Incorrect recipe; (*b*) Incorrect temperature; (*c*) Too much pulling or working after it is pulled.
Fault 4. Poor colour.
Cause: (*a*) Rise in temperature was too slow; (*b*) Excess temperature.

The temperature of the boiled sugar is not the only guide to its condition because this alone will not tell the patissier how much of the sugar has become inverted, and therefore how its crystallizing and setting properties are affected. Only by experience under varying conditions can the patissier master this highly skilled work.

Sugar Boiling Method and Precautions

(1) Place sugar and water in a clean pan (preferably copper) and dissolve by stirring gently on low heat.

(2) Once dissolved, raise the temperature to boiling. If glucose or acid is used, add it at this point (moisten the acid with a little water first).

(3) Whilst boiling *do not stir*. Keep the sides of the pan and the thermometer continuously washed down with a little water to re-dissolve any sugar crystals which may form. Boil as rapidly as possible to the required temperature.

(4) If any scum appears on the surface remove it with a spoon.

(5) When the required temperature has been reached, remove the pan quickly from the heat and plunge it into a pan of cold water for a few seconds to prevent the temperature rising further due to heat absorbed by the saucepan.

Sugar Boiling Recipe for General Use

$1\frac{1}{4}$ *lb* (600 g) *granulated or cube sugar*
8 *oz* (240 g) *confectioners' glucose* (42–45° *Baumé*)
8 *oz* (240 g) *water*
This is a good general recipe.

Sugar Boiling Recipe for Storage

$1\frac{1}{4}$ *lb* (600 g) *granulated or cube sugar*
8 *oz* (240 g) *water*
A pinch of cream of tartar
Boil to 300°F (149°C).

This recipe is more suitable for storage purposes and for goods requiring a harder boil, e.g. pulled sugar work. It should be cast into blocks or sticks and stored in a screw-top jar. When required for use, it is just heated until it is pliable enough to be manipulated.

Spun Sugar (for Gâteau St-Honoré, etc.) (Figure 115)

(1) Prepare a site in the kitchen by placing two sticks to project beyond the edge of a table and laying plenty of sheets of paper underneath on the floor.

(2) Boil the sugar syrup to 310°F (154°C) and immediately arrest the rise in temperature by plunging pan into cold water for a few seconds.

(3) Use a fork, a bundle of wires, or a whisk with the ends cut off. Dip into the sugar and throw off the sugar picked up by the strands of wire, so that threads of sugar are formed across the two sticks.

(4) Repeat the process for as many times as is necessary for sufficient spun sugar to be made.

(5) Collect the spun sugar and use immediately to prevent spoilage due to dampness in the atmosphere.

Pulled Sugar

(1) Boil the sugar to the degree required, strictly observing the sugar boiling precautions.

(2) If the whole of the sugar is to be the same colour, add it in the pan (*beware of steam!*), shaking carefully and then pouring out. Otherwise pour out onto a clean, slightly oiled slab and add colour as required to various portions.

(3) When cool enough, fold the outsides to the centre. Continue to do this ensuring that no hard pieces are allowed to form. A uniform heat throughout is the aim.

Figure 115. Making spun sugar

(4) When cool enough to handle start pulling by holding the sugar with one hand and pulling with the other, folding over and over so as to incorporate air and develop a silky sheen. (As long as the sugar mass is kept moving, it refrains from setting, an important factor to remember.)

(5) Once the sugar is in a satisfactory condition, it may be placed either at the mouth (opening) of an oven or at a suitable distance under an infra red lamp.

(6) This is the bulk of pulled sugar with which to work. It must be kept turned every so often to maintain uniform heat and to keep it in a solid mass. Small pieces rapidly heat up and will cause the sugar to crystallize.

Making Flowers and Leaves

Boil the sugar syrup to 290°F (143°C).

Petals (Figure 116). Pull petals by squeezing, with thumb and first finger, the edge of a ball of sugar, making a curling twist to give a rounded edge. Pinch off with the nail of the thumb and forefinger. The edge must be as thin as possible. Ensure that the petals are cool enough to set into their pulled shape.

Roses. Make enough petal shapes to complete the rose. Build up the centre with two petals. Place three other petals around, sticking them to the centre stem by heating the base of each petal with a spirit flame. A good commercial rose may be made with five petals.

Carnations. The petals are pulled in a similar way to the rose. Cut the thin edge with inner part of a pair of scissors and quickly twist it into an S shape. Make a calyx with green sugar and onto this stick the petals in a circle. Alternate white and red petals make a good combination. For white carnations, red spots in the centre make an interesting flower.

Stems (Figure 117). For these, thin strong wire is required. It should be pulled through the warm pulled sugar and, as it is covered, quickly shaped. Galvanized wire should first be 'burned off'. 'Tendril' shapes may be made by coiling the sugar pieces around a rod.

Leaves (Figure 116). The sugar should be pulled into a leaf shape, i.e. round, pointed, etc. Mark in the veins of the leaf with the back of the knife and pinch round the edges if necessary. Autumn leaves can be made by partly mixing red and green sugars.

A mould can be made from metal which may be used to impress leaf shapes and veins.

Other Flowers. Many other flowers may be made by copying originals, e.g. pansies, violets, anemones, daisies, etc. Careful use of colour can make them look very natural.

Orchids are made by forming a calyx, two large and three long narrow petals. They may be formed to shape by use of a rolling pin. The pistil is formed from a roll of sugar. A realistic appearance can be obtained with the right shading of colour.

Figure 116. Petals and leaves:
    (a) A selection of rose petals and leaves with an assembled rose and a strip of ribbon.
    (b) Stretching the pulled sugar to make a petal.

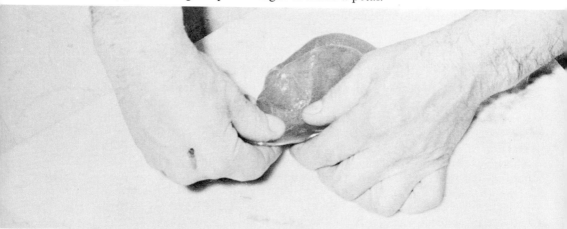

Figure 117. Stems: passing the hot pulled sugar through galvanized wire to make stems.

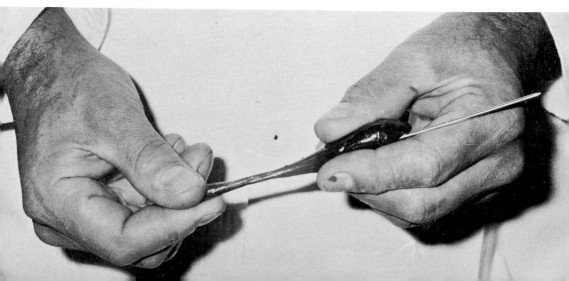

Butterflies

Delicate butterflies may be made from thin shaped pieces for wings attached to a shaped trunk and afterwards coloured. Royal icing may be used to make more complicated patterns.

Ribbons and Bows (Figure 118)

Boil the sugar syrup to at least 300°F (149°C). Use the Sugar Boiling Recipe for Storage.

(1) Make strips of sugar sufficiently thick of two or more colours, e.g. red and white.

(2) Press together and draw out carefully on a wooden bench. Make sure that the sugar is uniform in thickness and wide enough to pull out.

(3) Rub the piece down well to keep flat and uniform as the piece gets thinner and thinner.

(4) After pulling a little, cut into two and press the two white edges forming a red edged ribbon. For multi stripes repeat again.

(5) The ribbon must be pulled steadily at a fair speed, otherwise it will set and crack before it is thin or long enough.

(6) Cut into strips of pieces which can be handled, and when warm place in position.

(7) For bows, cut sufficient small pieces, warm, and make into loops, one for the centre and four for the bows.

(8) Warm with the spirit lamp and put the ends of the loops inside the centre loop.

Note. The pulled sugar can be cut by the use of an old knife heated over the spirit lamp so that it melts the sugar as it is cut.

Baskets (Figure 119)

These are usually displayed on a banqueting table filled with petits fours or pulled sugar flowers.

Simple Baskets. Roll out the pulled sugar and form it over an oiled tin shape. The edges may be pinched afterwards.

Woven Baskets (Figure 119). For these a base board is required fitted with an uneven number of pegs which are fairly loose and can easily be withdrawn. The board may be round or oval and both the board and the pegs should be oiled.

(1) Work the sugar into a ball and then a pear shape.

(2) Pull out a rope shape, keeping it uniform in thickness whilst coiling it in and out of the pegs. The thickness is kept uniform and at the same time the sugar is prevented from setting by twisting the sugar ball and rope end in the hand and pulling out at the same time. Once the rope end starts to set, break off and warm slightly or restart with another ball (Figure 119(*a*)).

(3) When the basket has been woven to a sufficient height, pull some sugar into long rods to the thickness of the pegs.

(4) Carefully remove the pegs and replace with the sugar rods, trimming the ends with a heated knife or a pair of small cutting pliers.

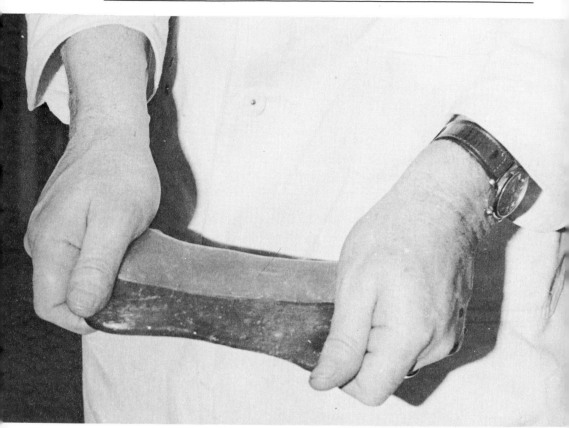

Figure 118. (*a*) Pulling two differently coloured strips of pulled sugar into a ribbon (*above*); (*b*) Multicoloured strip of pulled sugar being pulled to form a ribbon (*below*).

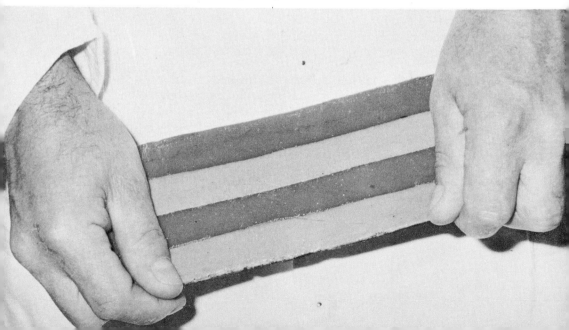

(5) Prepare a base, either by rolling out pulled sugar or casting sugar into the right shape (*see* later).
(6) Invert the basket and seal onto the base with liquid sugar.
(7) Coil a rope of sugar round the top and seal off the end.
(8) A handle can be made from strong flexible wire with pulled sugar coiled round in a spiral fashion (Figure 119(*b*)).
Alternative Methods.
(1) Attach the sugar pegs to the base and then weave the sugar strands round directly. Unless one is very skilled, this method does not result in such a well-shaped basket.
(2) Form the sugar into thin sheets and from this cut strips. Weave these strips in and out of either wooden pegs or the sugar pegs as suggested in (1) above.
  The basket may be completed by the use of ribbon wound around the handle or by placing pulled sugar flowers, leaves, and stems.
Note. For sticking sugar to sugar, sometimes it is easier to dip pieces into boiled sugar, or to use a rod of sugar melted over a spirit lamp. Simple joins are made by warming one piece over a spirit lamp and pressing it into the other.

Blown Sugar (Figure 120)

  For this we can use specialized equipment consisting of a rubber tube connected to a plastic nozzle at one end and a small hand pump at the other (Figure 120(*b*)). This is so that small quantities of air can be pumped through the nozzle. This is recommended for very large blown sugar goods. Alternatively, using a longer copper or wooden tube, the sugar can be blown with the mouth (Figures 120(*c*) and (*d*)). This gives easier control and is recommended for small blown sugar goods.
(1) Boil sugar syrup to at least 290°F (143°C).
(2) Pull the sugar as previously described but keep flattening the sugar to press out any large air bubbles.
(3) Select a suitably-sized piece of sugar, make into a ball, and press on the end of a suitably-sized oiled rolling pin. Roll this round to give an even thickness and then make it thinner at the edge (Figure 120(*a*)).
(4) Remove from the rolling pin, insert the plastic nozzle or tube, and attach the ends of the hollowed sugar piece. If necessary dip the end of the nozzle or tube in hot sugar to help it stick.
(5) Start blowing with short strong puffs and, as the sugar swells out, slow up with slight blowing.
(6) Ensure that it is of even thickness by feeling round the sugar bowl from time to time. Cool with a fan if the size increases too rapidly and also if any part becomes too thin. With practice, shaping is made by cooling and warming slightly.

Figure 119. Basket:

> (a) Making the sides of a small basket by coiling the pulled sugar in and out of the wooded pegs. Note how the ball of pulled sugar is kept twisted during the operation to prevent it setting.

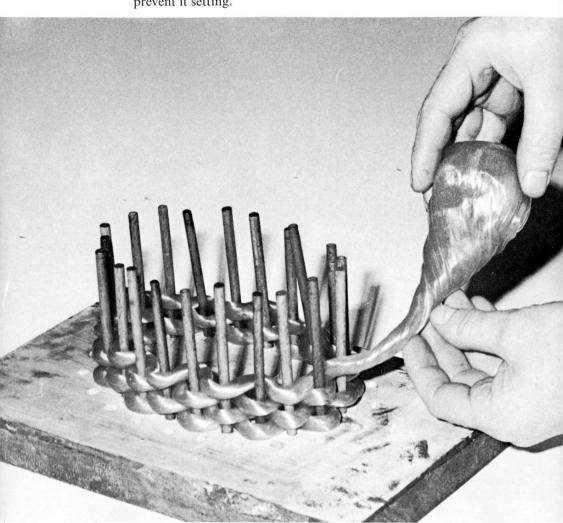

> (b) Coiling the pulled sugar around galvanized wire to form a handle.

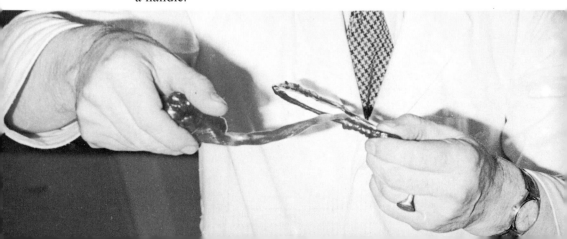

(*c*) This magnificent example of pulled and blown sugar was exhibited at Hotelympia in 1970.

The pulled sugar basket contains fruits made from blown sugar and is decorated with pulled sugar ribbon. (*Photograph by courtesy of Le Salon Culinaire International de Londres*)

Bowls and Vases

The base of the sugar ball will be thick but if this is required to be thinned out and to blow more of a ball shape, invert the sugar and tube and blow upwards. For a long necked vase, blow downwards and if necessary pull downwards as well (Figures 120(*c*) and (*d*)).

When the shape has been made, cool and when firm cut off with a warm knife.

If a vase is made it should be finished off by decorating with flowers on stalks. Handles may also be attached.

Other Shapes (Figure 121)

Fish. Pull to the appropriate length and shape. Fix on fins afterwards.
Fruits. Suitable ones are peaches, apples, and pears.
Swans. Made from a vase shape, the neck coiled round and shaped by careful warming and cooling. Wings are made by cutting and marking right-angled triangular pieces.
Elephant. Keep part of the vase shape thick and cut this into two. As blowing continues, these pieces will separate. The two are again divided and guided to separate as it is blown to form four legs. The neck end is curled over to form the head and trunk and a slit made for the mouth. Two large ears, two tusks and a tail make a good abstract elephant.
Birds. These are more difficult but are possible to do after practice.

Figure 120. Blown sugar work:
　　　　　　　　(*a*) Shaping the ball of pulled sugar over the end of a rolling pin, preparatory to blowing.

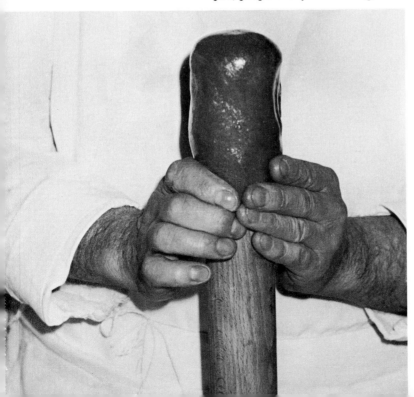

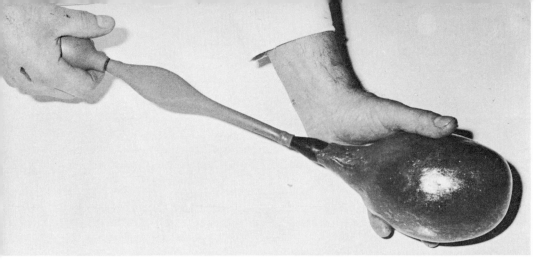

(*b*) Using the hand pump or bellows to pump air into the ball of pulled sugar.

(*c*) Shaping the ball of pulled sugar into a short vase shape by blowing upwards with the mouth.

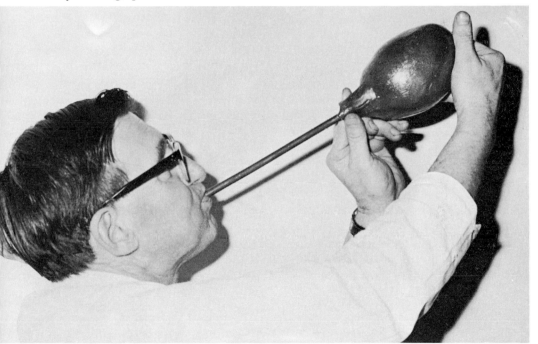

Cast Sugar Work (Figure 122)

The casting of sugar is a relatively simple procedure although it is not necessarily easy to produce good results. It is the method used to make complete models.

(*d*) Making a long vase shape from a ball of pulled sugar by blowing with the mouth and allowing the sugar to fall downwards.

We first need a mould made out of clay or plaster of Paris, constructed in sections, so that the sugar figure may be removed easily from the mould once cast.

The sugar is boiled to about 300°F (149°C) and then fondant is stirred into it so that the sugar will grain and solidify.

After pouring the sugar into the mould, allow time for draining and for it to solidify and then remove the mould section by section to release the sugar replica.

Using Non-grained Sugar

This is mainly used for flat moulds. These moulds are made from bent and formed 'band' metal, approx. $\frac{1}{2}$ in. (12 mm) wide, the strips being bent to a preconceived design with snipe-nosed pliers.

The shape is placed on oiled paper or film on a slab and the boiled sugar poured in to set (Figure 122). Use Sugar Boiling Recipe for Storage (page 273), boiled to 300°F (149°C).

If the sugar is clear it is possible to simulate 'stained glass windows'. For window displays it is usual to have an opaque sugar similar to the grained sugar. This is accomplished by mixing precipitated chalk into the sugar boil.

Different colours may be inserted by separating in sections; when one colour is cold, the other is poured in after removing the sectioning-off piece. Make sure any oil is wiped off to enable the sugar to join.

Other Methods.

1. Roll out plasticine, place on a design, and cut out. Oil the edges and pour in the sugar.

2. Cut out the shape in expanded polystyrene and line the shape with aluminium foil (Figure 122).

By the use of good design and colour, very attractive show and centre pieces may be made from this type of cast sugar.

Moulded Small Pieces for Gâteaux

A model of a flower or relief figure may be made in the following way.

First a relief mould of clay or plaster of Paris is made and from this an impression is made from solder metal. Before the hot metal sets a wire should be embedded.

Figure 121. Examples of blown sugar shapes suitable for display purposes

The sugar is now boiled, and the metal impression oiled and if necessary cooled in a refrigerator. It is now dipped into the boiling sugar, taking care not to allow it to lap over the edges. Hang up on the wire and just before the sugar sets, pull off the sugar figure. For flowers it may be necessary to produce several shapes in this way and assemble them together afterwards.

Many different shapes of pieces for decorative use may be made from the warmed scraps of sugar which may be rolled in castor sugar for a decorative effect.

Figure 122. Cast sugar being poured into moulds which have been made in polystyrene by cutting out the shape and lining it with aluminium foil. On the left of the picture is another set of moulds made from metal strip, secured to a base-board with plasticine which also makes a seal to prevent the liquid sugar from flowing underneath the strips

Poured Sugar Work

Boiled sugar may be used to decorate by piping. A tube with a $\frac{1}{16}$-in. ($1\frac{1}{2}$-mm) hole in the end of the handle may be used to pour lines over sugar pieces to form a design. Bright colours may be used to give sparkle to such work.

21. Preserves, Creams, and Icings

FRUIT PRESERVATION—JAMS, JELLIES, BOTTLED FRUIT, SUGAR PRESERVED FRUITS

In this technological age food preservation has been exploited to such an extent that all types of food are now available out of season and the patissier can usually buy most fruit, either dried, frozen, bottled, or tinned.

However, occasionally he may have to preserve a quantity of fruit for further use and in this case an understanding of this process is necessary.

Fruit may be preserved in the following ways:

1. Drying
2. Use of sugar
3. Sterilizing
4. Deep freezing
5. Use of preservatives.

Drying

This means the removal of water to the point at which micro-organisms and the natural process of decay cannot function or are slowed down. Not all fruits are suitable for this method of preservation although, with the comparatively recent advances in *accelerated freeze drying*, very good results have been obtained with fruits such as strawberries which were previously thought to be impossible to dry into an acceptable product. The drying process therefore, may be:

(a) *Normal hot air drying or natural sun drying*. This is reserved for products such as dried apricots, peaches, apples, figs, etc. Such dried goods usually require a prolonged soaking (up to 24 hours) before being cooked.

Goods like dates, raisins, sultanas, etc., are usually used in their dried state, although in some cases it is an advantage for them to be soaked prior to use. The drying of many of the products in sun drenched lands is done by exposure to the sun.

(b) *Accelerated freeze drying*. In this process, selected ripe fruit is first deep frozen. It is then placed into a vacuum oven between electrically heated plates. When the deep frozen fruit is subjected to gentle heat in a vacuum oven, the moisture is rapidly removed by evaporation but in such a way that the tissue of the fruit does not collapse as it does in the normal air drying process. The dried fruit, therefore, retains its shape and size and has a porous texture.

On reconstitution, the fruit behaves exactly like a sponge, mopping up the water it lost in the drying process in a matter of minutes instead of hours. All that is necessary is for a carefully measured quantity of water to be poured onto the fruit to bring it back to almost the same state as fresh fruit. Some loss of colour and firmness may be detected but this is a small price to pay for the advantage of having any desired fruit out of season.

In the future we shall see an increased range of products being preserved in this manner.

Use of Sugar

Sugar owes its powers of preservation to the fact that micro-organisms will not flourish in high sugar concentrations. Thus we can make jams and jellies which may be kept for a year or more. Confiture fruits and glacé and crystallized or candied fruits (*see* Chapter 20) may be kept much longer because they are impregnated with sugar to a very high concentration.

Sterilizing

This is the process adopted for bottling and canning. Since bottling is an easy and useful method for preserving fruit, fuller details are given below.

Fruit Bottling

General Rules.

1. Always use sound fresh fruit slightly under rather than over-ripe. Large fruits should be halved or quartered.

2. Bottle in syrup rather than water so that the preserving power of sugar may be used and is allowed to penetrate the fruit. (If bottled in water and sweetened afterwards, the added sugar would merely sweeten the juice and not the flesh of the fruit, e.g. pears.)

3. Make sure that the bottles or jars and their seals are clean, dry, and in good condition.

4. The fruit should be heated gently to prevent it from breaking or rising in the jar and to ensure complete sterilization.

There are four methods of bottling:
   Oven method
   Sterilizer with thermometer
   Sterilizer without thermometer
   Pressure cooker

Oven Method.

(1) Prepare the fruit and pack firmly, without bruising, into the clean dry bottles or jars.

(2) Cover with a metal lid or saucer.

(3) Place the jars, making sure that they do not touch, on slats of wood or an asbestos mat on a baking sheet in a low position in the oven. Alternatively, they may be placed in a shallow water bath.

(4) Allow fruit to cook in a slow oven until the skins of the fruit begin to crack (between $\frac{3}{4}$–$1\frac{1}{4}$ hours).

(5) Remove the jars singly onto a folded cloth in a tray. If fruit shrinks during cooking top up from another jar.

(6) Fill the jar gently with boiling syrup or water until it overflows.

(7) Seal at once by any of the following methods:

  (*a*) Metal screw top with rubber ring and glass top.

  (*b*) A commercially manufactured metal cap.

  (*c*) A synthetic skin.

(8) Leave undisturbed for 24 hours.

(9) Test seal by unscrewing top and supporting the weight of the bottle by the seal.

Sterilizer with Thermometer Method.

(1) Proceed as for Oven Method.

(2) Fill the jars to overflowing with either *cold* water or syrup.

(3) Seal according to type. If using a screw top seal, first tighten then unscrew a half turn.

(4) Making sure they do not touch, place the jars on a false bottom in a sterilizer, deep pan, or boiler.

(5) Cover with cold water.

(6) Apply heat and sterilize as follows:

Group	Fruit	*Temperature after* $1\frac{1}{2}$ *hours heating*	*Length of time to maintain temperature*
A	Apples Apricots Blackberries Currants (red, black, and white) Gooseberries Loganberries Mulberries Peaches Raspberries Rhubarb Strawberries	165°F (74°C)	10 minutes
B	Apples (solid pack) Cherries Damsons Greengages Plums	180°F (83°C)	15 minutes
C	Pears Quinces Tomatoes (whole in brine)	190°F (88°C)	30 minutes

(7) After cooking remove sufficient water to uncover the jars and lift them

out one at a time onto a cloth or slat of wood. Tighten the screw tops where necessary and leave undisturbed in a cool place. Re-tighten tops during cooling if required.

(8) Test the seal after 24 hours.

Sterilizer without a Thermometer Method.

(1) Proceed as for previous method but use *hot* water or syrup for filling the jars.

(2) Stand jars without touching in a water bath and completely submerge in warm water.

(3) Apply heat to raise the temperature to simmering in 30 minutes and maintain for the following specified time:

Group A 2 minutes.   Group B 10 minutes.   Group C 20 minutes.

Pressure Cooking. The use of a pressure cooker will reduce the cooking time to about one-third of that of other methods. It is particularly useful for the bottling of vegetables. Details of bottling are usually given with each pressure cooker.

Pulping. Where there is a large quantity of blemished fruit a pulp may be made and preserved. This is particularly useful for the manufacture of jams and jellies.

(1) Prepare the fruit by removing blemishes etc.

(2) Using the minimum amount of water, stew to a pulp for at least 30 minutes.

(3) Pour immediately into a very hot, dry jar and seal. Complete each jar before proceeding with the next.

(4) Immediately sterilize by placing it in a pan of boiling water to cover it completely. Allow to stand in the simmering water for 10 minutes.

(5) Finish off as previously described.

JAMS AND JELLIES

Rather than give a large number of individual jam recipes, the process of jam making is explained as well as the factors which influence the formation of a jam recipe.

Jams and jellies are made by boiling together two basic ingredients – fruit and sugar in approximately equal quantities. The quality of the jam, however, and especially its ability to set, will depend upon the strength of a naturally occurring jellying agent called *pectin*. However, the concentration of sugar, presence of acid, and amount of moisture present also have an influence.

Pectin

This jellying agent is present naturally in all fruits but some fruits, such as strawberries and cherries, are deficient in this agent, whilst in others such as apple there is more than sufficient (*see* chart opposite). The pectin is extracted from the fruit during the boiling process but more will be extracted in an acid medium. In jam-making, fruits which are naturally deficient in pectin should always have an organic acid like tartaric or citric (or lemon juice) added. In commercial manufacture of jam, pectin derived from apple or citron may be added to fruits naturally deficient in this agent.

Sugar

The concentration of sugar needs to be between 63 and 66% to make a firm product and also one with sufficient preserving qualities. Below this concentration, jam is more likely to attack by wild yeasts which will ferment it (*see* later). However, since the sugar contributes to the setting quality of the jam, the actual quantity used will be dictated by the type of fruit used and its pectin content.

FRUIT AND VEGETABLE JAMS

CHART

Fruit and Vegetable	*Acid Content*	*Pectin Content*
Apple, cooking, sour	xx	xxx
Apple, dessert, acid varieties	xx	xx
Apple, crab	xx	xxx
Apple, sweet, full-ripe	0	0
Apple, sweet, full-ripe, some varieties	x	x
Apricot, ripe	x	0
Banana, unripe	0	x
Barberry	x	x
Bilberry	x	x
Blackberry, early, ripe	0–x	0–x
Blackberry, late	000	0
Blackberry, unripe, red	x	x
Bullace	xx	xx
Cherry, acid, Morello and May Duke	x	x
Cherry, cooking	0	0
Cherry, sweet, ripe	00	00
Cherry, sweet, unripe	x	x
Cranberry	xx	xx
Currant, black	xxx	xx
Currant, red or white	xxx	xxx
Damson	xx	xx
Elderberry	0	0
Fig, ripe	00	00
Fig, unripe	0	x
Gooseberry, green	xx	xxx

Fruit or Vegetable	Acid Content	Pectin Content
Grape, unripe	xx	xx
Greengage	x	x
Japonica	x	x
Lemon	xxx (in juice)	xxx (in pith and some in juice)
Lime	xx (in juice)	xx (in pith and some in juice)
Loganberry	xx	xx
Marrow (vegetable)	000	000
Medlar	00	0
Melon	0	x
Mulberry	xx	x
Nectarine	0	0
Orange, bitter	xxx (in juice)	xxx (in pith)
Peach, ripe	00	00
Peach, unripe	0	0
Pear, cooking	0	00
Pear, dessert, ripe	000	000
Pineapple	xx	00
Plum, ripe, firm	x	x
Pomegranate	x	000
Pumpkin	000	000
Quince, ripe	00	xx
Quince, unripe	00	xx
Raspberry	0	0
Raspberry, some varieties, unripe	x	x
Rhubarb	0–x	0
Rowan, mountain ash berries	xx	x
Sloe	xx	x
Strawberry	x	000
Strawberry, some varieties	x	0
Tomato	x	0

x = high   xx = very high   xxx = extremely high content
0 = low   00 = very low   000 = extremely low content

Sugar quantity	*Amount of sugar per lb (480 g) fruit*
Fruits rich in pectin (apple, gooseberry, black currant, damson, red currant, etc.)	1¼ lb (600 g)
Fruits with medium pectin content (greengage, apricot, plum, etc.)	1 lb (480 g)
Fruits deficient in pectin (strawberry, rhubarb, marrow, blackberry, etc.)	¾ lb (360 g)

Acid Quantity

Fruit deficient in acid should always have some acid added (*see* chart, opposite). The acid may be added as follows to each 2 lb fruit:

(*a*) $\frac{1}{2}$ lemon or 1 tablespoonful of lemon juice.

(*b*) $\frac{1}{2}$ level teaspoonful of citric or tartaric acid.

(*c*) $\frac{1}{8}$ pint (75 g) gooseberry or red currant juice.

Water Quantity

For hard fruits, such as plum, damson, apricot, and gooseberry, up to $\frac{1}{2}$ pint (3 decilitres) of water should be added and the fruit stewed gently before the sugar is added in order to soften the skins. Soft fruits, such as strawberry, raspberry, apple, and blackberry, require no water.

General Method for Making Jam

(1) Select sound ripe fresh fruit. The fruit is better under-ripe than over-ripe.

(2) Wash and prepare. Large fruits need halving or quartering.

(3) Place the fruit (and acid if used) in the boiling pan and, if it is a hard fruit, give a preliminary stewing.

(4) Add the sugar and gently heat until the sugar is completely dissolved. Stir to prevent sugar burning on bottom of pan.

(5) Once the sugar has dissolved, boil as rapidly as possible until the setting point of the jam is reached.

(6) The setting point of the jam will vary according to the type of fruit used and may be between 2–20 minutes. Test as follows:

(*a*) Remove the spoon with some jam and allow it to fall off back into the pan. When setting point is reached the last cooled drops of jam should form a flake.

(*b*) Test by allowing a few drops of jam to fall onto a dry plate and leave in a cool place to set. If pushed with the fingers the surface of the jam should wrinkle.

(7) Once setting point has been reached, skim carefully and remove stones.

(8) Allow jam to cool slightly to thicken so that whole fruit, e.g. strawberries, will remain evenly suspended and not rise to the top of the jar.

(9) Stir and then fill clean, dry, warm jars.

(10) Cover surface of jam at once with a waxed paper disc.

(11) Lastly put on the final cover, label with the type of jam and date of manufacture, and store in a cool place.

Faults in Jam

1. *Sugar Crystallizing.* This will happen if:

(*a*) Concentration of sugar is too high.

(*b*) There is insufficient acid present.

(*c*) Jam has been insufficiently boiled.

(*d*) Jam has been too long in storage.

2. *Mould Formation on Surface.* Mould growth will occur on almost any medium which is moist and left in still air. It only requires one mould spore to find its way to the jam before it is covered for a luxurious growth of mould to appear eventually. The jam must be sealed whilst still very hot to prevent contamination by the mould spores floating in the air. Jam contaminated with mould is not harmful. The mould can be removed from the surface of the jam which will leave the remainder quite wholesome and fit for use.

3. *Fermentation.* This is caused by the presence of wild yeast cells which will reproduce on the jam causing an evolution of carbon-dioxide gas. It can be traced to contamination at the covering stage, although jam already opened is much more likely to be attacked and to ferment.

Watery jams, where the sugar concentration is low, are much more prone to attack of this kind.

If jam is opened for any length of time before it is used, it is always a wise precaution to bring it to the boil before use.

Fermented jam is usually completely spoiled, having an objectionable sour acid taste.

4. *Too Thick.* (*a*) Too much sugar. (*b*) Insufficient water.

5. *Too Watery.* (*a*) Not enough pectin. (*b*) Insufficient sugar. (*c*) Insufficient acid. (*d*) Too much water added.

6. *Poor Colour.* All fruits lose a certain amount of colour when they are cooked and this is reflected in the jam they produce. Most jam manufacturers use artificial colours to make their jam brighter and the private producer can do the same. However, the presence of a dirty colour in jam is usually because it has not been boiled properly or it has become contaminated by a dirty pan.

7. *Opaqueness.* Jam and jellies should be clear and almost transparent. Opaqueness is a sign that the boiling was unduly prolonged or that there is some contamination. Premature crystallization of the sugar will also cause this to happen.

SOME SELECTED JAM RECIPES

Apricots (made from dried apricots)

  8 *oz* (240 *g*) *dried apricots*
  $1\frac{1}{2}$ *pt* (9 *dl*) *water*
  Juice of $\frac{1}{2}$ *lemon*
  $1\frac{1}{2}$ *lb* (720 *g*) *sugar*

(1) Wash the dried fruit thoroughly.
(2) Place in a basin with the water and allow it to soak for at least 24 hours.
(3) Place the fruit and the liquor in which it has been soaked in a preserving pan and add the lemon juice.
(4) Bring to the boil and boil gently for $\frac{1}{2}$ hour, stirring occasionally.
(5) Add the sugar and continue boiling until the setting point of the jam has been reached. Stir constantly.

(6) Fill the jars and immediately cover.

Note. This jam can be sieved to make an ideal purée for glazing and other purposes.

Greengage/Apricot/Peach/Plum/Damson

1 *lb* (480 g) *fruit*
1 *lb* (480 g) *sugar*
$\frac{1}{4}$ *pt* (1$\frac{1}{2}$ *dl*) *water*

Same method as for Apricot Jam, using water to stew and soften fruit before adding sugar.

Green Gooseberry/Black Currant

1 *lb* (480 g) *fruit*
1$\frac{1}{4}$ *lb* (600 g) *sugar*
8 *oz* (240 g) *water*

Same method as for Apricot Jam, using water to stew and soften fruit before adding sugar.

Strawberry

1 *lb* (480 g) *fruit*
$\frac{3}{4}$ *lb* (360 g) *sugar*
Juice of $\frac{1}{2}$ *lemon*

(1) Cut strawberries in half. This helps in the extraction of their limited pectin content.

(2) Gently simmer with the lemon juice.

(3) Add sugar and boil rapidly until setting point is reached.

Notes.

1. Instead of lemon juice, $\frac{1}{16}$ oz (2 g) tartaric acid may be used or 2 oz (60 g) red currant juice.

2. Because of this jam's poor setting properties, it is often blended with jams which are rich in pectin, e.g. apple, red currant, etc.

Strawberry (using red currant to aid setting and increase bulk)

1 *lb* (480 g) *strawberries*
8 *oz* (240 g) *red currants*
1 *lb* (480 g) *sugar*

(1) Wash and string the red currants, place them into a pan with a little water, and simmer gently until tender.

(2) Pass through a cloth or hair sieve to obtain the juice.

(3) Add to the washed strawberries and sugar and proceed to make the jam as previously described.

Raspberry/Loganberry

1 *lb* (480 g) *fruit*
1 *lb* (480 g) *sugar*

Same method as for Strawberry Jam.

Note. It is best to use under-ripe fruit for this recipe.

Raspberry and Red Currant

> 8 *oz* (240 *g*) *raspberries*
> 8 *oz* (240 *g*) *red currants*
> 1 *lb* (480 *g*) *sugar*
> $\frac{1}{3}$ *pt* (2 *dl*) *water*

(1) Wash and string the red currants and place in the preserving pan with the raspberries.

(2) Add the water and simmer on gentle heat until the fruit is cooked.

(3) Add the sugar and proceed to make the jam as previously described.

Marmalade

> 1 *lb* (480 *g*) *seville* (*bitter*) *oranges*
> 3 *lb* (1440 *g*) *sugar*
> 3 *pt* (18 *dl*) *water*
> $\frac{1}{2}$ *lemon*

(1) Wash, wipe the oranges and cut in half.

(2) Remove the pips, tying them in a muslin bag.

(3) Slice or shred the fruit and place it together with the pips in the preserving pan.

(4) Boil until the rind is tender and the contents of the pan reduced to about half. This will take $1\frac{1}{2}$–2 hours.

(5) Remove the bag of pips.

(6) Add the sugar, stir to dissolve, and then boil briskly until setting point is reached.

(7) Allow to cool slightly for marmalade to thicken. Fill the jars and cover.

JELLIES

Preparation of Fruit

Soft Fruits. It is unnecessary to remove currants from the stem or top and tail gooseberries, etc. Wash, place in pan, and add sufficient water to barely cover the fruit. Stew until fruit is reduced to a pulp.

Hard Fruits. It is unnecessary to peel or core such fruits as apples. Wash, cut the fruit into small pieces, place in pan, and well cover with water. Stew until fruit is reduced to a pulp.

Straining. Place the fruit pulp in a bag or muslin cloth and suspend to allow the juice to strain through.

Jelly Making

(1) For fruits low in pectin add $\frac{3}{4}$ lb (360 g) sugar to 1 pt (6 dl) juice. For fruits rich in pectin, add 1 lb (480 g) sugar to 1 pt (6 dl) juice.

(2) Place sugar and juice in pan and allow sugar to dissolve.

(3) Rapidly boil until jelly sets.

(4) Skim the jelly during boiling.

(5) Pour at once into hot jars and seal.

Lemon Curd

> 6 *oz* (180 g) *sugar*
> 3 *oz* (90 g) *butter*
> 4 *oz* (120 g) *eggs*
> *Zest and juice of* 1 *lemon*

(1) Warm the butter in a saucepan.
(2) Add the other ingredients.
(3) Cook slowly, stirring continuously until the mixture thickens.
(4) Remove, transfer to a jar, and store in a cool place until required.

Orange Curd

As above but replacing the lemon with orange.

Marshmallow

This is really a boiled meringue which has been stiffened with the addition of a jellying agent, i.e. gelatine or agar.

> 8 *oz* (240 g) *sugar*
> 8 *oz* (240 g) *confectioners' glucose* } (A)
> 3 *oz* (90 g) *water*

> $\frac{3}{8}$ *oz* (12 g) *gelatine* }
> 6 *oz* (180 g) *water* } (B)

> 2 *oz* (60 g) *egg whites* (C)

(1) Whisk the egg whites (C) to a stiff foam.
(2) Boil the ingredients of (A) to 260°F (127°C).
(3) Dissolve the gelatine and water (B) with a little heat.
(4) Remove boiling sugar from the heat, plunge pan into cold water to cool the syrup, and then pour onto the whisking whites.
(5) Add the gelatine solution.
(6) Continue whisking until the mixture becomes thick.
(7) Use either immediately before the mixture sets or pour into a container and store in a cool place.
Note. Marshmallow is best made on a machine. To use marshmallow after it has been made and stored, slightly warm and whip using a machine.

CREAMS AND ICINGS

Buttercream – Crème au Beurre

Recipe 1. (German).

> $4\frac{1}{2}$ *oz* (135 g) *fresh eggs*
> $3\frac{1}{2}$ *oz* (105 g) *castor sugar*
> 8 *oz* (240 g) *unsalted butter*

(1) Whisk egg and sugar to a thick sponge.
(2) Cream the unsalted butter.
(3) Beat (1) into (2) in about four portions.
Recipe 2. (Boiled).

> 8 *oz* (240 *g*) *sugar*
> 2½ *oz* (75 *g*) *water*   } (*A*)
> ½ *teaspoonful lemon juice*

> 5 *oz* (150 *g*) *egg whites* } (*B*)
> 4 *oz* (120 *g*) *castor sugar*

> 12 *oz* (360 *g*) *unsalted butter*   (*C*)

(1) Boil the ingredients listed under (*A*) to 245°F (118°C) (soft ball degree).
(2) Meanwhile whisk ingredients under (*B*) to a meringue.
(3) Pour boiled sugar onto the whisking egg whites to make a boiled (Italian) meringue.
(4) Soften and cream the butter.
(5) When the meringue is sufficiently cold, add it to the butter and beat well in.
Recipe 3.

> 8 *oz* (240 *g*) *unsalted butter*
> 9 *oz* (270 *g*) *fondant*

Recipe 4.

> 6 *oz* (180 *g*) *marshmallow*
> 6 *oz* (180 *g*) *unsalted butter*
> 2 *oz* (60 *g*) *fondant*
> 1 *oz* (30 *g*) *icing sugar*

Method for Recipes 3 and 4. Bring ingredients to room temperature and beat together making sure that there are no lumps.

Notes.

1. Margarine may be substituted for butter to give a filling cream. This will fulfill all the functions of buttercream but is lacking in flavour.

2. The consistency of buttercream is influenced by temperature. If it is too hard to spread or pipe, it will need to be slightly warmed, and conversely if too liquid, it will need to be chilled.

3. Since buttercreams are emulsions containing water and fat, it sometimes happens that they curdle and the water separates out. The German Recipe 1 is especially prone to this. When separation occurs, warm the buttercream to approx. 80°F (27°C) and beat well, when a smooth homogeneous mixture can again be formed.

4. Colour may be added as well as flavours (*see* opposite).

Storage. Buttercream must not be stored for longer than is necessary because of the perishable nature of the butter itself. It should be stored in a sealed container in a cool place (a refrigerator can be used, but remember that cream stored thus will need heat applied to bring it to a working temperature). Also it must be kept away from strong odours with which it is likely to become contaminated.

Buttercream will blend with a very large variety of flavouring materials most of which are listed here:

1. *Natural and Artificial Essences, Essential Oils, and Extracts.* If these are of fruit extraction, i.e. lemon oil or essence, tartaric or citric acid should be added to simulate the natural acidity of the fruit.

2. *Fruit Extracts, Juices, and Concentrates.* These are very true flavouring materials and are excellent for use in creams.

3. *Curds* made from lemons, oranges, and pineapple will blend well and impart an excellent flavour to cream.

4. *Chocolate.* This has to be first melted and stirred in whilst still warm. The cream too must not be too cold, otherwise the chocolate will solidify before it is dispersed. For very sweet creams the use of block cocoa or unsweetened chocolate is recommended. Chocolate may also be shredded and stirred in.

5. *Praline.* This is a paste made from roasted nuts and sugar. To blend it uniformly throughout the cream, it needs to be softened by first creaming it with a little buttercream before blending it into the rest.

6. *Chestnut Purée.* To make this, the chestnuts are boiled in water until soft. The husk and skin are then removed and the soft meat mashed to a purée. This may be sweetened and used as a filling cream on its own or added to the buttercream. (Chestnut purée may be purchased in tins.)

7. *Crushed Nuts.* Any type of nut may be crushed and added.

8. *Crushed Fruit.* This makes a delicious addition to buttercream but care must be taken to exclude as much juice as possible because this will separate out. Glacé fruits, e.g. cherries, angelica, pineapple, may also be added but are not as attractive in flavour as tinned or fresh fruit.

9. *Spirits and Liqueurs.* Any type may be added but the choice is usually limited to the liqueurs derived from fruits which would be used in combination with such fruits, e.g.

Kirsch, Maraschino, and Cherry Brandy   – Cherries
Apricot Brandy   – Apricots
Peach Brandy   – Peaches
Grand Marnier, Curaçao   – Oranges
Tia Maria   – Coffee
Crème de Cacao   – Chocolate

Rum, being derived from sugar, blends well with a variety of different flavours but it is especially good with chocolate and, therefore, ganache.

Some fruits are so strong in flavour that the use of a liqueur in combination would be uneconomical, e.g. lemon.

10. *Coffee.* Liquid or the powdered instant variety.

11. *Milk.* Evaporated or condensed milk may be added to make a

smoother buttercream and simulate the flavour of fresh cream.

12. *Malt.* Malt extract or dried malt extract may be added.

13. *Eggs.* The use of eggs, especially yolks, helps to enrich the butter-cream. The use of egg whites is solely to make the cream lighter and smoother.

14. *Butter.* The name 'buttercream' means a cream made with butter. Many imitations however can be made with margarine or vegetable fats. For true buttercream, a good quality *unsalted* butter must be used. Its flavour will effect the overall flavour of the cream; therefore the initial choice is worthy of consideration. The presence of salt will interfere with the delicious flavour of a true buttercream, hence the use of *unsalted* butter.

Fruit Cream

> 3 *oz* (90 g) *fruit pulp*
> 3 *oz* (90 g) *castor sugar*
> ½ *oz* (15 g) *cornflour*
> *Juice of* ½ *lemon*
> 6 *oz* (180 g) *cider*

(1) Place ingredients in a saucepan.

(2) Heat gently, constantly stirring until mixture thickens.

(3) Transfer to a china basin and allow to cool.

(4) Cover over with a damp cloth to prevent formation of a skin.

Note. Some or all of the cider may be replaced with milk, water, fruit juice, or wine.

Wine Cream

Recipe 1.

> 9 *oz* (270 g) *dry white wine*
> ½ *oz* (15 g) *egg yolk*   } *(A)*
> 2 *oz* (60 g) *sugar*
> *Juice of* 1 *lemon*

> 4 *leaves gelatine (soaked)*   *(B)*

> ½ *pt* (3 *dl*) *whipped sweetened double cream* *(C)*

Recipe 2.

> ½ *gill* (2½ *oz*, $\frac{1}{16}$ *litres*) *dry white wine*
> ½ *oz* (15 g) *egg yolk* (1)
> ½ *oz* (15 g) *sugar*   } *(A)*
> 1 *teaspoonful lemon juice*
> ¼ *oz* (8 g) *cornflour*

> 2 *leaves gelatine (soaked)*   *(B)*

> ½ *pt* (3 *dl*) *whipped sweetened double cream*   *(C)*

(1) Place the ingredients listed under (*A*) in a clean saucepan and cook the mixture carefully, using a whisk to prevent the formation of lumps.

(2) To the above paste add the gelatine (*B*) and stir until dissolved.

(3) Whip and sweeten the cream (*C*) and add to the mixture. Carefully blend into a smooth cream.

Notes.

1. The consistency of this cream can be adjusted by altering the quantity of wine, or using single cream instead of double, or adjusting the gelatine content.

2. The wine may be replaced by cider if desired.

Pastry Cream – Crème Pâtissière (Yield 8 covers)

$1\frac{1}{2}$ *pt (9 dl) milk*
8 *oz (240 g) sugar*
8 *egg yolks*
4 *oz (120 g) flour*
Vanilla

(1) Whisk the eggs and sugar.

(2) Add the flour and mix to a smooth paste.

(3) Bring the milk to the boil.

(4) Allow to cool slightly and gradually add to the egg and sugar mixture stirring well.

(5) Return to a clean pan and bring to the boil stirring continuously.

(6) Pour into a basin, cool, and cover with greaseproof paper. Castor sugar may be sprinkled over the top to prevent a skin from forming.

Cream St-Honoré – Crème St-Honoré

Pastry Cream (as above).
10 *egg whites*

(1) Whisk the egg whites until stiff.

(2) Add the pastry cream gradually whilst still boiling, whisking continuously.

Note. In very warm weather four sheets of soaked gelatine may be added to the custard whilst still hot.

Water Icing

1 *lb (480 g) icing sugar*
$2\frac{1}{2}$ *oz (75 g) water or stock syrup*
Colour and flavour

(1) Heat the water or stock syrup.

(2) Whisk in the sieved icing sugar to a smooth icing.

Note. The consistency will vary according to requirements but can be adjusted with stock syrup. This icing may be thinned and used as a glaze. It may be coloured and flavoured in the same way as fondant (*see* page 262).

Apricot Glaze

Recipe 1. (Clear).
>   *Apricot jam*
>   *Water*

(1) Mix together.
(2) Bring to the boil.
(3) Pass through strainer.
(4) Use hot.

Note. Consistency is adjusted by ratio of water to jam.

Recipe 2. (Opaque).
>   *Apricot purée*
>   *Fondant*

Use equal quantities in same method as Recipe 1. Adjust consistency with stock syrup.

Red Glaze

(*a*) Use sieved red currant or raspberry jam or jelly instead of apricot.
(*b*) Colour arrowroot glaze (*see* below) with red colour.

Arrowroot Glaze

>   1 *pt* (6 *dl*) *fruit juice*
>   1 *oz* (30 *g*) *arrowroot*
>   *Sugar (depending on sweetness of fruit)*
>   *Colour and flavour*

(1) Mix arrowroot with a little of the fruit juice.
(2) Boil the remainder and gently pour it on the diluted arrowroot stirring continuously.
(3) Pass through a strainer.
(4) Use whilst still hot.

Jelly Glaze

>   1 *pt* (6 *dl*) *water*
> $\frac{3}{4}$ *oz* (21 *g*) *gelatine*
> $\frac{1}{8}$ *oz* (4 *g*) *citric acid*
>   6 *oz* (180 *g*) *sugar*
>   *Colour and flavour*

(1) Heat the water and stir in the gelatine.
(2) Add the sugar, acid, and flavour.
(3) Use when the glaze is near to setting.

Royal Icing – Glacé Royale

>   3 *oz* (90 *g*) *egg whites* (3)
>   1 *lb* (480 *g*) *icing sugar*
>   *Lemon juice*

(1) Beat the egg whites with two-thirds of the sugar and the lemon juice until white and thick (approx. 10 minutes continuous beating).

(2) Add the remaining sugar and beat until stiff.

(3) Keep covered with a clean damp cloth to prevent skinning.

Notes.

1. The more beating the mixture has in (1), the less it will require in (2), and the easier it will be to beat.

2. Royal icing should not be too aerated, stiff enough to hold its shape and yet feel soft when piped out. When exposed to the atmosphere it will set very hard and brittle. If this is not required, a teaspoonful of glycerine may be added to the above recipe which will cause the icing to set much softer.

3. Royal icing may be used for the decoration of all types of cakes, nougat baskets, petits fours, etc.

22. Ices

PROCESS OF MAKING ICES

Scrupulous cleanliness must be observed in every stage of ice-cream making because the materials used can so easily become contaminated and give rise to the development of food poisoning organisms. For the production of ice-cream, a special compartment should be reserved, appropriately fitted-out and kept solely for this purpose. Moreover, the equipment used should also be reserved solely for ice-cream making. An abundant supply of hot and cold water for washing purposes is also essential.

Hand Tub Freezers

These consist of wooden tubs into which fit metal containers, small enough to allow a quantity of ice to be packed around them when placed in the tubs. The metal container is fitted with a lid and a paddle which can be made to rotate inside by cranking a handle. Before being used, wooden ice-cream tubs should be thoroughly soaked in cold water for 24 hours so that the wood can swell and close any gaps which, if left, would cause the ice mixture to seep out and make a watery mess wherever the tubs are left to stand. At the same time the ice mixture would run away.

The ice-cream mixture is placed in the metal container, the paddle is inserted, and the lid is replaced. The whole is then inserted in the tub and layers of crushed ice and salt are placed round. The function of the salt is to lower the freezing point of the water formed by the melting ice, thus giving a more efficient freezing mixture.

The paddle is now rotated continually whilst the ice-cream mixture freezes. As it freezes, it becomes thick in consistency and a considerable quantity of air is incorporated, increasing its bulk by about a third to a half. When the paddle becomes difficult to turn, the ice-cream is ready. The lid is opened, the paddle is removed, and the ice-cream may be served immediately or removed to a deep freeze for future use.

Electric Tub Freezers

Today special small tub freezers are on the market which take away the drudgery by turning the paddle with an electric motor. The equipment is the same as the hand tub freezer except for this refinement.

Other Mechanically Operated Freezers

In this equipment the paddle is not only mechanically operated but the container is also placed in a special refrigerated jacket, cooled by a refrigerant as used in the normal refrigerator.

Causes of Faults

Good quality ice-cream should be perfectly smooth, free from any lumps, ice crystals, or sugar crystals, and be nicely aerated.

Lumps.

1. Mixture was not sieved before placing in the freezing container.

2. Paddle does not make absolute contact with the sides and base so that some of the mixture is not being stirred.

3. Hard ice-cream is mixed with soft, i.e. not all the mixture is of the same temperature.

Ice Crystals.

1. The action of the paddle is to break up and disperse the ice crystals as they form. If the mixture is left unstirred in a frozen condition in the initial stages of making, ice crystals will form.

2. The size of the ice crystals depends upon the speed and hence the temperature at which the mixture is frozen. The quicker the operation, the finer these crystals will be and the less risk of their detection in the finished ice-cream.

3. Sometimes water gets into the finished ice-cream (especially with tub equipment). In these circumstances, it is obvious that such water will form ice and this can become dispersed throughout the mixture.

The presence of small ice crystals in ice-cream is called 'sandiness' because this describes how the ice-cream feels and tastes. Slow freezing is usually the cause.

Sugar Crystals. Since an ice-cream mixture contains sugar in solution, it follows that under certain circumstances, if the mixture contained too much sugar, the sugar could crystallize out. This rarely happens when the ice-cream contains glucose or acid, as in lemon ice-cream. If the mixture is made properly and then quickly frozen, this fault should not appear.

The use of the saccharometer to adjust the density of the sugar solution is described on page 258.

Storage of Ice-cream

Ice-cream should be stored at the lowest temperature possible but in any event not higher than $-5°F$ ($-20°C$). However, at this temperature the ice-cream is very hard and unsuitable for service. It should be brought out of storage deep freeze the day prior to service and stored at normal refrigerator temperature of $10-20°F$ (-12 to $-6°C$) according to the type of ice-cream used and the consistency required for service.

Types of Ices

Cream ices	– contain cream and/or milk.
Fruit or water ices	– made from fruit purée or pulp and stock syrup.
Fruit cream ices	– made from fruit purée or pulp, sugar, and cream and/or milk.
Special ice mixtures	– bombes, gâteaux, cassatas, etc.
Other preparations	– coupes, sundaes, baked Alaska.

Yields

The number of portions obtained from ice-cream depends upon the size of the server used and the amount of aeration the ice-cream has received in its manufacture.

Many patissiers rely upon commercial ice-cream which can now be obtained in a good variety of flavours and combinations and is always of an excellent uniform standard. However, such ice-cream has to be economically produced to be sold at a competitive price and thus the variety tends to be limited and the quality restricted. Ice-cream made by the patissier can be of superior quality and a very good reputation can be built with specialities of the house. The following ice-cream recipes are of continental origin and well recommended for a first class restaurant.

ICE-CREAM

Vanilla Ice-cream

> 1 *pt* (6 *dl*) *milk*
> 5 *oz* (150 *g*) *cream*
> 1 *oz* (30 *g*) *confectioners' glucose*
> 5 *oz* (150 *g*) *sugar*
> 4 *oz* (120 *g*) *egg yolks*
> *Vanilla essence*

(1) Whisk together the egg yolks, sugar, and essence.
(2) Add the glucose to the milk and bring to the boil.
(3) Whisk the boiling milk into the yolks and sugar and thoroughly blend together.
(4) Transfer to a clean saucepan and gently heat (*do not boil*).
(5) Stir the mixture continuously until it coats the back of the spoon.
(6) Pass mixture through a fine sieve.
(7) Leave to cool and then add the cream.
(8) Freeze immediately.

Several different flavoured ice creams can be made from this basic recipe by deleting the vanilla and substituting other flavours as follows.

Chocolate Ice-cream

Using 4 oz (120 g) chocolate couverture make a thick sauce with $1\frac{1}{2}$ oz (45 g) stock syrup (*see* page 265). Stir this into hot milk, prior to it being added to the egg yolks and sugar.

Coffee Ice-cream

Add $\frac{1}{2}$ oz (15 g) instant coffee to the hot milk.

Praline Ice-cream

Add a little of the hot milk to 2 oz (60 g) of praline paste and mix to a smooth thin paste. Mix this into the yolks and sugar before the hot milk is whisked in.

Pistachio Ice-cream

Add:

    2 oz (60 g) ground almonds
    2 oz (60 g) ground pistachio nuts
    1 oz (30 g) fondant
    Maraschino essence
    Green colour

Stir the mixed ground nuts into the yolks and sugar before the boiling milk is added. Dissolve the fondant in the boiling milk. Add appropriate quantity of flavour and colour to the mixture just prior to incorporating the cream.

Caramel Ice-cream

Melt the sugar and glucose and heat until amber shade is reached. Add hot milk, a little at a time until the caramel mixture is dissolved. Add this to the beaten egg yolk and continue as previously described.

FRUIT ICES WITH CREAM

Strawberry or Raspberry Ice-cream

    To the Vanilla Ice-cream recipe add:
    ½ pt (3 dl) strawberry or raspberry pulp
    2 oz (60 g) sugar
    Red colouring

Stir into the warm milk and egg mixture prior to adding the cream.

Banana Ice-cream

    5 large ripe bananas
    1 pt (6 dl) stock syrup (see page 308)
    ½ pt (3 dl) cream
    Juice of ½ lemon

(1) Mash the bananas into a fine pulp and pass through a sieve.
(2) Add the stock syrup to the bananas and adjust the density to 17°B with water (*see* page 258).
(3) Add the lemon juice and lastly stir in the cream.
(4) Freeze in the usual way.

Basic Fruit Ice Recipe

    1 pt (6 dl) fruit pulp
    1 pt (6 dl) cream
    1 pt (6 dl) milk
    Sugar (see next page)
    1 lemon (juice only)
    Colouring

(1) Heat the fruit pulp, lemon juice, and sugar to about 200°F (93°C) stirring constantly.
(2) Leave to cool.
(3) Mix in the cream and milk and necessary colour.
(4) Freeze.

Because different fruits contain different amounts of sugar, the sugar content of this recipe has to be adjusted accordingly as follows:

Raspberry and strawberry	12 oz (360 g) sugar
Pineapple	10 oz (300 g) sugar
Peach	10 oz (300 g) sugar
Black cherry	8 oz (240 g) sugar
Black currant	12 oz (360 g) sugar
Orange and tangerine	10 oz (300 g) sugar
Apricot	12 oz (360 g) sugar

Stock Syrup for Ice-creams

$\frac{1}{2}$ *pt* (3 *dl*) *water*
1 *lb* (480 *g*) *sugar*

(1) Bring the sugar and water to the boil.
(2) Remove any scum.
(3) Store in a clean jar for future use.

WATER ICES

To obtain the best results with water ices, it is important that the mixture contains the correct concentration of sugar. This can only be accurately judged by the use of a saccharometer (*see* page 258) which measures the density of a sugar syrup. Fruit ices should not register more than 18°Baumé, otherwise they will be difficult to freeze and mould. Most water ice mixtures register 16°B or 17°B before freezing.

Lemon Ice – Glacé Citron

1 *pt* (6 *dl*) *stock syrup*
2 *lemons*
1 *egg white*

(1) Extract the zest and juice of the lemons and add to the stock syrup.
(2) Stir in the egg white.
(3) Pass through a fine sieve.
(4) Test with the saccharometer and adjust with water to register 17°B.
(5) Freeze in the usual way.

Orange or Tangerine – Glacé Orange: Glacé Mandarine

Same recipe as Lemon Ice but using 2 large oranges or 4 tangerines.

Strawberry Ice – Glacé Fraises

Same recipe as Raspberry Ice.

Raspberry Ice – Glacé Framboises

1 *pt* (6 *dl*) *stock syrup*
1 *lb* (480 g) *strawberries (or raspberries)*
1 *lemon*
1 *egg white*
Red colouring

(1) Crush the fruit and pass through a sieve to make a purée.
(2) Add the zest and juice of the lemon, egg white, stock syrup, and colour.
(3) Text with the saccharometer and adjust with water to 18°B.
(4) Freeze in the usual way.

Pineapple Ice – Glacé Ananas

1 *lb* (480 g) *pineapple*
½ *pt* (3 *dl*) *pineapple juice*
1 *pt* (6 *dl*) *stock syrup*
1 *lemon*
Yellow colouring

(1) Mash the pineapple and pass through a sieve with the pineapple juice to form a purée.
(2) Add the juice only of one lemon, the syrup, and colour.
(3) Test with the saccharometer and adjust to 17°B with water.
(4) Freeze in the usual way.

Sorbet

This is a very light semi-frozen ice which is served with black Russian cigarettes after the entrée and before the roast in order to refresh the palate. It is also served as a refreshment at cold buffets. It is made with syrup and wine, liqueurs, or fruit juice which is frozen and then mixed with Italian meringue.

1 *pt* (6 *dl*) *stock syrup*
1 *pt* (6 *dl*) *fruit juice or wine*
1 *lemon*
1 *oz* (30 g) *egg white into Italian meringue*

(1) Mix the syrup, fruit juice or wine, and juice of the lemon.
(2) Strain through a fine sieve.
(3) Test with saccharometer and adjust with water or dry wine to 17°B.
(4) Freeze in the usual way.
(5) Make an Italian meringue from the egg white (or use 3 oz (90 g) meringue).
(6) When the water ice has frozen, combine it with the Italian meringue.
(7) Continue to freeze until light and fluffy.
(8) Pipe in the form of a pyramid into well-chilled sorbet glasses or silver coupes to serve.

Punch à la Romaine (Yield 8 covers)

This is the classical name given to sorbets in which dry, white wine or champagne is used for the mixing and rum (3 oz (90 g)) is added afterwards or poured over the sorbet prior to service.

Note. If a special fruit juice has been used, the sorbet may be named according to the fruit used, e.g. Lemon Sorbet – Sorbet au Citron.

Liqueur Ice – Glacé aux Liqueurs

> 1 *pt* (6 *dl*) *stock syrup*
> 2 *oz* (60 *g*) *liqueur*
> *White wine or water*

(1) Mix the liqueur with the stock syrup.

(2) Test with the saccharometer and adjust to 18°B by adding white wine or water.

(3) Freeze in the usual way.

(4) When served, a little of the liqueur may be sprinkled on.

Granites

Made in the same way as ordinary water ice but the density is adjusted to 12–14°B with water or wine. They should be granular in texture after freezing.

Marquises

These are sorbets in which the meringue has been replaced by unsweetened whipped cream.

COUPES AND SUNDAES

Coupes and sundaes are made up from ice-cream, fruit, and a suitable sauce, and decorated with fresh whipped cream, fruit, nuts, etc. The fruit may be flavoured with liqueur or spirit. Coupes are served in special tall glasses or silver cups, whereas sundaes are served in shallow dishes. Both are usually accompanied with wafer biscuits or petits fours. It is wise to use cups or dishes which are large enough to prevent the contents spilling over the sides when they are eaten. The make-up of each coupe varies little but there are two basic ways as follows.

Method 1.

(1) Place the fruit in the base of the cup.

(2) Cover with a scoop of ice-cream.

(3) Pour over a suitable sauce.

(4) Decorate with cream.

(5) Garnish with fruit, nuts, chocolate, etc.

This method is usually reserved for macédoine of fruit.

Method 2.

(1) Place a scoop of ice-cream in the base of the cup.

(2) Cover with the fruit.

(3) Proceed as outlined in Method 1.

This method is used where whole or halves of fruit are used.

Notes.

1. Fruits must always have their stones, pips, and skin removed before putting into coupes or sundaes.

2. Where liqueur is mentioned this can also refer to wine or spirits. Fruit such as cherries and diced fruits is usually allowed to soak in the liqueur some hours beforehand. The liqueur is only poured onto solid fruit such as pear and peach halves.

3. Where two or more ice-cream mixtures are used, it is usual to place the fruit between.

4. Since many of the recipes are of continental origin, pistachio nuts are often mentioned. These are difficult to obtain and expensive, but an acceptable alternative is green coloured nib almonds.

Varieties of Coupes and Sundaes

The variety of coupes and sundaes which it is possible to make is enormous when one considers the number of permutations which can be made in the use of various flavoured ices, types of fruit, liqueurs, and sauces. A number of them are summarized on the following six pages.

COUPES

Name	Ice	Fruit Base	Liqueur	Sauce	Decoration
Abricotine	Apricot	Apricot halves	—	Apricot	Whipped cream
Adelina Patti	Vanilla	Cherries	Brandy	—	Rosettes of whipped cream
Alexandra	Strawberry	Macédoine	Kirsch	—	Whipped cream and strawberries
Alphonse	Pistachio	Raspberries	—	Mousseline	Whipped cream and wild strawberries
Andalouse	Lemon	Orange	Maraschino or Curaçao	—	Whipped cream and orange segments
Antigny	Strawberry	Half peach	—	—	Spun sugar
Arlésienne	Vanilla	Diced glacé fruits and half poached pear	—	Apricot	—
Bébé	Half raspberry, half pineapple	Fresh strawberries	—	—	Whipped cream and crystallized violets
Belle Dijonnaise	Black currant	Black currant	—	Black currant	Whipped cream and blackcurrants moistened with egg whites and rolled in sugar
Berlinoise	Vanilla and chocolate	Macédoine	Rum	—	Rosettes of whipped cream, glacé cherries, and chocolate cutout disc
Black Forest	Vanilla	Morello cherries and chopped walnuts	Cherry Brandy and Kirsch	—	Whipped cream in cone shape. Rolls of chocolate. Serve with wafers covered in chocolate dots
Brasilienne	Lemon	Diced pineapple	Maraschino	—	Cherries and angelica
Camargo	Coffee and vanilla	Diced pineapple	—	—	—
Châteaubriand	Vanilla and apricot	Strawberries	Brandy	—	—
Cléopatra	Maraschino and crushed praline	Strawberries	—	Strawberry mousseline	Small meringue mushrooms
Clicquot	Peach	Strawberries, peaches, and pineapple	Champagne	—	Piece of pineapple and strawberry
Coppelia	Coffee and praline	Cherries	Maraschino	—	—
Coucher de Soleil	Strawberry mousse	—	—	Grand marnier with cream	Roasted nib almonds
Cressone	Vanilla	Fresh sliced peaches	—	Kirsch flavoured apricot	Whipped cream
Cryton	Vanilla	Half peach	—	Curaçao mousseline	Whipped cream and wild strawberries

Diable Rose	Strawberry	Strawberries	Kirsch	—	Raspberry whipped cream and chopped glacé cherries
Edna May	Vanilla	Cherries	Kirsch	Melba	Raspberry whipped cream
Elizabeth	Vanilla	Cherries	Cherry Brandy	—	Whipped cream and crushed crystallized roses
Emma Calvé	Praline	Cherry compote	Kirsch	Raspberry	—
Eugénie	Vanilla	Crushed marron glacé	Maraschino	Strawberry purée	Whipped cream and crushed crystallized violets
Favorite	Vanilla and pineapple	—	—	Strawberry	Whipped cream
Fiammetta	Apricot	Stoned and skinned grapes	Brandy	—	Brandy, whipped cream, and grapes
Germaine	Vanilla	Cherries	Kirsch	—	Marron glacé and whipped cream
Gladstone	Vanilla with diced preserved ginger	Diced fresh pears	Gin	—	Whipped cream, glacé cherries, and angelica
Gressac	Vanilla	Peach and macaroons	Kirsch	Red currant	Whipped cream
Herriot	Vanilla with diced glacé fruit and apricot	Thin disc of sponge	Brandy and Cherry Brandy	—	Whipped cream and candied walnuts
Jacques	Lemon and strawberry	Macédoine	Kirsch or Maraschino	—	Whipped cream, half lemon, half strawberry, and grapes
Jamaïque	Coffee	Diced pineapple	Rum	—	Whipped cream
Japonaise	Peach	Raspberries	—	Tea flavoured mousseline	Nibbed or flaked almonds and crystallized orange blossom
Java	Coffee and chocolate	Morello cherries	Brandy	—	Rosettes of whipped cream, glacé cherries, and flakes of chocolate
Jeannette	Pistachio	Strawberries	—	Strawberry	Whipped cream, wild strawberries, and crystallized violets
Joséphine Baker	Chocolate	Diced pineapple	Cointreau	—	Whipped cream, glacé cherries, chopped pistachio, with a chocolate cutout
Jubilée	Vanilla	Cherries	Kirsch	Melba	Raspberry whipped cream
Léonora	Chocolate and vanilla	Broken marron glacé	Curaçao	—	Whipped cream and whole marron glacé
Lucullus	Vanilla and pistachio	Macédoine of fresh fruit and crushed macaroons	—	—	Whipped cream in cone shape, shredded pistachio nuts, glacé cherries, and leaf shaped wafers

313

Name	Ice	Fruit Base	Liqueur	Sauce	Decoration
Madeleine	Vanilla	Diced pineapple	Kirsch or Maraschino	Apricot with Kirsch or Maraschino	Whipped cream
Malmaison	Vanilla	Peeled and stoned grapes	—	—	Whipped cream, crystallized violets, and spun sugar
Marguerite	Strawberry	Half peach	—	Curaçao mousseline	Whipped cream and wild strawberries
Marie Brizard	Coffee and anisette	Cherries	—	—	—
Marie Louise	Vanilla	Raspberries	—	Raspberry	Whipped cream
Marquise	Vanilla	Strawberries	—	Melba	Whipped cream and wild strawberries
Mercédès	Vanilla	Apricots	—	—	Chartreuse whipped cream and shredded chocolate
Metternich	Raspberry	Diced pineapple	—	—	Vanilla whipped cream
Mexicaine	Tangerine	Pineapple	—	—	
Midinette	Vanilla	Half peach on small meringue shell	—	Kirsch-Melba	Whipped cream
Mireille	Half vanilla, half red currant	Stoned nectarines and white currants	—	—	Whipped cream
Miramar	Pineapple	Diced pineapple and tangerine	Kirsch	Chartreuse mousseline	Serve with savoy biscuits
Miss Helyett	Raspberry	Apricot	—	—	Vanilla whipped cream
Mistinguette	Almond and strawberry	Macédoine	Cointreau	—	Rosettes of whipped cream and a green cherry
Mizette	Vanilla	Half peaches	Curaçao mousseline	—	Whipped cream and strawberries
Monte Carlo	Pistachio	Macédoine	Kirsch	—	—
Monte Cristo	Lemon and pistachio	Diced peach, orange, and banana	Kirsch	—	—
Montmorency	Vanilla	Cherries	Kirsch	Melba	Raspberry whipped cream
Montreville	Vanilla	Half peach	—	Apricot	Whipped cream
Morland	Apricot	Diced melon	—	Apricot	Whipped cream
Moscovite	Almond with chopped glacé	Cherries	Kümmel	Raspberry	Whipped cream and roasted nib almonds

Name	Ice cream	Fruit	Spirit	Sauce	Topping
Mozart	Vanilla and almond	Sliced peaches	—	Raspberry	Whipped cream and roasted nib almonds
Nébuleuse	Chocolate	Cherries	—	Kirsch—raspberry	Whipped cream, praline nibs, and crystallized violets
Niçoise	Orange	Macédoine	Curaçao or Grand Marnier	—	—
Nina	Vanilla	Strawberries	—	Curaçao mousseline	Whipped cream. Cover with spun sugar
Orientale	Pineapple	Diced pineapple	—	Apricot	Whipped cream and roasted nib almonds
Petit Duc	Vanilla and lemon	Red currants and half peach	—	—	—
Princesse	Praline and orange	Raspberries	—	—	Whipped cream and strawberries
Princesse Olga	Apricot	Strawberries	—	Kümmel mousseline	Whipped cream and crystallized violets
Rêve de Bébé	Pineapple and strawberry	Strawberries soaked in orange juice	—	—	Whipped cream and crystallized violets
Rose Chéri	Pineapple	Strawberries	—	White wine sabayon	Crystallized roses
Royale	Vanilla	Macédoine	—	—	—
Sans Gêne	Vanilla	Red currants	—	—	Whipped cream
Savoy	Coffee and praline	Raspberries	—	Anisette mousseline	Crystallized violets
Silésienne	Vanilla	Marron glacé	Kirsch	—	Whipped cream
Stella	Vanilla	Half apricot on meringue shell	—	Apricot	Pistachio nuts
Suzanne	Pineapple	Diced pineapple	Rum	Red currant	Whipped cream
Tétrazzini	Pistachio	Half peach	—	Raspberry mousseline	Whipped cream and orange segments
Thaïs	Vanilla	Macédoine and marron glacé	Kirsch	—	Whipped cream
Tripolitaine	Strawberry and lemon	Diced peach, orange, and strawberry	—	—	—
Tutti Frutti	Strawberry, pineapple, and lemon	Macédoine	Kirsch	—	—

Name	Ice	Fruit Base	Liqueur	Sauce	Decoration
Vénus	Vanilla	Half peach	—	Curaçao mousseline	Whipped cream, strawberries, and spun sugar
Verdoot	Vanilla	Half peach, strawberries, and raspberries	—	Quince jelly	Crystallized violets
Victoria	Half strawberry, half pistachio	Macédoine	Champagne	—	—
Zaza	Raspberry	Quartered fig	—	Apricot	Whipped cream

SUNDAES

Name	Ice	Fruit Base	Liqueur	Sauce	Decoration
Créole	Lemon	Diced pineapple and banana	Rum	—	Chantilly cream
Banana Royal	Vanilla	Banana split lengthwise	—	—	Whipped cream, crushed pineapple, chopped walnuts, and glacé cherry
Imperial Palace	Ginger and pistachio	Stoned and diced lychees	—	—	Maraschino whipped cream and chopped walnuts
Longchamps	Vanilla and pistachio	Three savoy biscuits soaked in Benedictine	—	Purée of strawberries	Benedictine flavoured whipped cream and chopped pistachio nuts
Morocco	Chocolate	Pistachio with whipped cream and nougat	—	—	Chantilly cream and chocolate petal shapes
Ninon	Vanilla	Morello cherries	Rum	—	Chantilly cream
Osborne	Vanilla	Sliced banana	—	Maple syrup	Whipped cream and finely chopped figs
Peach Royal	Vanilla	Sliced fresh peaches	—	Crushed pineapple	Whipped cream with nougat nibs and glacé cherry
Pineapple	Vanilla	Diced pineapple	Kirsch	—	Chantilly cream
Rainbow	Pistachio and strawberry	Split banana	—	—	Whipped cream, orange segments, and chopped pistachio nuts

Strawberry Whip	Strawberry	Crushed strawberries with whipped cream	—	Raspberry	Whipped cream
Temptation	Vanilla, strawberry, and chocolate	—	—	Chocolate	Chantilly cream, chopped pistachio nuts, and glacé cherries
Tutti Frutti	Strawberry, lemon, and pineapple	Diced candied fruits	Kirsch	—	—
Viennese	Coffee ice cream softened with sweet black coffee or Chocolate ice cream softened with ganache	—	—	—	Chantilly cream

ICE BOMBES

Like coupes, ice bombes too can be prepared in a great number of combinations.

The preparation is as follows.

(1) Thoroughly chill the bombe mould by placing it on crushed ice or in the deep freeze compartment.

(2) Line the mould with the frozen ice cream to a depth of approx. $\frac{3}{4}$ in. (2 cm). This is best done with the fingers, pressing the mixture to the sides of the bombe mould.

(3) Fill to the top with the bombe mixture into which glacé fruit, chocolate, praline, nuts, etc., may be mixed.

(4) Cover either with a sheet of white paper, or preferably a disc of thin sponge cut to the same size as the mould.

(5) Seal the mould with fat and freeze, either in ice and freezing mixture or in the deep freeze compartment.

(6) When required for use, dip the mould into warm water for a few seconds, remove the base plug to release the vacuum, and allow the bombe to slide out.

(7) Decorate and serve immediately.

Note. Treat the fruit used in the same way as for coupes. Where liqueur is mentioned, it is either incorporated in the basic bombe filling or used to marinade fruit if used.

Basic Bombe Fillings (Parfait) (Yield 4–5 bombes)

Recipe 1.

    $\frac{1}{2}$ *pt* (3 *dl*) *stock syrup* (*see page* 308)

    6 *egg yolks*

    $7\frac{1}{2}$ *oz* (225 *g*) *cream* (*slightly whipped*)

Recipe 2.

    $\frac{1}{2}$ *pt* (3 *dl*) *stock syrup*

    11 *egg yolks*

    $\frac{1}{2}$ *pt* (3 *dl*) *cream* (*slightly whipped*)

(1) Mix the yolks and stock syrup gradually together.

(2) Heat the mixture in a bain-marie, whisking continuously until it becomes thick like the consistency of mayonnaise.

(3) Remove, place on ice, and continue whisking until the mixture is cool.

(4) Add any desired flavour, liqueur, etc., and fold in the cream. In some recipes it is recommended that the cream should be stiffly whipped to increase lightness and bulk. This makes it very difficult to blend in the other ingredients; therefore excessive whipping is not recommended. Continue whisking until mixture is perfectly smooth.

In the following list, unless otherwise stated, the filling used is the basic one above.

Name	Ice	Filling	Decoration
Aboukir	Pistachio	Praline with pistachio	—
Abricotine	Apricots	Kirsch layered with apricot jam	—
Africaine	Chocolate	Vanilla	—
Aïda	Strawberry	Kirsch flavoured	—
A glon	Strawberry	Chartreuse flavoured	—
Alexandra	Pineapple	Vanilla with crystallized fruits	—
Alhambra	Vanilla	Strawberry	Strawberries soaked in Kirsch
Alméria	Anisette	Grenadine	—
Alsacienne	Pistachio	Half vanilla, half chocolate	Pistachio nuts
Américaine	Strawberry	Tangerine	Sliced peaches and raspberries
Anglaise	Nougat	Red currant with brandy	—
Andalouse	Apricot	Vanilla	—
Archiduc	Strawberry	Vanilla with praline	—
Armida	Pineapple	Strawberry	—
Aurélie	Vanilla	Strawberry with glacé fruits, marinaded in Maraschino	Pineapple and orange segments dipped in caramel sugar
Aurore	Strawberry	Kirsch with cherries soaked in Kirsch	—
Baroda	Coconut	Chocolate	Chantilly cream and chocolate rolls
Batavia	Pineapple	Strawberry	Diced ginger
Bénédictine	Raspberry	Bénédictine flavoured	Crushed crystallized violets
Bernoise	—	Anisette with macédoine of fruit	Glacé fruits
Bordelaise	Apricot	Strawberry	—
Bourdaloue	Vanilla	Anisette flavoured	Crystallized violets
Bragance	Lemon	Alternate layers strawberry and rum flavoured	—
Brésilienne	Pineapple	Vanilla with rum and diced pineapple soaked in rum	—
Camargo	Coffee	Vanilla	—
Cardinal	Red currant and raspberry	Vanilla with praline	Crystallized rose petals
Carnot	Raspberries		—
Carnival	Lemon with macédoine of glacé fruits	Maraschino Strawberry	Vanilla custard sauce
Ceylon	Coffee	Rum flavoured	—
Chantilly	Chocolate	Kirsch and Maraschino flavoured	Chantilly cream
Châteaubriand	Apricot	Vanilla	—

319

Name	Ice	Filling	Decoration
Chinoise	Praline	Pineapple with candied pineapple	—
Clarence	Pineapple	Violets	—
Columbia	Kirsch	Pear	Glacé cherries
Comtesse Marie	Strawberry with Kirsch	Vanilla	—
Comtesse Sarah	Vanilla and Kirsch	Kümmel mousse with crystallized rose petals	—
Confetti	Vanilla	Kümmel with crushed violets	—
Coppelia	Coffee	Praline	—
Créole	Pineapple	Strawberry and pineapple	—
Cressane	Vanilla	Pears	—
Cyclamen	Pistachio	Kirsch flavoured	—
Cyrano	Praline	Cherries and Kirsch flavoured	Whipped cream and glacé cherries
Czarine	Vanilla	Kümmel flavoured	Crystallized violets
Dame Blanche	Vanilla	Almond	—
Danicheff	Coffee	Kirsch flavoured	—
Dauphine	Lemon	Pistachio with broken macaroons and finely cut candied fruit soaked in Maraschino	—
Dauphinoise	Pineapple	Chartreuse flavoured, with diced savoy biscuits soaked in Chartreuse	—
Délicieuse	Peach	Champagne flavoured	—
Derby	Lemon, flavoured with brandy	Anisette flavoured	Crystallized violets
Diable Rose	Strawberry	Kirsch flavoured, with glacé cherries	—
Dioclétian	Vanilla with diced glacé cherries soaked in Maraschino	Grand Marnier flavoured, with diced savoy fingers soaked in Cognac	Chocolate ornament (or cutout) and small leaf shaped wafers
Diplomate	Vanilla	Maraschino flavoured, with candied fruits soaked in Maraschino	—
Duchesse	Pineapple	Pear flavoured Kirsch	Cover with spots of red currant jelly
Dora	Pineapple	Vanilla	Whipped cream, orange segments, and chocolate shavings
Ecossaise (Scotch)	Orange with chopped candied orange peel	Whisky flavoured	—
Emperor	Chocolate	Pineapple	Whipped cream, orange segments, and chocolate shavings

320

Espagnole (Spanish)	Coffee	Vanilla and praline with red currants	—
Esperanza	Orange	Kirsch and praline flavoured	—
Esterhazy	Vanilla	Chantilly cream with diced glacé fruits soaked in Kirsch	Vanilla ice
Falstaff	Praline	Strawberry	—
Fanchon	Praline	Kirsch flavoured, with coffee drops (sweets)	—
Fanfreluche	Vanilla	Tangerine	—
Fédora	Orange	Praline	—
Fellah	Pistachio	Orange	—
Figaro	Chocolate	Orange mousse ice	—
Florence	Orange	Maraschino flavoured	—
Florentine	Raspberry	Praline	—
Françillon	Coffee	Champagne flavoured	—
Frou-Frou	Vanilla	Rum flavoured and candied fruits	—
Gabrielle	Peach	Vanilla	—
Georgette	Praline	Kirsch flavoured	—
Gismonde	Praline	Anisette flavoured and white currants	—
Gladstone	Ginger	Gin flavoured, with diced preserved ginger and angelica	—
Grand Duc	Orange	Bénédictine flavoured	—
Grande Duchesse	Pear	Chartreuse flavoured	—
Hamlet	Tangerine	Vanilla with diced preserved tangerines	—
Havanaise	Coffee	Vanilla with rum	—
Hilda	Avelines	Chartreuse and praline avelines	—
Hollandaise	Orange	Curaçao flavoured	—
Hernani	Coffee	Walnut flavoured	Chantilly cream with half walnuts dipped in caramel sugar
Impérial	Tangerine	Raspberry	—
Italienne (Italian)	Pistachio	Vanilla with candied fruit flavoured with Maraschino	—
Jaffa	Praline	Curaçao flavoured	—
Jamaique	Pineapple flavoured with rum	Orange	—
Japonaise	Peach	Tea flavoured mousse	—
Javanaise	Coffee	Chocolate	—

321

Name	Ice	Filling	Decoration
Jeanne d'Arc	Vanilla	Chocolate and praline flavoured	—
Jocelyn	Peach	Maraschino flavoured	—
Joinville	Chocolate with chopped almonds	Maraschino flavoured, with chopped cherries	—
Joséphine	Coffee	Pistachio	Serve with brandy cherries flambée
Jubilée	Vanilla	Vanilla	Whipped cream, chocolate ornaments
Kranzler	Pineapple with diced pineapple	Pistachio flavoured with chopped pistachio and praline	(cutouts), glacé pineapple, and cherries
La Vaticane	Vanilla	Apricot mousse flavoured Maraschino	—
Léopold	Vanilla	Kirsch flavoured, with wild strawberries	—
Liverpool	Vanilla	Raspberry mousse ice	—
Madeleine	Almond	Vanilla with diced glacé fruits soaked in Kirsch	—
Madrilène	Coffee praline	Vanilla	—
Maltaise	Blood orange	Mandarine flavoured chantilly cream	—
Mandarinette	Tangerine	Tangerine flavoured with Curaçao	—
Maréchale	Strawberry	Pistachio, vanilla, and orange	—
Margot	Almond	Pistachio	Vanilla ice
Marie Brizard	Vanilla	Vanilla with candied fruit and macaroons soaked in anisette	—
Marie Louise	Raspberry	Vanilla	Piped baked chou paste ornament, glacé
Marquise de Sévigné	Apricot	Bénédictine flavoured, with diced savoy fingers soaked in cognac	pineapple, and glacé cherries
Mascotte	Peach	Kirsch flavoured	—
Mathilde	Coffee	Apricot	—
Médicis	Vanilla flavoured with Cognac	Raspberry	—
Ménélik	Tangerine	Rum flavoured	—
Méphistophélès	Apricot	Rum and Curaçao flavoured	Flambé with kirsch before service
Mercédès	Apricot	Chartreuse flavoured	—
Mignon	Apricot	Hazelnut praline	—
Milanaise	Vanilla	Praline	Whipped cream and praline
Mikali	Pineapple	Kirsch with red currants	—
Mireille	Red currant	Strawberry, Kirsch, and Maraschino flavoured	—
Miss Helyett	Raspberry	Vanilla	—

Name			Garnish / Note
Mogador	Coffee	Kirsch flavoured	—
Moldave	Pineapple	Curaçao flavoured	—
Monte Carlo	Orange	Praline flavoured with Bénédictine	—
Monte Cristo	Raspberry	Vanilla	—
Montmorency	Vanilla	Kirsch and vanilla mousse with candied cherries	—
Moscovite	Kümmel	Bitter almonds and candied fruit	—
Mousseline	Strawberry	Whipped cream and strawberry purée	—
Nabob	Praline	Champagne flavoured and candied fruits	—
Nélusko	Praline	Chocolate	—
Néron	Vanilla caramel	Vanilla mousse and chocolate drops	Unmould on slice of sponge, coat, and decorate with Italian meringue
Nesselrode	Chestnut	Vanilla	—
Niçoise	Orange	Tangerine	Whipped cream and violets
Nina	Strawberry	Vanilla with crushed violets	
Odessa	Apricot	Strawberry	
Odette	Vanilla	Praline	
Orientale	Ginger	Pistachio	
Oskar	Vanilla	Apricot mousse ice	
Otéro	Apricot	Black currant	
Othello	Praline	Peach	
Parisian	Chocolate	Vanilla with macaroons soaked in Maraschino	
Parisienne	Strawberry	Walnut	
Patricienne	Vanilla	Hazelnut and red currants	
Pékin	Tea flavoured	Vanilla	
Polonaise	Orange	Praline with candied fruit	
Pompadour	Pistachio	Praline flavoured with Maraschino	
Portugaise	Tangerine	Curaçao flavoured	
Prince de Galles (Wales)	Chocolate	With chestnut purée and diced marron glacé	Whipped cream
Princesse	Anisette	Vanilla	—
Princesse Béatrice	Pineapple	Curaçao flavoured	—
Princesse Olga	Vanilla	Kümmel flavoured	—
Printanier	Strawberry	Strawberry mousse and mixed fruits	—
Prophète	Strawberry	Pineapple	—
Queen Olga	Pineapple	Praline mousse ice	—

Name	Ice	Filling	Decoration
Queen Victoria	Pineapple	Strawberry flavoured with Kirsch	—
Reine	Vanilla	Vanilla and marron glacé	Serve with coffee drops (sweets)
Richelieu	Rum flavoured	Coffee	Palm leaf wafers, chocolate ornament (cutouts), glacé cherries, and Chantilly cream
Rivièra	Orange	Lemon sorbet flavoured Curaçao and roasted almond nibs	—
Rosette	Vanilla	Whipped cream and red currants	—
Royale	Kirsch flavoured	Chocolate and praline	—
Russe	Praline	Kümmel flavoured	Whipped cream and pieces of marron glacé
Saint Laud	Raspberry	Half melon and half whipped cream	—
Santiago	Cognac flavoured	Pistachio	—
Sappho	Strawberry	With wild strawberries soaked in Kirsch	—
Sélika	Praline	Curaçao flavoured	—
Siçilienne	Lemon	Vanilla and praline	Roasted almonds
Singapore	Pineapple	Vanilla with diced candied pineapple soaked in Maraschino	—
Skobeleff	Vodka flavoured	Whipped cream flavoured kümmel	—
Solférino	Vanilla	Tangerine flavoured with Curaçao	—
Strogoff	Peach	Champagne flavoured	—
Succès	Apricot	Chantilly cream with diced apricots soaked in Kirsch	—
Suisse	Vanilla	Strawberry	Sugared strawberries flavoured with Kirsch
Sultane	Chocolate	Praline	—
Suzanne	Rum and coloured pink	Vanilla and red currants	—
Tokio	Tea flavoured	Tangerine flavoured with Curaçao	—
Tortoni	Praline	Coffee	Coffee drops (sweets)
Tosca	Apricot	Maraschino flavoured, with diced glacé fruits	Lemon ice
Trocadéro	Orange with chopped candied orange peel	Chantilly cream with diced sponge soaked in Curaçao	—
Tutti Frutti	Strawberry	Lemon with diced candied fruit soaked in Kirsch	—
Tzigane	Praline	Pistachio with sliced grilled almonds	—
Valencia	Orange	Orange	—

324

Valençay	Vanilla and praline	Kirsch flavoured whipped cream and a layer of apricot jam —
Vénitienne	Half vanilla and half strawberry	Maraschino flavoured —
Victoria	Strawberry	Pistachio —
Vivianne	Praline	Coffee flavoured with anisette —
Volcano	Vanilla	Vanilla — Pistachio flavoured whipped cream. Whipped cream. Serve with compote of hot cherries and flambé with Kirsch
Westphalienne	Tangerine	Vanilla with diced macaroons and candied peel soaked in Kirsch —
Wilhelmina	Tangerine	Strawberry mousse ice —
Zamora	Coffee	Curaçao flavoured —
Zanzibar	Coffee	Curaçao flavoured and mixed with ground almonds —

Iced Charlottes – Charlottes Glacées

These are made in charlotte moulds in the same way as charlotte russe or royal. The mould is lined with sponge fingers or Swiss roll and then filled with various ice creams, bombe or mousse mixtures with fruit, etc., and then deep frozen until required. They are often served with a cold sauce.

Ice Gâteaux

These are ice cream mixtures made in the form of a gâteau which is first frozen and then served in slices or wedge-shaped portions.

The make-up of these is as follows:

Two or three layers of thin sponge (roll mixing) are sandwiched with ice cream mixtures to which fruit, nuts, etc., may be added. The sponge may be splashed with liqueur. Once frozen the gâteau may be decorated with whipped cream, fruits, nuts, chocolate, etc.

Rolls

These consist of ice cream mixtures in the form of a roll around which is wrapped a thin sponge roll mixing. They are cut into slices for serving.

Bricks

Ice cream mixtures frozen in brick-shaped moulds. Also served in slices. If a bombe mixture is used and frozen into a brick shape it is called 'Iced Biscuits' (Biscuits Glacés).

Note. For sponge recipes *see* Chapter 4, page 74.

ICED MOUSSES

Iced mousses are used either on their own or as a centre for the iced bombes. There are two types: cream and fruit.

Cream Ice Mousse (Yield 8 covers)

$\frac{1}{2}$ *oz* (15 g) *water*
7 *oz* (210 g) *icing sugar*
5 *egg yolks*
3 *egg whites*
1 *pt* (6 *dl*) *whipped cream*
Flavouring

(1) Beat the egg yolks, water, and sugar together in a bain-marie over gentle heat until it is foamy.

(2) Transfer to ice and continue whisking until cold.

(3) Whisk the egg whites to a stiff snow and add to the mixture with the flavouring.

(4) Fold in the whipped cream.

Note. The flavouring may be chocolate, coffee, praline, vanilla, liqueurs, etc.

Fruit Ice Mousse (Yield 8 covers)

$\frac{1}{2}$ *pt* (3 *dl*) *stock syrup*
$\frac{1}{2}$ *pt* (3 *dl*) *fruit purée*
Few drops lemon juice
1 *pt* (6 *dl*) *whipped cream*

(1) Mix the stock syrup with the fruit purée and lemon juice.
(2) Gently fold in the whipped cream.

Note. This type of mousse can only be made with fruits such as bananas, peaches, apricots, raspberries, strawberries, etc., which give a thick purée. Watery fruits like melons, oranges, etc., are unsuitable.

ICED SOUFFLÉS–SOUFFLÉS GLACÉS

Ice soufflés are made in special soufflé moulds or straight sided silver timbales. Around the edge at least 2 in. (5 cm) higher is wrapped a strip of greaseproof paper and secured with a piece of thread. The mould is filled to within $\frac{1}{2}$ in. (12 mm) of the top of this greaseproof paper band and frozen. When the soufflé is served it looks as if it has risen $1\frac{1}{2}$ in. (4 cm) above the mould as a baked soufflé is expected to do.

Usually the mixtures used for soufflés are either the iced mousse or bombe but other mixtures can be used as shown below. Besides fruit, broken sponge fingers soaked in liqueur, crushed nougat, etc., may be incorporated.

Iced Fruit Soufflé – Soufflé Glacé aux Fruits (Yield 8 covers)

1 *lb* (480 g) *Italian meringue (see page* 86)
$\frac{1}{2}$ *pt* (3 *dl*) *fruit purée or pulp*
$\frac{3}{4}$ *pt* (4$\frac{1}{2}$ *dl*) *whipped cream*

Add the fruit purée to the meringue and fold in the whipped cream.

Iced Chocolate Soufflé (Yield 8 covers)

$\frac{1}{4}$ *pt* (1$\frac{1}{2}$ *dl*) *stock syrup*
1 *oz* (30 g) *unsweetened chocolate*
5 *oz* (150 g) *Italian meringue (see page* 86)
1 *pt* (6 *dl*) *whipped cream*

(1) Melt the chocolate.
(2) Blend in the stock syrup.
(3) Mix in the Italian meringue.
(4) Gently fold in the whipped cream.

Other Varieties of Iced Soufflés

The Iced Chocolate recipe may be used for other varieties as follows.
Coffee. In the above recipe substitute $\frac{1}{2}$ oz (15 g) soluble coffee powder for the unsweetened chocolate.
Liqueur. Replace the unsweetened chocolate with 1–2 oz (30–60 g) of the required liqueur according to its strength.
Praline. Replace the unsweetened chocolate with 3 oz (90 g) of crushed praline or praline paste.

Cassata

These are usually made in bombe moulds, being first lined with three different types of ice, with the final filling a meringue/cream mixture containing a good quantity of glacé fruits, and then frozen.

Filling.

8 *oz* (240 *g*) *Italian meringue*	8 *oz* (240 *g*) *finely diced glacé fruits*
5 *oz* (1½ *dl*) *whipped cream*	*Flavouring*

VARIETIES

Name	Ice Creams	Mix with Cassata Filling
Napoletana	Vanilla, Chocolate, Strawberry	Diced glacé fruits
Siciliana	Lemon, Orange, Chocolate	Diced angelica, halved pistachio nuts, and crystallized water melon
Tortoni	Praline, Pineapple, Chestnut	Noyau and diced marron glacé
Tosca	Pineapple, Apricot, Praline	Glacé cherries and pineapple

Baked Ice-creams (Baked Alaska)

These are ice-cream sweets which are covered with meringue and placed in a hot oven for a minute or so, for the meringue to take on an attractive colour (flashing).

(1) Prepare a base of thin sponge (roll mixing). This may be sprinkled with liqueur.

(2) Mould the ice-cream to the shape of the sponge base and pui back into the freezer for a little while.

(3) Cover with Italian meringue (page 86) using a savoy bag. Simple decoration can be applied using a star tube.

(4) Immediately place in a hot oven at 450°F (232°C) until the meringue is coloured.

(5) Serve immediately.

Individual Alaska with Fruit

(1) Prepare a base of sponge about ½ in. (1¼ cm) larger than the fruit which is to be used, i.e. peach, pear, etc.

(2) Place the fruit on the sponge base.

(3) Cover with a scoop of ice-cream.

(4) Place in the freezer for ½ hour or so.

(5) Cover with Italian meringue and flash off in a hot oven.

(6) Serve immediately.

Ice-cream and Meringue – *see* page 89.

Ice-cream with Fruit – *see* page 216.

Glossary

Fruits

Almond	*Amande*
Apple	*Pomme*
Banana	*Banane*
Blackberry	*Mûre de ronce*
Cherry	*Cerise*
Chestnut	*Marron*
Cranberry	*Cannenberge*
Currant	*Raisin de Corinthe*
Currant, white	*Groseille blanche*
Currant, red	*Groseille rouge*
Currant, black	*Cassis*
Date	*Datte*
Fig	*Figue*
Filbert	*Aveline*
Gooseberry	*Groseille verte*
Grapes	*Raisins*
Greengage	*Reine-claude*
Hazelnut	*Noisette*
Lemon	*Citron*
Melon	*Melon*
Mulberry	*Mûre*
Nectarine	*Brugnon*
Nut	*Noix*
Olive	*Olive*
Orange	*Orange*
Tangerine Orange	*Mandarine*
Peach	*Pêche*
Pear	*Poire*
Plum	*Prune*
Pomegranate	*Grenade*
Quince	*Coing*
Raspberry	*Framboise*
Strawberry	*Fraise*
Walnut	*Noix*

329

Others

Bomb	*Bombe*
Cakes	*Gâteaux*
Chilled	*Frappé*
Cream	*Crème*
Dried	*Sec (Sèche)*
Fingers	*Tranchettes*
Fritters	*Beignets*
Iced	*Glacé*
In cases	*En caisses*
Jelly	*Gelée*
Panada	*Panade*
Patties (small)	*Bouchées*
Patties (large)	*Vol-au-vent*
Paste	*Pâte*
Pastry	*Pâtisserie*
Pie	*Pâté*
Pudding	*Pouding*
Rolled	*Roulé*
Rolls	*Paupiettes*
Salted	*Salé*
Savoury Jelly	*Aspic*
Souffle	*Soufflé*
Wafer	*Gaufre*

Culinary and Technical Terms used in Patisserie

(Not all the terms explained here appear in this book but they are included to assist the practising patissier.)

Absorb – To take in.

Aerate – Incorporating air or carbon dioxide gas during one or more stages of production to make goods more palatable and digestible. Air can be introduced by whisking, beating, or mixing. Carbon dioxide gas is introduced by the use of either baking powder or yeast. The expansion of air and steam during baking also contribute to the total aeration.

Albumen – One of many proteins. Generally it refers to the whites of eggs.

Aspic – Savoury jelly.

Bag – Unit of 140 lb in which flour is delivered from the miller.

Bain-marie – (i) A container of water in which foods may be placed either to cook or to keep hot.

(ii) A double jacketed saucepan the lower part of which contains water and the top, material to be heated.

Bake blind – Baking unfilled flan or tartlet cases for filling later.

Baking – Cooking in an oven at correctly controlled temperatures.

Baking powder – Chemicals which when moistened and heated generate gas (usually carbon dioxide) which aerates bread and cakes.

Baking sheet – A metal plate on which cakes, etc., are baked.

Batch – Entire mixing or contents of oven.

Batter – Soft completed cake mixture.

Bavarois – A light sweet dish which includes gelatine and cream.

Bay – A well, made in a heap of flour or other dry materials, to receive liquid ingredients of a mixing.

Beat – The aeration of materials by beating together.

Béchamel – A basic white sauce.

Beignets – Fritters, sweet or savoury.

Blackjack – The dark, caramelized sugar syrup used for colouring rich fruit cake mixings.

Blanch – Removing the skins of nuts by plunging them first into hot water and then into cold.

Bloom – The healthy sparkle on baked goods. Fats and sugar bloom (*see* Chapter 18, page 249).

Bombe – Ice cream speciality of different flavours in a bomb shape.

Bouchées – Small puff pastry open cases.

Bun – A small cake aerated either chemically or by yeast.

Bun wash – A liquid brushed on yeasted buns immediately on removal from the oven to impart a glaze.

Cake – Baked mixture of fat, sugar, eggs, flour, etc.

Cake hoop – A metal ring in which a cake is baked.

Cake tins – Metal shapes in which cakes are baked.

Canapé – A piece of toast or biscuit on which various savoury foods are served, either hot or cold.

Candied – Preserved by immersion in super-saturated sugar solution. Subsequent drying results in a coating of sugar crystals.

Caramel – (i) Sugar heated above its melting point.
        (ii) Sugar solution boiled above 312°F (155·5°C) until it turns amber brown.

Caramel fruits – Grapes, orange segments, etc., dipped in sugar solution boiled to at least 280°F (138°C).

Caramelize – Change in the sugar during baking a cake causing crust to colour (see *Caramel* above).

Caramels – Toffees composed of butter, cream, etc.

Carbonate of ammonia – Known as VOL to the baker and confectioner, it is a mixture of ammonium bicarbonate and ammonium carbamate. When heated it changes to carbon dioxide and ammonia gases which aerate certain goods, e.g. biscuits and chou pastry.

Carbon dioxide (CO_2) – A heavy gas produced by baking powder or yeast fermentation which aerates cakes, buns, etc. It is also incorporated under pressure in fruit drinks to make mineral waters and carbonated refreshments.

Cassata – An ice cream speciality.

Celsius – Temperature scale (constructed by Celsius, 1701–44) in which 0° represent the freezing point and 100° the boiling point of water at normal atmospheric pressure. The degree Celsius is very often called the degree Centigrade, as they are the same thing; however, 'degree Celsius' is the preferred term.

Centres – Moulded fondants and other sweet meats ready for dipping into chocolate couverture or boiled sugar to make sweets or petits fours.

Charlotte – Kind of pudding made in a special shape for which a charlotte mould is required.

Cheese curd – A curd produced by adding rennet to warm milk or by souring. When set, the whey is drained away to leave the curd.

Chinois – A fine meshed conical strainer.

Chocolate vermicelli – Polished granules of chocolate used as a decorative medium.

Clarify – (i) Removal of all extraneous material from a liquid or jelly in order to improve its transparency.

(ii) Removal of water from butter, etc. by gentle heating.

Coagulate – Partial or complete solidification of a protein in suspension. This may be caused by heat or acid.

Coat – Cover a cake with icing, paste, chocolate, etc.

Coffee drops – Small sweets resembling coffee beans.

Comb scraper – A plastic scraper with a serrated edge used to create patterns on icings, chocolate, etc.

Compote – Stewed fruit.

Compound fat – A fat, white in colour, made from hydrogenated oils. It is almost 100% fat.

Cones – Rice or maize, coarsely ground, used as a dusting medium for dough.

Constituent – One ingredient or component part of the whole.

Coralettes – Small nibs made of almonds, etc., and coloured.

Coupe – An individual serving bowl.

Couverture – Chocolate, either plain or milk, made from the cocoa bean.

Cream – (i) To beat two or more ingredients together to a creamy, light, and fluffy consistency, e.g. fat and sugar.

(ii) Fresh dairy cream – fat content of fresh milk.

(iii) Generic term used to describe buttercream, etc. In Great Britain, confectioners can only use this term to describe dairy cream.

Cream of tartar – Potassium hydrogen tartrate. One of the acid components of baking powder in which two parts are mixed with one of sodium bicarbonate.

Cream powders – Refers to many types of organic acids sold as substitutes for cream of tartar for use in baking powder.

Crème – Cream.

Crêpes – Pancakes.

Crimping – Giving a decorative edge to various pastes, e.g. shortbread, almond paste, etc., either with the thumb and finger or with special pincers.

Croquant – Melted sugar with nuts. The mixture can be moulded into shapes when hot or crushed when cold. It may also be made into a paste known as praline paste or nougat.

Crystallization – Formation of crystals deliberately in various sugar boiling operations.

Cup cakes – Small cakes baked in small paper cases.

Curd – A cooked mixture like a custard, e.g. lemon curd.

Curdle – Separation of the emulsion formed when fat, sugar, eggs, etc. are beaten together to form a cake batter. It is usually caused by adding the liquid too quickly or too cold.

Cut-outs – Units cut out of a mass of paste, etc., with either a knife or a cutter.

Cutters – Implements used to cut out pastries, etc. in various shapes. They may be plain, fluted, or made in a special shape, e.g. holly leaf or flower.

Dariole – Special shape of mould.

Decorate – (i) To add fruits, nuts, sugar, etc. to goods to embellish them.
(ii) Adding royal icing, fondant, etc. in patterns or to form a design.

Deep freeze – Refrigerating goods to below the freezing point of water, usually − 5°F (− 20°C) to preserve them. Defrosting returns the goods to their original state.

Demi-glace – Equal quantities of espagnole and brown stock reduced by half its bulk.

Deposit – Placing portions of cake batter etc. in cake tins either by hand or by the use of a machine known as a depositer.

Develop – Thoroughly mixing a dough to increase its elasticity through complete hydration of the gluten.

Dilute – Reduce the strength of a fluid or mixing by adding water, milk, etc. Sometimes it refers to mixing (custard, cornflour, arrowroot) with water.

Docker – An implement with spikes which can mark and decorate goods prior to baking. It also provides holes for the escape of steam in goods, e.g. puff pastry.

Doily – A fancy lace mat made from paper, fabric, or plastic, on which goods are presented.

Dough – Usually refers to a mixture of flour and water either fermented or not.

Dragées – Small sweet balls coloured silver or gold used as a decoration.

Drain – To remove the liquid content in goods by placing in a colander or sieve.

Dredger – Small container with a perforated lid used to sprinkle sugar, flour, etc.

Drumming – Stretching greaseproof paper across the bottom of a cake hoop. It is secured in position by twisting the paper around the rim of the hoop. A drummed hoop prevents the bottom edge of the cake from becoming overbaked and prevents a fluid mixing from flowing out from underneath the hoop.

Dust – (i) Sprinkling flour or sugar on a table to prevent dough or paste from sticking.

(ii) Sprinkling sugar etc. over a cake or pastry as a form of decoration.

Egg wash – Beaten egg (usually diluted with water) used to produce a glazed surface on baked goods.

Emulsion – Intimate mixture of two immiscible liquids, e.g. oil and water, brought about by breaking up the liquids into very fine particles and the use of an agent called an emulsifier. Fat and egg form an emulsion in a cake batter, the lecithin in the egg being an effective emulsifier.

Enrichment – The addition of enriching agents such as fat, sugar, eggs, etc., to doughs and pastries, etc.

Enrobe – Coating of cakes, biscuits, ices, etc. (e.g. with icing, chocolate).

Essences – Compounds used for flavouring sweets, confectionery, etc. They can be either natural, synthetic, or blends of both.

Essential oils – Aromatic oils of fruits, nuts, flowers, etc., extracted and used as flavouring materials.

Fahrenheit – Temperature scale in which 32° represents the freezing point of water and 212° the boiling point of water at normal atmospheric pressure.

Fancies – Small decorated cakes.

Feathering – *See* Marble icing.

Ferment – Mixture of water, yeast, yeast food, and flour allowed to ferment at a controlled temperature. Used as a starter for rich fermented goods.

Fermentation – The action of yeast on sugar in solution which produces carbon dioxide gas, alcohol, and other by-products. This gas causes aeration in fermented goods; the alcohol and other by-products play a part in the resultant flavour.

Fingers – Finger-shaped rolls, cakes, etc.

Flaked – Cut into thin slices.

Flambé réchaud – A small charcoal or spirit-heated stove.

Flan – Open pastry case baked in a flan hoop in which fruit is arranged and afterwards glazed.

Flash – Placing a cake decorated with meringue or almond in a very hot oven in order to impart a golden colour, e.g. rout biscuits.

Fleuron – Small piece of crescent-shaped puff pastry.

Fondant – An icing made from boiling sugar, water, and glucose to 240°F (115°C) and then agitating to form a mass of minute crystals when cooled.

Frappé – Chilled.

Friandises – Petits fours.

Friture – A pan which contains deep fat.

Ganache – A paste made from a mixture of fresh dairy cream and chocolate.

Garnish – Embellish with parsley, etc.

Gâteau – A large decorated cake which can be cut into individual portions.

Gaufre – Wafer.

Gelatinization – Heating starch with water to form a thick jelly on cooling.

Genoese (Genoise) – Good quality plain cake or sponge used for making into fancies, gâteaux, etc.

Glacé – Ice or ice-cream.

Glaze – (i) To impart a gloss by coating with an agent such as apricot purée. (ii) Caramelizing sugar by the use of the oven or salamander.

Gloss – The fine reflective surface on goods such as chocolate and fondant.

Glucose, confectioners' – A thick, viscous, colourless syrup used in boiling sugar preparations, etc.

Gluten – The insoluble protein of wheat after it has been hydrated. It is the elastic substance which assists in trapping the carbon dioxide gas in a dough, thereby enabling it to be aerated.

Glycerine – A colourless and odourless syrup with a sweet taste, used in cakes for its hygroscopic property in order to delay staling.

Graining – Re-crystallizing a super-saturated sugar solution by agitation.

Grease – Brush or cover baking tins with fat.

Gum paste – Special paste made from icing sugar, starch, water, and gum tragacanth, used for modelling purposes.

Hard flour – Flour containing a good quantity of gluten. A strong flour.

Hors d'oeuvre – Appetizing dishes served as a first course.

Hotplate – A heated flat metal plate on which certain goods like pancakes can be baked.

Hydrometer – An instrument for determining the approximate specific gravity of a liquid at a certain temperature.

Hygroscopic – The power of attracting moisture, e.g. glycerine.

Icing – Sugar mixtures used for coating and decorative purposes, e.g. royal icing, fondant, etc.

Icing sugar – Finely powdered and sieved sugar.

Jelly – A soft, stiff, semi-transparent food chiefly derived from gelatine or other gummy substances. In patisserie there are several different types of jellies, namely aspic, pectin, piping, starch, gelatine, etc.

Jigger – A tool with a serrated wheel used for cutting pastry with a crinkled edge. It may be made of either brass or wood.

Jus-lié – Gravy which has been thickened.

Lamination – Formation of a number of layers as in the making of puff pastry.

Lecithin – A powerful emulsifying agent.

Macédoine – (i) A mixture of fruit or vegetables. (ii) Cut into $\frac{1}{4}$-in. (3-mm) dice.

Macerate – To steep in a liquid to soften. Generally applied to fruit which is sprinkled with liqueur to improve flavour.

Maidenhair fern – A fern which is dried and pressed and used in the decoration of cakes.

Manipulation – Term used to describe handling and shaping of a dough, paste, etc.

Marble icing – Decorative effect caused by inlaying one coloured icing into another in the form of a design. Also called 'feathering'.

Marzipan – A cooked paste made from two-thirds blanched almonds and one-third sugar.

Masking – Covering a cake surface with icing, buttercream, roasted nuts, etc.

Maw seeds – Seeds from a species of poppy, used for sprinkling on rolls etc. Available as either 'blue' or 'white'.

Menu – Bill of fare.

Mincemeat – Mixture of dried fruit with apples and suet flavoured with spice, lemon juice, and rum or brandy.

Mise en place – Basic preparations prior to the service.

Mould – (i) Shaping of a dough or paste.

(ii) A hollow form made from metal, plaster, plastic, wood, etc. in which pastes like marzipan may be cast.

(iii) Special hollow forms by which chocolate goods may be moulded.

(iv) Minute fungi which grow in damp conditions.

Mousse – A dish which is light in consistency, served either hot or cold.

Musty – A taint which develops usually in raw materials when stored under unsuitable conditions.

Nibs – Small fragments, such as almond or sugar nibs.

Nougat – (i) A confection made from sugar, honey, and egg whites, with added glacé fruits and nuts, e.g. Montelimar.

(ii) Mixture of melted sugar and almonds ground to a paste and mixed with chocolate.

(iii) Mixture of melted sugar and almonds known also as praline – croquant.

Orange flower water – A delicate flavoured distillate obtained from the flower of the orange tree used for flavouring almond and ices, etc.

Palette knife – A special knife having a thin flat blade with a rounded edge used for spreading purposes.

Parfait – Ice cream mixture made from syrup, egg yolks, and cream, and frozen in moulds.

Pastillage – Paste made from icing sugar and gum tragacanth or gelatine mucilage.

Pastries – Term used to describe all goods made by the pastrycook and confectioner.

Pasty – Small savoury containing meat and vegetables.

Patty – Small pie baked in a patty pan.

Pectin – The natural jellying agent found in most fruits and vegetables. It is available processed in either a liquid or a powder form. Used in cold set jelly and in jam and jelly recipes in which fruit used is naturally deficient in this agent.

Peel – (i) A flat wooden or metal blade attached to the end of a long handle. Used for setting and drawing bread and cakes, etc., from the oven.

(ii) The candied rinds of citrus fruits. Available either as halves (*caps*) or cut into small dices.

Petits fours – Very small pastries which can be placed in the mouth in one piece. There are two types:
(i) *Petits fours secs* – dry biscuit types.
(ii) *Petits fours glacés* – finished with icing.

Pie – A dish covered with pastry and containing fruit, meat, fish, etc.

Pincers – A tool consisting of two springy metal prongs, the ends of which are either shaped or serrated. They are used to pinch a design onto the edge of various pastes.

Pinching – Use of the above tool or the use of the thumb and forefinger to give a decorative edge to various pastes.

Pinning – Rolling out a paste with the rolling pin.

Piping – The operation of forcing a mixing from a bag through a small orifice which may be plain or shaped (cut) to leave a decorative impression.

Plaiting – The weaving of a rope of dough, paste, boiled sugar, etc., into an ordered design.

Plaster moulds – Moulds made from plaster of Paris.

Poach – Simmer dishes gently in boiling water or liquid without allowing the contents actually to boil.

Praline – Croquant which has been milled into a smooth paste. Used for flavouring purposes.

Precipitate – To throw out of solution. Deposit of a solid from a solution.

Prove – The aeration of a yeasted dough with gas prior to its being baked.

Prover – A cabinet in which yeasted goods are placed to prove before baking. A warm, humid atmosphere must be provided for this purpose.

Pudding – A soft mixture, either sweet or savoury, baked or steamed in a basin or dish.

Puff pastry – Laminated structure built up from dough and butter or fat.

Pulled sugar – A solution of sugar containing glucose or weak acid, boiled to at least 300°F (149°C), poured onto a slab, and then pulled to attain a sheen. Used for fashioning ornamental shapes for table decoration and display pieces.

Punch – Frozen mixture of fruit syrup and Italian meringue.

Réchauffer – To re-heat.

Recipe – Formula containing weights of materials used for a particular type of dish. Yields, temperatures, times, etc., should also be recorded.

Recovery time – The time required by doughs to lose their toughness, brought about by manipulation.

Reduce – Concentration of a liquid by boiling.

Rennet – An infusion from the stomach of a calf which contains the enzyme rennin. Used to coagulate milk for the manufacture of curd and cheese.

Retardation – Arrest of the activity of fermented goods usually by keeping them at a low temperature of 34–38°F (1–3°C).

Rice flour – Rice milled into a fine flour. Used in some mixings and also for dusting purposes.

Ripening – Usually refers to the mellowing of the gluten in fermented goods, making it less tough and more extensible. May be brought about by the action of fermentation, manipulation, temperature, or use of additives.

Rock sugar – An aerated decorative material made from boiling sugar and royal icing.

Rolls – Small shapes made from bread. They may be soft or crisp and of any shape.

Roux – Flour and fat cooked into a thick mixture.

Royal icing – Mixture of icing sugar and egg whites used for decorative purposes.

Sabayon – Sauce made from the yolks of egg and either water or wine.

Saccharometer – A special hydrometer for determining the density of sugar solutions. They are usually calibrated in degrees Baumé.

Sack – Unit of 280 lb in which flour is invoiced from the miller. It is delivered in two 140-lb bags.

Saffron – Dried stigmas of the saffron crocus. The deep orange coloured infusion is used for flavouring and colouring various specialities.

Salamander – A type of grill heated from above.

Salpicon – Mixture of small diced foods.

Sandwich plates – Shallow round metal tins in which sponge sandwiches are baked.

Saturated solution – A solution holding the greatest amount of another material without precipitation occurring. Usually it refers to a sugar solution.

Savoy bag – A cone shaped bag of cloth, nylon, or plastic in the end of which a tube can be inserted. Used to deposit or pipe all types of soft mixtures onto baking sheets or for decorative purposes.

Savoy tube – A nozzle made of metal, nylon, or plastic, either plain or shaped, through which various mixtures may be forced in either plain or decorative shapes.

Scaling – Operation of weighing dough or cake into units before baking.

Scoop – Small shovel for handling small quantities of dry materials.

Scraper – (i) A flat piece of flexible plastic material used to scrape mixings from the sides of the mixing bowl.

(ii) A flat piece of rigid metal fixed into a wooden handle and used for scraping baking tins or bench surfaces.

Either type of scraper may be used to smooth the sides of cakes coated with royal icing, buttercream, etc. Patterns cut into the edge of such a scraper may be used to give decorative effects.

Season – Dulling the shining surface of new pans and baking tins by leaving them in a hot oven for a few hours. This is to improve their heat absorption properties.

Seasoning – Adding a mixture of salt and pepper with other aromatic flavouring substances to savoury dishes.

Setting – Filling an oven with bread or cakes.

Sherbets – Very light ices made from fruit juice.

Shortpastry – A friable mixture made from flour and fat with either egg, milk, or water to bind. It may be either sweet or savoury.

Shredded – Cut into fine strips.

Sieve – Utensil with a mesh made of either wire or nylon, through which dry or liquid materials and mixtures can be strained. It can be used to screen small particles from larger ones.

Skinning – The hard surface which is formed if dough is left uncovered, due to the evaporation of moisture.

Slab cake – Cakes baked in large frames weighing about 5–7 lb (2½–3 kilos).

Slack dough – A dough containing extra water to make it soft.

Snow – Term used to describe the foam caused when egg whites are whipped.

Sodium bicarbonate – The alkali constituent of baking powder which liberates carbon dioxide gas in the presence of the correct quantity of acid.

Soft flour – A flour with a weak gluten content.

Sorbet – A very light fruit ice.

Soufflé – A very light dish. It may be hot or cold, sweet or savoury.

Spatula – A flat wooden spoon-shaped utensil used for mixing purposes.

Splash – Sprinkling water or liquid over goods.

Sponge – (i) A light cake made by beating eggs and sugar and then blending in the flour.
(ii) A thick fermented batter.

Spun sugar – Threads of sugar formed from a boiling sugar solution. Used for decorative purposes.

Stencil – A pattern cut from suitable material through which icings or mixings may be deposited in a certain shape.

Stock syrup – Solution of sugar and water used to reduce fondant etc.

Strong flour – A flour containing a strong gluten.

Sugar paste – A paste made principally from sugar.

Sundaes – Ice cream dishes to which fruit is added.

Super-saturated solution – A highly saturated solution in an unstable condition which, when agitated, will rapidly crystallize.

Tart – A baked pastry case filled with fruit or some type of mixing.

Tea bread – Small yeasted goods made from an enriched dough.

Tight dough – Stiff dough containing insufficient water.

Turntable – A piece of equipment upon which a cake can be rotated in order to apply an even coating of icing or cream.

Velouté – A basic sauce made from stock.

Vol-au-vent – A large case made of puff pastry.

Wafer paper – Edible paper-like sheets on which macaroons etc. may be piped. Sometimes referred to as rice paper.

Wash – To brush goods with eggs, milk, or water prior to baking, or to apply icing or a glaze on baked goods.

Washbrush – Soft haired brush used for applying the wash etc. to goods.

Whip – Rapidly aerate by beating with a whisk.

Whisk – An implement made from wire used to whip mixings.

Yield – Quantity of units calculated from any particular recipe.

Zest – The coloured outside rind of citrus fruits. This contains the essential oils of the fruit.

Temperature Conversion Table

The numbers in heavy type can be either °C or °F. If the heavy type number is °C, the equivalent in °F is on the right. If the heavy type number is °F, the equivalent in °C is on the left.

°C		°F	°C		°F	°C		°F	°C		°F
−40	**−40**	−40	−1·1	**30**	86·0	18·2	**65**	149·0	43	**110**	230
−34	**−30**	−22	−0·6	**31**	87·8	18·8	**66**	150·8	49	**120**	248
−29	**−20**	−4	−0	**32**	89·6	19·3	**67**	152·6	54	**130**	266
−23	**−10**	+14	0·5	**33**	91·4	19·9	**68**	154·4	60	**140**	284
−17·7	**−0**	+32	1·1	**34**	93·2	20·4	**69**	156·2	65	**150**	302
−17·2	**1**	33·8	1·6	**35**	95·0	21·0	**70**	158·0	71	**160**	320
−16·6	**2**	35·6	2·2	**36**	96·8	21·5	**71**	159·8	76	**170**	338
−16·1	**3**	37·4	2·7	**37**	98·6	22·2	**72**	161·6	83	**180**	356
−15·5	**4**	39·2	3·3	**38**	100·4	22·7	**73**	163·4	88	**190**	374
−15	**5**	41·0	3·8	**39**	102·2	23·3	**74**	165·2	93	**200**	392
−14·4	**6**	42·8	4·4	**40**	104·0	23·8	**75**	167·0	99	**210**	410
−13·9	**7**	44·6	4·9	**41**	105·8	24·4	**76**	168·8	100	**212**	413
−13·3	**8**	46·4	5·5	**42**	107·6	25·0	**77**	170·6	104	**220**	428
−12·7	**9**	48·2	6·0	**43**	109·4	25·5	**78**	172·4	110	**230**	446
−12·2	**10**	50·0	6·6	**44**	111·2	26·2	**79**	174·2	115	**240**	464
−11·6	**11**	51·8	7·1	**45**	113·0	26·8	**80**	176·0	121	**250**	482
−11·1	**12**	53·6	7·7	**46**	114·8	27·3	**81**	177·8	127	**260**	500
−10·5	**13**	55·4	8·2	**47**	116·6	27·7	**82**	179·6	132	**270**	518
−10·0	**14**	57·2	8·8	**48**	118·4	28·2	**83**	181·4	138	**280**	536
−9·4	**15**	59·0	9·3	**49**	120·2	28·8	**84**	183·2	143	**290**	554
−8·8	**16**	60·8	9·9	**50**	122·0	29·3	**85**	185·0	149	**300**	572
−8·3	**17**	62·6	10·4	**51**	123·8	29·9	**86**	186·8	154	**310**	590
−7·7	**18**	64·4	11·1	**52**	125·6	30·4	**87**	188·6	160	**320**	608
−7·2	**19**	66·2	11·5	**53**	127·4	31·0	**88**	190·4	165	**330**	626
−6·6	**20**	68·0	12·1	**54**	129·2	31·5	**89**	192·2	171	**340**	644
−6·1	**21**	69·8	12·6	**55**	131·0	32·1	**90**	194·0	177	**350**	662
−5·5	**22**	71·6	13·2	**56**	132·8	32·6	**91**	195·8	182	**360**	680
−5·0	**23**	73·4	13·7	**57**	134·6	33·3	**92**	197·6	188	**370**	698
−4·4	**24**	75·2	14·3	**58**	136·4	33·8	**93**	199·4	193	**380**	716
−3·9	**25**	77·0	14·8	**59**	138·2	34·4	**94**	201·2	199	**390**	734
−3·3	**26**	78·8	15·6	**60**	140·0	34·9	**95**	203·0	204	**400**	752
−2·8	**27**	80·6	16·1	**61**	141·8	35·5	**96**	204·8	210	**410**	770
−2·2	**28**	82·4	16·6	**62**	143·6	36·1	**97**	206·6	215	**420**	788
−1·6	**29**	84·2	17·1	**63**	145·4	36·6	**98**	208·4	221	**430**	806
			17·7	**64**	147·2	37·1	**99**	210·2	226	**440**	824
						37·7	**100**	212·0	232	**450**	842
									238	**460**	860
									243	**470**	878
									249	**480**	896
									254	**490**	914
									260	**500**	932

Index